Knowledge Generation, Exchange, and Utilization

About the Book and Editors

In spite of the knowledge explosion and the emergence of
information societies, existing knowledge is often not applied
appropriately to help solve societal problems. Inequities in
the access to and distribution of knowledge and the weaknesses
in systems for accessing and applying knowledge are startling.
In response to these concerns, a group of scholars and practitioners have linked theory and practice in the development of
a new field known as knowledge generation, exchange, and utilization. In this book, leading experts present a survey of
the state of the art in the field. Using a holistic, and often
a systems, approach, they present current models that conceptualize the entire process of knowledge creation, access, and
utilization. In addition, they address such critical questions
as the role of linkages, ethical issues in knowledge utilization, and the application of various research methods for
planning the utilization process to secure more effective use
of knowledge for policy and social change.

George M. Beal is research associate at the Institute of
Culture and Communication, East-West Center. Wimal Dissanayake
is assistant director at the same institution. Sumiye Konoshima
is a research information specialist at the East-West Center.

Knowledge Generation, Exchange, and Utilization

edited by George M. Beal,
Wimal Dissanayake,
and Sumiye Konoshima

Westview Press / Boulder and London

A Westview Special Study

This Westview softcover edition was manufactured on our own premises using
equipment and methods that allow us to keep even specialized books in stock.
It is printed on acid-free paper and bound in softcovers that carry the highest rating of the National Association of State Textbook Administrators, in
consultation with the Association of American Publishers and the Book Manufacturers' Institute.

Published in 1986 in the United States of America by Westview Press, Inc.;
Frederick A. Praeger, Publisher; 5500 Central Avenue, Boulder, Colorado 80301

Library of Congress Cataloging in Publication Data
Knowledge generation, exchange, and utilization.
    1. Communication. 2. Information science. I. Beal,
George M. II. Dissanayake, Wimal. III. Konoshima,
Sumiye. IV. Series: Westview special studies.
P90.K57   1986   001.51   86-7812
ISBN 0-8133-7242-9

Composition for this book was provided by the editors.
This book was produced without formal editing by the publisher.

Printed and bound in the United States of America

The paper used in this publication meets the requirements of the
American National Standard for Permanence of Paper for Printed
Library Materials Z39.48-1984.

6 5 4 3 2 1

Contents

vii

viii

Preface

The East-West Center is an educational institution located in Honolulu, Hawaii. Established by the United States Congress in 1960, the Center works to "promote better relations and understanding among the nations of Asia, the Pacific and the United States through cooperative study, training and research." Its permanent staff is multi-disciplinary and multinational. This staff is supplemented by short-term fellows, professional associates and interns. Its activities are organized around major problems of international concern as articulated through problem-oriented institutes.

Within this setting it is not surprising that there was a recognition of a major problem: despite the knowledge and technological explosion, all parts of the world and all sectors of societies are beset with unsolved problems to which existing knowledge could be addressed. The possibility that a newly emerging field dealing with a systems approach to knowledge generation, processing, dissemination and utilization might contribute to alleviating some of these problems was recognized.

It is also not surprising that within this setting the three editors of this volume found a common interest which brought together an interdisciplinary and cross-cultural approach.

Sumiye Konoshima comes out of a background of social psychology and library science. As a staff member of the Institute of Culture and Communication for more than ten years she has been responsible for developing a documentation/information/materials center on communication and development, especially population and family planning programs around the world. Special attention was given to collecting and disseminating information and materials not readily available through usual channels. She actively participated in worldwide networks, conferences, workshops and consultation dealing with knowledge accessing, processing and dissemination.

Wimal Dissanayake came to the Center from the University of Sri Lanka, where he was chairman of the Department of Mass Communication. He was trained in Sri

Lanka, the University of Pennsylvania and the University of
Cambridge. He is an ex-newspaperman and broadcaster and was
consultant to the Community Development Services Center of
Sri Lanka. He is primarily interested in the cultural and
humanistic aspects of knowledge generation, dissemination
and utilization. Thus Wimal's interest and experience have
ranged from the highly philosophical to the very pragmatics
of development communication. Equally important, he has
faced the problem of trying to evaluate the appropriateness
of Western knowledge for Eastern problems and the difficulties of trying to communicate relatively indigenous
developed Eastern strategies, e.g., the Sarvotaya Movement,
to Western audiences.

George Beal is a sociologist, perhaps best known for
his early and continuing work in adoption-diffusion of
technology, emphasizing agricultural technology. He has
been deeply involved in research, teaching and training in
that area throughout the United States and in several Asian,
South Pacific Island and Latin American countries. However,
this intense involvement in these specific elements of
dissemination and utilization led to the recognition of the
importance of understanding the more holistic, systems
approach and its environment encompassed by the entire
process of knowledge generation, processing, transformation,
product development, dissemination and utilization--a
paradigm he developed with Meehan in the mid-1970s.

These people, as individuals and together with
additional staff such as Larry Kincaid, Georgette Wang,
Betty Buck, and John Middleton, had dealt directly with the
problems of knowledge transformation, packaging, and
dissemination in their own writing, consulting, international conferences, workshops and program development.

Contacts with scholars and practitioners from the
United States who were beginning to coalesce around this
more holistic approach to knowledge generation-utilization
resulted in indications of strong interest in furthering the
development of the field. While the initiation of the
journal Knowledge Creation, Diffusion and Utilization in
1979 had helped provide a forum for exchange of ideas, there
was a definite feeling that an accepted organizing
conceptual framework did not exist and that most work was
being done on an individual and often isolated basis--there
was need for more interaction among those committed to the
field. Contacts with our Asian and Pacific Islands
colleagues indicated many activities directly related to
knowledge transformation and dissemination were being
carried out at the practitioner level, but little attention

was given to the more general level of conceptualization, paradigms or models, nor was there much awareness of the emergence of the field of knowledge generation-utilization. However, there was great interest expressed in the field and there was personal and institutional interest expressed in wanting to contribute and participate in planning and carrying out activities related to the development of the field in Asia and the Pacific Island area.

Out of this background, a project titled Transnational Knowledge Generation and Utilization was developed in the East-West Center's Communication Institute (now known as the Institute of Culture and Communication). To provide some beginning parameters to the project it was decided that initial focus would emphasize the communication and organizational aspects, would deal with transnational but would also include within-nation processes. Further, most activity would focus on knowledge that was judged to be ultimately of use to people at the local community and village level. Such knowledge would impact their development and quality of life in areas such as food and nutrition, health, education, welfare and social participation. At the beginning, emphasis would be on the content area of agriculture and health.

The project was planned for five years. The first 18 months were to help further establish the "state of the art" of the field, the second 18 months were for research on knowledge generation-utilization systems (codification of existing research, stimulating new research, and developing collaborative projects), and the third 18 months were planned for further codification, transformation and preparation of materials (possibly including training materials) for dissemination.

This book is largely the product of an international conference on the state of the field held at the East-West Center in April 1982. At the end of the conference, participants were involved in developing an outline for an edited book that would be one slice of the present state of the art in the field. This outline became the basis for contacting outstanding scholars in the field (many of whom attended the conference) to submit chapters to be included in the book. A number of people who presented papers and made an excellent contribution at the conference do not have chapters in the book. Their contribution is gratefully recognized. Staff colleague Larry Kincaid was a strong supporter and contributor to this project from its inception. His paper, "Networks as Knowledge Generation-Utilization Systems," as well as his active participation in

the conference added additional dimensions to the discussion. Staff colleague Georgette Wang reminded us of the
importance of indigenous knowledge and knowledge systems in
the overall scheme of knowledge generation-utilization.

John Woods, then director of the UNDP Asia Pacific
Program for Development Training and Communication Planning
(DTCP), Bangkok, and Rogelio Cuyno, director of communications for the Philippine Council for Agriculture and
Resources Research and Development (PCARD), Los Baños, both
presented applied models of knowledge generation-utilization
based on their vast real-world field experience and
responsibility.

Joseph Ascroft, international consultant and evaluator
on development and development communication made a major
contribution to the conference with his paper and discussion
of the problems of Western development and communication
trying to impact developing nations. In addition, his
suggestions for improved communication models are included
as a part of Wimal Dissanayake's chapter on communication
models. The presence of Bob Rich, editor of the Knowledge
Creation, Diffusion and Utilization journal, was felt
throughout the conference. John Brien, University of
Sydney, enriched the conference from his vast background of
research, consulting and extension training in Australia and
the South Pacific Islands. John Tait and Eric Abbott of
Iowa State University presented preliminary findings from
their Inter-American Development Bank study of the interface
between the agricultural research and extension systems of
23 Latin American countries and the international
agricultural research centers.

In addition to those mentioned above, many other people
have contributed to this project, the conference and the
preparation of this book.

Of special note is John Middleton, who played a very
influential role in the early stages of the development of
this project. A staff member of the Communication Institute
at that time, John's contribution was made from his Peace Corps
experience in Korea and his great experience and skill in
systems analysis, communication planning and learner-
centered materials development.

Most of all is the contribution of Ron Havelock. At an
early stage in the project, Ron was brought to the Communication Institute for a series of seminars on the status and
prospects for the field. He also helped develop the structure and suggested participants for the conference. He
stayed on briefly after the conference to help evaluate it
and develop preliminary plans for the edited book. In

addition to his three chapters in this book, he has prepared
several working papers that have aided in the entire
development process leading to this book.

Four East-West Center interns also contributed to our
project and the development of this book: Mirella Gotangco,
Linda Rose, Mimi Nichter and Pearl Takemoto. Special thanks
to Pearl for final paper editing and working with authors on
citations. Institute editor Michael E. Macmillan was
helpful in the final formatting and preparation of the
manuscript for publication.

And finally our secretarial and support staff thank
the technological world for word-processing and duplication
equipment, but we thank our friends for their interest,
motivation, creativity, care and attention to detail far
beyond the machines and normal expectations. Milly Gates
Ring was the overseer and keeper of all correspondence,
drafts and details. Thanks to Joann Oshima, Janice
Morikawa, and Michelle Rousseau, who did the draft-by-draft,
day-by-day and late-afternoon and Saturday work. Louise
Ishibashi took us through the final revisions and formatting
for camera-ready copy.

Most of all, thanks to our colleagues who prepared,
revised, edited and chased down citations for the chapters
in the book—a labor of love. We have come to know them in
their good (mostly) and bad moments. We are sure we speak
for each of them in hoping that in some small way we have
made a contribution to the development of an important new
field. If a few more bits of relevant knowledge get
produced, transformed, packaged, disseminated and used to
alleviate, at least just a little bit, some of the problems
of our world, our rewards will be great.

George M. Beal
Wimal Dissanayake
Sumiye Konoshima

Contributors

GEORGE M. BEAL is a research associate at the Institute of
Culture and Communication, East-West Center, Honolulu,
Hawaii. He studied sociology, agricultural economics, and
social psychology at Iowa State University, where he earned
his Ph.D. degree. He served on the faculty at Iowa State
from 1947 to 1977. Beal's special interests include
adoption-diffusion, development communication, knowledge
generation-utilization, and organization effectiveness. He
has had experience in India, Thailand, Guatemala, Mexico,
and the Pacific Islands and is currently doing research and
consulting on a project on information and knowledge
exchange among agricultural research, dissemination, and
producer systems in selected South Pacific Islands. He is
the coauthor/editor of six books, ninety monographs, and
numerous book chapters and journal articles.

WIMAL DISSANAYAKE is assistant director and research
associate, Institute of Culture and Communication, East-West
Center, Honolulu, Hawaii. Educated in Sri Lanka, at the
University of Pennsylvania, and at the University of
Cambridge, he formerly served as chairman of the Department
of Mass Communication at the University of Sri Lanka and as
a consultant to the Community Development Services Center of
Sri Lanka. He is interested primarily in the cultural and
humanistic aspects of knowledge generation, dissemination,
and utilization. His interests and experience range from
the high philosophical to the pragmatics of development
communication. He has been directly concerned with
evaluating the appropriateness of Western knowledge for
Eastern problems and with communicating indigenous developed
Eastern strategies to Western audiences.

WILLIAM N. DUNN is professor in the Graduate School of
Public and International Affairs, University of Pittsburgh.
He is author and editor of books and articles on planned
social change, knowledge utilization, and public policy
analysis, including Public Policy Analysis (1983) and Policy
Analysis: Perspectives, Concepts, Methods (1986). His
current research includes the investigation of individual

and collective frames of reference and their effects on
knowledge utilization by policymakers, the development and
testing of new methodologies for structuring ill-structured
problems, and the construction of systems of indicators for
assessing the impact of science on society. He is editor of
the journal Knowledge: Creation, Diffusion, Utilization.

RONALD G. HAVELOCK is the author of many books and studies
on the process of knowledge utilization. His 1969 volume,
Planning for Innovation through the Dissemination and
Utilization of Knowledge, was the fist major work to explore
this field in depth and to identify the major research
traditions from nearly 5,000 sources. His subsequent
comparative studies of research utilization have spanned
such diverse fields as education, medicine, libraries,
rehabilitation, highway safety, computer technology, and
Third World Development. He has also written practical
handbooks for change agents and has conducted numerous
workshops and seminars on diffusion of innovations and the
planning of change through knowledge transfer and use in the
United States, Canada, Europe, and Asia. He is currently
research professor at George Mason University and is
carrying on research on the diffusion of innovations among
libraries, the use of knowledge by small businesses, and the
transfer strategies of major technology-producing agencies
of the U.S. government.

SUMIYE KONOSHIMA is a research information specialist at the
East-West Center, Honolulu, Hawaii. She earned her
bachelor's degree in English literature and psychology at
Hope College, a master's degree in social psychology at
Teacher's College, Columbia University, and a master's
degree in library studies at the University of Hawaii.
Since 1963, she has been involved with activities in
documentation and information storage, retrieval, and
dissemination/networking at the East-West Center. She has
been coordinator and project team member of numerous
workshops and conferences on information networking,
documentation, computerization of information centers,
information needs and uses, and training internships. She
also has been a consultant to agencies and institutions in
Asia and the Pacific.

BRUCE KOPPEL is a research associate with the East-West
Center Resource Systems Institute. He received his
doctorate in rural sociology from Cornell University in
1973. His major interests are in the interactions between

public policy, science and technology, and social change.
He has pursued these interests through a number of academic
and applied activities in Asia and the United States. He
has considerable experience writing about and doing
technology assessment, evaluation, and impact analysis with
special emphasis on agriculture and agricultural research.

JUDITH K. LARSEN is a senior research scientist with Cognos
Associates in Los Altos, California. Her research has
focused on how information is used by local organizations,
and what impact the information has on the organization's
activities and services. Larsen is currently conducting a
national study of knowledge utilization in community mental
health centers, including factors affecting change in
centers. She also has conducted research on technology
transfer in high-technology industry in Silicon Valley.
This research includes studies of information exchange among
engineers, long-term policy options in the semiconductor
industry, changing lifestyles in postindustrial society, and
the impact of technology on people.

HERBERT F. LIONBERGER, professor emeritus of rural sociology
at the University of Missouri-Columbia, is an inter-
nationally recognized researcher of information generating-
distribution-use systems and the diffusion of new ideas and
practices. He is the author or coauthor of some sixty
journal articles and book chapters and of three books
relating to these subjects. He is a frequent resource
person in international conferences where the dissemination
and utilization of science-based information for developmental purposes is an issue. He served as an agricultural
communications consultant to the Indian government's
agricultural and family planning programs and on the joint
USAID-University of Missouri agricultural research programs.

PETER MEEHAN received his B.S. in English and journalism at
Iowa State University in 1972. After a number of work
experiences, including program director for a YMCA in Sri
Lanka, he returned to Iowa State and earned master's degrees
in anthropology and journalism and mass communication.
While pursuing these degrees, he was a research associate
with George Beal, and they worked together in the field of
knowledge generation-utilization and published "Knowledge
Production and Utilization: A General Model, Third Approximation," in 1977. Meehan pursued his Ph.D. at the University of Michigan in 1979 under Peter Clarke in the interdisciplinary program on communication, sociology, political

science, and psychology. He became ill and died of cancer
in September 1980 at age 30. Meehan is listed as coauthor
with George Beal on the models paper in this volume, not
only because of his initial contribution to the development
of the model presented, but to, in a small way, honor him
for his high motivation, scholarly ability, warm and
outgoing personality, and great potential, cut short by his
untimely death.

EVERETT M. ROGERS is Walter H. Annenberg Professor of
Communications and associate dean for doctoral studies,
Annenberg School of Communications, University of Southern
California, where he teaches and conducts research on the
diffusion of innovations. Rogers has been involved in such
research for more than thirty years, both in the United
States and in several Third World nations. He is the author
of Diffusion of Innovations (1983), the third edition of his
work on this topic. His current interest is the diffusion
of new communication technologies, especially those
involving computers. With Judith K. Larsen, he is the
author of Silicon Valley Fever: Growth of High Technology
Culture (1984). He recently published Communication
Technology (1986).

JACK ROTHMAN is professor in the School of Social Welfare,
University of California, Los Angeles, where he heads the
Macro Intervention Program. He has been a researcher,
teacher, and practitioner in human services for more than
twenty-five years. He holds a Ph.D. in social psychology
from Columbia University and an M.S.W. from Ohio State
University. A continuing theme in his work has been the
systematic application of social science knowledge to
contemporary issues of policy and practice. He is the
author of thirteen books, including works on organizational
innovation and change, community organization, and race and
ethnic relations. He has taught at the University of
Michigan and the University of Pittsburgh and has lectured
in Europe and the Near East. He has been a recipient of the
Gunnar Myrdal Award for Distinguished Research in Human
Services of the Evaluation Research Society.

NIELS G. RÖLING is professor and head, Department of
Extension Education, Agricultural University, Wageningen,
the Netherlands. He obtained his B.Sc. and M.Sc. degrees in
rural sociology at the Agricultural University in
Wageningen, the Netherlands (1963) and a Ph.D. degree in
communication at Michigan State University (1970). He spent

two years as a lecturer with the University of Ibadan,
Nigeria, and subsequently joined a MSU/AID research project
on the diffusion of innovations in rural societies in Enugu,
Nigeria. He has also participated in a field experiment
that attempted to control the factors affecting the
utilization of agricultural knowledge by farmers in Kenya
(1973) and in a working party on the small farmer and
development cooperation, funded by the Netherlands
Directorate General for Developmental Cooperation.

CAROL H. WEISS is senior lecturer and senior research
associate at the Harvard University Graduate School of
Education. She is the author of Social Science Research and
Decision-Making (1980), Evaluation Research: Methods of
Assessing Program Effectiveness (1972), and other books on
evaluation research and the utilization of research in
policymaking. She has published scores of papers in such
journals as Evaluation Review, Policy Analysis, New
Directions in Program Evaluation, Journal of Higher
Education, American Sociological Review, and Public Admini-
stration Review, and she serves on the editorial boards of
Society, American Behavioral Scientist, Policy Studies
Journal, and Knowledge: Creation, Diffusion, Utilization,
among others. The winner of the Evaluation Research
Society's Myrdal Award for Science in 1980, she was
president of the Policy Studies Organization (1983-84) and
was the first Congressional Fellow of the American
Sociological Association (1983).

GERALD ZALTMAN has a Ph.D. degree in sociology from the
Johns Hopkins University and an M.B.A. degree in marketing
from the University of Chicago. He is the Albert Wesley
Frey Distinguished Professor of Marketing, University of
Pittsburgh. He is also co-director of the University of
Pittsburgh Program for the Study of Knowledge Use and
director of the Pittsburgh Research Institute for Studies in
Marketing. Zaltman is active as a researcher and as a
consultant to numerous firms and nonprofit agencies in the
United States and abroad. His special interests focus on
the responses of individual consumers and organizations to
new products and services and the development of product
management strategy. Zaltman is coauthor or editor of
twenty-seven books and monographs and is a frequent contributor to professional journals and conferences. He is a
past president of the Association for Consumer Research and
is on the editorial boards of numerous journals in
management and the social sciences.

PART ONE

Introduction

Introduction

The generation, acquisition and application of knowledge and information are crucial elements for social, economic and cultural development of societies. The world is especially conscious of this axiom in the context of today's emerging information society and the knowledge explosion. Indicative of this phenomenal growth within the past four centuries are the following statistics from just one small part of the spectrum of knowledge fields.

In 1665, there were two scientific journals in existence. In 1965, the National Lending Library for Science and Technology in England (The Library attempts to collect all periodicals that might contain materials of interest to the practicing scientist or technologist) identified 26,235 periodical titles in science and technology. By 1974, titles received or on order by the Library was 49,440. The number of books in the field of science increased more than 40 percent in a ten-year period. Patents issued in the United States alone between 1960 and 1974 numbered 60 percent of the total number of U.S. patents issued up through 1960.

The emerging information society is witnessing also the increasing dominance of knowledge industries in the economies of many countries and the heightened socio-economic interdependence among nations of the world. Concurrently with changes in the information environment, there has been rapid growth in communication and information technologies.

In spite of the technological developments and the knowledge explosion, however, all countries of the world still have unsolved problems in most facets of societal life, to which existing knowledge and information could be applied for solutions. Gross inequities in access,

1

distribution and use of knowledge and information exist
within and among societies today. Groups that control and
have access to the technologies and the information and
knowledge resources possess a strong power advantage over
competing groups. Weaknesses in systems for accessing and
applying knowledge and information to solve problems persist
even in technologically advanced countries. These
inequities and discrepancies in access, distribution and
application of information and knowledge in relation to the
emerging power position of the information/knowledge
industry sector have resulted in heated discussion on a
number of critical international issues--e.g., technology
transfer, information imbalance, the new world information
order, the new international economic order, etc.--and
underscore the importance of knowledge and information
generation, dissemination and use systems for social,
economic and political development.

The field of knowledge generation and utilization as
conceived today can trace the roots of its history and its
emergence to the flurry of post-World War II activities in
international transfer of resources, knowledge, technology,
personnel, and skills for development purposes. It has
become apparent during the process of carrying out these
programs that knowledge utilization systems have not been as
effective as they might be and that there are a number of
major critical issues and problems that need to be
investigated and solved if knowledge is to be optimally
utilized for the betterment of the human condition.

THE RESEARCH PROCESS PROBLEM

In contemporary society, research is perceived as primary in generating knowledge and in providing information
for solutions to problems. Presumably, research results in
knowledge and information which ought to be applied toward
action for development and improvement of societies. However, costly research continues to be underutilized. Knowledge use systems have failed in incorporating mechanisms to
strengthen the probability of research use.

One problematic factor has been the defining of the
problem to be researched. Definition of the problem will
determine what kind of knowledge will be generated.
Political and economic factors and decisions will influence
the process of defining the research problem. Who defines
the problem, and for whom and for what purpose the research
is conducted will affect the output of research knowledge.

As a consequence of these influences impinging upon the research process, many of the "real world" problems cannot look to research findings and their application for solutions. Solutions offered in the context of one segment of society have been found to be inappropriate for other segments of society. Thus, the inability of systems to correlate research information needs with research output hampers the potential for full and optimum utilization of knowledge generated by research.

THE INNOVATION, CHANGE AND DEVELOPMENT BIAS

In the initial enthusiasm of fostering development in various countries following the end of World War II, the transfer of knowledge and technology in the name of innovation and change for development was vigorously promoted among aid recipients under the assumption that innovation and change were "good" and ought to be accepted and used. Even though criticism of this approach and attitude to knowledge transfer and use has surfaced during the past few years, remnants of the bias persist, resulting in inappropriate application and rejection of particular knowledges and technologies.

KNOWLEDGE RESOURCES: QUANTITY, KIND AND ACCESS

There is no lack of knowledge in terms of quantity. The sheer volume and variety of formats of informational materials existing and generated in the world creates enormous problems for acquiring, handling, storing, updating, disseminating and using knowledge. Even though substantial advances have been made in information and communication technologies, vast quantities of knowledge are inadequately organized and stored, and consequently the probability of their use is diminished.

A basic problem for knowledge utilization is the task of identifying and locating the appropriate knowledge out of the multitude of resources. In seeking information and knowledge users generally think of and turn to recorded information, especially in the developed and industrialized world. An important resource that is often overlooked is people. There is a kind of knowledge contained within persons and their minds, gained from experience and tradition, that proves to be as useful and valuable as documented scientific knowledge. The ethos of science and

its bias that only scientific knowledge is valuable and
useful compounds the underutilization of "people" resources
and undermines the potential application of "folk" and
indigenous knowledge and systems of communicating knowledge
which might be more appropriate and useful in some
situations.

The ability to access resources is crucial to knowledge
use. Potential users of knowledge resources are faced with
a number of hurdles related to access before they can
acquire and apply knowledge. Communication between user and
source may be difficult because of distances between them or
because of inadequate channels or means of communication.
Where access technology is available, the control of that
technology can also prevent access to knowledge resources
and dictate what resources can be accessed.

These above-mentioned environmental factors peripheral
to any particular core information system are only part of
the access problems. Knowledge and information resource
centers also have deficiencies and weaknesses which hamper
access and create problems for users. The resource base may
be disorganized, or organized in such a way so as to make it
difficult for the user to identify and retrieve information
appropriate for his needs. The resource base system may not
provide approaches to searching the knowledge base so that
only the appropriate and required information is retrieved
from the vast quantity of information available in the
resource base.

PROMOTING KNOWLEDGE USE--COMMUNICATION AND
DISSEMINATION

Lack of concern for how and in what form knowledge and
information should be presented to specific potential users
has impeded use of available knowledge. Although some
strides have been made in presenting information in language
understandable to the user and in formats that enhance the
learning process, there is still a need to investigate the
nature of the knowledge and its transformability and
adaptation in relation to the user and use and to test
knowledge products for their desired effects.

Information and knowledge cannot be utilized unless
communication takes place between the source of that
knowledge and the potential user of that knowledge.
Dissemination as part of the communication process is
therefore critical for optimum use of knowledge and
information. Many knowledge utilization systems either have

no active dissemination program or planned strategies to
reach potential users. Others are not prepared to mobilize
needed knowledge that already exists. Some are contained
within institutions where the prevalent attitude toward and
perception of information sources and centers are that of
archives for the storing and safekeeping of knowledge for
posterity. Information-seeking behavior patterns have not
been fully institutionalized.

PROBLEMS OF THE KNOWLEDGE UTILIZATION FIELD

The field of knowledge utilization has derived its
concepts and theories from psychology, sociology,
communication, education, information science and other
fields of learning in the natural sciences, social sciences
and humanities. The development of concepts and theories
has been fragmentary. Individual researchers have tended to
focus and work on the subfields of generation, diffusion and
utilization separately. It is only recently that these
researchers have begun to work with each other and to
discuss and investigate the knowledge generation-utilization
process within a conceptual framework of "systems."
Although a journal devoted to the topic and some empirical
studies have emerged during the past few years, there has
been no concerted effort to produce a comprehensive overview
and state of the field. The articulation of critical
issues, concepts and models on knowledge utilization is just
beginning.

Current knowledge utilization research addresses these
critical issues and problems and attempts to find some
answers and solutions. It examines processes and factors
that impinge upon the generation, exchange and use of
knowledge. It asks, how do systems work? Why don't they or
why do they work? It asks, what are the prevailing
theories, models, and systems? What strategies can be
developed to improve systems and what can we learn from
research to improve systems? Answers to these research
questions in knowledge utilization will provide answers not
only for the development of this knowledge field but also
for communication and information issues and problems that
seriously impact social and economic progress.

The purpose of this book then is to provide a forum in
which the various facets of knowledge utilization can be
considered and discussed, and to present an overview of the
state of the field.

OVERVIEW

Any basis for discussion of a field of study requires a definition of what constitutes this field. The first section of the book provides this basis, offers a definition and places the study of knowledge utilization in context with related fields of study and historical events. The second section reflects the evolving concepts and theories and the development of some of the more prominent models of knowledge utilization systems. These models are primarily derived from observation and analysis of processes in actual experiences of knowledge generation, dissemination and use. Since a systemic approach is common to these models, crucial for this approach is the concept of linkage of the generator of knowledge to the user of knowledge, which is discussed in Part 3. Knowledge use systems operate within an environment that impacts knowledge generation use processes. Therefore, environmental factors are considered in Part 4 as recognition of their importance for understanding better knowledge-use systems and the interaction and relationship between systems and the total situation in which they operate. Knowledge generation and utilization as a field of study does have a history of research. In Part 5 the state of research in the field, the central concepts and methodologies are assessed and discussed. And finally, for what purpose do we study this field of knowledge generation and utilization? Part 6 examines implications of knowledge gleaned from research for application in societal development and change.

Definition and Scope

In Chapter 1, Ronald Havelock, certainly to be regarded as one the of the "founding fathers" of the field, presents his ideas on the definition and scope of this new domain. He begins by dealing with different definitions and categorizations of knowledge per se. He then presents a six-category knowledge process taxonomy: generation, verification, transformation, transfer, reception and utilization. This is followed by identifying some of the different attempts to order or model these processes. Another section deals with how this domain relates to other domains. The latter part of the chapter deals with "major debates" and issues in the field and ends with his ideas of some of the major trends in research and applications in the field and a cautious look into the future.

Models

In order to provide an understanding of the entire
process of knowledge generation, dissemination and utilization, general theoretical models have been developed. Basic
questions that may be raised regarding the models in Part 2
include: do they reflect reality, are they bound by time and
space, and can they be generalized?

In Chapter 2, Everett Rogers critically reviews the
dominant models of knowledge transfer and use. He discusses
the elements of the agricultural extension model and the
weaknesses and strengths of its extension into other areas
and the diffusion model. He suggests that the pervasiveness
of underlying assumptions of the agricultural extension
model have hampered the development of the knowledge
transfer field.

In Chapter 3, Dissanayake describes and analyzes the
development of communication models in relation to the
expansion of thinking on knowledge generation and use. He
identifies three main stages in the evolution of communication models and shows how each stage led to a particular
perspective on knowledge utilization.

In Chapter 4, Havelock, in an updated and revised
version of his original general-level model, provides an
approach to the knowledge generation-utilization process in
systems terms.

Lionberger in his chapter discusses a diffusion model
based on experience in knowledge generation and use of the
land grant universities in the United States. This model
incorporates both the independence and the interdependence
of social systems at the macro and micro levels.

Beal and Meehan in Chapter 6 present a theoretical
communication model that focuses on intermediaries in the
knowledge generation and utilization process.

Rothman's chapter illustrates how the general principles of the research and development model might be
adapted to social knowledge utilization.

In Beal's "user-driven" model, the focus is on the
user, the user's definition of reality and the user's social
sub-system. Knowledge will more probably be adopted and
used if it is developed and tested in the user's physical,
social and perceptual environment.

Linkages

The linkage concept is a central concern in the

knowledge utilization field. In the main chapter of Part 3, Havelock summarizes current thinking and conceptualization in the concept of linkage. The link-chain metaphor is used to describe the knowledge system and to analyze the connection between any two subsystems or "worlds."

Röling discusses the dichotomy between "man-the-scientist" and the use of technical knowledge for control of the environment and "man-the-villager" and the use of social process knowledge. Effective linkages between users and these systems are needed to promote knowledge use for solving the problems of society. He suggests approaches, guidelines and strategies for creating these linkages.

Environment

The importance of environmental factors in the knowledge utilization process has been recognized by scholars in recent years. Environment is used in this context to indicate the need for a holistic approach for fuller understanding of the knowledge generation-use process. Knowledge generation and use take place in a social-cultural environment as well as a physical environment. These environments are systemically interrelated. Change in any aspect of the environment will result in disequilibrium in the social system and will require adaptation by aspects of the environment to attain a new state of equilibrium. Knowledge emerges out of this environment and takes on unique meaning because of the particular environment from which it emerges.

Dissanayake, in Chapter 11, suggests a hermeneutical approach to knowledge dissemination—a perspective in which knowledge is transposed and absorbed within the values and meaning contexts of the interpreter of that knowledge. Within a hermeneutic framework, knowledge generation and use is an interactive process contingent upon social, cultural and environmental factors.

In Chapter 12, Konoshima defines and describes the key concepts and components of the newly emerging field of information science as they relate to the environment in which knowledge utilization takes place, and how they impact the processes of transfer of knowledge from generator to the user.

Koppel, in the concluding chapter of Part 4, examines the ethical dimension of the knowledge generation and use enterprise. He identifies the reasons why research and development enterprises have difficulty in coming to terms

with ethical issues. He suggests posing some questions the
answers to which would facilitate the development of a
mechanism for assessing the ethical dimension of the
environment as well as explaining the value choices
involved.

Research

   Scholars working in knowledge generation utilization
recognize that a solid foundation of research is needed if
the field is to develop. Such a research program is
lacking. Part 5 assesses the state of research in the field
and makes a number of suggestions for conceptual and
methodological approaches.
   In Chapter 14, William Dunn discusses the central
concepts in the field of knowledge and knowledge use. He
believes past research has been based on oversimplified and
misleading conceptions of these central terms. He presents
a number of dimensions upon which knowledge and knowledge
use can be classified and suggests several principles which
should contribute to conceptual refinement and clarification
in the field.
   In Chapter 15, Larsen goes beyond these central
concepts to present other general-level variables important
in knowledge utilization research and provides an example of
their use in a field study.
   In Chapter 16, Dunn reports on a long-term study of
knowledge utilization research. After profiling these
studies, Dunn then describes in some detail research
methodology/procedures under these general types:
naturalistic observation, content analysis, and questionnaires and interviews. He also includes a number of scales
and indices. He concludes with an assessment of methodological strengths and weaknesses and suggests ways to
resolve some of these problems. An extensive bibliography
is included.

Implications for Policy and Social Change

   Part 6 deals with the role of knowledge utilization in
policy formation and social change. Weiss sees social
science knowledge contributing to a number of facets of the
decision making process and its context. Policy positions
and decisions are seen as the result of three main forces:
ideologies, interests and information. To expect informa-

tion to have an immediate and independent impact on policy making distorts the reality of how decisions are made.

Zaltman sees knowledge utilization as a part of the well-established broader topical area of social change. He takes a number of concepts and propositions from planned social change and demonstrates how effective knowledge utilization facilitates effective social action. Zaltman emphasizes the "user" rather than "knowledge product" orientation and concludes this orientation will result in more successful knowledge generation and utilization leading to desired social change.

Future Prospects

The final chapter in this volume looks into the future and considers the prospects for development of the knowledge utilization field.

1

The Knowledge Perspective: Definition and Scope of a New Study Domain

Ronald G. Havelock

Definition of a field might be a risky business if people took it seriously. It would be the intellectual version of staking out claims to land. We would have to be very careful that we knew who all the other stakeholders were and where they had staked, or else we would have to be prepared for nasty squabbling, endless and expensive legal battles and maybe even a bit of shooting. In the intellectual world there can be bitter disputes too, of course, but the legal battles tend to come over very specific word uses and who had priority. When it comes to staking claims for intellectual territory, the larger the domain, the less venom is likely to be involved, because nobody has to take the claim seriously. At that level of generality, intellectual claims do not have to be taken very seriously unless they are backed up by hundreds or even thousands of venerated advocates, and even then only when the new claims threaten to undermine old territorial prerogatives.

It is likely that with the proclamation that is made here, that "knowledge generation, exchange, and utilization" represents a very important new territory in the intellectual world, a new perspective that either will have or should have important consequences in altering our thinking about human cultures and where they are going. The territory is, indeed, very large, and the venerable scholars have not yet flocked to its banner in large numbers. Furthermore, it is not well-marked and it may not turn out to be a real territory after all. Given all that, there are still a few of us, many represented in this volume, who would like to see the new territory marked and recognized and then, perhaps, even heralded. The purpose of this chapter is to begin that marking process and to do so eclectically and

12

inclusively, if possible, so that most of the people I would
consider "knowledge perspectivists" can at least recognize
themselves if not their description.

I begin with the term "knowledge perspective" but only
with great intellectual discomfort because that is not what
I really mean. The focus of concern thus appears to be
"knowledge" and this is true up to a point but still misleading because this new field has significance not because
of its focus on "knowledge" (which is not at all new) but
because of its focus on how knowledge is processed. Hence
the more awkward but more accurate expression: "knowledge
generation, exchange, and utilization (KGEU). Just five
years ago a journal was founded with the similar and
similarly uncatchy title Knowledge: Creation, Diffusion,
Utilization. The idea is the same, and the territory which
we are trying to mark out is the same, but we are still
waiting for the right banner.

What follows is essentially a taxonomy of the knowledge
perspective. It is divided into six sections. The first
deals with definitions and categorizations of knowledge, per
se, an ancient and quasi-philosophical pursuit, but nonetheless one that still excites some interest. The second
section contains what might be considered the heart of the
taxonomy, a breakdown of knowledge processes into six categories: generation, verification, transformation, transfer,
reception, and utilization. Next, identification of the
different "models" of KGEU, where the different ways in
which the KGEU processes are ordered and related by different scholars are discussed. The following section is
concerned with the "major debates" within the field, the
issues that are discussed, researched, and argued most
vehemently. In some ways, these debates give the field its
energy and its momentum. The next section tries to indicate
how the domain of the knowledge perspective relates to other
domains, past and present. Some of its roots are clear,
some obscure; and some fields that were roots still coexist
and perhaps compete with KGEU for territory in terms of
public and academic recognition. The final section contains
some perceptions of the author regarding important trends in
the evolution of KGEU studies and applications which portend
a more prominent future for the field.

DEFINITION AND DIFFERENTIATION OF THE TERM "KNOWLEDGE"

The term "knowledge" is, indeed, the centerpiece of
this narrative, and I think I know what it means. It is the

collective achievement of the human race, nothing less.
"Cogito ergo sum" could mean "I think, therefore I am" but
more likely it means "I know" or "I have knowledge, therefore, I am." Knowledge is the one thing that accumulates
among humans, that can be passed from one human to another
almost intact (in the best of circumstances) and that can be
stored from generation to generation or perhaps for an
infinity of generations in some non-human form to be redis-
covered by the infinity-plus-one generation, to be carried
in those infinity-plus-one heads more or less in the form
that it was originally offered. Not exactly a definition
but obviously something very important. Let us proceed.

Definitions of "Knowledge"

The definition of the term "knowledge" is a much
steamier topic among philosophers and especially
sociologists than the casual observer could ever imagine.
In fact, there has been much written on this subject alone.
The very topic "the sociology of knowledge" as originally
coined by Karl Mannheim very largely revolved around
definitional issues, specifically whether knowledge existed
as a human product independent of its creators or merely as
a by-product of the particular people or culture from whom a
particular body of knowledge derived. It is not the purpose
of this chapter to resolve or even enter into this argument
(although we have strong opinions on the subject) but rather
to note that this, the definition of knowledge, is one of
the provinces of the territory of the knowledge perspective.

Related Concepts

The closest relative of "knowledge" conceptually is
probably "wisdom," but wisdom is clearly the possession of
individuals rather than a culture, and it cannot exist
independently of its holder while "knowledge" can. "Facts"
are a type of knowledge, to be sure, but clearly sub-
ordinate, having only the order that could be imparted to
them either by a "wise" person or a body of "knowledge."
Without order or relation to other facts and other aspects
of life, facts have very little independent meaning.
"Ideas" is a broader and looser term for cognitions, things
people think. Ideas may be passed on, like knowledge, but
they may also be very particular. When ideas are verified
in some way they become knowledge; when ideas get together

and get powerful they become "ideologies." Ideologies,
according to some authorities but not all, are the essence
of knowledge.

"Information" is another term that has to be understood
from the knowledge perspective. Information is clearly a
broader term and includes all knowledge. To some extent the
knowledge perspective has roots in theories of information
(discussed later in this chapter). On the other hand,
"information" has no cultural status. Any ant has information and so do all forms of life, including plant life,
according to classic information theory. Somehow or other,
"information" has come down to us as a purer term than
"knowledge," something more acceptable and manipulable in
scientific terms, less freighted with cultural baggage, but
it also means less. The term "message," which I used
liberally in a previous publication (Havelock 1969), is
something like "information" with the exception that the
attribute of transferability from one point to another is
stressed. In fact, I rather like the term "message" because
the notion of transfer seems to me to be so central to the
entire realm of KGEU. Perhaps "knowledge messaging" is a
phrase that would serve as an umbrella term for the
knowledge perspective at some future date, but our loose
consensus has not yet reached those heights.

Other terms such as "concept," "theory," "construct,"
"paradigm," "language," and so on deserve explication and
comparison to the focal construct, but this again is a task
that belongs in another paper, probably by another author.
The need here is to point out the domain and the relevance
of such discourse to the domain.

Knowledge Types and Typologies

As the primary cognitive content of culture, knowledge
includes all facts, concepts, theories, and artifacts that
are passed from one generation to another. This would
certainly include all religion, literature, art, archi-
tecture, law, medicine, science, engineering, education,
special skills of all kinds, folkways, mores, myths, and
beliefs that are shared. Reviewing such a list, many
readers may feel some discomfort already at the lack of
ordering. In this list there is no distinction between good
and bad, truth and falsehood, fiction and fact. There are
probably two dimensions of consideration which are of
greatest interest to knowledge perspectivists. One is
"verifiability," the extent to which the knowledge can be

subjected to various tests of empirical truth. Religious
and literary knowledge, for example, can be judged to be
profoundly true and universally valid in some sense, but
such knowledge is not really verifiable empirically, and
such tests are usually protested by true believers as
irrelevant. Certain philosophies, ideologies, and professional practices can also fall into this category if their
adherents choose to put them there. Indeed, empirically
discredited knowledge that has been widely held is likely to
have a very long post-empirical life in a culture. Such
phenomena are of great interest to some knowledge perspectivists. There are also many scholars who concern themselves with the generation, exchange, and utilization of all
kinds of unverifiable knowledge. Nevertheless the mainstream of the new movement is concerned primarily with
knowledge in the verifiable category.

The other major dimension is "utility." Utility can be
Note that "verifiable" is not the same as "verified."
Some knowledge perspectivists have primary interest only in
knowledge that is already empirically verified or in the
processes of verification. This would include the sociology
of science and the study of the transfer and utilization of
new technologies and validated innovations. Verification as
a knowledge process is further discussed in the next
section.

The other major dimension is "utility." Utility can be
defined most broadly as the extent to which knowledge has
the power to enhance human lives. Note that by this
definition unverifiable knowledge can have just as much
utility as verifiable and verified knowledge. Thus there is
nothing of higher utility than a religious belief which
elevates the spirit, provides comfort and solace from grief
and pain of all kinds. Judging utility, however, is no
simple matter. Almost all knowledge has potential utility
to someone. Thus, more rigorous knowledge perspectivists
are inclined to require some sort of empirical test of
utility as well as validity in other senses. For some the
utility test is primary. The utility dimension also lends
itself to almost infinite sub-categorization, and such
efforts have been pervasive in the recent KGEU literature.
Rich (1977), for example, has made a good deal of the
distinction between "conceptual" use and "instrumental" use,
partly with the intent of reminding us of the great
importance and high frequency of the former.

Another way to divide up knowledge is by the culture
from which it originates. This is an especially important
distinction to make when the context of KGEU is international, east-west, north-south, or Third World develop-

ment. Cultural relativism of knowledge has been argued back
and forth vehemently since the time that Mannheim coined the
term "sociology of knowledge," but the controversy takes on
a new coloring in these pages. To the extent that knowledge, including scientific and technical knowledge, is
culture bound, to that extent the value of its intercultural transmission can be questioned and is. While I
have definite views on the issue, for the purposes of this
paper it suffices to note its importance. Knowledge
relativism appears in many guises. The most global is that
the great bulk of contemporary science and technology is
"western" and thus somehow or to some degree irrelevant or
inappropriate for other cultures in the east or in the
developing world generally. A narrower and more generally
accepted version holds that much, if not all, knowledge has
a cultural context that is partly specific. Thus it is
important to identify that part for what it is and in the
process of intercultural transfer to make adaptations and
reinterpretations such that the receiving culture is both
protected from cultural invasion and at the same time
allowed to benefit most fully and appropriately from the
utility value inherent in the knowledge.

Knowledge Characteristics

It is possible to classify items of knowledge on many
different dimensions, and a persisting theme among KGEU
researchers is that these dimensions are important. Some
characteristics are difficult to distinguish from "types" as
discussed above. For example, the degree of scientific
validation, or utility, or culture-boundedness could each be
viewed as a characteristic of any piece of knowledge. Other
characteristics commonly cited are "complexity," "relative
advantage" (applicable mostly to instrumental knowledge
uses), "divisibility" (signifying for technical innovations
the extent to which separate components are separately
communicable and adoptable), "communicability," "acceptability" (to a receiving culture), and "adaptability."
Various researchers have developed classification schemas
and then have tried to correlate these to various outcomes,
so far without notable success, but the effort still appears
to be worthwhile and persists as a KGEU theme.

Knowledge Processes

"Knowledge generation, exchange, and utilization"
implies that there are three major processes that the
knowledge perspectivists are concerned about. Actually I
think there are at least six main categories, each with many
sub-categories. These are: (1) generation, (2) verification, (3) transformation, (4) transfer, (5) reception, and
(6) utilization.

Generation. Perhaps the most significant split within
the knowledge perspectivist community is between those who
are interested in the creation of knowledge and those who
are interested in what happens to it after it is created.
There is, indeed, a respectable literature on the psychology
of creativity which is almost never cited by KGEU scholars.
We also find this split to some extent in the contributors
to the journal Knowledge.

Restricting the discourse primarily to scientific and
technological knowledge, it is fairly safe to say that the
act of pure de novo knowledge creation is rather rare. Most
acts that are taken (quite properly) as creations are really
transformations of one kind or another, for example, uses of
knowledge in new contexts, novel juxtapositions and
syntheses, and so forth. Genuinely new creations can be
grouped under seven headings as follows:

(1) Discoveries: the identification and labelling of
entirely new phenomena, as when Galileo looked through his
telescope and discovered the moons of Jupiter. Few discoveries in science occur completely out of the blue. Many,
if not most, are deduced from theory or from other bits of
evidence, as in the discovery of atomic particles.

(2) Definitions: vastly underrated as important
creative acts by non-philosophers of science, definitions
represent the bedrock of empirical knowledge. They represent the attachment of observable phenomena to language,
thus allowing many types of higher order knowledge-building
operations such as abstraction, communication as concept,
ordering, quantification, etc.

(3) Distinctions: the subdivision of definitions,
i.e., the discovery that one defined phenomena is really two
or more. Distinctions may be purely conceptual-linguistic
or may be empirical as well as conceptual (combining the
notions of "discovery" and "definition"). In either case,
the generation of distinctions is a vital aspect of the
knowledge-building process. "Differentiation" is a nearly
equivalent concept.

(4) Relations: just a half-step beyond distinctions

is the positing or determination of connections or relationships between defined concepts and phenomena. The simplest
form of relation is the assignment of two defined elements
to the same category, but relations can be of any complexity. The ordering of elements on a scale of time,
shape, size, location, etc. represents a fairly primitive
form of relating. Theories represent the more elaborated
forms of positing relations.

(5) Quantifications: efforts to specify relations in
precise terms that can be measured empirically. Most forms
of instrumentation, validation, and theory testing
necessarily involve quantification.

(6) Syntheses: in some ways the opposite of distinctions; the bringing together of previously disparate knowledge elements including discoveries, definitions, and
relations of all kinds. Strictly speaking synthesis is also
a type of relating.

(7) Rearrangements: the dissolution of previously
accepted relations and syntheses and the construction of new
ones; perhaps the most refined form of creative knowledge
building. It was exactly this kind of knowledge building
that was represented in the proposal by Copernicus that a
simpler and more elegant formulation of planetary motion
would have the sun and not the earth at the center. Thomas
Kuhn (1970) has made a good deal of the notion of "paradigm
shift" as a massive reorientation of a scientific field
which results when particularly crucial rearrangements are
made and then come to be accepted by the elite members of
that field, as happened in the case of Copernicus.

The seven hardly represent an exhaustive listing of the
processes of knowledge generation. We have not begun to
consider how knowledge other than scientific knowledge is
generated, nor have we considered the generation processes
for knowledge that does not appear in conceptual form, such
as tools and instruments, skills, and technological devices.
A complete taxonomy would require elucidation of all these
types.

Verification. A crucial feature of scientific knowledge processing is verification, the effort to establish
and confirm the truth of a generated piece of knowledge,
whether it be a discovery, a definition, a distinction, a
relation, a quantification, a synthesis, or a rearrangement.
Verification involves the combined application to all these
knowledge forms of logical reasoning and various sets of
rules for the collection and presentation of evidence. To a
remarkable extent, the rules of logic are accepted by
educated persons worldwide as a proper foundation for valid

knowledge, but other rules and procedures are more controversial. They are especially controversial in the social
sciences and outside the confines of science in general.

Verification processes are the foundation stone of
science. Without them there would be no science, regardless
of how many discoveries, definitions, and distinctions were
made, and regardless of how many relations were posited.
This is why the lack of consensus on rules of evidence in
the social sciences is such a continuing issue and why
social science is widely questioned as a "science" by
physical scientists and laymen alike.

Transformation. In further discussions of "generation," knowledge processes that might be considered fully
creative were listed. On close examination, however, it is
very difficult to distinguish de novo creativity from transformation. Almost all created knowledge is created out of
some other knowledge or derived, even by opposition, from
other knowledge (e.g., again in the case of Copernicus there
was no new knowledge involved, strictly speaking, and
Copernicus did not discover anything. He did not even challenge the basic Ptolemaic theory of epicycles!). Be that as
it may, the knowledge perspectivists usually regard transformations as distinct from generation processes, per se.
Again we might posit at least seven distinct types of
transformation.

(1) Collection: perhaps the simplest form and perhaps
not a transformation at all, nevertheless an important type
of knowledge manipulation which can lead in all sorts of
directions including the most elaborate theory-making.
Obvious collection forms are files, data banks, libraries,
compendia. For at least 2,000 years the book has been the
most convenient and otherwise successful form for collected
knowledge.

(2) Summarization: most other knowledge manipulations
including effective transfer and utilization would not be
possible without summarization. There is no limit to the
extent to which knowledge can be summarized although debates
continue to rage about the cutting point beyond which all
meaning or essential meaning is lost. The full potential of
the summarization of language is probably only fully appreciated by those who write headlines and headings for
newspapers.

(3) Sorting: the placing of knowledge in categories
(usually guided by ordering relations or theory), a significant transformation process, central to such scientific
fields as biology and geology. Collection is generally of
little value without both summarization (titles, abstracts)

and sorting (cataloging, indexing, shelving, etc.)

While the very young professional field of library science is one of the central supporting disciplines of the knowledge perspective, its highest concentration of concern has been with transformations and particularly with collecting, summarizing, and sorting. One of the promising trends in the emergence of the knowledge perspective has been the inclusion of library science within a broader spectrum of knowledge processes and the expansion of concern and interest by library professionals into other related knowledge processes, including generation, verification, transfer, and utilization.

(4) Translation: in the narrowest sense from one language to another; a crucial task for worldwide knowledge transfer and utilization and for generation of knowledge worldwide which is truly based on existing knowledge. The term "translation" also fits those knowledge processes that involve the transformation from one style of presentation to another, from one context to another, and from one medium (e.g., print) to another (e.g., graphic).

(5) Materialization: when the "translation" is from more conceptual to more concrete, from more ideal to more practical, from more basic to more applied, the transformation is of a more radical kind. In many ways, these kinds of transformations are just as creative as any other type of knowledge generation. Making ideas and concepts into products, practical tools, and skills is sometimes referred to as "development," as in the expression, "research and development." This term is only related to "development" of individuals and nations in a purely semantic sense, but the meanings are sometimes confused.

(6) Abstraction/generalization: the reverse of the materialization process; a crucial step in making specific knowledge relevant in other settings and contexts and hence more widely useful.

(7) Adaptation: the modification of knowledge to fit a particular context other than the one in which it was generated. It is often proposed by knowledge perspectivists that adaptation is the key to utilization of knowledge that has been transferred.

Transfer. Perhaps the most salient of the parent disciplines of KGEU is "communication," itself a modern hybrid of psychology, sociology, and professional journalism. Thus a crucial aspect of the new field is the process by which knowledge gets communicated from one person to another, from one organization to another, from one social system to another, and from one culture to another. Of special

interest is the process by which knowledge is communicated
or transferred from generators to would-be potential users.
Sub-issues within the transfer category are the relative
effectiveness and appropriateness of different types of
media, the social structures and networks through which
knowledge flows and the speed of that flow given different
receiving cultures and different knowledge types, and the
use and effectiveness of various types of mediating roles
and agencies.

The term "transfer" can be used either narrowly or
broadly. The narrow definition would restrict meaning to
the movement of intact knowledge items from one point to
another. This is the way we are using the term here. The
other, more expansive definition includes almost everything
else covered in this chapter with the exception of knowledge
generation and verification. According to this interpretation, true transfer cannot be said to have taken place
until the receiver has fully integrated the new knowledge,
adopted it, incorporated it in thought and action. This
broader definition is clearly intended when the more common
expression "technology transfer" is employed, but it was
also intended when we established a research unit at The
American University in Washington, D.C., called The Knowledge Transfer Institute (founded in 1978 as a part of the
university, the Institute became independent in 1982). I
revert to the narrower meaning here because the opportunity
has been provided to describe the full range of processes of
knowledge to which transfer should be related and which
provide an appropriate context.

The terms "dissemination" and "diffusion" also deserve
mention here as potential synonyms. Both have been used as
rough synonyms of each other, "dissemination" more common
when the knowledge is in conceptual form (as in books,
speeches, etc.) and "diffusion" more common when a product,
practice, or folkway is the object of concern. "Diffusion"
may also lend itself better to the broader definition
discussed above, and it is distinctive in conveying an image
of knowledge spreading out like a wave or a ripple from a
splash. The study of the "diffusion of innovations", a
special branch of communication which has its primary roots
in rural sociology, is probably the most important precursor
to the KGEU field.

An important and often neglected aspect of transfer is
what might be called "meta-communication" about transfer,
the many types of transmissions that are required to set up
a transfer, negotiate its contents, costs, time, place, and
so forth. Much of this meta-communication takes place in

dialog form, much of it is informal, a great deal is probably unconscious. Meta-communication is probably important enough to deserve a separate "process" category, and as the field of KGEU expands, I would predict that it will take an ever more prominent role.

Reception. Sending and receiving are usually thought of as part of the same process. Actually, they are adequately different and deserve separate consideration and elaboration. "Reception" is a term used here to refer to a sequence of receiver responses of progressively increasing intensity starting with mere attention to the stimulus to full agreement with its contents. These are identified below.

(1) Attention: the minimum temporary response to a stimulus, orienting the receiver to be ready and to receive a message. Although not meaningful in and of itself, the capturing of attention is a crucial first step in any campaign and cannot be achieved without forethought and planning, particularly when the intended audience is widely dispersed and inaccessible by most media, as is often the case in rural areas of developing countries.

(2) Recognition/perception: the first stage of actually receiving a message and the result usually of successful meta-communication about the message, giving the receiver some sense of its purpose and content and perhaps the identity of the sender.

(3) Awareness: the capacity to recall a perception. Awareness has long been posited by rural sociologists as the first step toward the adoption of an innovation. In political and marketing terms, it is equivalent to name recognition. Usually to achieve awareness a stimulus/message must be presented more than once.

(4) Interest: often identified as the second step toward adoption of an innovation; the receiver's identification of the incoming message with a need or a motive which makes its reception and utilization potentially relevant and worthy of consideration.

(5) Understanding: the recognition of the essential contents and meaning of the message; the evidence that knowledge transfer has taken place. It is possible to have understanding without interest and interest (perhaps mistaken) without understanding.

(6) Apperception: defined by English and English (1958) as "the final stage of attentive perception in which something is clearly apprehended and thus is relatively prominent in awareness." Although this term has fallen into disuse, it represents rather precisely the last stage of

reception when the new message becomes integrated with what the receiver already knows and understands (sometimes referred to as the "apperceptive mass").

(7) Agreement/disagreement: the attitude the receiver takes toward the received message, which may come at any stage of understanding and apperception. The term "acceptance" is also used in this sense but has the alternative meaning of merely receiving the message. Agreement represents the receivers re-verification of the sender's message. It usually depends on the credibility that the sender has established, the extent to which alternative channels provide confirmation. If there is only weak agreement, utilization will be problematic. On the other hand, perceived positive results of use obviously strengthens agreement.

Utilization. The primary reason for the growth of the knowledge perspective in recent years has been the dawning realization that substantial social good can come from the utilization of science-based knowledge. This has nowhere been more clearly demonstrated than in the widespread diffusion and utilization of technologies related to the growing of high-yielding varieties of rice and other grains in Asia; but what constitutes "utilization"? This is a question that has grown in complexity as it has been studied. As Larsen notes (1981, 150), "the question of what constitutes utilization is one of the most salient issues in the field." She goes on to say (1981, 151), "Studies limited to a single indicator of utilization, and one which is action-based, measure one narrow dimension and may be expected to miss whole classes of outcome."

A taxonomy of utilization probably should start with types and here there has been much discussion centering on the distinction between "conceptual" and "instrumental" generally first credited to Caplan, Morrison and Stambaugh (1975) and widely espoused by Rich (1977). The main point of the distinction is that utilization should be thought of in broad terms. Knowledge affects thinking and action in very complex ways yet it has traditionally been studied and measured in terms of specific behavioral responses (e.g., "innovation adoptions") to specific sets of message stimuli (knowledge of the innovation). At least four types of utilization deserve separate consideration, although each is related to the other to some degree.

(1) Communicative utilization: the use of received knowledge in further transmission of that knowledge to others. This includes the primary function of the teacher or the reporter or the extension agent as one who passes knowledge from generators to ultimate users or consumers.

Being able to use knowledge in further communication is
generally regarded as a test of understanding and is thus
widely used in the educational process. Communicative
utilization does not necessarily lead to other types of
utilization and is not a prerequisite for other types.
However, knowledge that cannot be re-communicated easily
cannot be widely diffused and utilized in other senses.
Re-communication seldom occurs without some amount of
transformation of the knowledge (refer to the section on
transformation above), either intended or not.

(2) Confirmatory/disconfirmatory utilization: the use
of knowledge to strengthen or weaken previously acquired
knowledge, previously accepted beliefs, and previously
adopted behaviors. Few knowledge messages are powerful
enough by themselves to induce behavioral or even major
conceptual changes. Most have a cumulative incremental
effect, either supporting or weakening what is already
known. In measuring the effectiveness of knowledge transfer
these important micro and sub-behavioral effects are usually
ignored.

(3) Conceptual utilization: any use of newly acquired
knowledge that changes the way the user thinks about his/her
world, and the ways he/she subsequently formulates decisions
and actions. This would include changed sense of priorities, different ways of formulating problems and needs, new
perspectives on self and others, and so forth. Most behavioral uses are embedded in conceptual use, and conceptual
use may often be prior to behavioral use. The relationship
between the two is complex, but one can arrive at either one
without the other. Furthermore, a conceptual use can have
vastly greater long-term consequences, as for example, in
the adoption of a positive attitude toward innovations or
innovative technology in general which may pave the way for
innumerable specific adoptions and behavioral changes. Just
as most innovations have a knowledge component, so most
adoptions have a conceptual component, and the conceptual
component may ultimately be far more important than the
specific behaviors involved in adoption.

(4) Behavioral utilization: the transformation of
received knowledge messages into specific behavior. Behavioral use deserves much for the breakdown in terms of
degrees or depth of behavioral effects. This breakdown is a
major concern to many knowledge perspectivists.

> Adoption: the traditional designation of the end
> point in the study of the diffusion of innova-
> tions. This term is now almost obsolete. It

assumes that there is a discrete set of behaviors
that represent behavioral acceptance of an innovation and that a specific time can be designated
as the point at which these behaviors are in place
in a given person or social system. Simple adoption could also be seen as the first or minimal
level of behavioral utilization.

Adaptation: combining the ideas of adoption and
transformation; sometimes posited as an alternative to adoption and sometimes as the next step
beyond it. It is something like the behavioral
equivalent of apperception, the merging of new
behavior with the existing repertoire.

Implementation: signifies a great number of
specific actions which must take place after an
adoption decision has been made; another term
which suggests the complexity of the utilization
process. Many authors stress the importance of
distinguishing implementation from adoption,
seeing the former as far more important and far
more difficult to achieve in a satisfactory
manner. The long and largely sad history of
development efforts around the world testifies to
the importance of the distinction. Within
implementation, further distinctions can be made,
and the term also has overlapping meaning with
"adoption" and "adaptation."

Routinization: beyond implementation some researchers are now concentrating more and more on
what keeps behavioral changes in place, embedded
in the person or the system. This embedding
process is variously labeled "internalization,"
"integration," "incorporation," and "institutionalization." Evidence of routinization is provided
by indices such as achievement of official recognition, survival through annual budget cycles,
continuance after the turn-over of leadership, the
establishment of regular and reliable lines of
supply and maintenance, and the provision of
training for new staff.

MODELS OF KNOWLEDGE PROCESS RELATIONSHIPS

In the previous discussion of the different knowledge
processes, we have inevitably engaged in a good deal of
modeling, simple in the way in which the concepts were
ordered. Underlying the KGEU field are a number of models
of how all the elements go together. "Knowledge-into-use,"
the proposition that knowledge processes can be viewed as a
more-or-less linear sequence of interlocking processes which
lead from de novo generation to ultimate widespread behavioral use, is the implicit model that has been used here.
However, there are many others, some overlapping, some
contradictory. Mannheim's (1936) original proposition was
that all knowledge derived from specific cultural and
historic circumstances. As Shils (1982) has pointed out,
however, Mannheim's assertion tends to undercut the possibility of objectively and scientifically studying the
phenomena of knowledge. This may partially account for the
fact that while Mannheim is widely acknowledged as the
founder of the sociology of knowledge, the topic was not
pursued with any depth during his lifetime.
Robert Rich (1982) has expounded on the "two world"
hypothesis, which has been heuristically very useful in
positing relations between groups and cultures representing
fundamentally different orientations. Snow used the
metaphor to discuss relations between the sciences and the
humanities (Rich 1982). In a subsequent chapter of this
volume, I will employ essentially the same metaphor in
expounding on the notion of "linkage" between the worlds of
scientific knowledge building and of practical applications
and problem solving in social systems.
Problem-solving and decision-making models have also
been used as organizers for KGEU concepts. In the linkage
model, each "world" is further defined as a problem-solving
system unto itself employing interrelated processes of need
arousal, search, solution finding, and solution application
or implementation.
The several "models" proposed in this volume suggest
major alternative conceptualizations of relations, yet the
common elements across models are also striking. There is
even considerable correspondence between models intended for
practical use as didactic tools with practitioners and
models that are primarily intended for conceptual purposes
and as guides to research.

THE MAJOR DEBATES

Apart from the designation and study of various categories and models of KGEU, the field is dominated by consideration and argument regarding a number of unresolved issues. Five should be singled out as particularly important and troublesome: (1) the designation and measurement of "outcomes," (2) misuse and negative effects, (3) natural versus planned KGEU processes, (4) need pull versus technology-knowledge push, and (5) general versus special KGEU.

Outcomes

If is often said that the "proof of the pudding is in the eating." In KGEU the proof that the whole effort is worthwhile resides in the effects on humanity generally and individual users in particular. However, the issue is very complicated. First of all, if we think about it, the proof of the pudding is not really in the eating but in the pleasurable effects that the eating creates in the mind of the eater and then perhaps the nutritional effects it has later on the body of the eater, not to mention the intervening gastric and digestive effects. With knowledge there is a near infinite regress of effects, and the determination of the point that represents the outcome or even the most important outcome can be quite arbitrary.

However, from the point of view of those who support KGEU efforts, the outcome question is crucial. How can expenditures and manpower allocations on KGEU be justified if we cannot answer the question "so what?" Thus, it is very helpful to have outcome measures that are obvious, quantifiable, and obviously beneficial. In agriculture, productivity has traditionally served the bill. In education the outcome is rather more elusive and, what is most important, is hotly debated. Yet even productivity has recently been questioned as the most appropriate outcome measure for agriculture as surpluses mount and as economies get wildly out of balance through overinvestment in particular programs.

In the abstract, it is not difficult to propose desirable outcomes (e.g., raising living standards, improving health, increasing educational and nutritional levels), but the more difficult task is measuring such outcomes in such a way that findings are unequivocal and clearly consequent of KGEU actions.

Misuse and Negative Effects

Many KGEU scholars are concerned almost exclusively with the harm that can come to people and cultures through the use and misuse of knowledge and through the mismanagement and misapplication of KGEU processes. Critics of cooperative extension in the United States, for example (e.g., Hightower 1972), argue that this system is set up to serve the needs of large landowners and agribusinesses exclusively and to the detriment and relative deprivation of small farmers and consumers alike. Similar arguments have been made more recently about agricultural development programs in the Third World. Although such claims may be exaggerated at times, they are made loudly enough and frequently enough that they have to be attended to seriously.

Even those who generally accept the value of planned KGEU efforts have noted the need to look at negative as well as positive effects. There is also a special concern in some areas where risk factors are high for premature knowledge use, overuse, and misuse of knowledge.

Some authors (e.g., Caplan and Nelson 1973) have pointed to the wholesale distortion of knowledge building in certain fields resulting from the professional socialization of researchers. Such studies represent contemporary re-evocations of the Mannheim hypothesis regarding the dependence of knowledge on ideology and of ideology on specific cultural context.

Natural versus Planned KGEU

Through all history up to a few generations ago knowledge accrued, was exchanged, and was utilized without much deliberate planning or self-conscious analysis and consideration. For many scholars, that "natural" process continues to be the way things should be. The argument goes that to attempt improvement in what is essentially an organic process is either futile or harmful. While the naturalist argument has less and less currency when knowledge generation and verification processes are at issue, it rages hotly when exchange and utilization processes are at issue. The saying goes: "build a better mousetrap and the world will pave a path to your door." In other words, the worth or practical value of a new piece of knowledge will somehow or other advertise itself such that those who need it will get it and use it soon enough. However, the assumption rests on the full availability of channels of communication and the full capacity of users to match needs with available knowledge.

A special version of the planned-natural controversy within KGEU relates to the use of knowledge specifically generated out of KGEU studies. Is KGEU merely another academic subject or does it provide a knowledge base that is itself vitally useful in the design, development, adjustment, and improvement of KGEU activities? The writers of the contributions to this volume are mostly optimistic on this point, but some are non-committal and others skeptical.

Need Pull versus Technology/Knowledge Push

Economists who contribute to the knowledge perspective are particularly interested in the question of how useful knowledge gets generated and how successful channels toward use develop. The controversy here revolves around the question of the nature of the initiating stimulus. Do innovations (and knowledge related to them) emerge because a societal need for them first arises, or do they arise out of the current state of knowledge which suggests new possibilities. Instances seem to be found on both sides. The experience of rapid innovation in wartime suggests that highly aroused and articulated needs greatly accelerate innovation processes, but seemingly they cannot create what is not already available in the knowledge base in some form. On the other hand, innovation is also greatly accelerated by individuals who act as entrepreneurs and product champions, perceiving market voids and potential needs where none previously existed.

General versus Special KGEU

To a large extent the knowledge perspective rests on the assumption that there are knowledge processes that are generic, that is, that are applicable regardless of the type of knowledge in question and regardless of the culture in question. Yet this assumption is also challenged vigorously and often. If cooperative extension works for agriculture, does that mean it will also work for education? If it works in the United States, does that mean it will work in Costa Rica? The answer to such challenges comes hard and slow, and the evidence is not yet clearly in. If the field of KGEU is allowed to grow and flourish over the next several years, the answer will become clearer. On the other hand,

it will never be a "yes-no" type of answer. Undoubtedly
there are many ways in which fields and cultures are comparable and some ways in which they are distinctive and
require distinctive KGEU processes. It should be our task
to find both and make the best of both in designing
appropriate exchange processes.

Roots and Relatives

From the outset we have noted that KGEU is a hybrid.
To some extent each letter derives from a different parent
discipline. Perhaps sociology is the dominant parent field.
Within sociology, however, at least three distinct special-
ties make major contributions: the sociology of knowledge,
the sociology of science, and rural sociology, especially
the diffusion of innovation studies. Holzner has proposed
that there is a new discipline developing which he calls the
"sociology of knowledge application" (Holzner 1978; Holzner
and Marx 1979). Medical and educational sociology also
contribute something, again through studies of communication, innovation, and diffusion of knowledge and technology
within those fields.
Another important contributor is psychology, in particular social and organizational psychology. Classic studies
on persuasive communication were conducted by experimental
social psychologist Carl Hovland and his colleagues at Yale
University over a number of years. Field theorist and
Gestalt psychologist Kurt Lewin made very influential
contributions to the social processes involved in changing
group attitudes and behavior. Lewin disciples Ronald
Lippitt and Kenneth Benne pioneered the study of "planned
change" in organizations and communities and contributed to
early studies which defined and conceptualized the field of
"knowledge utilization" in the early 1960s (see Havelock
1969). Organizational research and organization development
conducted by psychologists have provided a major stimulus
for thinking about communication within organizations,
including scientific organizations (Pelz and Andrews 1966).
These are all strands that are loosely related but
somehow come together in KGEU. It is not our intention to
provide complete and systematic treatment of these various
roots and relatives but only to hint at their complexity and
at the inherent eclecticism of the field. Mention could
also be made of forays by economists into KGEU led by the
monumental works of Machlup (1962; 1980), and by political
scientists, most notably Rich (1981). Between the first and

second editions of his book synthesizing research on the
diffusion of innovations, Everett Rogers noted that separate
research traditions were opening up their "paper curtains"
to the extent that he could assert "Diffusion research is
thus emerging as a single, integrated body of concepts and
generalizations, even though the investigations are conducted by researchers in several scientific disciplines"
(1971, 47). We hope that the same can soon be said of the
knowledge perspective.

TRENDS IN THE EVOLUTION OF THE KNOWLEDGE PERSPECTIVE

We close this chapter with a look toward the future
based on some apparent trends in the recent past. All these
trends seem to be positive and promising for a future
blossoming of this field.

More Concern for Utilization

The earliest studies in the tradition of the sociology
of knowledge and the sociology of science (e.g., Mannheim
1936; Merton 1973) were highly academic in their orientation
and paid scant attention to issues either of exchange or
utilization. The reverse has generally been true of recent
studies and orientations. This has partly been the result
of governmental sponsorship. Knowledge studies have
expanded rapidly in the last 15 years as government agencies
have turned more and more urgently to the question of how to
get adequate dissemination and use out of sponsored R & D.
The trend, I believe, has been a positive one on the whole,
forcing knowledge studies to be more pointedly relevant to
practical concerns.

More Empirical Research on Knowledge Processes

Quantitative social research has made great strides
since the beginning of World War II, and the knowledge
perspective has benefitted ultimately from that larger
trend. Early writings were more predominantly theoretical,
conceptual, and anecdotal. More recently a variety of
survey techniques have been applied to all aspects of KGEU.
KGEU has also benefitted greatly from the strong empirical
tradition of its parent field, the diffusion of innovations.

Application of KGEU Models to More Social Problem Areas

As KGEU processes have been spelled out with greater
clarity and precision, their application to more problem
areas has become obvious. Thus in the last five or six
years, KGEU analyses have been conducted for criminal
justice research, handicapped research, housing, poverty,
and most particularly third world development (e.g.,
Havelock and Huberman 1978).

Application of KGEU Concepts and
Research in Government Policy

In at least one field in the United States, education,
KGEU concepts and findings have significantly influenced
policy decisions and have led to the development, for
example, of a "National Diffusion Network" for validated
innovative practices, and the widespread acceptance and
utilization of the Educational Resource Information Center
(ERIC).

The Development of More Sophisticated Research,
Development, and Diffusion Programs and Infrastructures

Some of the more practically oriented papers in this
volume attest to the greater sophistication that is seen
today in the design and planning of extension services and
research and development (R & D) utilization strategies the
world over. This trend is just beginning. It is important
that current KGEU thinking be brought to the attention of
planners and policy makers, particularly in the international community and in the bilateral development aid
organizations.

KGEU Is Becoming a Model for Cultural Enhancement and
Advancement and for Inter-cultural Exchange

As the knowledge perspective becomes more sophisticated, it may point the way toward an enriched view of
development, with knowledge flow and transformation as the
basic commodity, perhaps even taking precedence over natural
resources and finances. There is a growing realization that
investments in research and development eventually pay off
in a generally healthier economy and society, but the

connections are still obscure and the path between science
and progress uncertain. With the expansion of KGEU
knowledge, the path may be much clearer and the will to go
the knowledge route stronger.

REFERENCES

Caplan, N., A. Morrison, and R. J. Stambaugh. 1975. The
Use of Social Science Knowledge in Policy Decisions at
the National Level. Ann Arbor: Center for Research on
Utilization of Scientific Knowledge, Institute for
Social Research, University of Michigan.

Caplan, N., and S. D. Nelson. 1973. "On Being Useful: The
Nature and Consequences of Psychological Research on
Social Problems." American Psychologist 28, no. 3:
199–211.

English, H. B., and A. C. English. 1958. A Comprehensive
Dictionary of Psychological and Psychoanalytical Terms.
New York: Longmans, Green & Co.

Havelock, R. G. 1969. Planning for Innovation: through the
Dissemination and Utilization of Knowledge. Ann Arbor:
Center for Research on Utilization of Scientific
Knowledge, Institute for Social Research, University of
Michigan.

Havelock, R. G., and A. M. Huberman. 1978. Solving Educational Problems: The Theory and Reality of Innovation
in Developing Countries. New York: Praeger.

Hightower, J. 1972. Hard Tomatoes, Hard Times: The Failure
of America's Land Grant College Complex. Washington,
D.C.: Agribusiness Accountability Project.

Holzner, B. 1978. "The Sociology of Applied Knowledge."
Sociological Symposium 21: 8–19.

Holzner, B., and J. H. Marx. 1979. Knowledge Applications:
The Knowledge System in Society. Boston: Allyn and
Bacon.

Kuhn, T. 1970. The Structure of Scientific Revolutions, 2d
ed. Chicago: Univ. of Chicago Press.

Larsen, J. 1981. "Knowledge Utilization: The Current Issues." In The Knowledge Cycle, ed. R. F. Rich. Beverly Hills, Calif.: Sage Publications.

_____. 1962. The Production and Distribution of Knowledge in the United States. Princeton, N.J.: Princeton Univ. Press.

Machlup, F. 1980. Knowledge and Knowledge Production. Princeton, N.J.: Princeton Univ. Press.

Mannheim, K. 1936. Ideology and Utopia: An Introduction to the Sociology of Knowledge. New York: Harcourt, Brace and World.

Merton, R. K. 1973. The Sociology of Science. Chicago: Univ. of Chicago Press.

Pelz, D., and F. Andrews. 1966. Scientists in Organizations. New York: Wiley.

_____. 1977. "Uses of Social Science Information by Federal Bureaucrats: Knowledge for Action vs. Knowledge for Understanding." In Using Social Research in Public Policy Making, ed. C. H. Weiss. Lexington, MA: Lexington Books.

Rich, R. F., ed. 1981. The Knowledge Cycle. Beverly Hills, Calif.: Sage Publications.

_____. 1982. "Knowledge Utilization and the Rationalistic State: Revisiting C. P. Snow's Two Cultures." Paper presented at the Conference on Knowledge Utilization: Theory and Methodology, Communication Institute, East-West Center, Honolulu, April 26-30, 1982.

Rogers, E. M., with F. F. Shoemaker. 1971. The Communication of Innovations: A Cross-Cultural Approach. New York: Free Press.

Shils, E. 1982. "Knowledge and the Sociology of Knowledge." Knowledge: Creation, Diffusion, Utilization 4, no. 1: 7-32.

PART TWO

Models

2

Models of Knowledge Transfer: Critical Perspectives

Everett M. Rogers

The field of knowledge transfer today has much reason to view its past accomplishments with considerable pride. In the last couple of decades this field of scholarly activity has attracted a growing number of dedicated researchers and theorists, several outstanding books have appeared that synthesize work on this topic, and a number of university-level courses and programs of graduate-level have been launched. On the pragmatic side, most government agencies (both in developing and in industrialized nations) recognize their responsibility for conducting knowledge-transfer activities. In fact, many agencies see knowledge transfer as one of their <u>main</u> activities.

CRITICAL PERSPECTIVES

Recently, I met with representatives of a dozen U.S. government agencies (in health, mental health, education, public transportation, etc.) to review their knowledge-transfer strategies. Each was allocating a portion (albeit small) of its total budget for knowledge transfer, and each had an office or division established to carry out knowledge-transfer functions. Significantly, each of these U.S. government agencies was, in its activities, questioning certain aspects of the conventional wisdom about knowledge transfer.

I regard this as a healthy sign. Scholarship and practice on knowledge transfer have advanced to the point where we should be questioning our past models, and searching for improved alternatives, rather than just "doing more of the same." It is in the light of such critical perspectives that the present chapter is written.

A theme of this chapter is that a fundamental shift may have occurred in recent years as we have realized gradually that centralized knowledge-transfer systems are not "the only wheel in town." While such centralized approaches have advantages under many conditions, in certain cases a more decentralized model of knowledge transfer may be more appropriate.

Every field of scholarly activity makes certain simplifying assumptions about the complex reality that it studies. Such assumptions are built into the intellectual paradigm that guides every field. Often these assumptions are not very fully recognized, even as they affect such important matters as what is studied and what is ignored and which research methods are favored and which are rejected. So, when a scholar follows a theoretical paradigm, he or she puts on a set of intellectual blinders that help the researcher avoid seeing much of reality. "The prejudice of training is always a certain 'trained incapacity': The more we know about how to do something, the harder it is to learn to do it differently" (Kaplan 1964, 31). Such trained incapacity is, to a certain extent, necessary; without it, a scholar could not cope with the vast uncertainties of the research process in his field. Every research worker, and every field of science, has many blind spots.

The growth and development of a research field is a gradual puzzle-solving process by which important research questions are identified and eventually answered. The progress of a scholarly field is helped by realization of its assumptions, biases, and weaknesses. Such self-realization is greatly assisted by intellectual criticism. Unfortunately, the field of knowledge transfer has not been subjected to much critical review, a deficiency that we hope to remedy in this chapter.

WHAT IS KNOWLEDGE TRANSFER?

Past scholarship on issues of knowledge generation, exchange, and utilization grew out of several different disciplines, each of which favored certain theoretical viewpoints, research approaches, and terminologies. While the general trend is toward integration of this intellectual diversity, such academic unity is yet far from being accomplished. Perhaps a certain degree of difference in approach is a good thing, at least up to a certain point, but one area in which diversity still causes troublesome problems is in terminology. What I loosely refer to in this chapter as "knowledge transfer" is also known as knowledge, utilization, technology, transfer, and the diffusion of innovations (although these concepts are not exact synonyms).

We often use "innovation," "technology," and "know-ledge" as synonyms, but in fact they are not the same. An innovation is an idea perceived as new. A technology is a design for instrumental action that reduces the uncertainty in the cause-effect relationships involved in achieving a desired outcome (Rogers 1983, 12). A technology usually has two components: (1) a hardware aspect, consisting of the tool that embodies the technology as a material or physical object, and (2) a software aspect, consisting of the information base for the tool. Both the hardware and software dimensions of a technology encompass knowledge, but of course there are many other kinds of knowledge besides the new knowledge that is involved in an innovation or a technology. Nevertheless, most of the past studies of knowledge transfer have actually been researches focusing on innovation or technology transfer.

The scope of knowledge transfer that has been studied in the past has been the process through which technological information resulting from an R & D system is transferred by a linking system (e.g., an agricultural extension system) to a user system (e.g., farmers). This conception of knowledge transfer implies that it is mainly a one-way process; in actuality (or at least ideally), the R & D may have been initiated at the request of the user system, or at least in order to meet certain of their needs. Further, once the users have received the knowledge and put it into use, feedback (as to how well the knowledge meets the pre-existing needs) may be conveyed back to the R & D system. So it is an oversimplification to think of knowledge transfer as a one-way, top-down process.[1]

THE AGRICULTURAL EXTENSION MODEL

Any discussion of models of knowledge transfer must begin with agriculture extension, both for historical reasons and because the agriculture extension model has so influenced all of our thinking about this topic. While our intellectual dependence upon this model was mainly func-tional in the past, we have also been unfortunately limited in the scope of our conceptualizations about knowledge transfer. The first step in breaking outside the bounds of our prior thinking is to realize that certain alternative models may be possible. Of course, it may be advantageous to combine certain elements of a relatively centralized model like agricultural extension with parts of a decentralized model to formulate a knowledge transfer system that is especially suited to a set of particular conditions. This contingency approach to knowledge transfer is more academically sound than the numerous descriptions of a knowledge transfer system in the past, which stated or implied that that system was the best alternative for a wide range of conditions. For example, it has been claimed that the agricultural extension model could be effectively applied to solve knowledge transfer problems in education, family planning, vocational rehabilitation, and so forth. An examination of these "extensions" of the agricultural extension model, however, has shown them to be relatively unsuccessful unless major modifications were made (Rogers, Eveland, and Bean 1984).

The agricultural extension model is a set of assumptions, principles, and organizational structures for diffusing the results of agricultural research to farm audiences in the United States. This "model" is based directly on the experience of the U.S. government agency responsible for diffusing agricultural innovations; it closely parallels the conventional conceptions of a research and development/diffusion/utilization process.

Eight main elements constitute the agricultural extension model:

1. A critical mass of new technology, so that the diffusion system has a body of innovations with potential usefulness to practitioners.

2. A research subsystem oriented to utilization, as a result of incentives and rewards for researchers, research funding policies, and the personal ideologies of the agricultural researchers.

3. A high degree of user control over the knowledge transfer/research utilization process, as evidenced through client participation in policy determination, attention to user needs in guiding research and diffusion decisions, and the importance accorded feedback from clients on the system's effectiveness.[2]

4. Structural linkages among the research utilization system's components, as provided by a shared conception of the system, use of a common "language" by members of the system, and by a common sense of mission.

5. A high degree of client contact by the linking subsystem, which is facilitated by reasonable agent/client ratios and by a relatively homogenous client audience.

6. A spannable social distance across each interface between components in the system (where social distance might occur in levels of professionalism, formal education, technical expertise, and specialization). Generally, these variables decrease as one moves from the research subsystem (where Ph.D.'s are usually employed), through linkers, to the client subsystem.

7. Evolution as a complete system, rather than the knowledge transfer system having been grafted on as an additional component to an existing research system.

8. A high degree of control by the system over its environment, thus enabling the system to shape the environment rather than passively reacting to changes. Such a system is less likely to face unexpected crises or competitors, and is able to obtain adequate resources. The degree of control is expressed through the system's power base, its perceived legitimacy, and its policial-legal influence.

The following generalizations are offered about the agricultural extension model:

1. In response to alterations in the environment, the agricultural extension model has changed considerably since its origin in the United States in 1911. To a large extent, these adjustments are a reason for its relative success.

2. The agricultural extension model is based on client participation in identifying local needs, program planning, and evaluation and feedback.

3. Agricultural research activities are oriented toward potential utilization of research results. This pro-utilization policy facilitates the linking function of the extension workers.

4. State-level extension specialists are in close social and spatial contact with agricultural researchers in their specialty, which facilitates their performance in linking research-based knowledge to farmer problems.

5. The agricultural extension model was more effective in diffusing agricultural production technology to farmers (such as in crop and livestock production) than in its latter-day extensions to farmers on other subjects and to non-farm audiences.

6. The agricultural extension model recognizes the importance of communication as a basic process-skill for extension change agents and provides communication training on an in-service basis.

7. The agricultural extension model includes not only a systematic procedure for the transfer of innovations from researchers to farmers but also an institutionalized means for orienting research activities toward users' needs.

Thus, the land-grant college/agricultural experiment station/extension service complex is a total knowledge utilization system, which includes innovation-diffusion as only one of its components.

The federal investment in agricultural extension represents a heavy commitment, compared to that in agricultural research. Federally funded extension activities represent about 40 to 60 percent of the annual federal investment in agricultural R & D. For example, the USDA recently allotted $423 million for R & D. This figure would be considerably higher (over $600 million) if state funding were also included.[3] The annual federal budget for extension was $200 million; with state and county government contributions, the total annual budget for the extension services was about $500 million. Thus the total extension budget almost approaches the total public agricultural R & D budget. Even if only the _federal_ investment is considered, extension receives about half the funding of R & D. Comparable figures for federal extension-type activities as a proportion of federally supported R & D are much, much smaller in other fields:

1. Law Enforcement Assistance Administration   14   %
2. National Institute of Education   10   %
3. U.S. Department of Labor   3   %
4. National Institute of Mental Health   2   %
5. National Aeronautics and Space Administration
                     (NASA)   0.17%

Undoubtedly one of the reasons for the success of the agricultural extension services is their relatively high, stable budget. The financial success is, in turn, aided by the support given to the agricultural extension services by the powerful American Farm Bureau Federation.

EXTENDING THE AGRICULTURAL EXTENSION MODEL

What factors drawn from the agricultural extension model can be applied to other knowledge transfer systems, and which are unique to the agricultural extension services? In other words, can the agricultural extension model be extended to other situations? Rogers, Eveland, and Bean (1984) compared seven selected attempts to extend the agricultural extension model on the eight main elements of the model (that we stated previously). The seven "extensions" occurred during the 1955 to 1975 period and represent cases with which the analysts were personally acquainted. These seven "extensions" have (in most cases) been extensively evaluated, and so rather definite conclusions are possible.

The general pattern of extension system development in the agricultural case, and the relative successes and failures evidenced in the other seven cases, suggest some broad conclusions about knowledge transfer. The historical development of the agricultural extension system stretches over about 100 years. Comparatively speaking, knowledge transfer efforts in education, vocational rehabilitation, and other fields appear woefully underfunded and to have been treated like unwanted children of over-expectant parents. Two experiences (agricultural extension and family planning) in the developing countries of Latin America, Africa, and Asia show a lack of understanding of the importance of cultural adaptation of elements of the agricultural extension model (even when the model is applied to agricultural problems).

The county extension agent in the United States was a product of commercial agriculture, not subsistence farming. Until American agriculture began to modernize, there was not much need for an extension service. Subsistence (precommercial) farming in developing countries has not embraced the agricultural extension model with much success, a fact that suggests that the successful introduction of a knowledge transfer system must be carefully timed so that a feeling of need for its services exists or can soon be developed.

Attempts to introduce one or two elements of the agricultural extension model to non-agricultural settings should not be undertaken without adequate appreciation of the difficulties involved. The time and resources required to permit these knowledge transfer elements to prove their utility and to become assimilated into the culture of the host system can be easily underestimated. The failure of modestly funded efforts to transplant specific elements of the agricultural extension model into other sectors suggests that an extension system approach needs to be taken. When only certain elements of the agricultural extension model were introduced without support from the other elements, they usually failed.

Knowledge cannot be transferred effectively unless the goals of such transfer are very clear. The goals of the agricultural extension services were fairly direct and unambiguous: to produce more food and to raise farm incomes. In education and in rehabilitation, for example, the goal situation is much more complicated, with multiple, conflicting goals for knowledge transfer.

The agricultural extension services begin with users' needs and problems, and the system operates to find useful information to meet these needs, while many other, less effective knowledge transfer systems take an opposite approach of conducting research largely in answer to researchers' needs, and then attempting to find some use for the results. Naturally, the research topics usually do not match with users' needs. An effective knowledge transfer system must begin with users' needs.

DECENTRALIZED DIFFUSION SYSTEMS

We have already implied that there is considerable flexibility in the way the eight elements of the agricultural extension model can be adapted in selected knowledge transfer systems. During very recent years, a diffusion system in marked contrast to the centralized diffusion system of the agricultural extension model has been identified: decentralized diffusion.

Centralized Diffusion System

In 1971, Professor Donald Schon of MIT wrote that "theories of diffusion have characteristically lagged behind the reality of emerging systems." Schon particularly singled out classical diffusion theory for criticism; he termed classical diffusion a "center-periphery model." This model, Schon (1971, 81) said, rests on the basic assumption that "An innovation to be diffused exists fully realized in its essentials, prior to its diffusion" and that the diffusion process can be centrally managed. The best-known example of a centralized diffusion system is the agricultural extension services.

In this classical diffusion model, an innovation originated from some expert source (often an R & D organization). This source then diffuses the innovation as a uniform package to potential adopters, who accept or reject the innovation. The role of the adopter of the innovation is that of a relatively passive accepter. This classical model owes much of its popularity to the success of the agricultural extension services and to the fact that the basic paradigm for diffusion research grew out of the Ryan and Gross (1943) hybrid corn study. Much agricultural diffusion in the United States is relatively centralized, in that key decisions about which innovations to diffuse, how to diffuse them, and to whom are made by a small number of technically expert officials near the top of a diffusion system. While recognizing that this classical model fits much of reality, Schon noted that it fails to capture the complexity of relatively decentralized diffusion systems in which innovations originate from numerous sources and evolve as they diffuse via horizontal networks.

During the late 1970s, I gradually became aware of diffusion systems that did not operate at all like the relatively centralized diffusion systems that I had described in previous publications. Instead of coming out of formal R & D systems, innovations often bubbled up from the operational levels of the system, with the inventing done by users. Then the new ideas spread horizontally via peer networks, with a high degree of re-invention occurring as the innovations were modified by users to fit their particular conditions. Such decentralized diffusion systems usually are not run by a small set of technical experts. Instead, decision making in the diffusion system is widely shared with adopters making many decisions. In many cases, adopters served as their own change agents.

Gradually, I began to realize that the centralized diffusion model was not the only wheel in town.

Comparing Centralized Versus Decentralized Diffusion Systems

How does a decentralized diffusion system differ from its centralized counterpart? Table 1 shows six of the main differences between centralized and decentralized diffusion systems. This distinction is somewhat oversimplified because it suggests a dichotomy, rather than a continuum, of centralized/decentralized diffusion systems. In reality, an actual diffusion system is usually some combination of the elements of a centralized and a decentralized diffusion system. For example, the agricultural extension services in the United States are nearer the more centralized end of the decentralized/centralized continuum, although they have certain characteristics of a decentralized system.

In general, centralized diffusion systems are based on a linear, one-way model of communication. Decentralized diffusion systems more closely follow a convergence model of communication, in which participants create and share information with one another in order to reach a mutual understanding (Rogers and Kincaid 1981). A fundamental assumption of decentralized diffusion systems is that members of the user system have the ability to make sound decisions

Table 1   Characteristics of Centralized and Decentralized Diffusion Systems

Characteristics of Diffusion	Centralized Diffusion Systems	Decentralized Diffusion Systems
The degree of centralization in decision-making and power.	Overall control of decisions by national government administrators and technical subject-matter experts.	Wide sharing of power and control among the members of the diffusion system; client control by local officials/leaders.
Direction of diffusion.	Top-down diffusion from experts to local users of innovations.	Peer diffusion of innovations innovations through horizontal networks.
Sources of innovations.	Innovations come from formal R & D conducted by technical experts.	Innovations come from local experimentation by non-experts, who often are users.
Who decides which innovations to diffuse?	Decisions about which innovations should be diffused are made by top administrators and technical subject-matter specialists.	Local units decide which innovations should diffuse on the basis of their informal evaluations of the innovations.

Table 1 (continued)

Characteristics of Diffusion	Centralized Diffusion Systems	Decentralized Diffusion Systems
How important are clients' needs in driving the diffusion process?	An innovation-centered approach; technology-push, emphasizing needs created by the availability of the innovation.	A problem-centered approach; technology-pull, created by locally perceived needs and problems.
Amount of reinvention?	A low degree of local adaptation and re-invention of the innovations as they diffuse among adopters.	A high degree of local adaptation and re-invention of the innovations as they diffuse among adopters.

Source: Rogers 1983, 335.

about how the diffusion process is managed. This capacity
of the users to run their own diffusion system makes the
most sense (1) when the users are highly educated and technically competent practitioners (for example, cardiovascular
surgeons), so that all the users are experts, or (2) when
the innovations being diffused are not at a high level of
technology (for example, home energy conservation or organic
gardening versus building a nuclear power plant), so that
intelligent laymen have sufficient technical expertise.

The fact that relatively decentralized diffusion
systems exist in a wide variety of fields and locations
suggests that in the past we may have severely underestimated the degree to which the user system was capable of
managing its own knowledge transfer process. Our understanding of decentralized diffusion systems is still
limited, owing to the general lack of investigations of such
user-dominated diffusion. However, it seems apparent that
certain elements of decentralized diffusion systems might be
combined with certain aspects of the centralized model to
fit a particular situation uniquely. In other words, the
classical diffusion model is being questioned in certain
very important ways.

Advantages and Disadvantages of Decentralized Diffusion

Decentralized diffusion systems have both advantages
and disadvantages. Compared to centralized systems, the
innovations that decentralized systems diffuse are likely to
fit with users' needs and problems more closely. Users feel
a sense of control over a decentralized diffusion system, as
they participate in making many of the key decisions, such
as which of their perceived problems need most attention,
which innovations best meet these needs, how to seek information about each innovation and from what source, and how
much to modify an innovation as they adopt and implement it
to their particular setting. The high degree of user control over these key decisions means that a decentralized
diffusion system is geared closely to local needs. Problems
of change agent/client heterophily are minimized. It is
mainly user motivations to seek innovations that drive a
decentralized diffusion process, and this may be more cost-
efficient than situations in which professional change
agents manage the diffusion process. User self-reliance is
encouraged in a decentralized system. Finally, decentralized diffusion is publicly popular; users generally like
such systems.

Several disadvantages, however, often characterize decentralized diffusion systems:

1. Technical expertise is sometimes difficult to bring to bear on decisions about which innovations to diffuse and to adopt, and it is possible for "bad innovations" to diffuse through a decentralized system because of this lack of "quality control." So when a diffusion system is disseminating innovations that involve a high level of technical expertise, a decentralized diffusion system may be less appropriate than a more centralized diffusion system.

2. Furthermore, extremely decentralized diffusion systems lack a coordinating role (that is, the "big picture" of the system, where problems exist and which innovations might be used to solve them). For example, a local user may not know which other users he or she could visit to learn about an innovation. Thus, completely decentralized diffusion systems suffer from the fact that local users, who control the system, lack certain aspects of the big picture about users' problems and about available innovations to meet these problems.

3. A highly decentralized system will not be appropriate for innovation for which potential users do not feel a need. An example is family planning in developing nations, which a government may regard as a high priority but which people may not want. There are very few decentralized diffusion systems for contraception in Latin America, Africa, and Asia.

Thus, our present discussion suggests that:

1. Decentralized diffusion systems are most appropriate for certain conditions, such as for diffusing innovations that do not involve a high level of technical expertise, among a set of users with relatively heterogeneous conditions. When these conditions are homogeneous, a relatively more centralized diffusion system may be most appropriate.

2. Certain elements of centralized and decentralized diffusion systems can be combined to form a diffusion system that uniquely fits a particular situation. For example, a diffusion system may combine a central-type coordinating role, with decentralized decisions being made about which innovations should be diffused and which users others should site-visit. Technical evaluations of promising innovations can be made in an otherwise decentralized diffusion system.

BIASES IN KNOWLEDGE TRANSFER

The constructive criticisms that have been made of
knowledge transfer models in very recent years help us
identify several biases in such work, and they also suggest
ways of overcoming such biases.

The Pro-Innovation Bias

The pro-innovation bias is the implication that an
innovation should be diffused and adopted by all members of
a social system, that it should be diffused more rapidly,
and that the innovation should be neither re-invented nor
rejected. Seldom is the pro-innovation bias straight-
forwardly stated in scholarly publications. Rather, the
bias is assumed and implied. This lack of recognition of
the pro-innovation bias makes it especially troublesome and
potentially dangerous in an intellectual sense. The bias
leads researchers to ignore the study of ignorance about
innovations, to underemphasize the rejection or discontinuance of innovations, to overlook re-invention, and to
fail to study anti-diffusion programs designed to prevent
the diffusion of "bad" innovations (like marijuana or drugs
or cigarettes, for example). The net result of the pro-
innovation bias is that we have failed to learn about
certain very important aspects of the diffusion of
innovations. What we do know about diffusion (and other
aspects of knowledge transfer) is unnecessarily rather
limited. But it need not be so.

How did the pro-innovation bias originally occur? Part
of the reason is historical. Undoubtedly, hybrid corn was
profitable for each of the Iowa farmers in the early Ryan
and Gross (1943) diffusion study, but most other innovations
that have been investigated do not have this extremely high
degree of relative advantage. Many individuals, for their
own good, should not adopt them. Perhaps if the field of
diffusion research had not begun with highly profitable
agricultural innovations in the 1940s and the 1950s, the
pro-innovation bias would have been avoided, or at least
recognized and dealt with properly.

During the 1970s, several critics of diffusion research
recognized the pro-innovation bias. For example, Downs and
Mohr (1976, 700) stated: "The act of innovating is still
heavily laden with positive value. Innovativeness, like
efficiency, is a characteristic we want social organisms to
possess. Unlike the ideas of progress and growth, which

have long since been casualties of a new consciousness,
innovation, especially when seen as more than purely
technological change, is still associated with improvement."
   What causes the pro-innovation bias in diffusion
research?
   1. Much diffusion research is funded by change
agencies; they have a pro-innovation bias (understandably
so, since they are in the business of promoting innovations), and this viewpoint has often been accepted by many
of the diffusion researchers whose work they sponsor, whom
they call upon for consultation about their diffusion
problems, and whose students they may hire.
   2. "Successful" diffusions leave a rate of adoption
that can be retrospectively investigated by diffusion
researchers, while an unsuccessful diffusion does not leave
visible traces that can be very easily studied. For
instance, a rejected and/or a discontinued innovation is not
so easily identified and investigated by a researcher by
interrogating the rejectors and/or discontinuers.
   As a general result of the pro-innovation bias, we know
much more (1) about the diffusion of rapidly diffusing
innovations, (2) about adoption than about rejection, and
(3) about continued use than about discontinuance. The
pro-innovation bias in diffusion research is understandable
from the viewpoint of financial, logistical, methodological,
and practical policy considerations. The problem is that
the pro-innovation bias is limiting in an intellectual
sense; we know too much about innovation successes and not
enough about innovation failures. While we have largely
discussed the pro-innovation bias here in terms of the
diffusion of innovations, it also permeates all other
aspects of the knowledge transfer process.
   How might the pro-innovation bias be overcome?
   1. Alternative research approaches to post hoc data-
gathering about how an innovation has diffused should be
explored in knowledge-transfer research. Diffusion research
does not necessarily have to be conducted after an innovation has diffused completely to the members of a system.
Such a rearward orientation to most diffusion studies helps
lead them to a concentration on successful innovations. It
is also possible to investigate the diffusion of an innovation while the diffusion process is still underway, or, in
fact, before it even begins.
   2. Researchers should become much more questioning of,
and careful about, how they select their innovations of
study. Even if a successful innovation is selected for
investigation, a scholar might also investigate an unsuc-

cessful innovation that failed to diffuse widely among
members of the same system. Such a comparative analysis
would help illuminate the seriousness of the pro-innovation
bias. In general, a much wider range of innovations should
be studied in knowledge-transfer research.

3. Researchers should investigate the broader context
in which an innovation diffuses, such as how the initial
decision is made that the innovation should be diffused to
members of a system, how public policies affect the rate of
diffusion, how the innovation of study is related to other
innovations and to the existing practice(s) that it re-
places, and how it was decided to conduct the R & D that led
to the innovation in the first place. This wider scope to
research studies would help illuminate the broader system in
which the knowledge-transfer process occurs.

4. We should increase our understanding of the motivations for adopting an innovation. Strangely, such "why"
questions about adopting an innovation have only seldom been
probed by diffusion researchers; undoubtedly, motivations
for adoption are a difficult issue to investigate. Some
adopters may not be able to tell a researcher why they
decided to use a new idea. Other adopters may be unwilling
to do so. Seldom are simple, direct questions in a survey
interview adequate to uncover an adopter's reasons for using
an innovation. But we should not give up on trying to find
out the "why" of adoption just because valuable data about
adoption motivations are difficult to obtain by the usual
methods of diffusion research data-gathering.

It is often assumed that an economic motivation is the
main thrust for adopting an innovation, especially if the
new idea is expensive. Economic factors are undoubtedly
very important for certain types of innovations and their
adopters, such as the use of agricultural innovations by
U.S. farmers, but the prestige secured from adopting an
innovation before one's peers may also be an important
factor. Certainly the first and most important step in
shedding a pro-innovation bias in knowledge-transfer
research is to recognize that it may exist.

The Individual-Blame Bias in Knowledge Transfer

In addition to a pro-innovation bias in much past
diffusion research, there has also been a source-bias, a
tendency for diffusion research to side with the change
agencies that promote innovations rather than with the
audience of potential adopters. This source-bias is perhaps

even suggested by the words that we employ to describe this
field of research: "Diffusion" research might have been
called something like "problem-solving," "innovation-
seeking," or the "evaluation of innovations" had the
audience originally had a stronger influence on this
research. One cannot help but wonder how the diffusion
research approach might have been different if the Ryan and
Gross (1943) hybrid corn study had been sponsored by the
Iowa Farm Bureau Federation (a farmer's organization) rather
than by an agricultural research center like the Iowa
Agricultural Experiment Station. And what if the Columbia
University drug study (Coleman, Katz, and Menzel 1966) had
been sponsored by the American Medical Association, rather
than by the Pfizer Drug Company? The source-sponsorship of
early diffusion studies may have given these investigations
not only a pro-innovation bias but may have also structured
the nature of diffusion research toward individual-blame.

     Individual-blame is the tendency to hold an individual
responsible for his or her problems, rather than the system
of which the individual is a part (Caplan and Nelson 1973).
In other words, an individual-blame orientation implies that
"if the shoe doesn't fit, there's something wrong with your
foot." An opposite point of view would blame the system,
not the individual; it might imply that the shoe manufacturer or the marketing system could be at fault for a shoe
that does not fit.

     Of course it is likely that some of the factors under-
lying a particular social problem may indeed be individual
in nature, and that any effective solution to the problem
may have to deal with changing these individual factors.
However in many cases the causes of the social problem lie
in the system of which the individual is a part. Ameliora-
tive social policies that are limited to individual interventions will not be very effective in solving system-level
problems. How a social problem is defined is an important
determinant of how we go about solving it, and therefore of
the effectiveness of the attempted solution. A frequent
error in defining a social problem is to overstress
individual-blame and to underestimate system-blame.

     System-blame may be defined as the tendency to hold a
system responsible for the problems of individual members of
the system. How else can the person-blame bias be overcome?

     1. Researchers must attempt to keep an open mind about
the causes of a social problem, at least until exploratory
data are gathered, and guard against accepting others'
definitions of knowledge-transfer problems, which often tend
to be in terms of individual-blame.

2. All the participants should be involved, including potential adopters, in the definition of a research problem, rather than just those individuals who are seeking amelioration of a problem.

3. Social and communication structural variables, as well as intra-individual variables, should be considered in knowlege-transfer research. Past diffusion studies largely consisted of audience research, while seriously neglecting source research. The broader issues of who owns and controls (1) the R & D system that produces innovations and (2) the communication systems that diffuses them, and to whose benefit, also need attention in future knowledge-transfer investigations.

As in the case of the pro-innovation bias in diffusion research, perhaps one of the first and most important ways to guard against the individual-blame bias is to be aware that it exists. To what extent does knowledge-transfer research have an individual-blame bias? It is difficult to assess the degree of individual-blame in past researches accurately, but, on careful reading, there seems to be a certain flavor of individual-blame in many of the resulting publications. An individual-blame orientation is not, in and of itself, always inappropriate. Perhaps individual-level variables are the most appropriate to investigate in a particular study. By no means do we advocate the complete discarding of all individual-level, psychological variables in knowledge-transfer research, but in almost all cases, such a psychological approach centering on individual-level variables is not a complete explanation of the behavior being investigated.

THE GENERATION OF INNOVATIONS

Knowledge transfer consists of much more than just diffusion. Past investigations have overlooked the fact that a great deal of relevant activities and decisions usually occurred long before the diffusion process began: A perceived problem, funding decisions about R & D activities that led to research work, invention of the innovation and then its development and commercialization, a decision that it should be diffused, transfer of the innovation to a diffusion agency, and its communication to an audience of potential adopters. Then the first adoption occurs.

This entire pre-diffusion series of activities and decisions is certainly an important part of the innovation-development process, of which the diffusion phase is but one

component. The importance of what happens prior to the
beginning of an innovation's diffusion (especially those
events that affect the nature of diffusion later on) has
been almost entirely ignored in past research.

The innovation-development process consists of all of
the decisions, activities, and their impacts that occur from
recognition of a need or problem, through research, development, and commercialization of an innovation, through
diffusion and adoption of the innovation by users, to its
consequences. Here we take up each of the main steps in the
innovation-development process, which corresponds roughly to
the process of knowledge transfer.

1. Recognizing a Problem or Need. One of the ways in
which the innovation-development process begins is by recognition of a problem or need, which stimulates research and
development activities designed to create an innovation to
solve the problem/need. In certain cases, a scientist may
perceive a forthcoming problem and launch research to find a
solution. An example is the agricultural scientist at the
University of California at Davis who foresaw a severe labor
shortage for California tomato farmers when the bracero
program ended and initiated an R & D program to breed hard
tomato varieties that could be machine-picked.

In other cases, a problem/need may rise to high
priority on a system's agenda of social problems through a
political process. Research and development to develop
safer cars and highways had been conducted and accumulated
for several years, but the results were not put into
practice until the mid-1960s when a series of highly
publicized legislative hearings and Ralph Nader's (1965)
book, Unsafe at Any Speed, called national attention to the
high rate of traffic fatalities. The social problem of auto
safety rose to a high national priority owing to higher
fatality rates in the early 1960s, when the annual death
rate reached 50,000. But the interpretation of this
dangerous trend was in large part a political activity.

2. Basic and Applied Research. Most innovations that
have been investigated in diffusion researches have been
technological innovations. Most such innovations are
created by scientific research activities, although they
often result from an interplay of scientific method and
practical operations. The knowledge base for a technology
usually derives from basic research, defined as original
investigations for the advancement of scientific knowledge
that do not have the specific objective of applying this
knowledge to practical problems. In contrast, applied
research consists of scientific investigations that are

intended to solve practical problems. Scientific knowledge
is put into practice in order to design an innovation that
will solve a perceived need or problem. Applied researchers
are the main users of basic research. Thus, an invention
may result from a sequence of (1) basic research followed by
(2) applied research leading to (3) development.

   3. Development. The abbreviation R & D corresponds
closely to the concept that it represents: "R" always
appears together with "D" and, moreover, always precedes
"D"; development is always based on research. In fact, it
is usually difficult or impossible to separate research and
development, which is why the term "R & D" is so often used.

   Development of an innovation is the process of putting
a new idea in a form that is expected to meet the needs of
an audience of potential adopters. This phase normally
occurs after research but prior to the innovation that stems
from research.

   4. Diffusion and Adoption. Perhaps the most crucial
decision in the entire innovation-development process is the
decision to begin diffusion of an innovation to potential
adopters. On the one hand, there is usually pressure to
approve an innovation for diffusion as soon as possible, as
the social problem/need that it seeks to solve may have been
given a high priority. Public funds may have been used to
sponsor the research, and such financial support is an
unrealized public investment until the innovation is adopted
by users. On the other hand, the change agency's reputation
and credibility in the eyes of its clients rests on only
recommending innovations that will have beneficial consequences for their adopters. Scientists tend to be cautious
when it comes time to translate their scientific findings
into practice.

   A novel approach to gatekeeping medical innovations is
followed by the National Institutes of Health through the
conduct of "consensus development conferences." Consensus
development is a process that brings together biomedical
research scientists, practicing physicians, consumers, and
others in an effort to reach general agreement on whether a
given medical technology is safe and effective (Lowe 1980).
The technology may be a device, a drug, or a medical or
surgical procedure. A consensus conference differs from the
usual state-of-the-art scientific meeting in that a broadly
based panel is constituted to address a set of predetermined
questions regarding the particular medical innovation under
review. A three-day consensus conference typically begins
with a series of research synthesis papers that are discussed by the expert investigators, users of the technology,

and their consumers. A consensus statement is prepared by
the panel and read on the final day of the conference to the
audience, who then react to it. The final consensus statement is then published by the U.S. Government Printing
Office and widely disseminated to physicians, the mass
media, medical journals, and the public.

Consensus conferences were begun in 1978 in recognition
of the fact that the medical field lacked a formal process
to assure that medical research discoveries were identified
and scientifically evaluated to determine if they were ready
to be used by doctors and other health-care workers. It was
feared that some new technologies might have been disseminated without an adequate scientific test, while other
well-validated medical technologies might be diffusing too
slowly. The consensus panels have, in fact, occasionally
recommended against using a given medical or surgical
procedure, device, or drug under certain conditions. So,
they serve an important function in gatekeeping the flow of
medical innovations from research into practice.

Some other fields also utilize a formal procedure for
deciding when an innovation should be diffused. Most
knowledge transfer systems however, do not evaluate
innovations for diffusion in such a rigorous way. Here,
perhaps, we see an example of how one knowledge-transfer
system can learn and adapt useful lessons from another such
system. Such transfer of knowledge-transfer methodologies
can be greatly facilitated by the world of scholars of the
knowledge-transfer process, as they engage in comparative
analyses and evaluations of knowledge transfer systems.

THE ENTREPRENEURIAL TRANSFER OF KNOWLEDGE

Previously in this chapter we argued that past research
on the knowledge transfer process has been unduly limited in
scope. There are many types of knowledge transfer that have
been ignored by scholars. One of these is technology
transfer that occurs between private firms and that is
driven by market forces, rather than by public policies
enacted through activities of a government agency. We
should not forget that most of what we now understand about
the nature of knowledge transfer is based, rather narrowly,
upon the transfer of innovations from a national government
agency to individuals; here again we see the considerable
influence of the agricultural extension model upon our
thinking about knowledge transfer.

Yet a great deal of knowledge transfer obviously must

take place in the context of for-profit firms that are
competitively seeking to market innovative products to
consumers. One spectacular illustration is provided by
Silicon Valley, the high-technology complex in Northern
California that is the world center of the microelectronics
industry. Silicon Valley produces the semiconductor chips,
microcomputers, video games, and lasers that are
transforming industrialized nations into information
societies.

At the heart of Silicon Valley is severe competition in
continuous technological innovation; each company tries to
gain an advantage over its competitors by being the first to
market (perhaps by only a month or two) with a new product.
In this setting, gaining technical information about a new
idea translates directly into profits. In the early days of
Silicon Valley (in the 1960s), much of the information came
from research laboratories at Stanford University. Today
much of the new information comes from R & D that is
conducted by the firms themselves. One reason for the high
rate of job mobility (estimated to be about 30 percent per
year) in Silicon Valley is that each firm tries to hire key
employees away from its competitors in order to learn
company secrets.

Further, one or several key employees frequently
spin-off of an established firm in order to start their own
company, which usually is in direct competition with its
parent. The new firm is usually organized around a new
product, which, if successful, can make the founders of the
start-up millionaires within a few years.

Here we see an entirely different type of knowledge
transfer from that represented by the agricultural extension
model. The U.S. government has not played a direct role in
the rise of Silicon Valley, nor in the dozen or so other
"Silicon Valleys" that are springing up around the United
States. Significantly, each of these new high-technology
complexes has a research university at its center (an
example is MIT in the Route 128 complex around Boston, the
University of North Carolina in the Research Triangle
complex, etc.).

So each of these high-technology centers represents an
example of a special kind of technology transfer. Perhaps
the research university represents today the central
institution in the emerging information society (Rogers and
Larsen 1983).

Much more needs to be learned about this entrepreneurial model of knowledge transfer. Perhaps it illustrates
an important lesson for scholars and practitioners of

knowledge transfer: that they need to broaden their definitions and conceptions of the knowledge-transfer process.

NOTES

1. This discussion of the concept of knowledge transfer raises the issues of what should be the main dependent variable(s) (1) in research on knowledge transfer, and (2) in practice, as an indicator of performance. In past studies of the diffusion of innovations, the usual dependent variable has been adoption versus rejection of a technological innovation. But there are many other possible dependent variables in knowledge transfer research and/or practice: Awareness-knowledge of a technological innovation or of another idea, development of a favorable or unfavorable attitude toward the innovation or another idea, or beneficial consequences of adoption or rejection of the idea (to meet the original needs).

2. While much rhetoric is given to this feedback about needed research from farmers through the extension service to agricultural scientists, it is actually a fairly rare occurrence.

3. The activities of the extension services over the years have focused somewhat narrowly on immediate technical problems in agriculture, rather than on the longer-range social, political, economic, and ecological consequences of technological change in U.S. agriculture (Hightower 1972).

REFERENCES

Caplan, N., and S. Nelson. 1973. "On Being Useful: The Nature and Consequences of Psychological Research on Social Problems." American Psychologist 28, no. 3: 199-211.

Coleman, J. S., E. Katz, and H. Menzel. 1966. Medical Innovation: A Diffusion Study. New York: Free Press.

60

Downs, G. W., and L. B. Mohr. 1976. "Conceptual Issues in the Study of Innovations." Administrative Science Quarterly 21, no. 4: 700–714.

Hightower, J. 1972. Hard Tomatoes, Hard Times: The Failure of America's Land Grant College Complex. Washington, D.C.: Agribusiness Accountability Project; and Cambridge: Schenkman.

Kaplan, A. 1964. The Conduct of Inquiry. San Francisco: Chandler.

Lowe, C. U. 1980. "The Consensus Development Programme: Technology Assessment at the National Institute of Health." British Medical Journal 280, no. 6231: 1583–1584.

Rogers, E. M. 1983. Diffusion of Innovations. New York: Free Press.

Rogers, E. M., and D. L. Kincaid. 1981. Communication Networks: A New Paradigm for Research. New York: Free Press.

Rogers, E. M., and J. K. Larsen. 1983. Silicon Valley Fever: The Rise of High-Technology Culture. New York: Basic Books.

Rogers, E. M., J. D. Eveland, and A. S. Bean. 1984. Extending the Agricultural Extension Model. Washington, D.C.: University Press of America.

Ryan, B., and C. Gross. 1943. "The Diffusion of Hybrid Seed Corn in Two Iowa Communities." Rural Sociology 8, no. 1: 15–24.

Schon, D. 1971. Beyond the Steady State. London: Temple Smith.

3

Communication Models and Knowledge Generation, Dissemination, and Utilization Activities: A Historical Survey

Wimal Dissanayake

The objective of this essay is to discuss the evolution of communication models in relation to knowledge generation, dissemination and utilization activities. Models are useful heuristic constructs that are frequently employed in the social sciences for explanatory purposes. However, we can best use them for explanatory purposes only if we are alive to their limitations, namely, that they are by no means a simulacrum of reality, but only a simplified image of it. Indeed, it is very important to stress this fact at the beginning of this essay.

Discussing the use of models in the social sciences, Karl Deutsch identified the following three advantages (Deutsch 1966). Firstly, they perform an organizing function, that is, they serve to order and relate systems to one another and give us an idea of the whole system which we might otherwise miss. In other words, a model affords us the opportunity to discern how a given system is organized. Secondly, models perform an explanatory function by pointing out in a somewhat simplified fashion how a system operates. The emphasis here is clearly on the nature of the process. Thirdly, models perform a predictive function in that they enable us to predict the outcome of actions and events. This has the advantage of allowing us the opportunity to formulate hypotheses for the purpose of research. Broadly speaking, we can classify the models employed in the social sciences into two groups: the structural and processual. The first type describes the structure and the second the process. The features that Deutsch talks about really apply to the processual models, and in this paper, we shall be largely concerned with the processual type.

When we examine the evolution of communication model-building, we can identify three main phases. In the first

61

phase the emphasis was clearly on linear, one-way communication, and the operative term was manipulation. The first model of communication that we find in Western culture is perhaps the model proposed by Aristotle in his Rhetoric. There, he talks of three important ingredients in the act of communication, the sender, the message and the receiver, and the objective of communication is to persuade the receiver or the listener in a way deemed fit by the speaker through the proper mastery of enthymemes. This tenor of thinking survived into the twentieth century. Many of the early models of communication bear the imprint of Aristotle's model of communication, and some like Beltran have gone so far as to characterize them as Aristotelian models (Beltran 1980).

Of the models that are associated with this first phase of communication model development, three will be discussed: Lasswell's, Shannon and Weaver's, and Berlo's models. These three have been selected from among many others because they are representative, both in terms of conceptualization and of influence of the early stage.

Harold Lasswell, the political scientist who was interested in communication, was one of the earliest social scientists to come up with a rudimentary model of communication. He said that the following questions enable us to understand the act of communication more clearly (Lasswell 1948).

Who
Says what
In Which Channel
To Whom
With What Effect

When we examine these questions we see that they add up to a simple, linear, one-way model of communication. Here the communicator and his message are all important. It is interesting to note that the concept of feedback does not figure in this model. However, Lasswell's model exercised a profound influence on the thinking of scholars in communication and allied fields.

The second model, Shannon and Weaver's model (1949), is also referred to as the mathematical model. This model was, of course, developed in relation to electronic communication, but later applied by many communication scholars to human communication. The essence of Shannon and Weaver's model can be diagrammatically represented as in Figure 3.1. Here we have an information source producing a message. This message is transformed into signals by the transmitter, and these signals have to be adapted to the channel. The

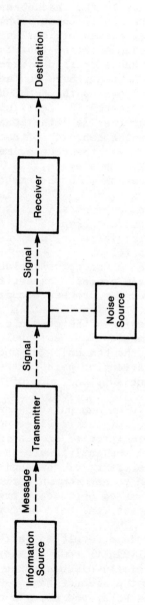

Figure 3.1 The Shannon and Weaver model of communication

receiver reconstructs the message on the basis of the signals and forwards it to the destination. The signal is susceptible to interference by the channel and hence the importance of paying attention to noise. Once again this is a model of linear, one-way communication.

The third model of communication that I wish to refer to is Berlo's model. It has exercised a far-reaching influence on communication researchers in the social sciences. This is referred to as the S-M-C-R model (Berlo 1960). Here Berlo is interested in identifying the elements of an act of communication that is intentionally designed to effect certain changes in the behavior of a receiver. The main elements of his model are the source, message, channel, receiver and the feedback. Once again this is a linear, one-way model of communication with the emphasis on the communicator.

These three models of communication, as indeed all other models that are representative of the first phase, share, from a contemporary viewpoint, many deficiencies. They can be enumerated as follows:

1. The inclination to conceptualize communication as a linear, one-way process, rather than see it as a circular and two-way process occurring over a period of time.
2. The heavy emphasis on the communicator's role in the act of communication, as opposed to the interaction between the communicator and the receiver.
3. An inadequate attention paid to the context, which in point of fact supplies much of the meaning in communication.
4. A heavy emphasis on manipulation and persuasion by the communicator of the receiver at the expense of mutuality and reciprocity in meaning generation.
5. The tendency to see individuals as atomistic as opposed to vital parts of the social structure.
6. The inclination to see communication in mechanistic terms as opposed to organic terms.

These different deficiencies, one need hardly add, are very closely intertwined.

The communication models developed in the second phase in many ways sought to eliminate some of these defects. In this regard, I wish to briefly discuss three models that are fairly representative of the second phase. They are Schramm's, Gerbner's, and Riley and Riley's models. The Schramm model originated with C. E. Osgood. This is a circular model where the emphasis is on the channels that link up the communicator and the receiver as opposed to on

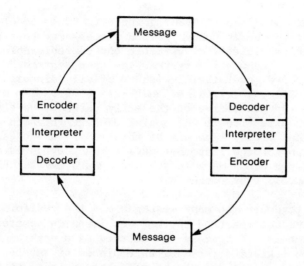

Figure 3.2   The Osgood-Schramm model of communication

the communicator as in the earlier models (Schramm 1954).
Here the emphasis is clearly on the organic nature of
communication as opposed to the mechanical transfer of
information. As Schramm observed in 1954, "it is misleading
to think of the communication process as starting somewhere
and ending somewhere. It is endless" (Schramm 1954). The
essence of the Osgood-Schramm model of communication can be
diagrammatically represented as in Figure 3.2. In addition
to the circular nature of communication in this model, the
encoding, decoding and interpreting functions of the
communicator and the receiver have been highlighted.
    Gerbner's model, which was developed in 1956, is
primarily concerned with perception and production of
messages (Gerber 1956). The essence of this model can be
represented in verbal form as follows:
  1. Someone
  2. perceives an event
  3. and reacts
  4. in a situation
  5. through some means
  6. to make available materials
  7. in some form
  8. and context
  9. conveying content
 10. with some consequences.

As McQuail and Windahl (1980) point out, "This model suggests that the human communication process may be regarded as subjective, selective, variable and unpredictable, and that human communication systems are open systems."

The third model that I wish to briefly discuss is the Riley and Riley model (Riley and Riley 1969). The models that were representative of the early phase of development paid scant attention to the social context in which communication takes place. The aim of this model was to gain recognition for the fact that mass communication is one social system among many in society. As Riley and Riley (1969) stated, they sought to

> fit together the many messages and the manifold individual reaction to them within an integrated social structure and process--formulated as a working model which organizes the available pieces of substantive knowledge in terms of the relevant theories of the social system.

This model can be diagrammatically represented as in Figure 3.3.

The communication models associated with the second phase of development represent a definite advance over the models associated with the first in terms of conceptualization. The linear, one-way, de-contextualized models have given way to circular, two-way and contextualized models. And the impact of this mode of thinking on knowledge generation and utilization activities, as we shall presently see, has been enormous.

The attempt at communication model-building characteristic of the third phase is reflective of the desire to further refine the already existing model and the conceptualizations that led to their creation. Areas of inquiry such as cybernetics and systems theory, semiotic and structuralist thought have yielded rich insights into the relationships between man and society which have inspired many contemporary communication theorists. It is indeed difficult to identify any one single model as being representative of the third phase of development, although the continuing efforts of such scholars as Barnlund, Kripendorff, Kincaid, Derwen, Clark and Delia, to name but a few, point toward the emergence of a newer set of models. One way of characterizing these efforts is to say that they all see communication as interaction in specific sociocultural contexts through shared meanings. (See chapter 11 in this book which urges a hermeneutical approach to

OVERALL SOCIAL SYSTEM

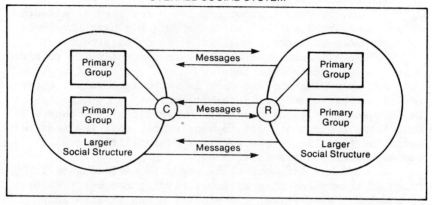

**Figure 3.3   The Riley and Riley model of communication
(from Riley and Riley 1969)**

knowledge generation, dissemination and utilization.) The
nature of meaning generation, the way information is
absorbed, the holistic as opposed to mechanistic and reduc-
tionist approaches to the art of communication, the way the
participants in the process of communication are constantly
changing, the importance of constructivism, and so forth are
important considerations that lie at the heart of contemporary communication model-building.

It is interesting to observe that these three phases of
communication model-building have had a profound impact on
the way we think of knowledge generation, dissemination and
utilization. As we examine the literature, we begin to see
that there was a great interest in questions of knowledge
creation and use in the forties and the fifties. The
research of such scholars as Ryan, Gross, Beal, Bohlen,
Lionberger, and Spaulding inspired many others to explore
this field. Knowledge dissemination is inextricably linked
to concepts of communication, and it is hardly surprising
that implicit in the work of many of the above-mentioned
scholars, and those who chose to adopt that tradition of
thinking, is an approach to communication that reflects the
communication models associated with the first phase.

What were the essential characteristics of communication endorsed by the early scholars of knowledge diffusion?
One can summarize them as follows:
   1.   Communication is manipulation of the receiver.
   2.   Communication is what the communicator does.

3. Communication is unilinear.
4. In the art of communication a far greater attention was paid to the individual and his psychological make-up than to questions of social structure.
5. The importance of context in communication received inadequate attention.
6. Communication was seen in mechanical rather than organic and processual terms.

It does not need great powers of perspicacity to observe that these assumptions fit in very neatly with the presuppositions that lie at the heart of communication models representative of the first phase.

As more and more questions began to surface both in terms of theory and of practice regarding the early efforts at knowledge generation, dissemination and utilization, scholars interested in this field began to think of alternate conceptualizations.

This quest for an alternative mode of conceptualizing communication was characterized by a desire to place greater emphasis on the context in which knowledge creation, diffusion and utilization takes place, the role of the user, the social structure of which he is a part, and the complexities of the process itself. Indeed this quest resulted in an epistemological change regarding knowledge utilization. It was seen that knowledge generation and knowledge utilization are society-centered rather than individual-centered, as was conceived by the earlier conceptualizers. The implications of this epistemological change for conceptualizing knowledge creation and use are profound and far-reaching. A number of new knowledge use and dissemination models were developed which sought to give theoretical expression to this epistemological change. In this regard, I wish to discuss briefly one model of knowledge generation and utilization which is fairly representative of this next approach, namely the Farming Systems model.

The Farming Systems model is a much-needed corrective to the earlier efforts of conceptualizing knowledge creation and use. It is an integrated, holistic approach to knowledge diffusion that appreciates the importance and value of the user. It also calls attention to the importance of paying greater attention to indigenous knowledge systems and cultural practices. (A fuller discussion of the Farming Systems model is found in chapter 8 of this book.)

The principles of communication implicit in the Farming systems model conform admirably to the presuppositions of communication models associated with the second phase. The

circular, two-way, contextualized models representative of
the second phase illustrate in pure communication terms what
the Farming systems models seeks to achieve in terms of
practical consequences.

When we talk of communication models representative of
the first phase and the second phase, we must be careful not
to make the distinctions too rigid. Imaginative researchers
can always make use of an earlier model by suitably modifying it to meet contemporary needs. Let us, for example,
take a communication model like that of Westley and MacLean
which is invariably associated with the earliest phase of
communication model-building. One can, with appropriate
adjustments, make use of it to deepen our understanding of
the processes involved in knowledge generation, dissemination and utilization (Westley and MacLean 1957).

In the Westley-MacLean model there is A, the communicator; B, the receiver; and X, the objects or events which
are the events in the world at large and which may be in the
memory field of A but not B. A may be motivated to select
and transmit the abstracted information of some Xs with the
idea of bringing about certain modifications in the attitudes or behavior of B towards those Xs. In this situation
X^1 becomes the message transmitted by A to B. It is indeed
the role of C which is the most innovative aspect of this
model. As Westley and MacLean observe:

> C is conceived of as one who can a) select abstractions
> of object X appropriate to B's need satisfactions and
> problem solutions, b) transform them into some form of
> symbol containing meanings shared with B and finally c)
> transmit such symbols by means of some channel or
> medium to B.

It is interesting to observe the way in which C's role
differs from that of A. A transmits purposive messages with
the objective of altering B's perception of an X. The message of C, on the other hand, is nonpurposive. When C is
interposed between A and B he assumes a role that Westley
and MacLean characterize as a channel role. By a channel
role, what they mean is not a mere conduit type of role, but
a more active gatekeeping one. One can reinterpret the role
of C in a modern context, say for example, that of a news-
paperman in the role of a development support communicator.

Although one can reinterpret the Westley and MacLean
model so as to be more in keeping with the general ethos of
the second phase of communication model-building, in my
judgment it is still essentially a model that is reflective

of the first phase. The role of B does not differ significantly from the role of the receivers in earlier models. However, the opportunity for reinterpreting older models always exists.

In discussing the third phase of the growth of communication model-building I made the point that what we observe is a deeply felt need to strike out in newer directions. We do not, as yet, have carefully constructed models that represent the concerns of this latest phase, although we do have a number of them in embryonic form. This is even more pronouncedly so in the field of knowledge generation, dissemination and utilization. (See chapter 11 of this book.)

In this regard, the convergence model of communication developed by D. Lawrence Kincaid is most interesting. It derives its strength from basic information theory and cybernetics. While repudiating the linear, one-way models of communication that have guided research in the past, Kincaid's conceptualization results in a model characterized by a cyclical process of convergence and divergence over time. This model maps out a new paradigm for research in the field of communication and knowledge generation that places greater emphasis on networks of human relationships that communication creates.

Realizing some of the deficiencies of the earlier attempts at formulating the issues and processes of knowledge diffusion unambiguously, and the need to take into consideration its manifold complexities, the latest theorists in the field are seeking to come up with more comprehensive explications. Their attempts are directed on two levels. They are:
1. The complexities of the process of knowledge diffusion.
2. The multi-layered nature of knowledge and how best it can be conceptualized.
These two dimensions, one need hardly add, are very closely interlinked.

First let us consider the conceptualization of the process of communication. Up until now it was a transportational framework that determined conceptualizations of knowledge diffusion. That is to say, the question that was uppermost in the minds of theorists was how can a body of knowledge be transferred from A to B where A and B could be either individuals or social systems. In contradistinction to this approach those theorists of knowledge diffusion who are associated with the third phase are primarily concerned not with the question of how knowledge is transported from A

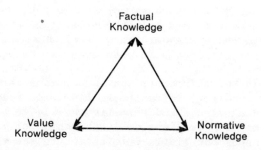

Figure 3.4   Relationships of three knowledge groups

to B, but how both A and B are involved in a joint enterprise of creation of meaning. Indeed, if one examines the
history of the growth of the social sciences, one would
realize that this is a concept that has been pushed into the
forefront of intellectual inquiry largely as a result of the
work of interpretive social scientists and humanities
scholars like Robert Bellah, Clifford Geertz, Charles
Taylor, H. G. Gadamer, and Paul Ricoeur. In other words,
the theorists of knowledge creation and use associated with
the third phase have begun to redefine the roles of
knowledge creators, disseminators and users.

   Secondly, one discerns a greater interest in seeking to
understand the multi-layered nature of knowledge and how
best it can be conceptualized. The distinction between
information and knowledge is clear enough, knowledge being
structured information. However, if we are to come up with
more intellectually stimulating and practically productive
models of knowledge generation, dissemination and utilization, we need to establish far finer distinctions. For
example some scholars (Drage 1983) have classified knowledge
into three groups (see Figure 3.4):
   1.   Factual knowledge
   2.   Value knowledge
   3.   Normative knowledge
Factual knowledge is seen as originating in the sphere of
primary experience of individuals and collective labor.
Value knowledge is conceptualized as that which makes it
possible for individual groups and the society in its
totality to choose between certain alternative ends for
their actions. Indeed, it is here that ideologies, world
views and delineations of reality are located. Normative
knowledge is that which enables one to arrive at a decision
as to which of the alternative values discernible in a value

knowledge is to be accepted as correct in a given situation, and it should be affirmed by means of action. Normative knowledge performs a standardizing function. That there is a dialectical relationship between each two categories is patently clearer.

So far in our efforts at conceptualizing knowledge in the field of knowledge diffusion we have paid scant attention to value knowledge and normative knowledge having fallen victims to a very narrow instrumentalist view of things. It needs but little imagination to see that even in the case of a purely instrumentalist view of knowledge, value knowledge and normative knowledge are of crucial importance. Therefore, the predilection of modern theorists of knowledge generation, diffusion and utilization to pay more and more attention to drawing finer distinctions within the generic term of knowledge is indeed a necessary and salutary step. The tenor of thinking is wholly consistent with the frame of mind that characterizes communication model-building in the third phase.

Many scholars in recent times have sought to address the issue of knowledge values and group interests. Among these the German scholar, Jürgen Habermas, is perhaps the most significant. In this regard his theory of cognitive interests merits very close attention indeed. He repudiates the "objectivist illusion" which urges us to perceive the world as a universe of facts that exists independent of the knower. He maintains strongly that knowledge and human interests are inextricably intertwined.

According to Habermas (1971), the process of human inquiry can be broadly categorized into three groups:
1. Empirical-analytical sciences
2. Historical-hermeneutic sciences
3. Critically oriented sciences.
In the first category will be included the natural and social sciences insofar as they seek to generate nomological knowledge. The historical-hermeneutic sciences comprise the humanities and the historical and social sciences insofar as they seek to understand interpretively meaningful configurations. The critically oriented sciences will largely include psychoanalysis, critical social theory and philosophy seen as a reflective and critical discipline. For each of these groups here Habermas posits a readily identifiable cognitive interest.

The approach of the empirical-analytic sciences incorporates a technical cognitive interest: that of the historical-hermeneutic sciences incorporates a

practical one; and the approach of critically oriented
sciences incorporates the emancipatory cognitive
interests (Habermas 1971).

In knowledge diffusion studies, and the communication
models that have been constructed so far to explain the
nature and process of knowledge diffusion, what Habermas
terms "cognitive interests" have hardly entered the
thinking. This is primarily due to the fact that communication models associated with the earlier two stages have
been operating under the "objectivist illusion." It is only
now that communication scholars have begun to give serious
attention to these issues. The work of the Frankfurt School
in general and Jürgen Habermas in particular has much to
offer to modern communication scholars who are seriously
interested in knowledge diffusion.

Another contemporary social thinker who is centrally
concerned with the question of knowledge and whose insights
can be a great impetus to communication scholars is the
French philosopher Michel Foucault. His interest in
knowledge is closely linked to his interest in the concept
of power. According to Foucault (1972), knowledge is not
ideal and abstract, but material and concrete. It cannot be
properly understood without taking into consideration the
workings of power throughout society. He makes every
attempt to emphasize the fact that knowledge is embedded in
power relations. Foucault seeks to gain recognition of his
belief that as knowledge is implicated in power, there
cannot exist any pure knowledge, and that knowledge will
remain undefined and amorphous without the exercise of
power. The writings of Michel Foucault, too, can throw
valuable light on the question of knowledge diffusion and
communication, and communication scholars should seek to
draw on them, although they are by no means easy to
understand.

Much useful work has been done in recent times in the
field of knowledge, the writings of Habermas and Foucault
being only two outstanding examples. If our communication
models seeking to explain the complexities of knowledge
generation, diffusion and utilization are to be productive
of newer insights, we should not remain innocent of the
various new developments taking place in the study of
knowledge.

In this paper, rather than making an inventory of communication models and knowledge diffusion models, I have
sought to identify the main historical trends by focusing
attention on a few representative ones. Given the brief

compass of the paper, such a method of approach I believe allows one to raise the key issues in a meaningful way.

REFERENCES

Aristotle. 1954. _Rhetoric_. Trans. R. W. Roberts. New York: Random House.

Beltran, L. 1980. "A Farewell to Aristotle: Horizontal Communication." _Communication_, 5, no. 1: 5–41.

Berlo, D. K. 1960. _The Process of Communication: An Introduction to Theory and Practice_. New York: Holt, Rinehart and Winston.

Deutsch, K. 1966. _The Nerves of Government_. New York: Free Press.

Drage, F. 1983. "Social Knowledge and the Mediation of Knowledge in Bourgeois Society." _Media, Culture and Society_ 5, no. 1.

Foucault, M. 1972. _The Archeology of Knowledge_. New York: Harper and Row.

Gerber, G. 1956. "Toward a General Model of Communication." _Audiovisual Communication Review_ 14: 171–199.

Habermas, J. 1971. _Knowledge and Human Interest_. Boston: Beacon Press.

Lasswell, H. D. 1948. "The Structure and Function of Communication in Society." In _The Communication of Ideas_, ed. Bryson. New York: Harper and Brothers.

McQuail, D., and S. Windahl. 1981. _Communication Models_. New York: Longman.

Riley, J. W., and M. W. Riley. 1969. "Mass Communication and the Social System." In _Sociology Today_, ed. R. K. Merton and others. New York: Basic Books.

Schramm, W. 1954. "How Communication Works." In _The Process and Effects of Mass Communication_, ed. W. Schramm. Urbana: Univ. of Illinois Press.

Shannon, C. E., and W. Weaver. 1949. <u>The Mathematical Theory of Communication</u>. Urbana: Univ. of Illinois Press.

Westley, B., and M. MacLean. "A Conceptual Model for Communication Research." <u>Journalism Quarterly</u> 34 (5): 31-38.

4

Modeling the Knowledge System

Ronald G. Havelock

It has been said often enough that no man is an island, but the aphorism is saved from banality by the paradox that all men <u>are</u> also islands. While some people in some circumstances prefer to emphasize the "no island" aspect of our existence, others in other circumstances tend to emphasize the "island" aspect. Of course, by "man" we refer to humankind in general in their various groupings, as individuals, families, organizations, communities, cultures, and so on. We are all partially interconnected but not totally so, and we are all separate and distinct entities but not totally so. There is, indeed, a continuous tension between our needs for independence and our needs for dependence or interdependence. It is a very serious tension. It can lead to all sorts of misunderstandings between people and it can even, on occasion, lead to revolutions. It should therefore be no surprise that what applies generally to human affairs also applies in a very central way to what can be called the "knowledge" system.

In some ways, the knowledge system can be thought of as a vast network of connections among people, indeed, including all the people on earth and not only those now living but all those millions of past generations who gave us their genetic material as well as what was transferable from their experience of life. It is almost too large and too sprawling to be described or understood, but we can try. It is usually helpful to initiate an analysis of this kind with some simple concepts from general systems theory.[1] All systems from the most rudimentary to the most complex are composed fundamentally of networks of <u>connected entities</u>. It is extremely important to keep in mind that understanding connections is the key to modeling the knowledge system.

GENERAL CONNECTING AND THE PERVASIVENESS
OF NETWORKS

"Entities" are the material things that populate the
universe; they can be of any size or description, and they
can be defined arbitrarily merely as points or specified
spaces regardless of any material referent. All entities in
the universe can be said to be related to one another, and
these relations can be thought of in spatial terms as
varying from most proximate to most remote or distal.
"Connections" are the various kinds of ties that may exist
between any two entities. Entities may or may not be
connected to other entities, and connections may be weak or
strong in a number of senses, for example, in the amount of
messages they carry, the variety of messages they carry, the
extent to which they influence the nature of either connected entity, their durability, and their resistance to
breaking influences.

Since connections can bind any two entities, the
possibility always exists that three or more entities will
be connected to one another either directly or through
intermediary entities. This line of reasoning leads us very
quickly to the notion of "networks" (i.e., connected sets of
entities). From networks we get to just about everything
else that makes up the knowledge system. Some networks are
more highly interconnected than others, and some parts of
networks are more highly connected and differently connected
than others. We have learned through countless studies of
diffusion processes that these connection patterns are very
important and very predictive of the flow of messages and
the adoption of innovations.

A most intriguing aspect of the study of connections is
the study of how connections come into being, how they get
stronger or weaker, and how they sometimes break or fade
away. This might be called the "dynamics of connections."
The formation of entirely new connections between previously
unconnected entities is especially difficult and important
in understanding the innovation process and the process of
knowledge transfer between cultures. The development of
connections between previously unconnected clusters of
connected entities (networks) is a crucial bridging process
that leads to a higher order of system development and
ultimately to a world system of knowledge generation,
transfer, and use.

THE RUDIMENTS OF SYSTEM

Systems are nothing more nor less than clusters of entities and their various connections. This is true regardless of the level of complexity of systems, their size, or their function. Organic systems, however, require a specific differentiation of entities and connections into six elements or features. As roughly illustrated in Figure 4.1 these are: (1) boundary, (2) sub-entities or subsystems, (3) subsystem connections, (4) an internal processing routine, (5) input, and (6) output. Organic systems require continuous input, internal processing and output of material from the environment in order to maintain themselves, to grow, to reproduce, and to achieve their various purposes.

"To achieve their various purposes" is admittedly a slippery phrase, but an all-important one, for a very special attribute of all organic systems and especially human ones is their purposive nature. We are always striving for something and often for many things. All species are seemingly programmed to strive for reproduction (i.e., preservation of the species). Humans and human cultures also seem to strive for a state of fulfillment which goes well beyond reproduction. It is from such a tendency that the notion of "progress" has evolved and the related notion of "development of culture." It is this

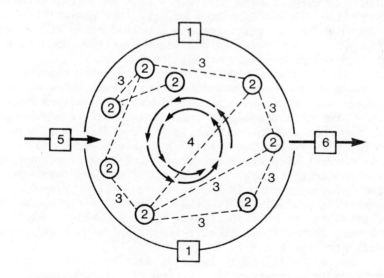

Figure 4.1 Essential elements of an organic system

special type of striving that seems to be the engine of what
I like to call the "knowledge system."

The "knowledge system" stands in relation to the human
race as the human brain stands to the system of the human
person. It is a subsystem, not at all self-sustaining,
wholly dependent on a larger system of gathering, synthesizing, and transforming matter and energy. Yet in many
respects, it can be studied and understood in its own terms.
This paper is intended as a brief tour through the knowledge
system, an examination of gross features and relationships
and a speculation on how it works and where it is taking us.

PARAMETERS OF THE KNOWLEDGE SYSTEM

To begin this discussion, we first have to deal with
the matter of scale. It is proposed that there is one great
worldwide knowledge system which envelops any number of
smaller knowledge systems and systems within systems. Most
of these smaller systems are more clearly delineated and
more powerful than the world system, so much so in some
cases that they obscure or throw into question the fact of
such a supra-system. Furthermore, it is not necessary to
assume a world system in order to fully understand the
functioning of the smaller systems. Indeed, most discussions on this subject focus on knowledge systems occurring
within a country or more narrowly within an organization or
a discipline. I propose, however, that the essential
processes and structural elements involved occur regardless
of the size of scale of the system in question, down to and
including the individual person. On the other hand,
discussion is greatly simplified by restricting consideration to a given scale, treating other levels below as
subsystem phenomena and other levels above as either
inter-system or supra-system phenomena. This is a very
understandable convention, but it has one serious flaw in
that all systems at whatever level or scale are highly
interdependent with other systems at the same level and at
higher and lower levels. This possibly endless continuum of
system interdependency is generally recognized by system
theorists, especially those like James Miller (1978) who
have attempted to describe living systems within a common
conceptual framework starting from the individual cell and
ascending to the society.

There are essentially two processes that have to be
understood to comprehend the essence of all knowledge
systems. These are (1) transmissions and (2) trans-

formations. Transmissions refer to the passage of messages
either between systems or into and out of systems. The word
"transmission" also implies that the message received is
essentially the same as the message sent. "Transformation,"
on the other hand, says nothing about relocation of the
message or messages but indicates that their essential
nature has been changed. Transformations are the result of
internal processing within systems. They can lead to
further transmissions (output) and they are, at least in
part, dependent on prior transmissions (inputs). However,
some systems such as newspapers, journals, clearinghouses,
television stations, and telephone companies specialize in
transmission, per se, sometimes priding themselves on their
ability to reduce transformation to the vanishing point.
Others, conversely, specialize in transformation; included
in this category might be research and development
laboratories, factories, and think tanks.

The transformation function is probably most difficult
to understand for two reasons: first, the possibilities for
transformation and the resulting products represent such a
bewildering range of phenomena, and second, because transformations change both the level and the nature of the
discourse. Thus, for example, when knowledge is turned into
the concept of a product, when the concept is turned into
the actual product, when the product is then marketed and
transformed into a margin of profit or loss for the
producer, when the product is subsequently used or consumed
and is transformed into improved or decreased well-being for
the consumer, we can see ourselves jumping from one realm of
discussion to another and another. Our mental faculties
rebel against such conceptual gymnastics and we say, "let's
keep the discussion on the level of economics" or "products"
or "scientific knowledge." Yet this is the challenge and,
for me, the fascination of efforts to describe the knowledge
system, because what we have here is not merely a mechanism
for moving words from one place to another but the very
means by which life is sustained and expanded.

The concepts of "transmission" and "transformation" are
much too broad and inclusive to represent anything approaching a "model" of knowledge systems, but they do divide the
conceptual territory into two huge domains. It is interesting that those who study one of these domains tend to
ignore the other and vice versa. This is perfectly understandable considering the size of each and the intricate
complexity of the issues involved. Yet adequate modeling
must recognize the interdependence of the two as much as the
separate importance of each. Toulmin (1969) proposed a

zoological evolutionary metaphor for the process of innovation as consisting of the three connected phases of
"mutation," "selection," and "diffusion." It is an
insightful proposal with much merit, but it has the flaw of
making us think in too linear a fashion about the total
phenomenon. The act of creation is too often conceived as
something that comes out of the blue, something that is
unpredictable and perhaps even random like a mutation.
Mostly, I believe, creation is no such thing. Sometimes it
is merely the application of a received idea in a new context. In other words, it is the direct result of the joint
reception and subsequent combination of two or more received
ideas (resulting from two transmissions). Toulmin's "selection" phase was considered by him to include the activities
of validation, verification, and experimental application of
innovative ideas and products after they had been initially
created, but in the real world diffusion does not wait for
verification unless someone takes specific steps to prevent
it, and many selection processes take place after diffusion.

Also lacking from Toulmin's formula is the concept on
which I began to stake my professional career twenty years
ago: utilization. What I argued then and feel more strongly
today is that the utilization of knowledge was a topic
distinct from either the creation or the diffusion of knowledge, and the same applies to technology or to the more
general term, "innovation" (Havelock 1964; Havelock and
Benne 1969). Utilization turned out to be a critical
mediating concept because it seemed to be a point of conjunction between two previously unlinked sets of concerns,
each represented in the literature of the social sciences by
coherent bodies of theory and backed up in many cases by a
long tradition of empirical research studies. Arrayed on
one side was the still young but rapidly growing field of
communication research. It included a group with which I
was already familiar from my graduate school training in
social psychology, those who had performed numerous carefully designed experiments on persuasive communication under
the leadership of Professor Carl Hovland at Yale (e.g.,
Hovland and others 1957; Hovland 1954). However, this was
only one branch. New to me at that time, but ultimately far
more influential in my thinking, was the work of the rural
sociologists who had specialized in studies of the diffusion
of new farm practices. The key figures here were Lionberger
(1960) and Rogers (1962), who were the first great synthe-
sizers of a new special field known as the diffusion of
innovations. What was special about this work to me was the
fact that a clear connection was made between patterns of

communication and the effects of those patterns on social change. These researchers, while coming from a communication perspective, were touching the edge of the issue of utilization, the issue with which I was trying to grapple.

The other social science domain that was linked by the concept of utilization was that concerned with group and organizational behavior. The leading intellectual light in this domain in the 1940s was probably Kurt Lewin (1951), whose field theory provided a challenging intellectual framework first for understanding how groups functioned and later for developing strategies to change group attitudes and improve group function. After establishing the Research Center for Group Dynamics and the National Training Laboratories in 1946 and 1947, Lewin died prematurely, but his work was carried on by a great many followers (e.g., Marrow 1969), many of whom became the founders and leading spokespersons for the specialty known as organization development (OD). OD actually had roots both in the field theory of Lewin, which was a kind of general systems theory, and in clinical psychology. It sought to translate the notion of healthy organic function from the individual to the organizational and sometimes even to the societal level. The focus of concern was on how human organizations can improve themselves through greater cohesiveness, mutual goal setting, and cooperative action. On the other hand, relations with the larger external environment were not much attended to, and the role of technical knowledge regarding innovation that might come from outside the organization in question was all but ignored. It thus appeared to me that there was a need for a wedding between the communication school and the human-relations oriented organization development school, and utilization seemed to be a promising vehicle to this end.

With the help of a rather handsome grant from the U.S. Office of Education in the late 1960s I undertook an eclectic and extensive analysis of these social science domains with a view to their eventual integration. The conceptual analytic work that paralleled the literature search and review led to the conclusion that there was not one but rather at least three paradigms or "perspectives" within which most theories of dissemination, utilization, and planned social change could be grouped. These were labelled as the "social interaction perspective" (representing the social communication group), the "problem-solver perspective" (representing the human relations - OD group), and the "research-development-diffusion" group (RDD), representing the point of view in vogue at the time of

macroplanning and systematizing the flow of knowledge from
research to development to practice. These distinctions are
still useful with some modifications. However, the professional isolation of the different areas is no longer so
marked, thanks in part to the increasing interest in
integrated perspectives and also to the fading of the RDD
model with the passing of the great society and with the
generally reduced enthusiasm throughout the society for
macroplanning and for large scale coordination of the
knowledge system.

Where I find these old perspectives most useful,
however, is as thought organizers for the main features of
the knowledge system. The problem-solving perspective helps
us to spell out some of the crucial issues that need to be
considered within systems, especially the transformations
and the sets of functions that are required to transform raw
knowledge inputs into problem solutions and need satisfactions. Communication research and particularly studies
of the diffusion of innovations help us understand inter-
system phenomena and the structures of connections we call
networks, which seem to underlie and explain so much for
which more elaborate explanations are expected but not
needed. Finally, despite its fall from fashion, I still
like the macromodelling efforts of the RDD perspective
because they provide a larger context for considering
particular knowledge systems as parts of a larger worldwide
enterprise I call the knowledge system.

INTRA-SYSTEM ROUTINES AND PROCESSES LEADING TO
SYSTEM MAINTENANCE AND SYSTEM DEVELOPMENT

In a sense, what goes on inside a system is not much
different from what goes on outside. Between systems there
are connections and there are patterns of communication
which can be represented as lattices and flow diagrams.
Likewise, within systems there are connections among
elements and patterns of flow of ideas, information,
material, and so forth. The difference lies partly in the
fact that inside messages are contained in a special
environment, an environment that is at the same time more
protected and more coherently organized. The parts or
subsystems of a strong and stable system are arranged in
such a way that the flow among them is orchestrated to
produce certain transformations necessary for either
maintenance or growth of the whole. In biological systems
the internal arrangement is mostly fixed for the life of the

organism and predetermined by the genetic code. For social systems, however, the configuration of elements can occur and can be changed in countless ways. In spite of long-standing traditions favoring one or another internal configuration, there is little scientific evidence and little agreement among social theorists regarding the relative merits of one structure or one configuration over another.

The internal flow pattern which dictates how knowledge and other material is transferred and transformed within the system can be referred to as the "procedural configuration." To some extent, such procedural configurations are kept in place by a prevailing ideology or long-standing tradition or both, but maintenance of important procedural configurations and most particularly the introduction of new ones also depend upon leaders who in some sense embody the idea of the system and personify the procedural configurations. Procedural configurations also depend upon the internal structure or infrastructure of the system. When a desired or leader-espoused procedural configuration does not correspond to or does not fit within the existing infrastructure, the system will experience internal tension and conflict. Realization of the procedural configuration not only requires leadership advocacy but also that the various subsystems or members be understanding, appropriately skilled, concerned, and committed both to the survival of the system and to the goals espoused by the leader. Hence a major internal system issue is always participation, and this issue has preoccupied the human relations-OD school more than any other.

Barriers and their Permeability

Reflecting again on Figure 4.1, we note that the most rudimentary system is not much more than a defined area, and what helps to define an area is a boundary line or a barrier, something that is supposed to keep most things out and let only a few relevant and necessary things in. Barriers preserve the integrity of systems, blocking invasions by other systems and by dangerous environmental elements, but also they allow survival through their very permeability. Barriers within a system also control flow, allowing messages to move in certain directions but not in others and allowing certain aspects of messages to be transmitted but not others. In fact it is within the permeable membranes of a system that we can unravel many of the mysteries of transformation. Many if not most membranes are semi-permeable.

Thus what enters on one side will never be the same as what comes out on the other side. Furthermore, within a system there are probably certain membranes or boundary regions that serve as crucial transformers for system survival, as when bodily deficits are transformed into articulated need messages, which then impel action in search of food or other life sustaining elements. The act of consumption may also be such a critical boundary transformation process.

System Differentiation and Integration

As systems grow, the number of subsystems within them generally grows also. This growth of subsystems is what is meant by differentiation in its most rudimentary form. Differentiation has two notable effects: it allows the performance of more complex procedural configurations, and it makes the overall flow of messages through the system slower and more difficult. Integration, on the other hand, refers to the coordination or orchestration of already existing subsystems and implies more rapid, more reliable flow of messages among subsystems.

Problem-solving as the Imperative Procedural Configuration for Any Living System

Living systems are characterized by a more-or-less continuing struggle for preservation and propagation, processes which require elaborate internal procedural configurations, a continuing stream of inputs from the environment, and the maintenance of a minimally turbulent internal environment. The term "problem-solving" can reasonably be used to describe these procedural configurations. The signals, which indicate requirements for new inputs, can be described as needs or problem situations; the materials, as they are brought in and transformed to meet those needs, can be referred to as solutions.

At the most primitive level, the problem-solving configuration of a system can be depicted as having two components: the problem component and the solution component. This is illustrated in Figure 4.2. The first thing to note is that the two components act as both transformers and transmitters. The problem component receives signals in some form from the need state and transforms these into communicable messages, which can be transmitted internally to the solution component and/or

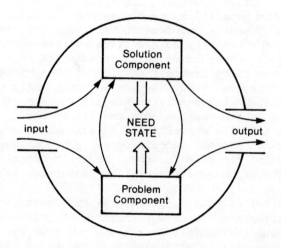

Figure 4.2   The simplest representation of a problem-solving system

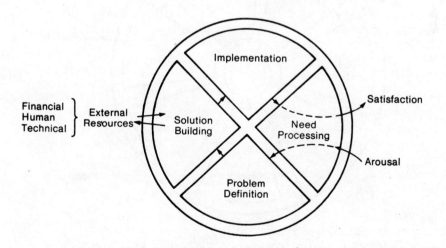

Figure 4.3   A four-component problem-solving configuration

externally to other systems. Likewise, the solution component has the capacity to send and receive messages from
the problem component and from the external environment, and
it also has the capacity to transform messages into signals
that somehow are responsive to the need state.

These two procedural elements might even correspond to
functional roles and relationships within a small organizational unit such as a family in which a newborn baby might
be construed as the problem unit and its mother the solution
unit. It could also describe the relationship between a
sick person and his/her doctor, or any group of needy people
who are turning for help to others in their organization or
community who might have the skills, resources, or willingness to help.

Typically, of course, procedural configurations for
problem-solving are far more elaborate. Figure 4.3 suggests
a minimal elaboration into four steps and four components.
Figure 4.4 suggests an extension to seven steps which might
be considered a rational sequence.

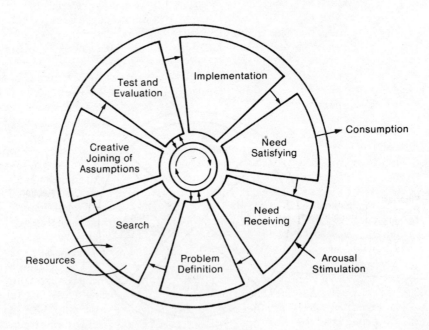

**Figure 4.4 A hypothetical model for rational problem-solving in
seven steps**

PARTICIPATIVE PROBLEM-SOLVING AS A DELIBERATE
STRATEGY AND AS AN ORIENTATION TO THE CHANGE PROCESS

It has become more and more fashionable in recent years
to emphasize the importance of local or indigenous initiative, responsibility, and capability in societal advancement
generally and in the development of Third World nations in
particular. The fundamental idea is very simple and
straightforward: "Development" has no meaning if it is not
directed toward the needs of the particular people and the
particular culture for their own self-actualization. Building on this idea, the strongest adherents of the problem-
solving approach say that people already have within
themselves most, if not all, of the ideas, resources,
capacities, and energy to bring about whatever change they
see fit. Furthermore, it is they, and only they, who have
the specific knowledge and the right to determine what their
own needs are in their own terms. Outsiders may be allowed
to play some kind of supportive or facilitative role with
temporary infusions of aid or technical assistance, but such
inputs are seen mostly as peripheral to the real change
process. Sometimes such outside assistance may appear in
the form of "process help," that is, advice and training on
the process of problem-solving, resource retrieval, problem
definition, solution fabrication, and so forth.

Figure 4.5 suggests some of these dynamics. The user
system is a world unto itself with sharply defined boundaries which are considered inviolate in many respects. Outside resources, outside agents, other systems, and externally generated knowledge are all viewed as peripheral and
probably most irrelevant to the main internal task. What is
important is first of all to bring the members of the
defined "system" together so that they can function as one,
solving problems collectively to the benefit of all members.

Perhaps the strongest argument for a thoroughgoing
problem-solver orientation is the fact that self-initiated
change has the firmest motivational basis and the best
prospects for long-term maintenance, other things being
equal, assuming that inside- and outside-generated
innovations have equal technical merits. Outside experts,
assuming they are not imperialists, are here today and gone
tomorrow. When they go, all their skills, understanding,
and enthusiasm for the innovation may go with them. Lasting
innovations are not merely accepted; they are embraced and
internalized by the user system. Clearly, the user system
will be more likely to internalize an innovation that it
sees as its own invention.

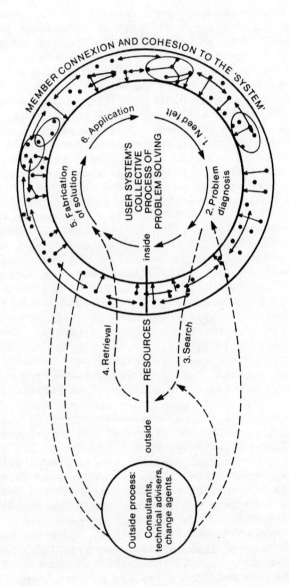

Figure 4.5 The problem-solving configuration as the focus of collective action and relations with would-be external helpers

On the other hand, a view of the innovation process that is limited to the problem-solving perspective has many serious flaws. First of all, it ignores the fact that users and user communities may not have the resources or the capacities to cope with certain problems that they do want to solve. Among the strongest advocates of this view there is an inadequate consideration and appreciation of the scope, variety, and rich potential of outside resources, and particularly outside expert knowledge on both the substance of needs and solutions and the process of problem-solving. It is indeed ironic that the world knowledge resource base was growing by leaps and bounds during the very period in the mid 1970s that it was being most denigrated and ignored by many Third World development advocates.

Another defect of the problem-solving perspective is the lack of a clearly articulated strategy for spreading innovations and their benefits to all members of the user system. Participation is a fine ideal, but participation in technical decision making by thousands or millions of people is at best something that can only take place vicariously. As Bagehot observed long ago, imitation is "the cake of custom" which binds together all but the strongest. Development of new forms, new technologies, and new ways of doing things are not realistically to be expected of all people equally (Allport 1954, 21-22). Thus we need to turn elsewhere for models of how new ideas spread through a population of users. This is why it is most important to integrate the concepts deriving from the human relations and organizational problem-solving tradition with those of the diffusion research tradition.

COMMUNICATION AS A DELIBERATE STRATEGY AND AS AN ORIENTATION TO THE CHANGE PROCESS

As noted earlier, all systems are fundamentally sets of connections between entities. The study of connections is the study of communication, and from such study we can learn a great deal about how systems work internally as well as how the inter-system environment functions. Communication research focuses more on the transmission of knowledge than on the transformation, but it should not be ignored or discounted for that reason. Of all the various sub-fields of communication, however, none is more important for understanding the change process than the research on the diffusion of innovations.

Although some of the underlying assumptions and

propositions of diffusion theory can be traced to anthropological studies of the 1920s and although classic studies
in different fields occurred in the 1930s and 1940s (Rogers
1962 and 1971), diffusion did not really become a distinct
and coherent discipline within sociology until the late
1950s when Beal at Iowa State University and Lionberger at
Missouri began to integrate the findings from what was
already a considerable accumulation of empirical studies
from the rural sociological departments of many land grant
universities (e.g., Beal and Bohlen 1957; Lionberger 1960).
In roughly the same period, there was a growing realization
that studies with a generally similar framework had been
undertaken in fields other than agriculture with very
similar conclusions. In 1961, Elihu Katz published a paper
entitled, "The Social Itinerary of Technical Change," in
which he carefully traced a comparison between his and
colleagues' research on the diffusion of new drugs in the
medical community and the classic study by Ryan and Gross
(1943) of "The Diffusion of Hybrid Seed Corn in Two Iowa
Communities." The similarities in approach and conclusions
were striking despite obvious disparities in innovation,
user population, time, and place. In the following year,
Everett Rogers's Diffusion of Innovations (1962), a classic,
left no doubt that there was an important new discipline
here with a substantial empirical base derived from studies
in diverse fields.

Of the many findings that have been reported consistently from the diffusion research tradition, at least six
stand out: first, that the individual user or adopter
belongs to a network of social relations which largely
influences his adoption behavior; second, that his place in
this network (i.e., his centrality, connectedness, peri-
pherality, isolation) is a good predictor of the time at
which he will be likely to adopt relative to the first
introduction of the innovation to the social system; third,
that informal personal contact is important for all adoption
decisions and crucial for later adopters; fourth, that the
mass media have an important awareness or alerting function
for all adopters but are primarily influential on the
decisions of a small minority who then exert interpersonal
influence on the majority; fifth, that group membership and
reference group identification are major predictors of
individual adoption and resistance to adoption; and, sixth,
that the rate of diffusion, plotted cumulatively, follows a
predictable S-shape pattern, being very slow at the
beginning, accelerating rapidly as key influentials adopt,
rising steeply as they are copied by others, and leveling

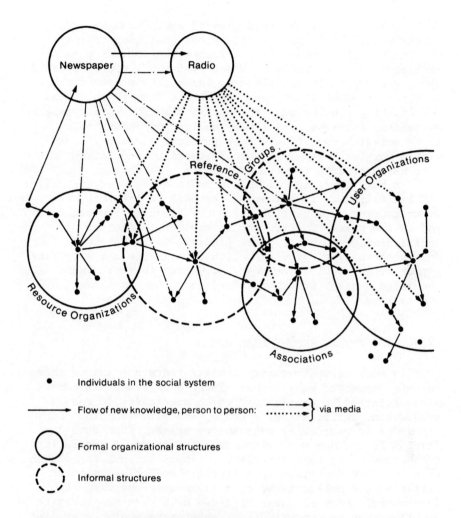

•   Individuals in the social system

⟶ Flow of new knowledge, person to person: ⋯⋯⋯⟶} via media

○ Formal organizational structures

⌒ Informal structures

Figure 4.6   Hypothetical model of the diffusion of an innovation within a small social system

off as the limits of the population of users are reached and as those remaining are stubbornly resistant, isolated, and oriented against innovation of any kind.

Figure 4.6 is intended to represent a hypothetical community of users being influenced by a diffusion strategy for an innovation which enters via the individual user (dot) on the extreme left side. The figure suggests both the strengths and the weaknesses of diffusion as an explanatory

model. It explains the phenomena of spread and imitation
rather well, but it says little about what goes on inside
the individual or what goes on inside the community as a
problem-solving mechanism. Procedural configurations within
users are typically conceived as orientations toward a pre-
existing external innovation, as stages through which the
user might go on the way to adopting that innovation (e.g.,
awareness, interest, trial use, evaluation, adoption,
implementation, etc.). It does not deal so well either
within complex intra-system configurations and infrastructures or with the transformation of messages.

In many ways, the diffusion model derives strength from
its limitations. If attention was paid to internal user
dynamics, to the invention and fabrication of innovations,
and to the place of diffusion in the larger context of
social problem-solving, there probably would not be a
consistent body of findings which illuminates one important
aspect of the whole. However, as we try to model the
knowledge system, we are required to go beyond these
limitations.

KNOWLEDGE SYSTEMS IN THE REAL WORLD

In complex contemporary society there are innumerable
loosely connected subsystems. These subsystems are sometimes referred to as "fields" which specialize in the
production, verification, storage, and dissemination of
knowledge in particular substantive areas. Each such
"field" is further subdivided or constituted of specialized
subsystems which take a variety of institutional forms such
as university departments, scientific societies, special
libraries and collections, clearinghouses, and research
institutes. Many of these "fields" have been subjected to
special study by communication researchers (notably studies
by Garvey and Griffith 1967; Hagstrom 1965; Crane 1972;
among others), and the results generally confirm the
patterns that emerge from diffusion research. As in studies
of diffusion, however, scant attention is generally paid to
consideration of these fields as problem-solving systems or
as transformers of knowledge. It is probably true that many
fields exist in large part as separate entities unto themselves, knowledge-building and sharing enterprises with no
agenda other than the further accumulation of knowledge in
that area. It is my preference, though, to view them as
parts of a larger societal enterprise, however loosely
constructed.

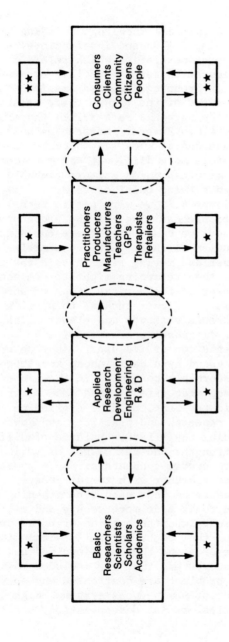

★ Intradisciplinary and interdisciplinary contacts.

★★ Other consumers, friends, acquaintances, neighbors, opinion leaders.

Figure 4.7 A paradigm for analysis of the knowledge macrosystem

What I propose is that all knowledge-building, transferring, and transforming fields and institutions can be
grouped into four general categories which relate to a broad
problem-solving configuration for the society as a whole.
Figure 4.7 depicts this grouping. We can imagine that
within each of the squares of the figure there exists a vast
complex of communication networks rather like those
represented in Figure 4.6. However, between each square,
substantial transformations of knowledge occur. These
connections are therefore more difficult and more complex
than those occurring within squares and are probably more
crucial from a problem solving point of view.

If in viewing Figure 4.7, we were not to recall the
prior discussion of problem-solving and the procedural
configurations involved, we could then trace out a number of
alternative need-solution circular paths by starting at the
right with the consumer and moving left through the other
functional groupings, then returning right to the consumer,
who is the ultimate user of the various steps of knowledge
processing represented. A figure such as this, of which
there could be innumerable variants and elaborations, has
value as a heuristic, diagnostic, or prescriptive tool,
depending on the orientation of its user. As a heuristic
tool it suggests one grand hypothesis about knowledge
systems: Are they discernibly connected in the manner
illustrated, and if so, what effects does such a structuring
have? As a diagnostic tool, it could be applied to
particular fields of research and practice, and questions
could be asked regarding the relative balance of different
components and the strengths and weaknesses of various
inter-system and intra-system connectors. As a prescriptive
tool, it could be used together with the diagnostic
information to propose areas that need strengthening and
connections that need to be made more secure and reliable.
It would also be of some importance to observe the problem-
solving configurations that occur naturally within this
framework, the number of steps that are involved and the
number of different subsystems that are included when major
social and technical problems are confronted and solved
(e.g., the development of new weapons systems, high-
yielding grain varieties, racial desegregation, etc.).

THE DELIBERATE PLANNING AND MANAGEMENT OF KNOWLEDGE SYSTEMS

Efforts have been undertaken by various interest groups
at various times to bring together the knowledge system

components within a given field and to make a more formalized system with designated roles and a clear division of
labor. Although it is still generally a matter of controversy as to whether such deliberate macroplanning is the
best way to improve on the informal knowledge system, some
major instances of such efforts have been in existence for a
long time, and many other efforts in nearly every field have
either been under development or under active consideration
within the last generation. It was with such a motive that
the U.S. Department of Education originally funded my work,
and a similar intent lay behind considerable interest in
mapping out research, development, and diffusion models in
the late 1960s.

The oldest, most elaborate, most ambitious, and
arguably most successful effort to develop a structured
macrosystem for knowledge development and use has been going
on in agriculture in the United States over the last 100
years. The land grant universities, their experiment
stations, and the Cooperative Extension Service together
comprise a coherent and well-coordinated system for the
generation, transmission, transformation, and utilization of
scientific knowledge about agriculture, home economics, and
to some extent community and youth development. These truly
amazing feats of knowledge production and use are realized
through an elaborate sequence of institutions and mechanisms, partly consecutive in mission, partly redundant. It
includes some unique institutions and roles such as the
extension specialist and the county agent, people who act as
linkers or boundary spanners between the worlds of research
and development and the world of routine everyday practice
(see, for example, Sanders 1966; Rogers, Eveland, and Bean
1976).

So successful was the U.S. agricultural model perceived
to be that it was, itself, diffused throughout the world and
imitated in whole or in part in a number of developing
countries. Even in the United States there have been many
attempts in education and other areas to adopt or adapt
various features of that model. The history of these
attempts at social engineering to improve knowledge systems
is a very important one. The wisdom that could be derived
from a careful and comparative analysis of these efforts
across cultures and across fields should bring us close to
the answer to a number of questions, such as how far can we
go productively in attempting to accelerate or otherwise
enhance diffusion and utilization of knowledge?

FORGING CRITICAL CONNECTIONS: LINKAGE

Again in reference to Figure 4.7, it has already been
noted that among the myriad of possible and actual connections that characterize any knowledge system, some are more
important than others. Most important and most difficult to
create are those between subsystems, between cultures,
between fields, and between functional groupings (e.g.,
researchers and developers or developers and practitioners).
In every case, however, what makes a connection more
difficult also makes it more important. Inter-system
linkages are more difficult because they are more likely to
involve transformations in addition to transmissions. They
are more difficult because they require the crossing of
stronger system boundaries. They are more difficult because
there are likely to be fewer pre-existing connectors and
fewer persons in the boundary region who can, as it were,
speak both languages. They are also more difficult because
the contexts and the need states of the sending and
receiving systems are fundamentally different. Yet, as
Granovetter has noted (1973, 1982), the value of the
information load carried by an inter-system bridge may be
very great indeed for the receiving system, even if the
connection is initially very weak and uncertain.
Because of the importance of intersystem bridges and
because of their difficulty and their tendency to be weak, a
major goal of social engineering of knowledge systems should

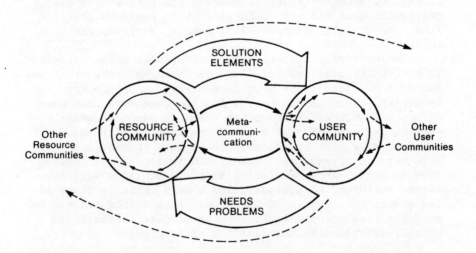

Figure 4.8   Elements of a linkage model of the knowledge system

be the determination of ways to make weak links stronger and ways to bring links into being where none formerly appeared to exist. Such an objective requires us to undertake a rather thorough analysis of what actually constitutes a satisfactory bridge between two systems that have different objectives, a central interest in different types of knowledge, and different ways of processing knowledge.

In a number of previous writings (Havelock 1969, 1971, 1974; Havelock and Lingwood 1973), we have developed the concept of "linkage" as a model which would help us understand this critical bridging function on the one hand and serve as a metaphor for how the knowledge system works as a whole. Figure 4.8 suggests some of the basic features of this model. It builds on two ideas: first, that the "communities" that are to be connected are separate problem-solving systems, and, second, that two-way communication between them is the essential prelude to any significant transfer of usable knowledge from one community to the other. The two communities are identified as "resource" and "user" only with respect to some designated problem and the knowledge resources relevant to that problem. The assumption is that the community on the left has knowledge of potential value to a problem confronting the community on the right. For another type of knowledge and another problem the roles might be entirely reversed.

The technical substance of the communication which is the end desired state could be described as "needs" and "solutions." "Solutions" or "solution elements" (i.e., knowledge that can be applied to a need state in the user community) presumably should be able to flow from the resource community to the user community. For this to happen, the resource community must have accurate perceptions of what the need state is in the user community, and this can only come through a counter-transfer of articulated need and problem messages. However, neither type of transfer can take place without a considerable amount of prior communication between the two communities and their members, communication that establishes channels, agendas, ground rules, appropriate media, and understandings of internal processes and contextual factors that must be understood by the other side. Within the figure, all these additional communicative elements are identified as "meta-communication" (i.e., communication about the communication, the message, the media, etc.). Clearly this meta-communication must also be two-way and must develop over time from very simple to very complex and multi-layered exchanges.

We will reserve for another paper in this volume a more extended consideration of the linkage construct. Our purpose here is to indicate how linkage might be seen as a way of integrating understandings and perspectives reviewed earlier. It should be understood in Figure 4.8 that each "community" also does its own problem-solving, utilizing its own resources and its own solution ideas. Furthermore, each "community" is also an extended network of sub-communities and individuals who similarly do their own problem-solving, while at the same time they are engaged in a continuous process of social influence which can best be understood in the terms provided by the diffusion researchers.

Figure 4.8 is also drawn to suggest that both resource and user communities have many other options for bridging relationships besides each other. Users may wish to communicate their needs to many different potential resource communities, never knowing for sure which one will really be able to provide the most valued return inputs. Likewise, resource communities may find many other user communities who are as appropriate or as interested in the solution elements they can provide.

LINKAGE AS THE GUIDING METAPHOR FOR THE KNOWLEDGE SYSTEM AS A WHOLE

Linkage should not be viewed as merely a two-communities process. Again considering Figure 4.7, adequate functioning of the total system requires a series of linkages among critical subsystems. Thus, the link becomes the chain. Even beyond this consideration, however, the notion of a bi-polar linkage process is a useful way of viewing knowledge systems in any field and of any scale, including the knowledge system representing all human knowledge relating to all human needs. Linkage combines the notions of a communication network and a problem-solving system, and the level of discourse is not critically important since the concept of "system" itself is a relative one with limits that can only be designated on an arbitrary basis. The knowledge system as a whole can be viewed, as in Figure 4.7, as an extended series of subsystems which conceive of and process knowledge in somewhat different ways. However, within this series we can also observe a polarity, which is consistent throughout, namely, that the leftward flow along the bottom of the figure expresses transformations into higher and higher levels of abstraction from raw human needs to the most esoteric formulations of problems in mathematics

and the physical sciences. The rightward flow along the top
expresses transformations of problem solutions from that
same esoteric level, by successive stages back into more and
more concretized and practically applicable solutions to
more and more specific need situations. Thus, if we
generalize the linkage model, we can interpret the entire
knowledge system as a kind of macro-dialog between knowledge
builders on the one hand (left side) and knowledge users on
the other. In other words, Figure 4.7 and Figure 4.8 are
trying to say the same thing in slightly different ways.
Modeling the "knowledge system" can legitimately be viewed
as a "two-world" phenomenon or as a multi-world connecting
problem.

The two-world imagery is probably especially useful
when we are focusing on relations between the developed and
the developing countries. Clearly every developing and
every developed country has its own internal "knowledge"
system," its own internal version of Figure 4.7. Just as
clearly, it would be most desirable if these many separate
systems could be linked together, not for one-way transfer
of technology nor for exploitation of one by the other, but
so that images of need and elements of solution could be
more widely shared for mutual gain. Simultaneous application of the knowledge system models presented in this
paper should lead to an understanding of how such linkage
could come about.

NOTES

1. A more extended discussion of the general systems
model in relation to knowledge utilization in developing
countries is contained in Havelock and Huberman 1978,
chapter 2.

REFERENCES

Allport, G. W. 1954. "The Historical Background of Modern
    Social Psychology." In Handbook of Social Psychology,
    ed. G. Lindzey. Reading, Mass.: Addison-Wesley.

Beal, G. M., and J. M. Bohlen. 1957. The Diffusion
    Process. Special Reprint #18. Ames: Iowa
    Agricultural Experiment Station.

Crane, D. 1972. Invisible Colleges, Diffusion of Knowledge in Scientific Communities. Chicago: Univ. of Chicago Press.

Garvey, W. D., and B. C. Griffith. 1967. "Scientific Communication as a Social System." Science 257: 1011-1016.

Granovetter, M. S. 1973. "The Strength of Weak Ties." American Journal of Sociology 78: 1360-1380.

_____. 1982. "The Strength of Weak Ties: A Network Theory Revisited." In Social Structure and Network Analysis, ed. P. V. Marsden and N. Lin. Beverly Hills, Calif.: Sage Publications.

Hagstrom, W. 1965. The Scientific Community. New York: Basic.

Havelock, R. G. 1964. Research Utilization Report: Analysis of Seminar Sessions. Report of a Ford Foundation Grant, R. Likert and R. Lippitt, principal investigators. Ann Arbor: Institute for Social Research, University of Michigan.

Havelock, R. G. 1969. Planning for Innovation through the Dissemination and Utilization of Knowledge. Ann Arbor: Institute for Social Research, University of Michigan.

Havelock, R. G. 1971. A National Problem-Solving System: Highway Safety Researchers and Decision Makers. Final Report to the National Highway Traffic Safety Administration, U.S. Department of Transportation. Ann Arbor: Institute for Social Research, University of Michigan.

Havelock, R. G. 1974. Ideal Systems for Research Utilization: Four Alternatives. Final Report to Social and Rehabilitation Service, U.S. Dept. of HEW. Ann Arbor: Institute for Social Research, University of Michigan.

Havelock, R. G., and K. D. Benne. 1969. "An Exploratory Study of Knowledge Utilization." In The Planning of Change, ed. W. G. Bennis, K. D. Benne, and R. Chin, 2d ed. New York: Holt, Rinehart, and Winston.

Havelock, R. G., and A. M. Huberman. 1978. Solving Educational Problems: The Theory and Reality of Innovation in Developing Countries. Paris: Unesco Press.

Havelock, R. G., and D. Lingwood. 1973. R&D Utilization Strategies and Functions: An Analytical Comparison of Four Systems. Final Report to the U.S. Department of Labor. Ann Arbor: Institute for Social Research, University of Michigan.

Hovland, C. I. 1954. "Effects of the Mass Media of Communication." In Handbook of Social Psychology, ed. G. Lindzey. Reading, Mass.: Addison-Wesley.

Hovland, C. I., W. Mandell, E. H. Campbell, T. Brock, A. S. Luchins, I. L. Janis, R. L. Feierabend, and N. H. Anderson, eds. 1957. The Order of Presentation in Persuasion. New Haven: Yale Univ. Press.

Katz, E. 1961. "The Social Itinerary of Technical Change: Two Studies in the Diffusion of Innovation." Human Organization 20, no. 2: 70-82.

Lewin, K. 1951. Field Theory in Social Science. New York: Harper & Bros.

Lionberger, H. F. 1960. Adoption of New Ideas and Practices. Ames: Iowa State Univ. Press.

Marrow, A. J. 1969. The Practical Theorist: The Life and Work of Kurt Lewin. New York: Basic.

Miller, J. 1978. Living Systems. New York: McGraw-Hill.

Rogers, E. M. 1962. Diffusion of Innovations. New York: Free Press.

Rogers, E. M., with F. F. Shoemaker. 1971. Communication of Innovations: A Cross-cultural Approach. New York: Free Press.

Rogers, E. M., J. D. Eveland, and A. S. Bean. 1976. Extending the Agricultural Extension Model. Stanford: Stanford University Institute for Communication Research.

Ryan, B., and N. Gross. 1943. "The Diffusion of Hybrid Seed Corn in Two Iowa Communities." Rural Sociology 8, no. 1: 15-24.

Sanders, H. C., ed. 1966. The Cooperative Extension Service. Englewood Cliffs, N.J.: Prentice-Hall.

Toulmin, S. 1969. "Innovation and the Problem of Utilization." In Factors in the Transfer of Technology, ed. W. H. Gruber and D. G. Marquis. Cambridge, Mass.: The M.I.T. Press.

5

Toward an Idealized Systems Model for Generating and Utilizing Information in Modernizing Societies

Herbert F. Lionberger

INFORMATION MACROSYSTEMS IN HISTORICAL PERSPECTIVE

For centuries man depended on individuals to develop new knowledge and technology. Under these conditions, new additions were slow in coming, unpredictable and sporadic. Also, there was almost no way to control what happened. One anthropologist estimated that 99 out of every 100 inventions got lost (Linton 1936, 322). However, in many that survived, a recurrent theory-to-use developmental sequence of activities was apparent in their emergence.[1]

Perhaps for the first time in the history of mankind, most of the theory-to-use capability was built into a single coordinated organization known as a land-grant university. These were initially established to teach agriculture and the mechanic arts to all who wanted to attend. They later added experiment stations to generate information needed to teach students in residence and outstate farmers.[2]

Later when an extension service was added, a capability to develop and deliver information to farmers was completed. Few innovations got lost and the whole developmental process was greatly accelerated. With this, man had created one of the most powerful inventions of all time. Thus an informational need in agriculture and the mechanic arts became a vehicle for originating a system capable of developing and supplying specialty information for many clienteles. Although of, by and for whom the system should work and "how" issues were not initially resolved, the potential for control of the entire developmental sequence was there. Creation of new knowledge and its distribution accordingly was on its way to becoming a business which now in the United States is probably second to none in terms of

105

people involved and the value of the product produced
(Paisley, Butler-Paisley, and Shapiro 1976).

With systems of this kind quickly built into at least
one land-grant university in each state and into many other
sectors of U.S. society, an enormous capacity to develop and
deliver information had been created. Collectively, these
informational macrosystems institutionalized and virtually
guaranteed change at an increasing rate. They laid the
basis for creating and sustaining an information society--
the full implications of which we are perhaps only beginning
to envision.

When:
  (1) Information supply problems emerged that the
       research, development and delivery mode (RD & D)
       of operation could not resolve,
  (2) public agencies were pressured into developing
       systems to innovate and use new ideas and
       practices,
  (3) industry had adapted the research, develop and
       deliver mode of operation to their own ends,
  (4) pressures grew to address urgent problems in
       society, and
  (5) mistakes mounted in attempts to adapt information
       development--supply systems that worked well in
       one place to other places and purposes--the stage
       was set (by the mid 1960s) for a concerted effort
       to discover or devise better and more adaptable
       models that would work.

THE SEARCH FOR MODELS

Directions Taken

This search took a number of directions. Some of the
searchers chose to inventory hundreds of relevant studies
that have a bearing on how information macrosystems should
be organized and operated (Meehan and Beal 1977; Havelock
1971). Some relied heavily on what they had seen happening
over the years (McDermott 1975; Lionberger 1977; Whyte
1981), while others relied heavily on how they thought these
systems should work (Guba and Clark 1975; Gideonse 1968),
and others concentrated on promising innovative new ones
(Nagel 1979; Kidd 1971).

Havelock (1971), who has researched these matters most
intensively, identified three model-like types:

(1)   a research, development and delivery one in which
      a guided theory-to-practice development sequence
      is implicit,
(2)   a problem solving perspective in which solving
      people problems is central, and
(3)   a social interactive one chiefly concerned with
      the process by which already existing innovations
      are diffused to the users' social system and are
      put to use.

It takes all three to achieve the theory-to-practice
research development and delivery capability plus an added
ability to address location specific problems for which
there are no readily available answers.

Aside from efforts concerned only with the diffusion of
innovations, modeling attempts for supplying specialty
information to users have tended either to a research,
development and delivery or problem solving stance.
Interestingly, these closely parallel the way "thought-out"
decisions start, i.e., with awareness of an innovation on
the one hand or a problem on the other (Campbell 1966;
Samonte 1970). The first is possible only when there is
something new (an innovation) to become aware of, as is
indeed often the case. Diffusion research findings testify
to the preponderance of this type of adoption decisions by
U.S. farmers (Rogers and Shoemaker 1971).[3]

The research, development and delivery feature built
into U.S. land-grant universities and into public agency and
industry systems in the U.S. has the capacity to deliver a
continuous assured supply of new information and technology.
Researchers in the system also have a strong inclination to
keep a portion of the research aligned with the needs and
desires of their non-academic user clientele. This they
have done quite well. Anyone who doubts the magnitude of
the supply of useful information generated and available to
people in our state from its land-grant university alone,
need only look at the voluminous collection of available
extension Guide Sheets and the long list of publications on
subjects of concern to farmers, gardeners, food processors
and homemakers. Literally, thousands of actual and
potential questions are answered.

By and large, the American farmer wants and gets
answers to a number of questions. So do many other people.
However, research cannot always be completed in time to
provide the necessary answers. A good case in point is
"Legionnaires" disease and cancer of the vital organs.
Sometimes the research route to solutions takes years. Thus
researchers must help anticipate problems, do the necessary

research and, if possible, find the answers before the need
arises. Research, development and delivery (RD & D) is the
route of most likely success.

Yet frequently there are situations where:
(1) The information available is either not suited for
    direct local use or simply is not available,
(2) potential users do not know what questions to ask
    and as a result may ask the wrong ones,
(3) professionals have only limited knowledge of the
    local situation and the informational needs of the
    potential users,
(4) all parties involved find it difficult to
    communicate with each other (Beal 1978), and
(5) conditions demand that something be done.

A different operation is needed for supplying informational
needs of this type, but not necessarily different subject
matter specialists or a different informational back-up
system. With the two informational needs always present and
systems in place to meet them, it is not surprising that
those looking for models quite consistently come up with
RD & D, and problem solving models, and thought-out
decisions of information users (Campbell 1966).

When some allowance is made for the exaggerated claims
made by the enthusiastic proponents of each, and the
limitations of the other, there is still much
complementarity in the way they operate and little actually
in conflict. Very often when problem-solving proponents
trace knowledge inputs back to their origins, they tie into
systems with research, development and delivery capability.
Proponents of the last invariably find problems they cannot
solve and people who will not wait. They then must address
the problems hopefully with the best expertise available.

Requirements and Assumptions

The position here is that a satisfactory model for
servicing the specialty informational needs of a diverse
clientele in a changing society, must be capable of:
(1) developing and delivering locally validated
    information and thus providing answers to most
    questions that people ask, e.g., in medicine,
(2) helping people generate location-specific
    information necessary to deal with issues and
    problems for which there are now answers readily
    available, and

(3)   retrieving knowledge and technology developed by
      innovative persons in one place for delivering it
      to others elsewhere.

These three things require, at a minimum, that the model
have both research development and delivery and in-field
problem solving capabilities. Implicit assumptions for
proposing a model with these capabilities are:

(1)   that a continuing supply of updated, science-based
      information is necessary for the informational
      needs of most people in modernizing societies,

(2)   that away-from-home specialized systems are
      required to supply it, and

(3)   the social setting in which they operate must
      include the necessary supply and service
      facilities to provide what users need to do, what
      they decide to do.

Other assumptions of a more general nature are that:

(4)   The degree of specialization and disassociation of
      the informational macrosystem from the supply and
      other servicing arrangements is a partial function
      of the state of development and availability of
      the other necessary support systems, and

(5)   the information macrosystems themselves must be
      thoroughly adapted to the social setting in which
      they operate, and be properly linked with other
      service and supply agencies that people must use.

An additional assumption is that a tripartite
sociological, organizational, normative and process
conceptualization provides a useful context for looking at
and describing any social systems model for generating,
developing and using information. The organization
component directs attention to the distinctive structural
features of the system, process to its distinctive mode of
operation and norms to the rules that specify how the system
should operate and the underlying values that specify why.

Like all models, the one proposed here is neither true
nor false and it is not complete. It focuses on a few
issues and omits everything else. Utility is its only
reason for existence. In any case, meaningful description
requires that there must be a conceptual scheme for
specifying what is important and must, as a minimum,
recognize and specify:

(1)   a science theory-to-practice or use developmental
      sequence of activities, and

(2)   the functions that must be performed to insure
      that the activity sequence will operate.

The Theory-to-Practice Continuum

Even when we depended on individuals to develop and disseminate new information and technology, the "science theory-to-practice" sequence prevailed. McDermott (1975) sees this as a natural process, i.e., one that just happens without direction from anybody. Indeed the sequence has been often repeated. If we trace the origins of hundreds of innovations from their basic science antecedents to where they were ultimately put to use, the sequence would probably look something like this:

1. People trying to extend the frontiers of knowledge with almost no thought of providing anything useful (basic science). For example,
   a. trying to find out why some plants have certain characteristics and others do not,
   b. why some come true to seed and some do not,
   c. why people get sick,
   d. what light is, what electricity is,
   e. how people learn,
   f. what is life.
2. Other people trying to exercise some control over what basic scientists found out. For example,
   a. can one intervene in the inheritance process,
   b. can we store electricity, control its flow or reverse its direction,
   c. can we bend light, project an image, or create an illusion of motion.
3. Other people (developers) trying to invent something useful, often just for the fun of it (Linton 1936). For example,
   a. a voice box (radio),
   b. a cotton gin,
   c. an electric light,
   d. a horseless carriage, etc.
4. Others (entrepreneurs) who take steps to exploit what has been developed, for fun, for personal advantage, for profit or even for the public good.
5. Maybe others or the developers themselves distribute what has been produced in the form of information, products or services.
6. Finally, you and I as consumers use it.[4]

If we trace the development of radios, television sets, cameras, high yielding wheat and rice varieties, communication strategies to bypass personal predispositions in the communication process or professionally prepared reading books for children, the sequence described would be apparent, often with surprisingly little overlap of people within categories along the continuum, let alone feedback. The time required for the developmental sequence to yield a useful product often exceeded a hundred years (DeFleur and Rokeach 1975, 34-105; Krugman 1972). As we have noted, information macrosystems put all of this together, potentially under the control of man.

This developmental sequence can be described in great detail as Meehan and Beal (1977) have chosen to do, or with considerable brevity as others have done (Nagel 1979; Guba and Clark 1975). Perhaps specification could also be in terms of elements or conditions essential for generating, transforming, and disseminating information (Lionberger, Pope, and Reddy 1979).

Succinctly the sequence of activities could be specified as basic research, applied research, development, distribution of the product, and utilization. In practice each of these has tended to become the responsibility of specialists and specialized subsystems. Even though the general inclination is to debate with self or others about whether there is a proper distinction between basic and applied research, the usual conclusion is that there is a difference and that they should be viewed as representing somewhat different but overlapping subsystems (Gideonse 1968; Meehan and Beal 1977; Nagel 1979). Thus, the activity and subsystem sequence tends to become:

(1) Basic researchers – extending the frontiers of basic science knowledge
(2) Applied researchers – intervening in the propositions and processes of science, to invent new things and adapt them to local use
(3) Developers – fabricating a useful innovation (information, produce or service) for distribution to potential users
(4) Disseminators – getting the locally adapted innovation to people
(5) The public – using the new information or technology

The Functional Requisites

The second feature of the model derives from the first; namely, what functions have to be performed to facilitate the theory-to-practice developmental sequence. These we have conceptualized as innovation, validation, dissemination, information, legitimation or persuasion, and integration. A reinforcement function is added for other reasons. The information, validation and dissemination functions were derived from the land-grant university experience in learning what had to be done to generate new science-based information and disseminate it. However, they could just as well have been conceptualized from an examination of the way information macrosystems operate (Havelock 1971).

The information and legitimation or persuasion functions are clearly apparent from "diffusion" research findings about the individual adoption process (Rogers and Shoemaker 1971; Lionberger and Gwin 1982). The integration function derives from what anthropologists have long known and demonstrated (Linton 1936) but which was overlooked by most diffusion researchers and professionals concerned with information development and use.

In a broad sense, functions may be defined as expected consequences of actions taken or in an instrumental sense, achievement of specified goals or purposes. For achieving them, more than one kind of activity or set of conditions may suffice.

Innovation. The first lesson from the land-grant university experience was that some means of generating new science-based information had to be found. This, it has been noted, was provided by adding experiment stations in addition to teaching students in residence. As here envisioned, the innovation function is presumed to include all of the basic science and applied research that is required to create usable new information and technology.[5]

Validation. This is the process by which the suitability of an innovation for local use is demonstrated. This means getting it as locally suited as the research methods of science will permit.[6]

Others like McDermott (1975) prefer to label this intervening stage as adaptation and the associated activity adaptive research. A few have included it in an amorphous category that they refer to as reinvention (Rogers 1983, 178; Rice and Rogers 1980). Validation as here envisioned continues adaptation and testing until the local utility of the innovation has been demonstrated. Important validation issues for any innovation are: Will they work for their intended purposes, are they locally feasible, and are they devoid of major undesirable consequences. In short, validations specifies that problems of "fitting in" have been reasonably well resolved.

One reason for singling this out as a separate function is the inclination to neglect or disregard it (Moseman

1971, 140). Too often, agriculturalists, for example, have assumed that information or technology developed and tested in one place is ready for transmission and use in others. Experience has repeatedly shown that the risks of doing so are unacceptably high (Rice 1974; Whyte 1981; Roling 1974).

However, proper validation does not mean that an innovation will be automatically accepted by potential adopters. Legitimation is required. This refers to the subjective process by which individuals finally decide that an innovation is (1) basically all right and (2) good for them. It requires the application of acceptance standards that they set for themselves. Usually, research evidence alone will not suffice.

Dissemination. Third, there must be a dissemination function even where adopters are relatively sophisticated and have high management ability (i.e., ability to relate abstract knowledge to own use). Information macrosystem modelers seem to have no doubt about the need for this function (Havelock 1971). The dissemination function, at the same time, requires some respecification of the information available and timely presentation of it to the user clientele.

Information and Persuasion (Legitimation). To insure that locally validated information and innovations are put to use, two additional functions must be performed by or on behalf of the adopting individual. These have been labeled the information and persuasion functions by Rogers and Shoemaker (1971, 99–106).

The information function refers merely to getting information to the adopter clientele; persuasion to bringing about an attitude change. I am inclined to label this function as legitimation instead of persuasion. Requirements for legitimating an innovation are imposed by the adopter. As such, it is a personal matter. It specifies requirements imposed for personal use acceptance.[7]

Integration. Guba (1968, 50) contends that innovations not designed for a specific situation will not fit. Thus, either the innovation or the environment or both have to be changed. The process by which this is done constitutes the integration function. When an innovation becomes so thoroughly a part of what it is built into that it is no longer regarded as new, integration has been achieved. This function approximates the adapting and installing activity specification of Meehan and Beal (1977).[8]

Even for simple practices presumed to fit in easily, integration may be very difficult. This is well illustrated by the adjustments that Iowa farmers had to make in switching from open pollinated to hybrid corn. In the open pollinated system, "good" farmers had devised ways for insuring that they would have an ample supply of seed for next year's planting. At harvest time, they carefully selected, by and large, ears with straight deep indented grains. The choice ears were usually put in a box at the front of the wagon. They were then stored during the winter to insure proper drying. In the spring, they were shelled for planting and the tips and butts were shelled off for livestock feed. The grains in the middle were graded by size of the holes in the corn planter plates and carefully shelled into containers for each of the sizes. The seed was then planted taking care to keep the rows three feet six or eight inches apart and grains no closer than eighteen inches in the row.

Use of hybrid seed required that they discard all of this technology which was a mark of a good farmer in which they took pride. Instead they had to pay five to ten times more for seed than they could get for the corn they raised. In addition, what they bought did not look like seed corn. There were grains of all sizes and they were hard and flinty. Farmers also wondered whether or not hogs would eat and thrive on it. In addition, they were expected to plant it perhaps twice as thick as they thought it ought to be and to put on what appeared to be huge amounts of fertilizer (by comparison to the amounts they were accustomed to). Thus, it is no wonder that some of the early adopters made their first trials away from the road where their neighbors could not see them.

No-till types of cultivation of today flies in the face of almost everything farmers traditionally have thought "good" farmers should do to grow row crops. Boiling water to kill germs is considered absurd in terms of ideas about hot and cold food, and asking Indian women to use one-hole secluded latrines means giving up the pleasant social association of going to the fields together for taking care of their toilet needs. Thus fitting in many new ideas and practices is often surprisingly difficult for potential users, particularly those who find it difficult to apply abstract knowledge to their own situation (i.e., people with low management ability). The implications of failure to attend to the performance of this function ought to be indelibly clear for managers of systems to develop and deliver new information and technology to people and get it used.

Reinforcement. Diffusion research suggests that people may cease to use new practices because they get no positive

support for innovating (Rogers 1983, 184). In fact, they
may be subjected to derision. Thus, they may cease to use a
new practice for the wrong reason. As generally recognized
in advertising, there is a need to supply the new adopter
with reasons why his initial use decision was a good one and
why it still is (i.e., reinforcement).

Governance. So long as man depended upon individuals
to develop new information and invent new technology and
interpersonal communication there was no system to control
the innovation-information disseminating processes.
However, when the research, development and delivery
activity was made a social system responsibility, man was
placed in a position to control the whole operation.
Decisions had to be made for whom and how the system should
work. Default was no viable option. Providing direction is
what is referred to as the governance function.

Further Conceptualization of Function Needed. As
systems for generating, transforming and using information
become more differentiated and sophisticated and their
operation better understood, further conceptualization of
features and functions will be needed and possible.[9] The
admonition here however is to concentrate on understanding
system qualities and specifying functions and how they must
vary with the state of development of need in the user's
social system.

Other Features

There are, of course, additional features about models
that must be considered. These include:
(1) how much organizational differentiation and
     specialization is needed in the system,
(2) how responsibility for the performance of
     functions should be assigned, and
(3) in agriculture in particular, what division of
     responsibilities for research development and
     distribution may be feasible within and among
     countries of the world.

A PROPOSED INFORMATION MACROSYSTEMS CONSTRUCT

The model being proposed is in a very real sense only
an institutionalization of what has been happening for
decades (McDermott 1975). As already noted, it envisions a
theory-to-practice continuum of activities as one dimension

and a specification of functions necessary to operationalize
their performance as the other. Moreover, the model
includes a problem-solving capability for addressing the
questions for which suitable answers are not available.

How to Graphically Represent It

If the egalitarian critics will permit, I prefer a
Figure 5.1 type of representation. If they will not, we had
better settle for one that arrays activities and functions
along a horizontal continuum. Note that except for
governance, functions are entered across the top in the
general sequential order in which they occur, along the
theory-to-practice continuum. Governance is intended to cut
across major subsystems and linkages that must develop.
Vertically along the left side is the
theory-to-practice continuum of activities which, as we have
noted, can be specified with little or much detail and
perhaps with some activities substituting for others. The
circles in the body of the model denote the major subsystems
that have tended to develop. These of course, could be
further specified inasmuch as subspecialties exist within
each of the subsystems noted. Solid lines indicate
directions of major communicative exchange. Two-way lines
across social subsystems are intended to denote interaction,
not the mere sending and receiving of messages (Berlo
1971).[10] Now that direction of the entire system is
possible, the time frame of the developmental sequence has
been shortened, interactive feedback from users is possible
and is essentially a must if it is to operate to address
their interests.
The loop within the body of the graphic indicates a
user information need reduction cycle, i.e., a special kind
of problem solving capacity which Nagel (1979) and Havelock
(1971) have properly stressed (Leithwood 1981). In another
sense, the RD & D sequence can operate in the same way and
often does when the governance is heavily vested in the
users' social system. It just takes longer to get the
answers. The problem-solving circuit is difficult to
illustrate graphically because of the diverse courses it may
take (Meehan and Beal 1977). In an elemental sense it
represents a situation dating back to a time when people as
information users performed all functions along the
developmental continuum (i.e., in a system totally
undifferentiated as to function). However, what seems to
have emerged and is working well under conditions of

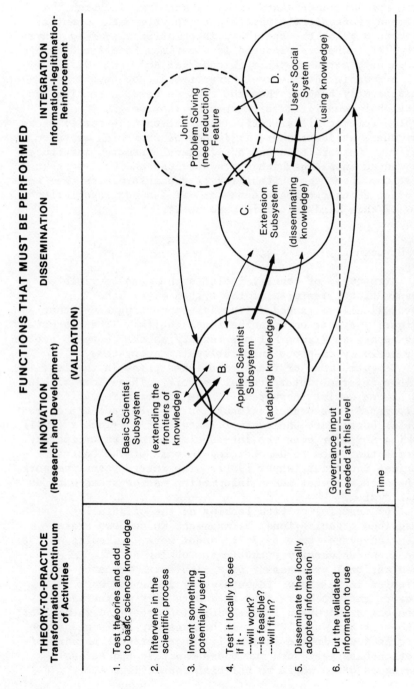

FUNCTIONS THAT MUST BE PERFORMED

| THEORY-TO-PRACTICE Transformation Continuum of Activities | INNOVATION (Research and Development) | DISSEMINATION | INTEGRATION Information-legitimation-Reinforcement |

(VALIDATION)

1. Test theories and add to basic science knowledge

2. Intervene in the scientific process

3. Invent something potentially useful

4. Test it locally to see if it -
   ---will work?
   ---is feasible?
   ---will fit in?

5. Disseminate the locally adopted information

6. Put the validated information to use

A. Basic Scientist Subsystem (extending the frontiers of knowledge)

B. Applied Scientist Subsystem (adapting knowledge)

C. Extension Subsystem (disseminating knowledge)

D. Users' Social System (using knowledge)

Joint Problem Solving (need reduction) Feature

Governance input needed at this level

Time

Figure 5.1   A systems model to generate, transform, and distribute specialty information and solve users' problems

informational uncertainty is an arrangement in which
selected professionals participate jointly with potential
users to develop the specialty information they need (Whyte
1981, 77). What is produced is sometimes location-specific
and sometimes transferable (Lionberger and Wong 1983).

Arrows in the theory-to-practice direction are
intentionally heavier than the reverse notwithstanding the
occasional need for greater reverse flow (e.g., in
problem-solving situations). Information necessarily flows
from where it is to where it is not or from high spots to
the low. Universities and agricultural research institutes
are indeed knowledge high spots notwithstanding important
questions about the suitability of the information they have
to offer to user clientele needs. If assumed information
flow of this kind is elitist, so be it.

Its Structure

Structure, of course, includes the readily visible
organizational features of the system (i.e., the
hierarchically arranged units with connecting lines that
ordinarily appear on organizational charts). The subsystems
that appear in Figure 5.1 are roughly as they seem to evolve
in relatively complete informational macrosystems.

However, most of the action takes place in the less
visible informal interpersonal network. These form within
and across social subsystems in the larger information
macrosystem (the organizational chart). Perhaps these, most
of all, constitute the central feature of Havelock's (1971)
linking model or even the interactive people participatory
schemes that seem to be emerging in some of the Central
American countries (Whyte 1981). The interpersonal network,
in essence, is what makes information macrosystems work as a
total system.

For example, critics looking at the officially
prescribed organizational arrangement in our own state
extension system have said it cannot work. Likewise,
land-grant university enthusiasts looking at the
organizational arrangement of agricultural research and
extension in Taiwan would surely say it cannot work.
However, the facts are that they both work very well
(Lionberger and Chang 1970, 1981; Lionberger and Cheng 1982;
Lionberger and Wong 1983). In both cases, the explanation
is to be found in the interactive interpersonal network of
relationships that form and operate within and across
subsystems often where no official connections are

specified. These tend to insure that proper linkages are
formed and maintained. Apparently neither researchers nor
extension workers in either the Missouri or Taiwan setting
felt obligated to go through official channels to get the
help they needed from the on-campus faculty.

In Taiwan these linkages were formed and maintained
across system boundaries where none were officially
prescribed. Agricultural technicians in the district
agricultural improvement stations and research institutes
under the Provincial Department of Agriculture and Forestry
had frequent contact with agricultural researchers in the
agricultural colleges under a separate Ministry of Education
(Lionberger and Chang 1970). They both were very much a
part of the agricultural information macrosystem. An
observation in the nature of a hypothesis is that once
formed and needed such relationships tend to maintain
themselves to the mutual benefit of the parties involved.

Also, the multiplying effect of people talking to and
influencing each other in the client system is enormous.
This, more than anything else, is responsible for adoption
of innovations at an increasing rate in the innovation
diffusion process (Rogers and Shoemaker 1971) and for the
success of developmental projects on the world scene (Morss
and others 1976). The McDermott admonition to start small
and grow big, if needed, surely applies to building
information macrosystems (McDermott 1971).

Process Considerations

Process considerations provide the framework for
observing and posing questions about how the system should
or does work. Of these there are many.

First and foremost we have noted that the system must:
a.   develop and deliver a continuing supply of updated
     science-based information ready for people to use
     with a minimum of additional local adaptation,
     i.e., it must supply ready-made answers to
     questions that people have.
b.   bring specialized informational resources to bear
     for resolving complex problems that they have.
     (This sometimes requires building and operating
     programs over extended periods of time).
c.   retrieve what people have learned on their own and
     feed it into the system for testing and possible
     use elsewhere (Emrick 1977; Sheridan 1981).

Issues about how the system performs these tasks must be
addressed. These, as a minimum, include
1. How administrative direction, control and
    constraints are exercised.
2. How interpersonal communicative networks are
    formed and operate within the system.
3. How research and extension problems originate and
    answers are arrived at and are processed through
    the system.
4. How necessary subsystem linkages are formed,
    operated and maintained.
Not until we understand how the emerging in-field system for
generating and utilizing information actually works (Whyte
1981; Wong 1981) can we really understand the significance
of innovative new informational macrosystem developments.
Otherwise, we are continually placed in a position of trying
to explain a system that we simply do not understand
(Moseman 1971; McDermott 1971).

Normative Considerations

        This refers to the values and philosophies that serve
as guides for deciding how the system should work, for whom
it should work, and for judging what it does. For land-
grant universities this approximates what knowledgeables
about these systems refer to as land-grant philosophy
(Lionberger, Pope, and Reddy 1979) or, in a somewhat different context, specifications for systems to generate and
utilize information for rural development (Lionberger 1982).
These norms are just as much a part of the system as its
organization and mode of operation (process). Since normative matters of informational macrosystems are often not
defined and may in fact exist only in the minds of knowledgeables who operate them, these norms are generally overlooked. In trying to introduce information macrosystems
into new situations, tangible organizational and process
features are emphasized. The rationale and specifications
for their being and operation tend to be left behind and
neglected.
        One set of contradictory of norms can well illustrate
how the same system could be run differently with different
results. While knowledgeables about land-grant universities
hold that these universities should become a repository of
knowledge second to none through free and diligent inquiry,
they also say they should operate on the premise that there
are extraordinary possibilities in ordinary people

(Lionberger, Pope and Reddy 1979).[11]

This means that the faculty and administrators must listen to what local people have to say, respect the indigenous knowledge that they possess, and take it into account when doing their research, planning their programs and trying to solve their operational problems. This kind of listening and response does occur (Lionberger and Cheng 1982).

The norms in systems such as land-grant universities are quite in contrast to views held by the social science and agronomy faculties in two leading Taiwan universities. Although the faculty had humanitarianism inclinations typical of land-grant university ways of thinking, they had little faith in the ability of ordinary people to solve their own problems. This was fortified by a belief that the university has an obligation to promote state views and philosophies. Collectively, this would seem to specify a paternalistic hard-sell stance with respect to the presumed less intelligent people they were willing to help. An "I'll talk while you listen" stance is suggested.

Observations and Conclusions

The proposed model provides a basis for understanding information macrosystems in the context of a conceptual scheme that specifies features central to their proper performance. It is assumed that it is generally applicable to situations where there is a mandate to provide specialty information to potential users systems and to assist them in solving problems for which there are no ready answers.

It is primarily an outgrowth of lessons learned in trying to meet the informational needs of users in situations where (1) administrators were charged with developing and supplying a particular kind of specialty information for them, (2) assured resources were provided for that purpose, (3) freedom to innovate existed, and (4) time was permitted to correct mistakes made. This was the nature of the situation in which U.S. land-grant universities and the so-called participatory types of informational macrosystems in Central America emerged (Edmond 1978; Gostyla and Whyte 1980; Lionberger and Wong 1983). Both developed a capacity to develop and deliver usable information to clients and ultimately a problem solving capability.

The problem-solving capability seems to inevitably emerge because even in the most judiciously planned and

operated RD & D system there always remain questions for
which there are no readily available answers and which must
be addressed before RD & D can deliver. Conversely the
systems that start with a local information-generating focus
(Hildebrand 1977; Sheridan 1981) either find they have
hidden RD & D connections or have to establish them.

The repeated appearance of similar informational
servicing arrangements to meet the specialty informational
needs of clientele plus reinforcement from judgments made
from research sources lends credence to the proposed ideal
systems model presented here.[12] It is adaptable to a vast
variety of places and conditions. The one presented here
could just as well have been the product of judgment made
from research results on and operational experience with
information macrosystems, as Havelock (1971) would seem to
suggest.

Many of the problems attributed to it had better be
attributed to (1) the way it is run, (2) the product it
tries to deliver, (3) the rules by which it is run (norms),
or (4) improper adaptation of the system itself to the
conditions that it is intended to address rather than to
system inadequacy. For the first two, there is no defense.
For the last two there are better explanations than system
blame.

The Elitist Charge Laid to Rest?

Run in a top-down manner without continued decisional
inputs from users, the systems will indeed operate in an
authoritarian elitist manner. So run, it can contribute to
increasing differences between the "haves" and "have nots"
and to reinforcing the structural conditions of societies
that create the division--as some have charged. The same
consequences, however, can accrue from a highly equalitarian
operation that specifies giving information and services
only to those who want and seek it and leaving others alone.
What the system does is a matter of governance, not of
system capability.

The inclination to blame the system rather than
governance errors (i.e., for undesirable consequences that
accrue for operating by the wrong set of rules or the way
societies are structured to keep the dispossessed
subjected), has led to:

(1) undue discounting of the potential of RD & D
     systems for human betterment, on the one hand
     (Sower 1962), and

(2)   an overemphasis on simple alternatives which also
        have their limitations.
Of the last, the extolled in-field problem-solving mode of
operation is typical. For sure, there is always an
unrealized potential in existing resource systems which when
properly activated, utilized and developed can contribute
materially to achieving locally defined goals and to
building institutions that will better serve the needs of
people (McDermott 1971). For this continuing need and
situations where there is no locally validated information
available for delivery and use, information generation and
use by extensive in-field involvement of professionals and
locals (the problem solving model) will surely offer more
immediate benefits than an RD & D type of operation
(Hildebrand 1977; Sheridan, 1981). As we have seen, there
are limits to this approach also.

The Matter of System Fit

     Like any innovation, a system to generate and utilize
information must be adapted to the situation and conditions
it is intended to serve. It must fit (be integrated into)
the structural arrangements within societies that service
the other needs of people. One crucial problem centers on
how differentiated (functionally and organizationally) the
informational system needs to be to fit in properly.
     At the least differentiated end of the continuum is a
situation in which all information macrosystems functions
are concentrated in the user. Under these conditions, what
anyone comes to know is the folk knowledge that already
exists or is developed there by its fellow members. Such
other needs as services, supplies and credit also tend to be
provided mostly within the users' own social system. Some
Third World situations of potential information users are of
this nature. Any system concerned mostly with information
generation and use must recognize and adjust to this state
of affairs. Here, a highly undifferentiated informational
subsystem mostly of a problem-solving, need-reducing nature
is surely most suited—i.e., one in which professionals, the
people to be affected and the agencies that have something
to contribute jointly define problems, consider
alternatives, adapt inputs, generate new information, make
plans and take joint action to meet the needs of the user
who maintains a high governance input over the entire
operation.[13]

The diffusion and linkage aspects of the system, sometimes alluded to as linkage models (Havelock 1971), are regarded as necessary parts of the research, development, and delivery system. Ultimately, the time comes when people want answers to their questions, not task forces to solve problems. As answers plus additional useful information are provided and people come to depend on the system for information, they come to expect it and are annoyed if it cannot deliver (Nagel 1979). For this the highly differentiated research, development and delivery mode of operation is most useful.

Thus in virtually all cases both are needed. Adapting the informational system to societal conditions and needs will mainly involve decisions about relative emphasis that needs to be placed on RD & D and problem solving capabilities, not which one.

In Defense of a Comprehensive Systems Perspective

For a time, some of the functions specified (along the theory-to-practice continuum) may seem to be unnecessary and neglected, seemingly without serious consequences to fulfilling the specialty informational needs of the public. However, ultimately the consequences are too costly. For example, the success of the problem-solving approach in providing locally generated solutions to problems may initially cast doubt on the need for an expanding body of basic science knowledge to meet the practical informational needs of the users in modernizing societies. For sure, there is always an additional utilitarian potential in the existing basic science knowledge base upon which to draw. Although its linkage to utilitarian use is often remote and unpredictable, its general neglect comes at a very high price. True, it does not determine what useful information and technology will be generated or where it sets limits on what can be done. Imagine, for example, what the potential would be if the nitrogen-building qualities of leguminous plants could be introduced into the nonleguminous food-producing ones or the vigor of some plants, now thought of as weeds, could be introduced into the edible crops of the world. Both seem to be very real possibilities (Burton 1976). Even though not necessarily in the same location or even the same country, the entire functionally interrelated information generating, transforming, utilizing system is necessary.

In Defense of Modeling Efforts

Systems to develop, transform and deliver information are a necessary part of modernizing societies. There are recent powerful social inventions of enormous unrealized potential for human betterment. Many of those who operate and even advise others on how to set up and use them have little or no knowledge of what research about them shows. Havelock (1971) made the translation of research results into practice much easier by analyzing at least four thousand of these studies in a context meaningful for information-system specialists and administrators who wish to apply the new knowledge.

One way of enhancing its utility is to identify models that have worked well and/or propose new ones that combine successful elements of those that have demonstrated superior performance with the view of making it easier for those who can use the information to do so. For the serious students of such systems, it is an intellectual "cop out" and practically foolish not to do so. Those who make such attempts will make mistakes, but it would be a much greater mistake not to try. This chapter is a third attempt on the part of the author to propose an ideal systems model or at least one that is better than most people have. Further improvements can be made by examining organizational and operational issues as they arise, in light of what the research shows plus the accumulated wisdom of practitioners. The net additive result of decisions made should be to build still better models. Trial-and-error learning and repetition of old mistakes should be a thing of the past.[14]

The Utility of the Model

Like all models, this one focuses on only a few issues and neglects most others. It accordingly offers no special advantage for addressing problems not represented in the conceptual scheme. However, the elements included and the special way in which they are interrelated are surely central to the performance of information generation—and supply systems generally. The postulated theory-to-practice developmental continuum and functional requisites provides a construct for much more definitively diagnosing operational problems and sharpening conclusions about the range in which recommended solutions will apply.[15]

Thus in place of simply saying that __the system failed__ we can say that:

1. the problem was with the people who ran it (a governance problem)
2. a locally unsuited product was delivered (a validation function failure)
3. proponents of the system erroneously emphasized its organizational arrangement as central instead of its functional requisites (a conceptualization and missed identity problem)
4. people with low managerial ability were asked to use something of demonstrated local utility but failed to make it work (a possible integration function problem)
5. autonomy from state government was achieved before user subsystem support for the system was established (a linking problem)
6. the system helped create and maintain an advantage for the "bigs" over the "littles" (a governance problem)
7. information developed from research is not getting to the subsystem that disseminates it (a linking problem)
8. knowing people for whom the locally validated information was developed will not use it (a legitimation problem), etc.

Research and investigation in the conceptual context proposed can begin to provide information that makes it possible to diagnose operational problems and apply corrective measures. The model permits us to focus on organizational and operational matters of central importance to the system and to obtain answers that provide the basis for improving its operational potential. This permits progressive movement in the direction of recommending an ideal systems model.

The writer is strongly of the view that the time has come when a concerted effort of this nature should be undertaken much as the Diffusion Research Committee of years past did for knowledge in that area by activating the network of knowledgeables and researchers concerned with generating, transforming and utilizing diffusion research findings.[16]

NOTES

1. For example, this is clearly apparent in DeFleur and Rokeach's description of the emergence of radio and motion pictures and in a communication strategy known as "learning without involvement" described by Krugman (DeFleur and Ball-Rokeach 1975, 34-105; Krugman 1972). The story of the development of the high-yielding wheat and rice varieties in agriculture is basically the same.

2. The land-grant university designation is about the most undescriptive term imaginable for these university-centered systems to generate and distribute information. They were initially given that name because the U.S. Congress gave states public land to help support at least one in each state. The land-grant designation persists to this date (Kellogg and Knapp 1966).

3. One study suggests that decisions of this type also predominate in Taiwan (Lionberger and Chang 1968).

4. To be sure, all innovations do not proceed along this developmental sequence; but to test its validity make a list of what you are now wearing, what you ate for dinner last night, and the medical care you have obtained during the past year. Classify them into an "invented by me" and "by others" column. Then trace the developmental origins of as many of the borrowed ones as you can.

5. Nagel prefers to divide this into (basic) research and a series of developmental activities designed to produce a usable product. The last he labels as operationalization (Nagel 1979).

6. This approximates Meehan and Beal's adapting and installing sequence and is virtually synonymous with McDermott's integration function except for his inclination to apply the integration concept to the bifurcated supply system also. (Meehan and Beal 1977; McDermott 1975).

7. The requirements that individuals set for each of these functions and the means they habitually use to become informed and persuaded provide important clues on how the information dissemination subsystem can aid potential users of new information and technology. Diffusion research shows that the two functions are conceptually different and that the requirements imposed for each are different.

8. It also includes a part of what Rogers and others have referred to as re-invention but delimits more precisely what is included (Rogers 1983, 176-184; Rice and Rogers 1980). Somehow some distinction must be made between making changes necessary to fit an invention into a local setting for a given purpose about which anthropologists have known for years and what constitutes a sufficient degree of innovative behavior to warrant the label of re-invention.

9. One addition will surely have to be how to account for a subsidiary information servicing activity to which Meehan and Beal (1977) direct attention in their information, generating, distribution and use model.

10. A central premise of the proposed model is that the functions cannot be comprised, i.e., that all must be performed, but that there are organizational alternatives and methods for doing so.

11. Lack of confidence in the ability of ordinary people among agricultural researchers and extension workers on the world scene is seen by Ensminger as seriously dysfunctional to the service functions of agricultural research and extension on behalf of farmers (Ensminger 1981).

12. After exhaustive assessment of research results on information macrosystems 11 years ago, Havelock stopped only a little short of recommending basically the same kind of model (Havelock 1971, chap. 11).

13. But when operated to maximize potentially useful informational inputs professionals who are either the product of or have connections with RD & D systems are represented (Sheridan 1981; Hildebrand 1977; Lionberger and Wong, 1983). When these necessary linkages are overlooked for whatever reason, the operation can easily be seen quite exclusively as a local problem-solving need-reducing model. Outside linkages are necessary because locals simply can neither anticipate nor address all of the important problems that must be resolved hopefully and sometimes necessarily before they occur (Havelock 1971, chap. 11; Nagel 1979).

14. The knowledge and experience base about the organization and operation of information macrosystems is now sufficient to avoid remaking old mistakes, arguing about false dichotomies, posing partial models, and reliance on

trial-and-error as an appropriate means of operationalizing
ones suited to specific places and needs. The time required
to build a combined "research development and delivery" and
"problem-solving" capability (of the type described) in
land-grant universities was almost a hundred years. More
recently under agricultural conditions similar to those in
the United States in the late 1800s and where administrators
had sufficient autonomy and assured financial support, the
time required to arrive at much the same kind of system was
much less. As results from the last are being used to build
new ones the time required will surely be diminished still
further (Whyte 1981).

15. In the interests of brevity, a discussion and
suggested resolution of twenty such issues was deleted from
this paper.

16. This would not be nearly so ambitious as setting up
a special institution for advising countries on how to
develop and operate their agricultural research and
extension services as envisioned by the International
Service for National Agricultural Research, established in
The Netherlands (1980).

REFERENCES

Beal, G. M. 1978. "Another Look at Knowledge Production
    and Utilization." Development Communication Report no.
    23: 1-4.

Berlo, D. K. 1971. "Interaction: The Goal of Interpersonal
    Communication." In Basic Readings in Interpersonal
    Communication, ed. K. Griffin and B. R. Patton, 94-119.
    New York: Harper and Row Publishers.

Burton, G. W. 1976. "Overcoming Constraints and Realizing
    Potentials in the Physical and Biological Aspects of
    Feeding People." In Proceedings of the World Food
    Conference of 1976. Ames: Iowa State Univ. Press.

Campbell, R. R. 1966. "A Suggested Paradigm of the
    Individual Adoption Process." Rural Sociology 31, no.
    4: 458-467.

DeFleur, M. L., and S. Ball-Rokeach. 1975. Theories of
    Mass Communication, 3d ed. New York: David McKay
    Company.

Edmond, J. B. 1978. The Magnificent Charter: The Origin
    and Role of the Morrill Land Grant Colleges and
    Universities. Hicksville, N.Y.: Exposition Press.

Emrick, J. A. 1977. Evaluation of the National Diffusion
    Network, Volume I: Findings and Recommendations.
    Prepared for the U.S. Office of Education, Department
    of Health, Education and Welfare, Washington, D.C.
    Menlo Park, Calif.: Stanford Research Institute.

Ensminger, D. 1981. "Extension's Mission." Paper prepared
    for publication in KIDMA, Israel Journal of
    Development. Jerusalem, Israel, 1981.

Gideonse, H. D. 1968. "Research, Development and the
    Improvement of Education." Science 162, no. 3853:
    541-545.

Gostyla, L., and W. F. Whyte. 1980. "ICTA in Guatemala:
    The Evolution of a New Model for Agricultural Research
    and Development". Ithaca, N.Y.: Rural Development
    Committee, Center for International Studies, Cornell
    University.

Guba, E. G. 1968. "Diffusion of Innovations." Educational
    Leadership 25, no. 4: 292-295.

Guba, E. G., and D. C. Clark. 1975. "The Configurational
    Perspective: A New View of Knowledge, Production and
    Utilization." Educational Research 4, no. 4: 6-9.

Havelock, R. G. 1971. Planning for Innovation Through
    Dissemination and Utilization of Knowledge. Ann Arbor:
    Center for Research on the Utilization of Scientific
    Knowledge, Institute for Social Research, University of
    Michigan.

Hildebrand, P. E. 1977. "Generating Small Farm Techniques:
    An Integrated Multidisciplinary System." Paper
    presented at the 12th West Indian Agricultural
    Economics Conference, Caribbean Agro-Economic Society,
    Antigua, 1977.

Kellogg, C. E., and D. C. Knapp. 1966. The College of
   Agriculture: Science in the Public Service. New York:
   McGraw-Hill.

Kidd, D. W. 1971. "A Systems Approach to Analyses of the
   Agricultural Extension Service of Western Nigeria."
   Ph.D. diss., University of Wisconsin.

Krugman, H. E. 1972. "The Impact of Television
   Advertising: Learning Without Involvement." In Mass
   Media and Society, ed. A. Walls, 158-163. Palo Alto,
   Calif.: National Press Books.

Leithwood, K. A. 1981. "Managing the Implementation of
   Curriculum Innovation." Knowledge: Creation,
   Diffusion, Utilization 2, no. 3: 341-360.

Linton, R. 1936. The Study of Man. New York: D. Appleton-
   Century Company.

Lionberger, H. F. 1977. "Developing and Disseminating
   Information for Modernizing Societies: Toward an Ideal
   Systems Model." Department of Rural Sociology,
   University of Missouri, Columbia. Mimeo.

_____. 1982. "Consensus or Schools of Thought Among
   U.S. Knowledgeables about Rural Development Information
   Macrosystems." Paper prepared for presentation at
   Rural Sociological Society Meetings, Rural Sociology,
   University of Missouri, Columbia.

Lionberger, H. F., and H. C. Chang. 1968. "Communication
   and Use of Scientific Farm Information by Farmers in
   Two Taiwan Agricultural Villages." Research Bulletin
   #940. Columbia: Missouri Agricultural Experiment
   Station, University of Missouri.

_____. 1970. Farm Information for Modernizing
   Agriculture: The Taiwan System. New York: Praeger.

_____. 1981. "Development and Delivery of Scientific
   Farm Information: The Taiwan System as an Organiza-
   tional Alternative to Land-Grant Universities - U.S.
   Style." Extension Education and Rural Development:
   International Experience in Communication and
   Innovations, ed. B. R. Crouch and S. Chamla, 155-175.
   New York: John Wiley and Sons.

Lionberger, H. F., and W. Cheng. 1982. Agricultural and Community Development Extension in Missouri from an Information Macrosystems Perspective. Research Bulletin #1041. Columbia: Missouri Agricultural Experiment Station, University of Missouri.

Lionberger, H. F., and P. H. Gwin. 1982. Communication Strategies: A Guide for Agricultural Change Agents. Danville, Ill.: Interstate Printers and Publishers.

Lionberger, H., L. A. Pope, and B. A. Reddy. 1979. Information Development and Flow: A Study of the Communication Behavior of Social Scientists in a U.S. Land Grant and Two Taiwan Universities. Research Bulletin #1033. Columbia: Missouri Agricultural Experiment Station, University of Missouri.

Lionberger, H. F., and T. S. Wong. 1980. "The Integration Function in Community Development: The Missouri System as a Case in Point." Journal of the Community Development Society 11, no. 1: 35-48.

_____. 1982. Information Developer-User System Linking Roles of Education Assistants in the Missouri Small Farm Family Program. Research Bulletin. Columbia: Missouri Agricultural Experiment Station, University of Missouri.

_____. 1983. An Alternative to Research Develop and Deliver: Rural Development in Missouri as a Case in Point. Research Bulletin #1052. Columbia: Missouri Agricultural Experiment Station, University of Missouri.

McDermott, J. K. 1971. "Extension institutions." In Institutions in Agricultural Development, ed. M. G. Blase, 151-161. Ames: Iowa State Univ. Press.

_____. 1975. "The Technology of Technological Innovation." Washington, D.C.: U.S. Agency for International Development, Technical Assistance Bureau.

Meehan, P. M., and G. M. Beal. 1977. Knowledge Production and Utilization: A General Model. Third Approximation. Project No. 2218. Ames: Iowa Agricultural and Home Economics Experiment Station.

Morss, E. R., J. K. Hatch, D. R. Mickelwait, and C. F. Sweet. 1976. Strategies for Small Farmer Development. Vol. 1, Final Report. Boulder, Colo.: Westview Press.

Moseman, A. H. 1971. "Research Systems." In Institutions in Agricultural Development, ed. M. G. Blase, 139-147. Ames: Iowa State Univ. Press.

Nagel, U. J. 1979. "Institutionalization of Knowledge Flows: An Analysis of the Extension Role of Two Agricultural Universities in India." Quarterly Journal of International Agriculture. Special series issue #30, 1979.

Paisley, W., M. Butler-Paisley, and K. Shapiro. 1976. Databook—The Status of Education Research and Development in the United States. Washington, D.C.: National Institute of Education, U.S. Department of Health, Education and Welfare.

Rice, E. B. 1974. Extension in the Andes: An Evaluation of Official U.S. Assistance to Agricultural Extension Services in Central and South America. Cambridge, Mass.: MIT Press.

Rice, R. E., and E. M. Rogers. 1980. "Re-invention in the Innovation Process." Knowledge: Creation, Diffusion, and Utilization 1, no. 4: 499-514.

Rogers, E. M. 1983. Diffusion of Innovations. New York: Free Press.

Rogers, E. M., and F. F. Shoemaker. 1971. Communication of Innovations, 2d ed. New York: Free Press.

Roling, N. G. 1974. "From Theory to Action." Ceres 39 (May-June): 22-25.

Samonte, V. P. B. 1970. "An Application of the Campbell Paradigm to the Adoption Process of Farmers in Selected Areas in the Philippines." Ph.D. diss., University of Missouri.

Sheridan, M. 1981. "Peasant Innovation and Diffusion of Agricultural Technology in China." Ithaca, N.Y.: Rural Development Committee, Center for International Studies, Cornell University.

Sower, C. 1962. "The Land-Grant University 'Development Organization' in Transition: The Case of the Cooperative Extension Service." In Directing the Cooperative Extension Service, 12-159. Selected papers presented at the Seventh National Cooperative Extension Administrative Seminar, Madison, Wisconsin, 1962.

Whyte, W. F. 1981. Participatory Approaches to Agricultural Research and Development: A State-of-the-Art Paper. Ithaca, N.Y.: Rural Development Committee, Center for International Studies, Cornell University.

Wong, T. S. 1981. "Toward a Rural Development Oriented Information Macrosystem: A Case Study of a Social Innovation." Ph.D. diss., University of Missouri.

6

Communication in Knowledge Production, Dissemination, and Utilization

George M. Beal and Peter Meehan

There are many frames of reference from which knowledge and communication and their interrelations can be viewed. The major concern in this chapter is with communicators, communication systems and the structure, functions, roles and activities needed to define knowledge needs and produce or search out, develop, adapt, disseminate and secure the use of relevant knowledge fitted to user needs. A pragmatic orientation focusing on knowledge production and utilization is emphasized. In its simplest form, we see this process as including (adapted from Meehan and Beal 1977):

> a communication system in which knowledge is generated by scientists, clients and other system-participants and is systematically incorporated into the design, production, adaptation, dissemination and use of information, technology, products and programs to meet user needs.

Historically, relatively simple conceptualizations of communication systems have been used, such as, research-linking-client systems (Rogers and Jain 1969). A number of criticisms have been leveled at the various explicit and implicit communication system models extant. Among those criticisms are (1) the assumption of linearity, with knowledge flowing only from research, through technology to users (Gideonse 1968; Guba and Clark 1975); (2) the major assumption of one way communication "down" through the system, largely authoritarian, persuasive or manipulative (Schutjer and Van Der Neen 1976; Wharton 1969; O'Kelley 1977; Cummings 1977); (3) based on the above points, the perception of the creation of dependency (rather than collaborative) relationships (Schumacher 1973; Röling 1974;

Cummings 1977; Darling 1977); (4) the assumption that only
scientific research knowledge is relevant to problem
solution (Havelock et al. 1969; Handler 1960; Röling 1973;
Hathaway 1977; Williams 1978; Beal and Meehan 1978); (5) the
assumption of technology transfer rather than an interactive
communication process resulting in adaptive, intermediate or
improved indigenous technology (Schumacher 1973; O'Kelley
1977; Gideonse 1969; Röling 1974); (6) heavy responsibility
placed on "linkers" without also placing responsibilities on
those to be linked (Guba and Clark 1975; Gideonse 1968;
Rogers and Jain 1969; Meehan and Beal 1977); (7) dependence
on "trickle-down" communication and lack of concern with the
distribution effects of this type of technology adoption
(Röling, Ascroft, and Chege 1976; McNamara 1977a; Williams
1978; Ruttan 1977; Darling 1977); (8) and probably most
important, is the dissatisfaction with the effectiveness of
many programs based on present information-communication
systems models (Schumacher 1973; Wharton 1977; Cummings
1977; McNamara 1977a, 1977b; Williams 1978; Darling 1977).

It is evident that each of these criticisms is deeply
embedded in concerns with communications. The student of
communication will immediately recognize the multitude of
more specific communication issues inherent in these general
criticisms.

It is only in the last two decades that emphasis has
been placed on the systematic study and conceptualization of
knowledge production and utilization communication systems.
Some of the more recent research, conceptualization and
communication system "model" building appear to counter some
of the criticisms of past systems. One "communication
system" paradigm is described in this chapter. It draws
heavily on the work of many scholars, especially Havelock
(1969, 1971, 1974), Guba (1970, 1974), Guba and Clark
(1975), Gideonse (1968), Rotham (1974), Kiehl (1970),
Lionberger and Reddy (1976), Coughenour (1976), Rogers
(Rogers and Jain, 1969; Rogers and Shoemaker 1971), and
Röling (1974; Röling, Ascroft, and Chege 1976).

Past experience and present roles tend to permeate the
conceptualization of each author. The present authors come
out of a tradition of the land grant university as producers
(basic and applied research) of knowledge, and as product-
practice developers and disseminators (e.g., Extension
Service). Their specific tradition is the adoption-
diffusion of technology. Thus, at first glance this
paradigm tends to appear research driven. It can be,
however, despite graphic presentation in linear form, it
will be noted, and illustrated by example, an iterative

paradigm, which emphasizes user needs, recognizes various types and sources of knowledge and the importance of interaction of many role players at various stages, and allows for initiative and entry into the system at many different points in the system.

The paradigm presented here describes six categories of interrelated functions, activities and processes. They are believed to be distinct enough to merit separated (stage or step) treatment, at least for heuristic purposes. While the importance of communicators and communication is evident throughout the paradigm, they are not specifically emphasized. If the general paradigm has merit, it appears that a further elaboration of the importance, roles and dimensions of communication in the process is in order. This paradigm is described more completely in a separate monograph (Meehan and Beal 1977). For the sake of brevity, a brief description will have to suffice here.

The six stages are thought to represent different sets of activities with varying outputs. They also require different skills for the successful carrying out of the processes. The specialized activities are thought to represent elements of the knowledge-production-utilization structure which must be permeated by continual communication of each relevant stage to contribute fully to the task of generating knowledge and making it functional and useful.

Although the ultimate user, in the product-adoption/utilization stage, is the target of communication and behavior change, actors in each stage must meet the needs of users in other stages (Gideonse 1968) if the needs of the ultimate users are to be fulfilled. Each of the stages between research and adoption/utilization is regarded as a knowledge production and utilization unit in itself. In each stage (as specified in the more detailed description of the paradigm) the actors are seen as beginning by identifying specific user needs, planning and producing outputs according to those needs, and packaging outputs to appeal to the specified clients (Gideonse 1968).

The term product is used often in this description. It is used to apply to a broad range of phenomena, including hardware, material and software "products," e.g., a research report, an information search package, a brochure, a radio program, a feedback procedure, a training module, a family planning campaign, a newly created advisory committee, and interorganizational coordination council with negotiated authority.

THE COMMUNICATION PARADIGM: SIX STAGES

Scientific Knowledge Production

Scientists, using the scientific method, produce knowledge in the form of verified statements of relationships
between and among variables. Scientific knowledge is produced primarily by carrying out basic and applied research.
Though the distinction made between basic and applied
research is not always clear, they can be seen as semi-
autonomous but in many cases complementary activities which
often must be interrelated or linked to provide information
related to user needs. Basic research is often seen as
oriented toward the production of knowledge for knowledge or
discipline sake, while applied research is seen as producing
or applying knowledge for solution of "real world" problems.
Both types of knowledge may be needed to provide full or
partial information to define or suggest possible solutions
for user problems or for the development of technology. The
presentation below highlights the tasks to be performed.

I

KNOWLEDGE-PRODUCTION

Basic Research (BR)	Applied Research (AR)
1. depict problem	1. identify user needs
2. review research	2. depict problem
3. relate variables	3. review research
4. conceptualize problem	4. relate variables
5. test hypotheses	5. conceptualize problem
6. conclude from tests	6. test hypotheses
7. package results	7. conclude from tests
8. communicate results	8. package results
9. evaluate method	9. communicate results
	10. evaluate results

Knowledge-Management

The main output of the knowledge-production stage
(previous stage) is a vast array of articles, reports,
papers, monographs and books presenting research findings.
If this knowledge is to be effectively utilized, it must be
monitored, screened, indexed, catalogued, packaged and
stored in a form that is readily retrievable at access
points for functional search, use and dissemination. These

activities may be designated as knowledge-management. The steps in knowledge-management may be identified below.

II

KNOWLEDGE-MANAGEMENT

1. identify user needs
2. monitor/screen research
3. catalogue
4. package
5. store
6. retrieve
7. disseminate
8. evaluate operations

Knowledge-Translation

Knowledge-translation involved the synthesis and conversion of scientific research findings into information useful to product-developers who attempt to formulate solutions to practical problems. This stage may be characterized as one of the specific "meeting points" of abstract, scientific knowledge with the practical knowledge and problem definitions of clients. Effective "meeting" usually takes place through the efforts of highly skilled translators or linkers with a "dual understanding" of the scientific and practical conception of the same problem—possessing the skills to code and recode back and forth between the client's formulation of a problem and relevant descriptors of available scientific knowledge. Scientific research is synthesized, generalized and operationalized to bear on the problems of clients and alternative products that may aid in problem solution. The outputs from this stage may be papers, reports, presentations or consultation containing guidelines and information highly relevant for product development. The activities in knowledge translation may be outlined as follows:

III

KNOWLEDGE-TRANSLATION

1. identify user needs
2. recode user problem
3. review research
4. synthesize/generalize research

5. recode generalizations
6. operationalize
7. package
8. disseminate
9. evaluate operations

Product Development

At the product development stage, translated (synthesized, generalized and operationalized) knowledge is combined with knowledge of user needs (existing or created),
and "products" are developed which are judged to have the
potential of meeting these needs. There are variations in
the orientation to product development: on the one hand,
there is emphasis on discovering needs and wants of target
audiences (often involving disseminators and linkers in this
process) and developing knowledge packages, materials, services or material products; on the other hand, the product
may be first developed, and then its use is "promoted."
Solutions ("products") may take the form of social or
material technologies--software or hardware. The following
is one way to conceptualize product-development.

IV

PRODUCT-DEVELOPMENT

1. identify user needs

2. formulate problem
   a. review research
   b. investigate user-system
   c. relate variables

3. invent solution
   a. draft performance/appeal specifications
   b. determine general function
   c. invent/design alternative solutions
   d. analyze/assess solutions
   e. select optimal solution
   f. design prototype
   g. review prototype

4. fabricate prototype solution
5. test, re-test prototype
6. fabricate marketable solution
7. package solution
8. transfer to disseminators
9. evaluate operations

Product-Dissemination

Once potential solutions to user needs or problems (existing or created) are developed, dissemination to clients or users is undertaken. Activities at this stage usually include understanding the product and its uses, designing dissemination and communication strategy, distribution of the product, adaptation and installation of products, and monitoring product performance. It may be conceptualized in the following manner:

V

PRODUCT-DISSEMINATION

1. identify user needs
2. communicate needs to developer
3. assist product-development
4. understand solution
5. design dissemination/distribution strategy
6. communicate product messages
   - advertise
   - publicize
   - promote
   - educate
   - demonstrate
   - consult
   - counsel
   - inform
   - sell
7. initiate distribution
8. adapt/install product
9. monitor product performance
   - service
   - repair
   - resell
   - replace
10. evaluate operations

Product-Adoption/Utilization

Product-adoption/utilization is the process by which users discover and diagnose problems, locate solutions, try-test solutions, adopt solutions and assimilate solutions into their existing systems in a manner to secure effective utilization of the solution. The stages of this process may be conceptualized as follows:

VI

PRODUCT-ADOPTION/UTILIZATION

1. live with current needs
2. discover problem
3. diagnose problem
4. search for solution
5. evince interest in solution
6. try-test
7. adopt (or not adopt) solution
8. adopt/install solution
9. institutionalize solution
10. evaluate solution—maintain/repair/replace

APPLYING THE MODEL

In some cases solutions to user needs or problems may already be available. The model argues for this situation setting off an interactive communication process that will penetrate the previously discussed stages until knowledge sufficient to solve the problem is found or generated and the knowledge is transformed into a solution which is packaged and communicated to relevant linkers until the ultimate user can test, adapt and incorporate it into his situation for effective utilization. Thus, the paradigm may have the appearance of being one-way, linear—this is not necessarily true.

To further illustrate this point, a hypothetical example is presented (see Figure 6.1).

The source of initiative for this particular path of utilization is the farmer in Stage VI who lives with his/her current needs (Stage VI, step 1) for pesticides, and then discovers a problem (Stage VI, step 2). The problem is that current pesticides do not control a certain insect; as a result the corn yield has been reduced significantly. The farmer and an agricultural service representative discuss the problem, and they identify the farmer's need (Stage V, step 1). Farmer and representative then jointly diagnose the problem (Stage VI, step 3). The agricultural representative communicates this need to a product-developer (Stage V, step 2) in a pesticide firm, who thereby identifies the problem (Stage IV, step 1) and sets out to formulate the problem by means of a research review of corn pesticides and further investigation of the social and physical environmental problems of the farmer (Stage IV, step 2a and b). In doing so, the developer contacts a

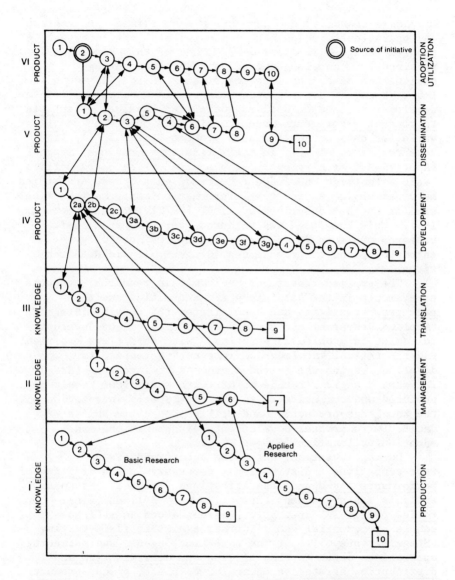

Figure 6.1   An interactive, dynamic model of knowledge production and utilization in agriculture

knowledge-translator to generate a synthesized, generalized and operationalized packet of knowledge on the corn pest problem (Stage III, steps 1-8). Much of this knowledge is received from knowledge-management services through designation of appropriate descriptors (Stage II, steps 1-6). However, certain questions remain unanswered, and the developer calls upon applied social and physical scientists to conduct experiments which clarify the operation of variables causing the farmer's problem [Stage I, (Applied Research) steps 1-9]. In their literature reviews [Stage I, (Applied Research) step 3], the applied researchers utilize basic scientific knowledge retrieved, catalogued, and stored by a nationwide agricultural information-management service similar to that described by Kiehl (1970) (Stage II, steps 1-6). This knowledge was gathered over time from basic research projects in chemistry, economics, sociology, entomology, and other sciences [Stage I, (Basic Research) steps 1-8].

The applied researcher reviews this research, conducts experiments in the laboratory and the field, and then packages, translates and communicates the results [Stage I, (Applied Research) steps 8 and 9] to the product-developer to assist in problem-formulation. With sufficient empirical and theoretical knowledge of relevant variables, the developer begins the extended process of invention (Stage IV, step 3 a-g). At this point (with sufficient knowledge produced and communicated to the developer), interaction on the knowledge-production-and-utilization chain shifts decidedly to product-development, dissemination, and adoption/utilization (Stages IV-VII).

During invention, extension agents and field representatives assist wherever necessary in the drafting of performance and appeal specifications (Stage IV, step 3a), analysis and assessment (Stage IV, step 3d), and final review (Stage IV, step 3g). Disseminators as well as a sample of potential users further assist in field-testing (Stage IV, step 5). At the same time, agents and marketing specialists begin to plan alternative dissemination and distribution strategies according to place, price, product, and promotion variables (Stage V, step 5). When the product is finally deemed market-ready, it is fabricated (Stage IV, step 6), packaged with instructions and an appealing appearance (Stage IV, step 7), and transferred to disseminators (Stage IV, step 8). Extension agents and salesmen study and learn about the use of the product until they understand the product (Stage V, step 4): and, if necessary, they revise and implement the previously designed dissemination/distribution strategy. Implementation occurs when product-messages are communicated to farmers through advertising, promotions, demonstrations, consultation and selling (Stage V, step 6). This is likely to involve a variety of personal and impersonal contacts with farmers over an extended period of time. Disseminators may encourage try-tests or even include free try-tests of the product in their dissemination/demonstration package (Stage VI, step 6). Farmers begin to purchase the new pesticide through conveniently located sales points in the distribution channels (Stage V, step 7). Agents and salesmen assist farmers in the final adaptation and installation of the pesticide in their particular farming systems (Stage V, step 8 and Stage VI, step 8). Based on continued need and satisfactory product-performance, the new pesticide is repurchased and finally institutionalized by farmers over time (Stage VI, step 9). Farmers evaluate the product while agents and salesmen monitor its performance, and action is taken by disseminators and users over the years to improve and perhaps eventually replace the pesticide with a better one (Stage V, step 9, and Stage VI, step 10).

An entire cycle of knowledge-production-and-utilization has been completed to illustrate the possible interaction of steps and stages on the utilization chain. In this case, initiative came from the client; knowledge-information was channeled through dissemination, development, translation, management, and production stages; and then came back to the client in the form of a solution to the original problem--a corn pesticide.

A FINAL NOTE

The production and utilization of knowledge for the solution of individual and social problems is seen as a complicated, interactive, iterative process involving a number of different "stages," roles, functions, activities, opportunities and constraints. Effective communication is at the heart of the process if relevant knowledge is to be generated, made available, integrated, adapted, packaged, disseminated and used.

The knowledge-production-and-utilization paradigm presented here attempts to take into account the various types of knowledge and sources of knowledge probably needed for problem definition and solution. It does not assume a linear flow of knowledge-information from basic research to

the ultimate user. It recognizes that initiative and
initiation of the communication process can start and/or
occur at any stage of the paradigm. There is a recognition
that the process is iterative in character and that
knowledge and communication flows back and forth within and
among stages--the process is often marked with repetition
and recurring interaction.

Emphasis is placed on knowledge management, knowledge
translation and the availability and use of relevant
knowledge in "product" development. The need was pointed
out for highly skilled translators or linkers with the dual
understanding of the scientific and practical conception of
the same problem--possessing the skills to code and recode
back and forth between the clients for mutation of a problem
and relevant descriptors of available scientific knowledge.
The role may be performed by newly trained specialized
linkers or communicators or by improving the conceptual and
communicative skills of those now found in these roles.

It may be noted that each stage in the paradigm can be
seen as a miniature knowledge need definition, production,
packaging and dissemination activity. That is, concern with
immediate (not only ultimate) client needs, preparing and
packaging information-products understandably and with
appeal, attention to dissemination communication strategies,
and helping test and secure utilization of the "product" are
seen as important functions at every stage--not just in
relation to the ultimate client or user.

The paradigm provides the opportunity for the
involvement of ultimate users and intermediate linkers and
their knowledge, conceptual and communication contributions
in defining problems, formulating and adapting solutions,
and integrating them into existing systems of actions. It
allows for collaborative knowledge production and
utilization, a move away from dependency relations and could
facilitate more equitable distribution of benefits. Thus
knowledge of various kinds, communicated from various
sources should contribute to the development of intermediate
technology, appropriate technology, selective technology,
and adaptive research, development and trials which will be
more effective in the solution of individual and social
problems.

The paradigm calls not only for a revised conceptualization, but in many cases for changes in philosophy and the
development of new functions, roles and responsibilities--
communicators are probably among those most affected. The
short-run utility of this paradigm rests on further discussion and clarification of its content and intent, and

further field testing in real world knowledge-production-utilization situations under different conditions. We hope it will be subjected to these evaluations.

REFERENCES

Beal, G. M., and P. Meehan. 1978. "Another Look at Know-ledge Production and Utilization." In Development Communication Report, No. 23 (July), Washington D.C., Clearing House on Development Communication, Academy for Educational Development.

Coughenour, M. 1976. "Review of D.M. Freeman's Technology and Society: Issues in Assessment, Conflict, and Choice." Rural Sociology 41, no. 2: 284-285.

Cummings, R. W., Jr. 1977. Minimum Information Systems for Agricultural Development in Low-Income Countries, Seminar Report. New York: Agricultural Development Council.

Darling, R. 1977. "A Return to Valid Development Principles." International Development Review 19, no. 4: 27-31.

Gideonse, H. G. 1968. "Research, Development and the Improvement of Education." Science 162, no. 3853: 541-545.

Guba, E. G. 1970. "Missing Roles in School Leadership: Matters Tended and Untended." In Frontiers in School Leadership, ed. L.J. Rubin. Chicago: Rand-McNally.

_____. 1974. A Diffusion Mechanism for the Center for Vocational and Technical Education. Columbus: Ohio State University.

Guba, E. G., and D. C. Clark. 1975. "The Configurational Perspective: A New View of Knowledge-Production-and-Utilization." Educational Research 4: 6-9.

Handler, P. 1960. Introduction to Knowledge into Action: Improving the Nation's Use of Social Sciences, National Science Board. Washington, D.C.: National Science Foundation.

148

Hathaway, D. E. 1977. "Alternative Institutions and Other Agents of Change for Increased Food Availability." In Proceedings, The World Food Conference of 1976. Ames: Iowa State Univ. Press.

Havelock, R. G. 1971. Innovations in Education: Strategies and Tactics, CRUSK (Center for Research on Utilization of Scientific Knowledge) Report. Ann Arbor, Mich: CRUSK Reprint.

Havelock, R.G., and others. 1969. Planning for Innovation Through Dissemination and Utilization of Knowledge. Ann Arbor: Center for Research on Utilization of Scientific Knowledge, Institute for Social Research, University of Michigan.

_____. 1974. A Comparative View of Six Federal R & D Information Systems. CRUSK Short Report. Ann Arbor, Mich.: CRUSK Reprint.

Kiehl, E. R. 1970. " An Information Network for the Agricultural Sciences." Agricultural Science Review 8: 11–15.

Lionberger, H., and A. B. Reddy. 1976. "Reference Group Influence on Extension Communication of Social Science Faculty." Rural Sociolgy 41, no. 1: 25–44.

McNamara, R. S. 1977a. Speech given to World Bank/ International Monetary Fund, Board of Governors, September 26, 1977. Reported in Society for International Development, Survey of International Development 14, nos. 4 and 5: 1–5.

_____. 1977b. "So Little Increase in Living Standards." An excerpt from annual address of Robert S. McNamara. Reported in A.I.D., War on Hunger 11, no. 10: 18–21.

Meehan, P., and G. M. Beal. 1977. "Knowledge Production and Utilization, A General Model: Third Approximation." Sociology Report No. 138. Department of Sociology and Anthropology, Iowa State University.

O'Kelley, E. 1977. "Intermediate Technology as an Agent of Change." In Proceedings, The World Food Conference of 1976. Ames: Iowa State Univ. Press.

Rogers, E. M., and N. Jain. 1969. "Research Utilization: Bridging the Communication Gap Between Science and Practice." Paper, Joint Session of Information Systems Division of International Communication Association and Speech Association of America, New York.

Rogers, E. M., with F. F. Shoemaker. 1971. Communication of Innovation. New York: Free Press.

Röling, N. 1974. "From Theory to Action." Ceres 7, no. 3: 22-25.

Röling, N., J. Ascroft and F. Wa Chege. 1976. "The Diffusion of Innovations and the Issue of Equity in Rural Development." Communication Research 3, no. 2: 155-170.

Rotham, J. 1974. Planning and Organizing for Social Change. New York: Columbia Univ. Press.

Ruttan, V. W. 1977. "The Green Revolution: Seven Generalizations." International Development Review 19, no. 4: 16-23.

Schumacher, E. F. 1973. Small is Beautiful. London: Blonde.

Schutjer, W. A., and M. G. Van Der Neen. 1976. Economic Constraints on Agricultural Technology Adoption in Developing Nations. University Park: Department of Agricultural Economics and Rural Sociology, Agricultural Experiment Station, Pennsylvania State University.

Wharton, C. R., Jr. 1969. "Risk, Uncertainty and the Subsistence Farmer: Technological Innovation and Resistance to Change in the Context of Survival." In Studies in Economic Anthropology, ed. P. Bohannon and G. Dalton. Washington, D.C.: American Anthropological Association.

_____. 1977. "The Role of the Professional in Feeding Mankind: The Political Dimension." In Proceedings, The World Food Conference of 1976. Ames: Iowa State Univ. Press.

Williams, M. J. 1978. "Development Co-operation: Efforts and Policies of Members of the Development Assistance Committee, 1977 Review, OECD, Paris." Society of International Development, Survey of International Development 15, no. 1: 1-8.

7

The Research and Development
Model of Knowledge Utilization:
Process and Structure

Jack Rothman

Knowledge utilization is conceived of in different ways
by different scholars. In an early discussion, Havelock
(1973) identified three different orientations: The "social
interaction" or diffusion model, the "problem solver" or
consultation model, and the "research, development and
diffusion" model, which is sometimes referred to as social
R & D. It represents, I believe, the most structured means
for systematically seeking and applying existing research
knowledge. It also provides a definite bridge between
knowledge producers (researchers) and knowledge appliers
(professional practitioners in various fields).

This chapter will deal with knowledge and its application for practical purposes, particularly social science
empirical research. It brings together ideas that I have
previously expressed[1] so they can be compared with other
approaches to knowledge utilization. Since my work has
focused on human service organizations and professionals as
the context for application, that perspective will infuse
this discussion. A specific model of knowledge utilization,
research and development (R & D), and the process that
characterizes it is presented. The discussion will draw on
the experience of the Community Intervention Project, a
long-term action research project focusing on utilization of
knowledge to design strategies and techniques for "change
agents" working at the community level. An analysis of the
model examines organizational considerations for implementation: roles, procedures, and structures.

THE RESEARCH-PRACTICE DICHOTOMY

The body of potentially useful social science knowledge

gathered by researchers over the years is vast and expanding rapidly. That potential is poorly and haltingly tapped by human service policy makers and practitioners. The nature of the responsibilities of the human services professionals is such that, as a practical matter, they do not have the time or the opportunity to search the knowledge pool for that which would be useful to them and to make systematic application of what is there. Swift, easy, and efficient access to knowledge in a usable form has, heretofore, not been available to them.

The basic researcher in social science and the human services professional are divided by a common need: the effective utilization of social science knowledge. That division has not been without its consequences. Practitioners wait impatiently for researchers to provide information in a practical form. Researchers offer abstract information through journals, books, scientific papers at conventions, monographs, and so forth. They believe themselves to be effective communicators of their results and are often puzzled and irritated that the practitioner does not take advantage of what is offered. An undercurrent of tension, mistrust, and lack of confidence pervades the researcher-practitioner relationship—a function of equally pervasive misperceptions of one another's roles and functions.

Social scientists see practitioners as placing low value on intellectuality and high value on action or change for its own sake. Instead of orderly, systematic examination of issues that requires time and scholarly objectivity, practitioners are seen to come to hasty conclusions and engage in actions not supported by adequate data. Practitioners, in the social scientist's view, are uninterested in self-criticism and are offended by outside criticism. They manifest a distrust and fear of research. This also is related to a narrow professionalism: such intense engagement in the specifics of a given problem situation that generalizations on a more abstract basis cannot be carried over from one context to another. Social scientists also resent the smugness of practitioners who feel that only they understand worldly problems or real people because of their direct, everyday engagement. In addition, social scientists maintain that it is not their responsibility but that of the practitioners to draw implications for policy and action from research.

Clearly, the social scientist's perception of the practitioner is distorted. There is an equal distortion, however, in the practitioner's view of the social scientist.

Practitioners see social scientists as engaged in studies of low social relevance. The subject matter areas are largely social, trivial, esoteric, or abstract, and reflect narrow scientism rather than humanistic concern. Quite often if there is a social value orientation expressed in the social scientists' work, it is one of conservatism. The whole systems theory approach, in the practitioner's view, for example, is indicative of this static orientation. Social scientists are seen as avoiding the policy implications of their work, and their failure to relate the outcome of the research efforts to important social issues is perceived as stemming either from arrogance or lack of compassion. There also is a kind of compromised intellectual integrity in the bending of research pursuits to such exigencies of the moment as the availability of federal or foundation grants or to subject areas that will yield the largest payoffs in dollars and professional prestige.

The social scientists' preoccupation with methodological "gimmickry" and the attendant overinflated jargon, in the eyes of the practitioner, serve only to alienate those who seriously wish to draw on social science knowledge. Social science writings are viewed as exhibiting a sponginess about conclusions that can be reached. Practitioners are interested in definite answers to specific questions; instead, they believe, they find inconclusive generalities about broad theoretical matters.

It is obvious that different styles and modes of thinking divide the researcher and practitioner, making communication difficult and the use of each other's contributions and products problematic. The social distance between them—characterized by mistrust, differing outlooks, and ostensibly contrasting goals—is formidable. In the past this has inhibited fuller articulation between the social scientist and the social practitioner.

Perhaps the fundamental difference is one of function. Social scientists have the primary function of comprehending the world: producing knowledge that permits them and others to understand it better. Practitioners have the key function of changing the world (or, more specifically, parts thereof): producing material effects that permit clients, organizations, or communities to behave more advantageously in terms of specific desired outcomes.

THE NEED FOR SYSTEMATIC LINKAGE BETWEEN
RESEARCH AND APPLICATION COMMUNITIES

Commenting on the usual modus operandi in developing
social programs, Etzioni (1976, 11) makes note of the lack
of a systematic, step-by-step planning and developmental
process:

> We have learned from the social programs of the '60s,
> the campaigns against drug abuse, crime and cancer and
> the recent drive to develop new energy resources, that
> in trying to use national resources to overcome our
> social problems, highly ambitious projects have often
> been attempted without a sufficient knowledge base or
> back up. Multibillion-dollar programs, conceived in
> Washington, D.C., were introduced based on verbal
> concepts and with little testing or prior research. We
> cannot afford, in human or financial terms, the
> expensive wrecks that result. We need fewer but
> better-researched and developed government programs.

Etzioni (1976, 11) goes on to recommend a way of
functioning that incorporates many of the basic features of
the social R & D/Research Utilization Model that I will be
elaborating in this presentation:

> It is fairly standard practice in the engineering of
> new spacecraft, weapons, airplanes, even toys, to move
> systematically from a theoretical concept to a pencil-
> and-paper design, to a small-scale model that is
> subject to various tests, leading to the production of
> one or a few full-scale prototypes—all before mass
> production is authorized. Normally, at each stage
> modifications are made on the basis of experience
> gained precisely because as a rule we cannot anticipate
> or reason out all reactions and developments. New
> government programs [and attempts at social problem
> solving] need to go through a full and as careful a
> process of research and development as new
> technologies.

Typically, researchers and action people berate one
another for failures in communication and deficits in
application. These ad hominem accusations result from a
lace of recognition that this is basically a structural
problem. There is an absence of a linking technology and
linking instrumentalities for connecting social theory to

social practice. The vast, complex network of engineering roles and institutions characteristic of the physical sciences is completely missing in the social field. It is as though a theoretical physicist at Princeton were expected to state his propositions and theorems in a form that could be put to use immediately by the factory foremen in Bayonne, New Jersey.

The major implication to be drawn from this analysis is that human service professions ought to move toward the creation of an engineering capability--that is, institution-alized linking roles and structures of various kinds that would serve to expedite the transition between research knowledge and social policy and practice. Some essential features of such an institutional pattern are suggested by Guba (1968, 39-40), an educational R & D specialist, in discussing the character of Bell Labs:

> A. T. & T. in its wisdom has interposed a vast organization between the knowledge producers and the ultimate consumers. This system, known as Western Electric, has its own coterie of engineers, who are themselves divided into specialties. Some of their personnel are concerned with developing prototype applications; others with testing these out and debugging them. Still others are concerned with designing these applications in ways that will make their production feasible and economical. And finally, of course, there are productive specialists who actually turn out the devices that will be installed and used by the Bell Telephone companies.

Guba points to the absence of corresponding linkers and conversion mechanisms in the social fields. This results in blockages and inefficiencies in knowledge utilization. This defect goes unrecognized within the professional structure itself. Instead, personnel tend to "write-off the research-practice gap as stemming from the uncooperativeness of the researchers or the laziness and ignorance of the practitioners, or both" (Guba 1968, 40).

When viewed in this way, it becomes obvious that in the social field a multiplicity of different gaps are discern-able and that various points of linkage and coupling are unattended. The way research is organized in the human service professions does not alleviate the problem. Scholars and doctoral students in the professional schools and the disciplines accumulate knowledge, reporting their results too often in the main to other scholars, and only occasionally suggesting in fairly rudimentary fashion some practice or policy implications of their findings.

Another avenue of research production is in agency settings of various kinds. Here, for the most part, we find operational research or program evaluation, studies that deal in a narrow way with a peculiar field problem and its solution with the situation. These studies reflect parochial empiricism for they are ordinarily not generalizable beyond the situation. Further, in many cases there is insufficient effort to draw upon existing social science theory and knowledge to illuminate the research task. Use is made of the technical methods of social research but not the cumulative substantive knowledge that has been produced by these methods.

Research sponsored by governmental bodies has taken the same bifurcated form. On the one hand, bureaus such as NSF or NIMH have typically emphasized grants to scholars to pursue basic or "pure" research. On the other hand, functional agencies such as HHS and HUD are relying increasingly on RFPs and contracts, where specifications are strictly delineated and geared to concrete operational problems. In countering a previous tendency to allow overly vague and abstract theoretical studies, these agencies are engaged in a pendulum swing toward overly rigid applied studies.

An alternative policy would be to give greater weight to the terrain that lies between basic research and agency practice: the domain of conversion, linkage, and application. In the material that follows I will describe our efforts to bridge the gap between research and agency practice by the creation and implementation of a Research Utilization Model. In the process of creating and implementing this model not only were we able to document the feasibility of such an undertaking, but we were also able to identify the need for further elaboration of organizational linking roles, procedures, and structures. This is discussed later in the chapter.

RESEARCH AND DEVELOPMENT AS A RECONCILIATION
AND LINKING PROCESS

The situation may be dissected through an analogy to a lumbering operation. The social science researchers have gone into the forest of knowledge, felled many a good and sturdy tree, and displayed the fruits of their good work to one another. A few enterprising, application-minded lumberjacks have dragged some logs to the river and shoved

them off downstream ("diffusion" they call it.) Somewhere
down river the practitioners are manning the construction
companies. They manage somehow to piece together a few
makeshift buildings with what they can find that has drifted
down the stream, but on the whole they are sorely lacking in
lumber in the various sizes and forms they need to do their
work properly. The problem is that someone has forgotten to
build the mill to turn the logs into lumber in all its
usable forms. The logs continue to pile up at one end of
the system, while the construction companies continue to
make do at the other end.

To carry this analogy one step further, there has been
governmental and foundation support for the logging operation. There has also been some support for the construction
companies. There has been almost nothing, however, for the
planning and running of a mill. In our view the social
science research and development methodology is that mill.
Fundamentally, R & D is a systematic process for bringing
the gap between research and application. It permits the
conversion of scientific principles to particular tools and
procedures for dealing with real-world problems.

Brooks (1965, 126) states the matter simply in the form
of a query:

> ...how to use the knowledge which has been gathered
> primarily for its own sake—fundamental research. How
> is this knowledge to be condensed, summarized,
> repackaged, and interpreted for use, and how is it to
> be communicated to those responsible for action—the
> decision-makers, the technological innovators, the
> service professionals, and the students?

Schutz (1970, 40), in his succinct definition, concentrates on "the gap between scientific knowledge and user
practices." The need for linkage is reinforced by Carter
(1968, 17):

> In evaluating contemporary problems in education and
> the social area generally, it seems there is a wide
> separation between the practitioners in these fields
> and those engaged in research in our academic
> institutions. We do not have the middleman who, as in
> the case of the engineer, is devoted to solving
> specific problems...Such people are lacking in the
> education and social fields.

The term "research and development" has been carelessly and imprecisely (but profitably) used. This carelessness and imprecision over the years worked its way into the common parlance to the point where today there are very few of the lay public who fully understand and appreciate the process. This has prompted such specialists as Roberts (1967, 5) to state that too often R & D, even for those engaged professionally in the field, "is based largely on facts and folklore, rather than on principles derived from facts." He deplores "the lack of true understanding of its processes, and a lack of an organized educational base for its managers." Schutz (1970, 6) likewise tells us that individuals in the technical fields that have thus far dominated R & D work have not been predisposed to conceptualize the methodological components of their own activities:

> [They] thus have given only modest attention to packaging their macro—strategies in a form readily cognizant to persons within the field or transferable to other fields such as education.... It is the methodology not the men of aerospace, architecture, business, engineering, and pharmacy that renders these fields ripe for contributing to the development in education [and the human services].

Schutz urges his readers to identify commonalities in intellectual endeavors across the fields he enumerates. That there are such commonalities is indicated by the fact that it is possible to generalize conceptually basic features of the R & D process, regardless of the particular field in which it is employed.

A useful point of departure in conceptualizing R & D is the set of definitions propounded by the National Science Foundation (1969b) and employed in its statistical surveys of the field. NSF lays out three relevant areas: basic research, applied research (which we shall call "design" for the sake of clarity and to reduce overlap with other concepts), and development. The definitions are as follows:

Basic Research:
Basic research is primarily motivated by the desire to pursue knowledge for its own sake. Such work is free from the need to meet immediate objectives and is undertaken to increase understanding of natural laws. Wide applications often come from gains in basic knowledge, or scientific concepts are extended or revised with far reaching effects. (NSF 1969b, 1)

Applied Research or Design:
Applied research is carried out with practical
applications in mind and may...be concerned with
"translating" existing knowledge into such applications...It differs from basic research in that it
seeks to show or indicate the means in which the first
pilot steps may be taken to reduce an abstract idea to
a useful purpose. [It] serves to further specific
agency missions, frequently as a forerunner to
development. (NSF 1969b, 15)

The sense of applied research as design, as we will
emphasize in this presentation, is brought by Holt (1975,
2:61), who defines applied research as follows:

Applied research is the systematic creation and
application of knowledge through the organized effort
of people working toward a specific [practical]
objective.... The purpose of applied research is to
find a solution in principle (design concept) for a new
or improved product, process, or material.

The third of the NSF definitions is that of
development:

Development:
In development the findings and understanding derived
from research are directed toward the production of
useful materials, devices, systems, or methods; such
work includes design and improvement of prototypes and
processes. Development activities, which are dependent
upon research results, usually involve engineering and
testing to advance a component, product, or process to
the point where it meets specific functional or
economic requirements;.... development is directed to
very specific and generally predictable ends. (NSF
1969b, 19)

The product of development, then, is something that is
user-ready. It has a purpose that is well-defined, and it
functions, ideally, in such a way as to fulfill that purpose
in an optimal manner.
Havelock (1973) introduces an additional key element to
research and development, namely, diffusion. If a new
product or tool or process is to be useful, it needs to be
disseminated (marketed, promoted) and put into active operation by potential users. A product and its diffusion may be

directed at a general population—for example, consumers,
listeners, readers, and so forth. Alternatively, they may
be aimed at a specialized, intermediary professional population such as physicians, broadcasting engineers, or human
service practitioners, and, later, directed through them
toward broader target systems: clients or constituents, for
example. By way of illustration, one can visualize the
development of new drug products for direct purchase and use
by consumers or for transmission by family doctors in their
practice. For the purposes of our own explorations of
social R & D, we elected to place emphasis on the development of intervention strategies for use by intermediary
practitioners.

When Havelock speaks of diffusion, he uses such terms
as "dissemination," "distribution," "installation,"
"adoption," and target system "integration." He also
defines two specialized roles in the diffusion: sender and
adopter. He sees the sender as engaging in activities such
as "promoting," "informing-telling," and "demonstrating-
showing." He views the adopter as engaging in collateral
activities such as "awareness," "evaluation," and
"installation."

Based on Havelock's (1973, 2:42) concepts, then, we can
now incorporate a fourth definition into this basic formulation of R & D:

Diffusion:
Once knowledge has passed through this development
phase, it is ready to be mass produced and diffused to
all members of society for whom it might be useful.

These, then, may be considered to constitute the basic
phases of all research and development endeavors: basic
research, design (or applied research), development, and
diffusion (which aims at wide utilization).

The phases in R & D are not precise, neither in definition nor with regard to the functions involved. Ansoff
(1961, 210) makes this quite clear:

The fact that the degree of uncertainty can vary over a
wide spectrum gives rise to a major difficulty in
defining clear-cut separation between applied research
and activities which precede and follow it.

Based on the Bell Laboratory experiences, Kelly (1950)
suggests a somewhat broader scheme than our own four-fold
formulation. The first two stages are identical to ours:

basic research and applied research (or design). He divides development, however, into what might be viewed as two substages: development and design and engineering for manufacture.

The staff of the Far West Laboratory for Education Research and Development (1973) drew from a number of their different project experiences to construct what they consider a general progress pattern of development process. That general pattern and its correspondence to our own efforts is as follows:

Develop a Preliminary Form of the Product
Do Preliminary Field Testing
Product Revision
Main Field Testing
Operational Product Revision
Operational Field Testing

According to the Far West Laboratory group, these activities are followed by a set of tasks in the diffusion stage.

A RESEARCH UTILIZATION-RESEARCH AND DEVELOPMENT MODEL

As part of our endeavor toward the understanding and application of research and development in the social sciences, we have formulated a working model of what we view as the basic flow of activity in social R & D. It is largely an empirical, inductive formulation both descriptive and normative. It grew out of actual experiences of the Community Intervention Project as we attempted to move between existing basic research findings and practical intervention tools. We believe it summarizes and organizes in an effective way the concepts we have been discussing thus far.

The model is composed of six material stages linked by five operational steps (see Figure 7.1). It starts with a social goal or a social problem that is of interest to some group or organization concerned with social welfare or the delivery of human services. The existing body of empirical social science knowledge is examined as a source of possible solutions for the social problem or as a source of possible direction toward achieving the social goal. The model moves along a continuum to wide application by human service professionals in the field. Each of the five operational steps, located with the arrows to indicate their more active

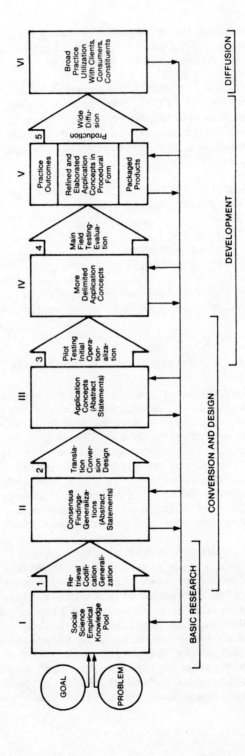

Figure 7.1 Schematic model of research utilization--R & D process

function, results in a material stage that is a landmark product. Such products might be experience, data, devices, operational guides, training manuals, and so on. Each material stage with its products, represented by the boxes in our model, leads in turn to the next operation and is the basis for that operation. In the rather detailed narrative description of each Material Stage and Operational Step that follows, it will help to refer to Figure 7.1. In this way you will be able to keep in mind where each of the various components fits in the larger design.

Material Stage I: Basic Pool of Social Science Research Knowledge

This is the reservoir of existing empirical research data available in the formal literature of the disciplines and professions. It also includes less formal sources, such as agency reports, dissertations, and project memoranda. Some of this material stands independently; some is referenced in index books or computerized data banks of various types, and other material is referenced and abstracted in index books or computerized data systems. Which other bodies of literature and data are selected for scrutiny depends on the nature of the social goals and/or problems that are being addressed through the social R & D effort.

Operational Step 1: Retrieval, Codification, Generalization

1. This step requires the location of pertinent research data sources in terms of presenting practice problems or objectives. Both primary and secondary sources can be used, including the use of stored information pools.
2. Those studies bearing on the problem or issue at hand must be selected from the source pool. Here one encounters problems of nomenclature, including the appropriate selection of descriptors. Problems of traversing the disparate taxonomies of knowledge in social science and social practice present themselves. Practice perspectives ordinarily need to be transplanted into typical scientific linguistic analogs in order for scientific sources to be exploited and later reconverted.
3. Data must be assessed for reliability, validity, and applicability.

4. Data must be codified into suitable categories of knowledge.
5. Work must be done toward discovering consensus findings or recognized uniformities within the selected data.
6. Work sometimes involves formulating generalizations and propositions from consensus findings.

Material Stage II: Consensus Findings, Generalizations, Propositions

As the previous description of tasks implies, the product here is one or more generalizations based on certain accepted scientific laws or principles, or on the convergence of the findings of a number of disparate research studies. Where numerous studies in varying circumstances, using different subjects and methodologies, are in substantial agreement, one can have a greater degree of confidence in the validity of these generalizations. This is particularly true when there are few, if any, findings with counter-conclusions.

The resulting generalizations will likely be abstract as a result of their tendency to synthesize diverse studies and to arrive at uniformities. They will also tend to describe social phenomena rather than prescribe methods of intervention. This is not surprising, since most social science research deals with describing and understanding the social world rather than changing it.

Consensus findings may be descriptive of a simple, empirical regularity, or they may be propositional in describing a constant relationship among two or more variables.

Operational Step 2: Conversion and Design—Formulating Application Concepts

The essential task here is cognitive application.
1. Translations now need to be made from scientific language back to language more suitable to the categories of normal usage in applied situations.
2. Conversion from descriptive to prescriptive formulation may entail making an "inferential leap" across the gap between generalizations and application concepts. A conversion construct entails consideration of the size of the

inferential leap and the direction of application
(toward achieving organizational stabilization or
organizational change, for example.)

3. "Reality" dimensions in designing implementation—
such as feasibility, or implementability, of a
given application, cost, limiting conditions, and
qualifiers that restrict or channel use—may be
weighted at this time.

Material Stage III: Application Concepts

These are the outputs of the translation-conversion-
design process. The prescriptive formulations we call
application concepts are representative of products in this
stage. These prescriptive statements, while now of more
immediate relevance to practitioners, are derived from broad
consensus generalizations. They tend also to be constituted
in rather abstract terms and in cognitive form. At this
level, the more concrete implementation of application
principles is left to the creative efforts of practitioners
unless the utilization process is carried forward into the
next stages. In industrial R & D, a fairly tight, mathe-
matically supported design may have been produced. Its
workability, impact, and economical feasibility remain in
question.

Operational Step 3: Initial Operationalization,
Pilot Testing

Operationalization involves more finite specification
of locations, contexts, materials, resources, and behaviors
for implementation. Two examples are the type of agency
setting and the types of people to whom the application
pertains. All empirical referents of the application
concept must be identified and worked with.

Operationalization may be partially a cognitive-
perceptual task, but it must include actual experimental
implementation, or engineering, including the conducting of
a pilot test in the intended implementation setting, or with
the materials, processes, and actors of that setting. Pilot
work is necessary in order to determine whether the
application concept will work under real conditions and
whether prototypes and models of implementation can be
realized. In this step, the practitioner functions in a
front end social engineering role.

Material Stage IV: Application Concepts in Delimited Form

Initial operationalization results in a much more
detailed, narrowed, practical exposition of application
concepts. It may involve greater concretization of each of
what have been identified as the key elements contained in
the application concept. In this form, application may be
discussed in mental health centers, for example, as compared
to city-planning agencies; large cities as compared to small
cities; agencies with sizable budgets as compared to those
with limited funding; and so on. Specific actors,
procedures, or resources may be indicated. Initial working
models or prototypes result from this early pilot work in
fabricating operational forms of the application concept.
Such an operationalized statement of implementation gives a
practitioner a great deal more direction and some confidence
in the workability of the application formulation.

Operational Step 4: Fuller Implementation—
Main Field Testing

1. This step assumes the availability of a preliminary
    procedural manual, working documents, audio-visual
    materials, etc. that can be put in the hands of
    "development engineers." These social engineers
    are expected to fabricate a detailed and durable
    operational form of the application concept. An
    expanded number of experiences and units are
    studied as compared to the pilot stage.
2. The R & D main field study seeks to modify, expand,
    and more clearly operationalize the application
    concept and to assess its effectiveness with
    respect to intended outcomes with a substantial
    number of clients, consumers, etc. Performance
    testing through careful evaluation of outcomes is
    especially important. Fairly firm specifications
    of the conditions, constraints, and procedures of
    application can be delineated. This step
    incorporates elements of evaluative research but
    places it in a more product-oriented R & D context.
    This form of reality testing, like that at each
    stage, may yield feedback that modifies the
    application concept or even the basic theory that
    generated it.
3. Field tasks may include selection of sites or
    users, recruitment and training of a social

engineering staff incentives for use, entry
problems, clarification of the role of field
practitioners and their relationship to the role of
applied researchers, etc.
4. Research tasks include designing a suitable
methodology for study and development of
instruments; monitoring; adjustment for special
problems such as practitioner-engineer resistance
or Hawthorne effects; evaluation of effectiveness;
and the development application concept.

Material State V: Practice and Policy Outcomes; Tested, and Refined Application Concepts; Diffusion Media

At this stage, several useful products should have been
brought into being. In the first place, it is now possible
to determine the impact of the application concept when
implemented by a cross section of actual ultimate users.
This type of assessment may be carried through by means of
formal research procedures, or less formal observational-
assessment approaches. Ordinarily, the product of main
field testing is given an additional operational field test
with potential users in order to remove remaining "bugs" and
to complete "fine tuning" of the tool, process or product.
It also may indicate problems and possibilities to be taken
into account in the subsequent diffusion stage.

Finally, based on the field experience, diffusion
materials incorporating results of the field work—
practitioner manuals and/or handbooks, audiotapes,
videotapes, documents, charts, etc.—may be crystallized.

The feedback between Stage V and Stage IV, may be heavy
and recurrent. There may be a number of cycles of trial,
modification, and retrial. The cyclical nature of development is particularly pronounced here.

Operational Step 5: Production and Wide Diffusion

This step includes:
1. The mass reproduction of media incorporating
operationalized solution strategies: handbooks,
manuals, charts, forms, etc. Production is
ordinarily "farmed out" to a printing firm or
media house that has the experience and resources
to carry out this technical task. It is not a

basic social science professional activity. In an
expanded version of the R & D model, one might
conceive of production as a separate step and
stage, as in the area of industrial R & D.

2. Isolation of a universe of specific practitioners
    or organizations who are potential target users.
    This should initially be done at the outset of R &
    D but needs further specification and reassessment
    at this time.

3. The determination of the attributes, attitudes,
    and needs of potential users must be made. This
    is, essentially, a form of marketing research.

4. Selection of appropriate informational and
    promotional approaches and further packaging of
    utilizational materials in an attractive,
    responsive way must be accomplished.

5. Potential users must be reached and motivated.
    High-intensity (personal contact) approaches such
    as workshops may be used. Alternatively, low-
    intensity (mass communications) approaches such as
    direct mailings or media advertising may be
    employed.

6. Functional gatekeepers, opinion leaders, or
    informal professional networks may be located to
    use as diffusion channels.

7. Users may need to be provided with initial
    training and reinforcement.

8. Procedures must be developed for scanning the
    results of wider application of the product.

Material Stage VI: Broad Practice Use

The end result of the process should be widespread use
of the developed application concept in the field. By this
time, the concept should have withstood testing, and means
of effectively communicating its appropriate and detailed
implementation to practitioners through operational and
procedural guides should have been developed. The eventual
beneficiaries are clients, consumers, and constituents in
the human service system. Broader experience with clients,
involving both method and outcome, should again hypo-
thetically feed back to the entire process, suggesting
modifications and refinements for every stage, right back to
basic research.

We have, quite understandably, focused this R & D
process on the human services practitioner. However, for

"practitioner-user" one may read "manager-user," "teacher-user," "politician-user," "labor union organizer-user," or any potential applier of basic social science research converted to an operational form through the social R & D process.

Interaction with R & D and Feedback

At the bottom of the model, the four basic phases R & D are indicated. They synchronize with the research coilization formulation in the following ways:
  Basic Research: Stage I, possibly also Step I and
        Stage II.
  Conversion & Design: (Applied Research). May overlap
        Step I and Stage II. Concentrated in Step 2 and
        Stage III. May overlap Step 3.
  Development: Step 3 through Stage V.
  Diffusion: Step 5 and Stage VI.
  Finally, feedback is indicated through the use of the arrows among all stages and steps of the research utilization process. The role of feedback in social science research is particularly critical.

A clarification of R & D-Research Utilization may be in order at this point. Our primary work in the Community Intervention Project was the development, field testing, and diffusion of prescriptive formulations for human service practitioners. We were not hypothesis testing in the traditionally accepted sense of the term. The generalizations upon which our action principles were based had already been established. Thus there was no question of "proving" or "disproving" the derived action principles.

TOWARD SOCIAL ENGINEERING

The creation and implementation of the research and development model described above made it possible for us to envision additional needs and opportunities for the future. It is my conviction that the efficient and effective implementation of our R & D Research Utilization Model require the establishment of a range of organizational linking roles, procedures, and structures to make the model I described function adequately. This undertaking will also involve a mixing and blending of scientific and applied interests and competencies. This is a large subject that I can touch upon only suggestively.

Linking Roles and Procedures

Looking back on the Research Utilization model, a number of derivative linking roles seem evident. Among these are:

1. Information retrieval specialists.
2. Program and policy design specialists.
3. Development personnel: program implementers, development researchers, performance testing technicians.
4. Media fabrication people.
5. Diffusion experts.

Some of these roles currently exist to some degree, but not in the explicit, structured, and interrelated way that has been suggested. For example, information specialists can be found in the human services. Diffusion staff may be found there also, performing training and literature dissemination roles. Indeed, salespeople in publishing firms are among the most active disseminators of social science findings and products. Some roles are extremely rare at present, especially the conversion-design specialist and the array of roles associated with the development process. Outside of educational R & D, development in the sense denoted here has been almost unknown in the social fields.

An interesting and potentially useful role is that of the "research utilization specialist." This role has been instituted within the vocational rehabilitation field and has been subjected to evaluative study by Glaser and Backer (1975, 388). According to these authors:

> The RUS job role was aimed at effecting change in the operation of the state rehabilitation agency that leads to sustained, worthwhile improvement in service delivery.... The RUS' mission included creating an improved organizational climate within which application of new knowledge would be likely to take place.

The listed activities that were performed included knowledge search, conduct of special projects, consultation to agency staff, holding conferences and workshops, and information dissemination. Glaser and Backer have delineated strength and weakness of the new role and have suggested some criteria associated with successful performance.

The research utilization specialist performs as a research application agent within an operating agency. A variation of this role is that of extension specialist who reaches out from a sponsoring knowledge-diffusion agency to other organizations in the community and to the community at large. This reformulation of the agricultural extension agent role has been advocated for the field of education, for example, by Clark (1962).

With regard to linking procedures, the research utilization conference has been suggested and used by a variety of organizations in such areas as poverty (Crisswell 1969) and pollution control (Crowe and Madancy 1974). In connection with these experiences, studies have been made concerning more effective ways of using the conference as a means of stimulating awareness and utilization of research findings by practitioners and policy makers. A variation here is the "traveling seminar project" that has been used by the System Development Corporation (Carter 1968, 8-11).

The Environmental Protection Agency indicates a variety of media they have used to stimulate action based on research. Among these they include design manuals, technical capsule reports, seminar publications, handbooks, process and project brochures, newsletters, videotapes, and motion pictures (Crowe and Madancy 1974).

Other linking roles and procedures have been used or can be envisioned. These few examples, however, should suffice to indicate the potentialities.

Linking Organizations--Locus and Structure

Several of the specified roles and procedures can be absorbed within existing organizational structures. For example, the information specialist can be part of continuing education programs or a specialized service of a social agency. On the other hand, it would seem desirable to create new organizational forms that would have a focused research and development function, cutting across several or all of the roles and procedures that have been previously described. In the physical sciences and in industry, such a specialized structure is the research and development laboratory. It would seem advisable and appropriate for the human service fields to create analogue structures. Such structures could be located within large service delivery systems related to mental health, aging, child welfare, and so on. Alternatively, they could be associated with professional schools.

In considering the establishment of an R & D lab, an important question is the kind of larger host organization

within which to locate it. Three obvious organizational
locations come to mind: (1) within a large human service
organization (i.e., an organization concerned primarily on
an on-going basis with providing services, etc.); (2) within
a university setting; and (3) within an independent
community-based R & D organization or consulting firm.

As Soloff and others (1975) have observed, industrial
R & D labs typically have production-service organization
type of sponsorship. In addition, governmental labs are
similarly supported, e.g., naval labs. In the human
services field, the Rehabilitation Service Administration
has financed a vocational rehabilitation research
utilization lab within the Chicago Jewish Vocational
Services agency and in other locations. As described by the
Soloff Team, these labs exhibit R & D tendencies.

Universities are common settings for certain types of
R & D efforts. The Educational Research and Development
Centers established by the Office of Education, for example,
had such a type of organizational arrangement. The Regional
Laboratories supported by the Office of Education were
placed within independent community-based organizations,
autonomous and separate from either the area educational
systems or from a university in the region. A voluntary
community board constituted the governing bodies. Contract
work let out by governmental bureaus to independent consulting firms having R & D programs (such as ABT Associates
and the RAND Corporation) take this form. In this instance,
there is a quasi-corporate structure with profit making
objectives for rendering R & D services.

Clearly, R & D work can and does take place under any
of these arrangements. Even in industrial R & D labs, mixed
arrangements can occur with some of the work given over to
external labs to a larger or smaller degree.

While there is no definitive answer to the question of
what organizational location is best, certain criteria
concerning optimal conditions may be advanced. For example,
wherever the lab is located, it needs both a measure of
independence and operative linkages. The Manpower Lab
Review Committee of the National Academy of Sciences (1974,
2-3) concluded that the setting in which a laboratory is
located has important consequences for its success. Certain
optimal conditions are suggested:

Laboratories located within organizations that share
their research orientation, sympathize with their
purpose, and provide support for their project
activities are more likely to make progress toward the

attainment of their objectives than those that do not.
The freedom of laboratories to establish and work
toward the attainment of their goals, to select their
staffs, to design their research programs, and to
report administratively to the Labor Department, rather
than the host-agency is emphasized for its importance
in decisions on their locations.

From the space craft experience, Sayles and Chandler
(1971, 128) extrapolate:

A kind of "sovereignty," not for the individual
components, but for the project as a whole is needed.
Autonomy appears to be a significant requirement for
the international project intent on excellence. And
financial autonomy is perhaps most important of all.

While these observers emphasize lab protection from
ongoing and inappropriate production pressures, it is also
necessary not to be insulated from these pressures, but
rather to have some connection to them and some involvement
in them. The lab staff in a social R & D undertaking needs
to know the problems, to suffer some of the travails of the
system it is attempting to assist and enhance. That staff
has to be in touch with the real world it is attempting to
affect. Morton's (1969) notion of "barriers and bonds"
applies to a certain degree here. The host setting should
ideally offer the opportunity for both of these conditions
to be at play.
We have suggested locating a model R & D structure
within a professional school of a university. This option
is supported in a special report of the National Science
Foundation (1969a, 21) on the use of social science
knowledge. The report states:

The professions--law, medicine, engineering, social
work, journalism, mental health work, and
education--are among the main social institutions
through which social science knowledge can be
translated into day-to-day practice...The professions
have a distinctive role in the translation of knowledge
into action.

We would specifically locate a human services R & D lab
within the graduate schools in human-service professions. A
sizable number of the faculty of such schools are made up of
individuals from the world of practice who teach practice

principles. Adjunct faculty members from other disciplines
or individuals with multiple department appointments are
part of the teaching staff of such professional schools.
This interdisciplinary attribute endows such schools with
great potential for the utilization of social science
research. That such potential is not always realized is of
far less importance than the fact that it exists. Our own
experience with the Community Intervention Project, located
within a school of Social Work, demonstrated, at least to
us, that such a setting can be conducive to productive R & D
work.

The setting of a professional school permits effort to
be focused on given social and human problems around which
the contributions of several disciplines may be organized.
A reality problem focus requires cutting across rigorous but
static discipline categories, for complex and multifaceted
phenomena are at work. This serves to soften the insularity
of academic department categories. For these reasons,
professional schools within universities are particularly
suited to undertake knowledge-linkage roles.

Staffing--Strains and Arrangements

An R & D capability requires a staff group that is
typically very diverse and fairly large. Diversity relates
to the many different types of tasks involved in various
aspects of the R & D process. People from a range of
specializations with differing competencies are necessary,
from those with the facility of working close to the margin
of science to those with ease in communicating with and
understanding the operational problems of people engaged in
application tasks. In addition, a wide variety of supple-
mentary technical and administrative staff play a role.

The cross pressures of requiring specialized capabilities and common endeavors are articulated by Schutz (n.d.,
32) as follows:

> A major paradox...is that effectiveness in development
> programs requires a high order of responsible autonomy
> and the opportunity to innovate and even to change
> plans. But large scale projects...also require
> unbelievably precise integration and coordination among
> the parts...Thus, a wide array of intellectual and
> economic commitments must be simultaneously focused on
> a very explicit task without destroying the motivations
> that release energy and commitment.

This paradox must be met by a delicately balanced R & D organization.

Another way of addressing this issue has been suggested by Jack A. Morton, who has served as Bell Lab's head of components research and engineering. According to Morton (1969), the operations of an R & D system must be analyzed in terms of organizational barriers and bonds. He suggests that the R & D process be thought of as a machine for processing information, a machine made up of a well-defined series of steps linked together in a precise order. Should any of these steps be missing, or fail to function properly, then the machine will fail to perform.

There is some difference of view within the R & D field concerning what type of structural arrangement will generate the kind of creativity and productivity discussed above. Shepard (1963) indicates that there are two basic structural approaches: Functional groups or project groups. Functional groups are organized around specialist criteria. Project groups are more ad hoc collectivities comprising of diverse specialists working on a given developmental undertaking.

According to Shepard (1963, 350), neither of the two approaches has been found to be superior to the other:

In most laboratories, some combination of functional organization and ad hoc team organization is used. Each appears to have its advantages and disadvantages from the point of view of administration, productivity, creativity, and satisfaction in work.

Individuals coming from such divergent backgrounds will expect different types of supervision from those above them in authority. In his studies of R & D supervisors, Pelz (1967) found that personnel performance was highest where the supervisor had a leadership style that gave neither complete autonomy nor excessive direction. Frequent interaction with staff and a participatory climate produced most effective work. Thus, both the extremes of laissez-faire and domination seem inappropriate. Dominating supervision brings forth apathy and resistance; laissez-faire leadership brings about dissatisfaction and low productivity. The preferred leadership may contain aspects of both "security" and "challenge," the climate Pelz found conducive to creativity. Pelz points out that it is the existence of both security and challenge at the same time, not a mid-point between them, that is effective. The challenge to R & D leadership is to find a way to keep a heterogeneous group of people

fixed on a predetermined common goal, and at the same time
to leave room for individual and group imagination and
autonomy. Leadership must somehow blend freedom and flexibility with structure and bureaucratic expectation. These
same requisites fall on the overall lab director.

Carter (1968, 16) states that "certain critical conditions are essential" for effective R & D. These conditions
by and large attach to the organizational stability and
sustenance within which R & D takes place. Among these are:

> A trained, motivated and experienced staff available
> for long-term application to the problem. Generally,
> the problem will not be solved in any short period of
> time, and those responsible must recognize that the
> same staff must be maintained over a number of years if
> the problem is to receive real attention and
> solution...Funding must be available not only to
> support the staff but often to make many physical and
> organizational changes with the setting in which the
> problem exists.

Carter writes as a systems expert who has been associated with R & D undertakings over a number of years. Almost
the identical set of conditions is cited by Klausmeier
(1968, 45), speaking from his experiences as an administrator of an educational R & D center:

> From the beginning, four conditions were regarded as
> essential to achieve the goal; first, educational
> researchers and developers with ideas and skills who
> were willing to work cooperatively in achieving the
> goal; second, time to plan and carry out research
> development activities; third, monetary support assured
> over an extended period of time, mainly for people's
> time and for supplies and equipment; and fourth,
> facilitative (applied) environments in which to carry
> out research and development activities and to
> demonstrate successful practice.

In previous works I have made note of the tumultuous
professional and technical climate in which R & D occurs.
Given the inherent restlessness, observers who have studied
the phenomenon suggest that a counter-balancing, secure
organizational base is necessary in order to achieve a
reasonable level of operational stability in the situation.
Three aspects of that organizational base are long-term
perspectives, sufficiency in staff, and adequate funding.

A SOCIAL ENGINEERING PERSPECTIVE

The term social engineering is used here in a
deliberate, precise, and consistent manner, rather than in
the global way it is often employed. This usage is conveyed
in a common dictionary definition of <u>engineering</u>: "The art
and science concerned with the practical application of
scientific knowledge, as in the design, construction, and
operation of roads, bridges...communications construction,
and operation of roads, bridges... communications systems,
etc." This accents the idea of converting basic scientific
knowledge toward useful purposes. I believe that <u>social</u>
engineering is identical in this connection to physical
engineering, and I look upon it in paraphrase form as: The
art and science concerned with the practical application of
social science knowledge, as in the design, construction,
and operation of programs, techniques, agency structures,
and so on.

It is obvious that there is some peril in the use of
the term, "social engineering." It has been used in the
past in an extremely loose and varied way. This may tend to
contaminate the concrete and delimited meaning we attach to
it here.

The purposes of social engineering, as I envision them,
are aimed at the solution of social problems and the
enhancement of the less powerful or less advantaged members
of society. It is my hope that social R & D would
particularly promote the more effective and humane provision
of services to members of the community. Tools to assist
people directly or indirectly toward these ends are viable
outgrowths of social R & D.

At the same time, it is true that any new technology
(nuclear energy, aerospace flight, new drugs) is, in itself,
value-neutral and can be employed by human users for
multiple purposes—evil or beneficial, destructive or
elevating of human worth. Social technology is no different
from physical technology in this respect. Scientists or
engineers who invent a new technological method cannot
control the way in which it is ultimately carried forward.
They can only communicate their intentions and hopes
regarding the eventual impact on human kind. There is a
chance that conveying a philosophical perspective may in
some way give direction to the way the technology is put to
work.

Engineering, for some, goes beyond mechanistic
neutrality to decided negativism. Indeed, the dictionary
carries this popularly held view of engineering: "To put

through or manage by contrivance: To engineer a
scheme...maneuvering."

There exists the danger that social R & D techniques
can be employed in this cynical way, but this need not be
inevitable. We have been able to avoid this in our own
program over a considerable number of years. Indeed, our
development of social R & D methods was predicated on the
assumption that they aid human service professionals to
bring about beneficial social outcomes in a more powerful
way then existing methods have been able to accomplish
through the planned and systematic application of social
science research knowledge.

CONCLUSION

The R & D model is only one of numerous approaches to
knowledge utilization that are represented in this volume.
It has a variety of merits and advantages that I have
attempted to set forth. At the same time, it may appear to
some to be too mechanistic, technical, and linear (despite
the series of feedback loops that are built into the model).
In my view, the model needs further testing and analysis in
order to arrive at a firmer grasp of its potentials and
limitations. In my own work, my associates and I have
proceeded through each phase, one step at a time, over a
period of time encompassing almost a decade. It is now
propitious to bring the entire process together dynamically
within a single organizational framework, such as an R & D
Lab, and to give it a trial as a reactive, faster-paced
knowledge utilization, problem-solving instrumentality
attached to one or more human service delivery systems.
Such a trial should not only evaluate its effectiveness as a
knowledge utilization mechanism, but should also further
clarify the phases and methods in the process. In addition,
it should investigate optimal organizational forms and
arrangements for implementation of social R & D. The paper
concludes, therefore, by suggesting a new kind of beginning,
with all the future issues, problems, and questions that
such an undertaking would generate.

NOTES

1. Refer to works from which this paper has been adapted: Social R & D: Research and Development in the Human Services, Englewood Cliffs, N.J.: Prentice Hall, 1980; Planning and Organizing for Social Change: Action Principles from Social Science Research, New York: Columbia University Press, 1974, and "Gaps and Linkages in Research Utilization: Enhancing Utilization through a Research and Development Approach," in Sourcebook on Research Utilization, edited by A. Rubin and A. Rosenblatt, New York: Council on Social Work Education, 1979.

REFERENCES

Ansoff, H. I. 1961. "Evaluation of Applied Research in a Business Firm." In Technological Planning on the Corporate Level, ed. J. R. Bright. Cambridge: Harvard Business School.

Brooks, H. 1965. "Scientific Concepts and Cultural Change." Daedalus 94 (Winter): 66–83.

Carter, L. F. 1968. "Knowledge Production and Utilization in Contemporary Organizations." In Knowledge Production and Utilization in Educational Administration, ed. T. L. Eidell and J. M. Kitchel. Columbus, Ohio: University Council for Educational Administration.

Clark, D. L. 1962. "The Function of the U.S. Office of Education and State Departments of Education in the Dissemination and Implementation of Educational Research." In Dissemination and Implementation, ed. K. Goldhammer and S. Elam. Bloomington, Ind.: Phi Delta Kappa.

Crisswell, J. H. 1969. "Research Utilization in Poverty Situations." Rehabilitation Record (March–April): 7–11.

Crowe, R. E., and R. S. Madancy. 1974. The U.S. Environmental Agency's Experience in Technology Transfer. Washington, D.C.: Office of Research and Development, U.S. Environmental Protection Agency.

180

Eash, M. J. 1968. "Bringing Research Findings into Classroom Practice." Elementary School Journal 68 (May): 410-18.

Etzioni, A. 1976. "An Earth-NASA: The Agency for Domestic Policy Development." Human Behavior 5 (December): 11.

Far West Laboratory for Educational Research and Development. 1973. A Training in Educational Development, Dissemination, and Evaluation. Berkeley, Calif.: FWLERD.

Glaser, E. M., and T. E. Backer. 1975. "Evaluating the Research Utilization Specialist." Rehabilitation Counseling Bulletin 19 (December): 388.

Gordon, G., and S. Marquis. 1966. "Freedom, Visibility of Consequences and Scientific Innovation." American Journal of Sociology 72 (September): 195-202.

Guba, E. G. 1968. "Development, Diffusion and Evaluation." In Knowledge Production and Utilization, ed. T. L. Eiddell and J. M. Kitchel. Columbus, Ohio: University Council for Educational Administration.

Havelock, R. G. 1973. Planning for Innovation Through Dissemination and Utilization of Knowledge. Ann Arbor: Center for Research on Utilization of Knowledge, Institute for Social Research, University of Michigan.

Holt, K. 1975. Product Innovation. Trondheim: University of Trondheim, Norwegian Institute of Technology.

Kelly, M. J. 1950. "The Bell Telephone Laboratories—An Example of an Institute of Creative Technology." Proceedings of the Royal Society 203, series A, no. 1074 (October): 287-301.

Klausmeier, H. J. 1968. "The Wisconsin Research and Development Center for Cognitive Learning." In Research and Development Toward the Improvement of Education, ed. H. J. Klausmeier and G. T. O'Hearn. Madison, Wis.: Dembar Educational Research Services.

Morton, J. A. 1969. "From Research to Technology." In The R&D Game: Technical Management and Research Productivity, ed. D. Allison. Cambridge: The MIT Press.

National Academy of Sciences, National Research Council. 1974. The Experimental Manpower Laboratory as an R&D Capability. Washington, D.C.: Government Printing Office.

National Science Foundation. 1969a. Knowledge into Action: Improving the Nation's Use of the Social Sciences. Washington, D.C.: Government Printing Office.

National Science Foundation. 1969b. Federal Funds for Research, Development and Other Scientific Activities, Fiscal Years 1966, 1967, 1968, Vol. 15. Washington, D.C.: Government Printing Office.

Pelz, D. 1967. "Creative Tensions in the Research and Development Climate." Science 157, no. 3785: 160-165.

Price, J. L. 1964. "Use of New Knowledge in Organizations," Human Organization 23 (Fall): 224-34.

Roberts, E. B. 1967. "Facts and Folklore in Research and Development Management." Industrial Management Review 8, no. 2 (Spring 1967): 5-18.

Sayles, L. R., and M. K. Chandler. 1971. Managing Large Systems. New York: Harper & Row Publishers.

Schutz, R. E. 1970. "The Nature of Educational Development." Journal of Research and Development in Education 3 (Winter): 39-64.

_____. (n.d.) "The Conduct of Development in Education." Unpublished internal report of Southwest Regional Laboratory for Educational Research and Development.

Shepard, H. A. 1963. "Nine Dilemmas in Industrial Research". In The Sociology of Science, ed. B. Barber and W. Hirsch. New York: Free Press of Glencoe.

Soloff, A., L. J. Goldston, R. A. Pollack, and B. White. 1975. "Running a Research Utilization Laboratory." Rehabilitation Counseling Bulletin 19, no. 2 (December): 416-424.

8

A User-Problem–Need-Driven Model: Farming Systems Research and Development

George M. Beal

Many different models and paradigms have been posed for prescribing or describing and understanding knowledge generation–utilization[1] by individuals from many different disciplines, and apparently based on quite different assumptions (see the analysis of Weiss 1978, 426–429, and Larsen 1981, 156–157). Many models assume or describe situations where actions are research(er) or knowledge driven. There is at present much discussion about the need for "user–problem oriented or driven" paradigms. However, in the literature there appear to be relatively few theoretical or empirical cases discussed where in fact the knowledge generation–utilization process, especially the research and development phase, is heavily user–problem based.

The experience of a number (10 or 15, depending on criteria used) of major programs over the past decade in various parts of the world dealing with developing, testing, and disseminating agriculture knowledge, practices and technology may represent an approach worthy of further analysis and discussion as an example approaching a user–problem oriented paradigm. This approach is called Farming System Research and Development (FSR&D).

We will begin this paper by viewing FSR&D briefly in the context of the debate revolving around the "old and new paradigms of development." We will then attempt to describe the essence of FSR&D, its activities, organizational structure and personnel. The main focus is on describing the seven main phases of FSR&D.

Finally, characteristics of the paradigm will be briefly analyzed in terms of some of the variables of the old and new paradigms of development debate.

Background: Search for a New Paradigm

The various paradigms of knowledge generation-
utilization may take on different importance and meaning
depending on the context in which they are placed. For
example, the several models of knowledge utilization may be
analyzed within the context of and, in fact, as an integral
part of, the current active debate around the world dealing
with the "old" and "new" paradigms of development. A major
part of that debate revolves around who generates technology, what kind of technology, with what motives, for what
purposes, to serve whose ends, how it is transferred, who
benefits and with what side effects--all involving knowledge
generation-utilization and often transnational knowledge
communication and utilization.

The debate over old and new paradigms of development is
far too complex to attempt to discuss or even summarize
here.[2] However, it is evident the battery of "old" paradigm
concepts such as high, complex, capital- and resource-
intensive Western technology; technology transfer;
industrialization as desired and inevitable; growth measured
as GNP; and trickle-down as the panacea for the masses are
being questioned. "New" paradigms place emphasis on:
appropriate technology; adapted technology; cheap
technology; renewable resource technology; "small is
beautiful"; indigenous knowledge, technology and practice in
itself and as a base for developing new technology; on-site
research, experiments and field tests; holistic, systems
approach. Data from the field of agriculture indicate much
of the technology developed and disseminated is appropriate
for large-scale, high-resource, commercial farmers and
entrepreneurs. Thus, its adoption brought negative effects
on equity and distribution. There is a felt need for
specially targeted programs for low-resource entrepreneurs
to improve equity, distribution, and quality of life and to
meet basic human needs.

As the debate rages on, there are those who argue that
there is only rhetoric, no reality, in most of the "new"
paradigm ideas dealing with: decentralization; local
participation; peasant involvement; self-sufficiency;
self-determination; low cost-resource technology;
appropriate technology developed out of an indigenous
practice, knowledge and experience and testing base;
technology representing a strong potential for special
targeting and utilization by broad populations of low-
resource entrepreneurs; technology and practices that take
into account household and national goals; and technology

and programs seen as interacting with the physical,
biological and socioeconomic environment. Real world
examples of these variables being incorporated into
successful program efforts are said to be difficult, if not
impossible, to find. There are those who say the Farming
Systems Research and Development approach may include many
of these "new paradigm" variables. After reading this
chapter, the reader can be the judge.

FARMING SYSTEMS RESEARCH AND DEVELOPMENT--ITS ESSENCE[3]

Farming Systems Research and Development (FSR&D) is an
approach to the research and development of technology and
practices which views the whole farm as a system and focuses
on (1) the interdependencies between components under the
control of members of the farm household and (2) how these
components interact with the physical, biological and
socioeconomic factors not under the household's control.

Farming systems are defined by their physical,
biological and socioeconomic setting and by the farm
family's goals and other attributes, access to resources,
choices of productive activities (enterprises), and
management practices (Shaner 1981a, 12).

FSR&D is farm system-based; attempts to understand the
farmers' indigenous practices, problems and opportunities;
is comprehensive in that it attempts to understand the whole
farm setting; is interdisciplinary in approach; complements
existing research and development activities; is iterative
and dynamic; and attempts to be responsible to both farmer
and society goals (Shaner 1981a, 16-17).

The FSR&D process is implemented by:

(1)   Selecting areas and groups of farmers with
      reasonably similar characteristics as targets for
      research and development;
(2)   Identifying and ranking problems and opportunities
      in the farming system and setting forth hypotheses
      for alternative solutions;
(3)   Planning experiments, studies, and procedures for
      data collection;
(4)   Undertaking experiments on farmers' fields, in
      conjunction with other research, to identify or
      generate improved technologies suitable for the
      farmers' conditions;
(5)   Coordinating the on-farm experiments and studies
      with commodity and disciplinary-oriented research;

(6) Evaluating the acceptability of the results of these experiments to the targeted farmers and society;

(7) Extending acceptable results widely to appropriate farmers within and outside the target area; and

(8) Focusing attention on ways to improve public policy and support services to assist both the targeted farmers and those operating under similar conditions.

The distinction between FSR&D and "conventional" research can be summarized in the following way. FSR&D looks at the interactions taking place within the whole farm setting and measures the results in terms of farmers' and society's goals. Traditionally, conventional research separates tasks into progressively narrower subject areas to be studied more or less independently and then evaluates results by standards within the discipline, not by their contribution to the whole. Furthermore, FSR&D places relatively more importance, than in the past, on integrating the social sciences into the research and development process. This is accomplished by considering such factors as household goals and preferences, community-norms, markets, public policies, and support services. (Shaner 1981a, 12-13)

The essence of FSR&D is claimed as being that the research problems and opportunities are defined by interdisciplinary field teams in interaction with household members on the farm, and most of the research is carried out and tested on the farmer's fields. However, an objective, broader view indicates there are a number of decision-making filters which the FSR&D program goes through before reaching this on the farm problem identification and research phase. They will be described in later sections.

ORGANIZATIONS, STRUCTURE AND STAFFING

Throughout the description of the basic philosophy, research and development related decisions and description of activities, reference will be made to various organizational units and persons involved. An understanding of these activities, relationships, and potential for success is somewhat dependent on a general-level understanding of these organizations, organizational

structures, and their personnel. This section will attempt
to provide information to further that understanding. FSR&D
structure and staffing will be discussed first, followed by
"Extension," Research, and Other Organizations.

FSR&D Structure and Staffing

It is recognized that development of an organizational
structure and substructures and securing and training of
personnel will be a complex, developing and dynamic process.
Structures, roles and levels of knowledge and skills will
probably vary from country to country and even within
country.

Here follows a very general and brief description of
one possible structure and staffing pattern. It assumes the
organization has been in existence sometime and is thus
operational.

Minister of Board of Directors. The highest level of
authority directly and specifically responsible for most
national FSR&D programs is either a minister or some form of
governing board. The governing board would usually be made
up of ministers (or their designates) from highly related
ministries or agencies within ministries and related
organizations (e.g., rural development, planning, economics,
universities, farmer organizations, etc.; Shaner 1981a,
248).

National Headquarters Team. Direct line authority and
responsibility usually rests with a director, director
general or executive director. At this level, there would
be the usual staff units such as budgeting, personnel,
planning, evaluation. Specific line responsibility usually
rests with a program director. Also at this level, one
usually finds disciplinary (technical and social)
specialists, commodity specialists, training specialists,
and so forth (Shaner 1981a, 250).

Regional Headquarters Team. A regional director is
responsible for managing a number of field teams in the
research areas. The director may or may not have authority
over experiment stations, farms and various staffs in the
area. In any case, an attempt is made to have cooperative
relations with experiment stations, universities and
relevant institutions at the regional level (Shaner 1981a,
250). There are also usually disciplinary and commodity
specialists who support field teams.

Field Teams. The field teams form the core of the
FSR&D program. They are in closest contact with farmers and

farmer groups, and are most directly involved in daily, local research, mainly on the farms. Each team has a designated team leader, responsible for the team activities.

Professionals on the field teams vary from two to seven members who are usually university graduates or people with comparable experience. They are predominantly agronomists (crops, soils), livestock, agricultural economists (preferably with some training in farm management and marketing), and social scientists (e.g., general social scientists, sociologists, anthropologists). Additional professionals are included depending on the characteristics of the research area or population (e.g., irrigation engineers, horticulturist, vegetable and small crops, rice, veterinary medicine, entomology, etc.; Shaner 1981a, 51).

Professionals are often supported by technicians. These tend to be people who have high school degrees, preferably with some vocational agriculture training (Shaner 1981a, 251). These technicians help the field professionals in many different ways, but especially in putting out, monitoring and keeping records on researcher and farmer manager trials. The number of technicians per professional can be as high as five to one.

A field team of five should be able to manage from 75 to 100 experiments on approximately that number of farms (Shaner 1981a, 38, 251).

Research Specialists. Research specialists have been mentioned at all levels. They may be specialized by discipline, applied science (e.g., agronomy, soils), by commodity (e.g., rice, maize, sheep) or problem (e.g., disease control, drainage). They may be employed by or assigned from universities, ministries, experiment stations, commodity programs, extension, or the private sector. Their input (direct or indirect, on request or by initiative) at the field team level is especially important. They can help interpret constraints and opportunities, state solution hypotheses, help plan field research, carry out special experiments, access information from higher echelons or beyond the system, and provide leads for important applied or basic research that needs to be done. They will also probably develop instructional materials and train team members. They can make it possible to operate FSR&D at the field level with staff that are not highly trained in research methodologies nor in depth in a discipline. At the same time, FSR&D specialists can work toward influencing more appropriate research at the experiment stations, universities, and commodity centers.

The levels of training of the specialists range from college B.S. to postgraduate, doctoral education in-country and in developed countries. In many cases, specialists will have attended special experience or training programs at national or international centers.

"Extension" Services

Most countries set up some form of extension service to carry out educational programs with various adult and youth audiences. Though the degree of emphasis and distinctness varies, most countries have a major agricultural extension educational program. Extension services are usually located at the national level in ministries of agriculture or community development. In some cases, extension services are an integral part of a university research-extension system. In other cases, they are separated from research activities.

The FSR&D program is heavily dependent on extension-type organizations for ultimate dissemination of technologies and developed practices. It is strongly recommended that extension service be involved in various and continuing roles all through the FSR&D process. It is also strongly recommended that a role, specialist in FSR&D, be established in extension service. These specialists would operate at all levels but be especially important at the regional level. Their major roles would be to assure coordination, assist with FSR&D, develop materials for extension, help train extension staff regarding philosophy and practices and technology of FSR&D, and take major responsibility for facilitating transfer of the function and information to extension at the dissemination stage.

"Traditional" Research

Most developing countries have an agricultural research structure and program. There are usually one or more agricultural universities or agricultural colleges in major universities. In most cases, there are regional universities and/or experiment stations.

Programs and staffs are organized differently. In many cases, emphasis is on discipline or applied fields (e.g., entomology, agricultural economics, agronomy, animal science). In other cases, it may be on a commodity basis (e.g., rice, maize, swine). Some research centers are organized around problem areas (e.g., dry land farming, tropical agriculture). There are more than fifteen international research centers organized around commodity (e.g., rice, maize) or problems (e.g., semi-arid tropics, animal disease).

There are two major perspectives from which FSR&D may view these more traditional research systems. (1) They, and what they have produced, represents a vast, important and available body of expertise and knowledge--links must be set up and maintained to tap that body of existing knowledge and to stimulate the development of additional knowledge. (2) However, there is a need for FSR&D to approach the farmer's problem from a systems point of view, based on the farmer-household level of operation, and develop and test practices and technology that are effective, appropriate and acceptable. The two R & D systems are seen as complementary. The complementarity pays off only if there is coordination and communication between FSR&D and the other research units.

Other Organizations

The FSR&D's system approach, with its emphasis on the social-economic and political environment, usually brings about an interface with many additional social systems. Only a very sketchy picture can be provided here.

There are usually a large number of additional government agencies directly related to or who have a role in FSR&D (e.g., credit, irrigation, transport, markets, cooperatives, health, family planning). FSR&D's attention to the social and political environment may also bring them in contact with legislative or administrative bodies who set and administer policy but also governmental units and officials at all levels may be relevant. In many cases, voluntary or pseudo government-voluntary associations such as farmers associations, commodity groups, irrigation associations, neighborhood or community development groups, political groups, may also be important.

BASIC ACTIVITIES

Farming systems research and development is a process that involves a large number of interrelated activities. Though these activities may vary from country to country, or by programs within a country, there appear to be a number of common elements. They may be conceptualized as (1) decision to try FSR&D, (2) target and subarea selection, (3) research area selection, (4) problem identification and development of base for research decisions, (5) planning on-farm research, (6) on-farm research and analysis, and (7) extension of results. Some of the activities are relatively straightforward and discrete (e.g., the first three and the last activities). However, problem identification, planning on-farm research, and on-farm research and analysis activities are highly related; flow directly one into the other; are highly iterative, and are played over many times, over highly varying time spans.

If we are to understand the dimensions, the functions and roles, the uniqueness of the FSR&D system of knowledge generation-utilization, we will have to understand what goes on during each of these sets of activities, who plays and what roles are played, the location where roles are played, what the frames of references are, what variables are taken into account, how and who makes decisions, what outcomes are expected and the criteria for evaluating outcomes. As we describe each activity, an attempt will be made to take these variables into account, especially as they relate to the knowledge generation-utilization process.

Decision to Try (Implement) FSR&D

In a sequence of activities, the first appears to be a decision to try or implement FSR&D. In most countries, there are probably one or more existing systems of research and development and extension. One way to approach an understanding of why policymakers or administrators might decide to try FSR&D is to look at <u>possible</u> shortcomings or dissatisfaction with existing systems. This is not to say all of those listed are relevant or accurate in specific situations, or can be overcome by FSR&D.

Some of the most common criticisms of existing systems of research and development include: lack of major contributions to agricultural production goals; too costly; policymakers, researchers and farmers do not communicate with each other or agree on research priorities; research systems are funded by the West and are Western solution-oriented; research systems are centrally located, controlled and have limited feedback systems, thus unresponsive to farming problems and needs; requires high-quality (scarce) and high-cost scientists who respond to basic research, profession and discipline reward systems.

There are also strong criticisms of the technology that is developed by current research systems, such as: being too complex; requiring too much capital or other scarce resources; designed for high-resource, large-scale farming; inappropriate to local needs, values and norms; too specialized, not seen in its relation to an interacting system; does not build on or take into account existing indigenous knowledge and technology.

Based on some of these (and probably other) reasons, a number of policymakers and administrators have made the decision to try FSR&D. It can be seen that the basis used in making this decision (i.e., what is expected to be accomplished by the FSR&D approach) will affect the objectives to be accomplished, what type of research will be undertaken and who will be served.

This decision is usually made by highly placed policy-makers and administrators, often with the advice of their staff members, researchers and extension personnel. Outside-country consultants, advisors and funding agencies will often influence the decision-making also.

Target and Subarea Selection

The choice of target areas and target populations is generally based on national priorities and policies reflecting national goals. Such goals may be: increased food production, more food for urban areas, or for international exchange; the production of specific crops or livestock; better use of resources to fulfill basic needs of people living in the area; alleviating land pressure (e.g., resettlement areas); increased income, income distribution and quality of life; political stability. In some cases, the target area is chosen because of specific problems or opportunities (e.g., soil erosion, deforestation, need for effective use of water). Target populations are populations of farmers with similar cropping and livestock patterns, methods of production, and potential. Most of the FSR&D programs activated around the world have emphasized a target population of low-income, low-resource, small-scale farmers (Shaner 1981a, 28). Additional criteria such as costs, access, and resources in terms of physical inputs, markets, manpower and organization are often considered.

Criteria such as these are used by policymakers and high-level administrators in agriculture, planning or finance to make decisions on target areas and target populations. These decisions are often based on information

and advice from their staffs, researchers, extension
workers, national task forces and in some cases outside
FSR&D consultants. In most cases, these decisions involve
political considerations (Shaner 1981a, 28, 59).

The decision-making process tends to be fairly
centralized, bureaucratic and authoritarian. It can be
easily observed that the decisions do influence where
research will be done, upon what it will be done, the focus
of the research, who should be served or benefitted by the
research and the basis for judging success of the program.

Figure 8.1 indicates the sequence of locations of FSR&D
work during the FSR&D process starting with selection of the
Target Areas. The figure also portrays multilocational test
areas, pilot production areas and the diffusion of
appropriate technology into additional areas, which will be
discussed later in this section.

Target Areas into Subareas. The target area and target
populations are usually divided into subareas and/or
subpopulations based on common physical, biological,
socioeconomic and farming systems characteristics. The
basic assumption behind this strategy is that such
homogeneity allows for the development of improved
technology applicable to similar farmers and conditions
throughout the target area (Shaner 1981a, 50-53). In many
cases, the technology is also applicable to similar
conditions outside the target area.

The selection of the subareas will be carried out
largely by national and regional FSR&D staff members working
with relevant extension and research staff members at
similar levels.

Research Areas within Target Subareas. Research areas
are designated within the target subareas. It is within
these research areas that improved technologies are
developed. Ideally, if research areas are representative of
the target area, then the technologies developed should be
relatively applicable to the entire target area. The
research area may be a single area or a number of selected
areas that, when combined, constitute a research area and
research population.

It is recognized that the process of choosing target
areas, subareas, research areas and then identifying
problems and gathering information as a base for research
decisions may not be broken into discrete stages--the interrelations and demand for consistency within the process are
required. Usually, the phase of choosing the research areas
is more intensive than previous phases, requiring more
information, both secondary and primary. This activity is

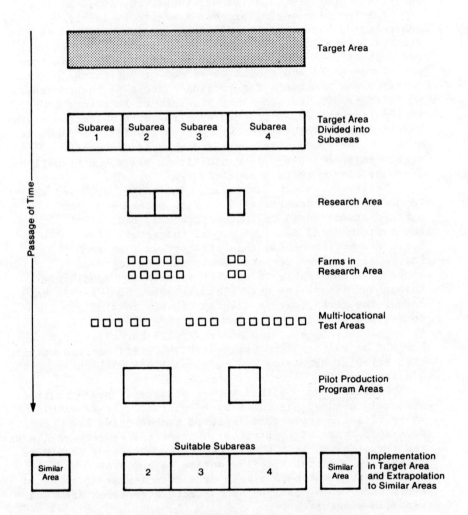

Figure 8.1 Sequence of locations of farm system research and development work during the FSR&D process (Shaner, Philipp, and Schmehl 1981a, 48)

usually carried out by experienced FSR&D staff with help
from specialists in agronomy, livestock production,
agricultural economics, sociology-anthropology and other
specialists, depending on the uniqueness and characteristics
of the subareas. Extension specialists and field staff
should be involved and input from commodity groups, farm and
business groups may be relevant (Shaner 1981a, 63-64). In
general, the major variables considered in selecting the
research areas fall within the following categories: (1)
physical environment, (2) biological environment, (3)
socioeconomic environment, (4) production systems, (5)
household systems.

The following phase, "Problem Identification," applies
these variables and involves many of the same people.
However this next phase is much more focused, intensive and
time-consuming.

Problem Identification and Development of a Base for Research Decision

Identification of problems and opportunities is an
iterative and dynamic process that continues throughout all
FSR&D activities. FSR&D focuses on and emphasizes this
frame of reference. Its objective is to discover and design
technologies and practices that are appropriate and
acceptable to the target populations. Its major approach is
understanding the farming system and the farmer's
environment. Three general-level steps are undertaken by
the FSR&D team: (1) identify existing farming systems,
existing practices and existing technology and attempt to
understand all this from the point of view of the farmer
within the context of his perceived and existing
environment; (2) identify problems (constraints) and
opportunities for improving the technology, system and
environment--the perceptions of both household members and
technicians--researchers are incorporated; and (3)
priorities for experimentation, research and actions are set
(Shaner, 1981a, 73).

This phase involves intensive field involvement of
FSR&D and related staff, intensive seeking out of
information (both secondary and primary), detailed analysis,
and decisions that set the direction and allocation of
resources for the major activities of FSR&D.

Information Categories. The variables used in
describing and understanding the farmer's environment will
probably include: (1) physical environment (e.g., climate,

soil, topography and water); (2) biological environment
(e.g., weeds, insects, diseases); (3) socioeconomic
environment, such as resource availability (e.g., land,
labor, inputs, cash, credit), infrastructure, markets,
transportation, sociocultural characteristics (e.g., land
tenure, ethnic groups, norms, cultural values), community
structure, and political and economic policy; (4) production
systems, such as enterprises, cropping systems, livestock
systems, management practices, technology and inputs used,
yields, production, entry into market, cash flow by seasons
and cropping-livestock cycles (Shaner 1981a, 76-78). From
these and related data on farming systems, flow models may
be developed ranging from the simple to very complex (Shaner
1981a, 83; 1981b, Appendix 5K); (5) the household system,
the ultimate integrator, consisting of the family structure,
family decision making, labor allocation, responsibility for
providing basic needs including food, roles, household
goals, knowledge, beliefs, attitudes (e.g., regarding
agricultural technology), off-farm work (Shaner 1981a,
78-79); and (6) household resources: land, water, labor,
capital, and management (Shaner 1981a, 80).

These categories of information do demonstrate the
breadth, scope and, as stated in FSR&D, the emphasis on
holistic, "bottoms up," "downstream," indigenous-based,
appropriate, applicable and acceptable technology and
practices. This is the essence of the FSR&D basis for
research decisions and thus strongly influences the
research-experimentation analysis and the technology and
practices that are developed and recommended.

Sondeo--An example of method and process. As indicated
above, this problem of identification and developing a base
for research decisions, is an iterative, dynamic and
continuing process. The prior paragraph illustrates the
type of information and data sought, some of which will be
available from secondary sources. The following illustrates
one early step approach used to develop some insights and to
gather some primary information.

This specific method falls under the more general
Reconnaissance Survey method. It is used in one Latin
American country program and is called Sondeo, Spanish for
reconnaissance survey.[4] Sondeo is used in the early stages
of problem identification. A Sondeo reconnaissance survey
group could be composed of: members of an existing or
developing FSR&D field team, specialists in appropriate
agricultural technology fields from regional headquarters,
experiment stations, commodity groups or extension, and
specialists in socioeconomics. Usually in a group of ten,

it would be equally divided between technical agriculture and socioeconomic members.

The primary objectives of the Sondeo is to acquaint the field team with the area in which they work, to begin to set the framework and operationalize the FSR&D approach, and to begin to establish working relations between team members and, to a degree, with specialists.

This is the first time in the FSR&D process that emphasis is focused on what farmers do and why they do it. The team members attempt to gain an understanding of what factors, such as knowledge, beliefs, obligations, goals and perceptions of risks, influence the farmer's decision-making in regards to household and farming systems. They also try to determine the rationale for, and conceptualization of, present farming practices and technologies and perceptions of constraints and opportunities. This reconnaissance should also familiarize the group members with concepts and terms used, local vernacular, units of measurement and analysis, modes of expressing problems, goals, needs, and so forth; more importantly, it helps to identify needs for further, probably more formal information gathering (Shaner 1981a, 97).

The six categories of information previously described in this section provide the general framework for data gathering. More specifically, the task is to discover the cropping and livestock systems and technologies of the farmers, the agro-socioeconomic conditions of the household and farm, which are most important in determining the present system, and in considering any modification of the system. It is also ". . . invaluable in acquainting the field staff with the realities of farming in the area" (Shaner 1981b, 469-470).

The Sondeo is usually carried out in a week or ten days, depending on local conditions. The first day is a general reconnaisance of the area by the group as a whole and includes group interviews with household members. Interviews are unstructured, open, broad ranging, information gathering, impressionistic -- emphasis is on eliciting the greatest amount of information, feelings, perceptions, constraints, from the household members. After each interview, survey group members meet together to exchange their information, perceptions and observations with each other to determine the degree to which different perspectives create different perceptions, definitions of the situation and possible solutions. Usually this discussion is also continued back at headquarters at the end of the first day.

On subsequent days the ten-person group is divided into pairs who continue intensive on-farm interviews with additional households. The pairs are rotated each day so each person, depending on his specialty area, is paired with each other person in the survey group. Again, after each interview, each paired team compares their perceptions, information, definitions of problems and opportunities and possible hypotheses for changes. At the end of each day, the entire team meets for similar comparisons and alternative hypotheses.

Near the end of the time period, a report outline is agreed upon and each team member is assigned to write up one or more segments of the report. As the report is drafted (usually one half day), an additional half-day is allowed for return to the field to confirm or gather additional information.

One half-day is allowed for the _first_ reading (reporting) of the various sections of the report. The final day is allowed for a second reading and drawing conclusions, action implications, and tentative priorities. The limitations on the completeness, quality and finality of the report is recognized. However, the field team continues to work in the area, and the report is a basis for subsequently more quantitative, complete and accurate data gathering analysis and conclusions. However, those who use this approach value the process as equally important as the product (Shaner 1981b, 466-480).

Hypotheses for Improvement. FSR&D uses the concept "hypotheses for improving the system" to describe the "next" function to be performed. "Next" is used in quotes to indicate that data gathering, analysis, listing and redefining are all parts of an iterative, dynamic, continuing process and do not occur at only one "next" step.

The collected information and data are analyzed to attempt to understand existing constraints on the household in reaching its household and production goals and to look for possible alternatives (opportunities) to alleviate constraints or capture potentials not now being considered and used. The attempt is made to develop meaningful hypotheses which help specify crucial variables and which can be used as the basis for experimentation and research to test their feasibility. This analysis-hypothesis development process can vary from a highly complex process using farming system models and highly quantifiable, interactive data to less formal and more impressionistic approaches (Shaner 1981a, 82-83).

A first step (from both the farmer's and technician-researcher's point of view) may be to look for factors limiting plant and animal growth and productivity. Second, analyze why farmers have not solved these problems; often, it has been found farmers have very good reasons for not using technology that at first glance appears to offer a solution to problems. Thirdly, opportunities are investigated; perhaps other innovative farmers have solved existing problems or seized opportunities that are generally applicable. Farmers may have limited abilities to see or understand problems or recognize opportunities. Thus, the technicians, field team researchers, extension workers and specialists, and research specialists will probably be able to see a wider range of opportunities. These sources can be tapped using many channels, media and techniques of communication including interpersonal communication. Problem and opportunity alternatives and hypotheses for improvement from all of these sources can be inputted into the process of setting priorities on problems and opportunities, which leads to the planning and carrying out of research.

Setting Priorities. The following suggested three general-level criteria have been operationalized in a very detailed and pragmatic way by those involved in farming systems. They are (Shaner 1981a, 89-90):

1. Seriousness of problem as viewed by farmers, technicians-researchers, and administrators.

2. Potential for solving the problem, capturing the opportunity, gaining acceptance of solution and ease of implementing the results.

3. Importance of problem or opportunity in an overall experimentation-research farming system-household strategy. Basically this is an attempt to not limit activities to only specific, possibly unrelated problems or opportunities, but when appropriate, to see problems and opportunities in a larger, interrelated context and develop an integrated research strategy (sometimes called a "development path") that can have a major impact on removing constraints or capturing opportunities.

Emphasis. This problem-identification phase, and the subsequent carrying out and analyzing of on-farm research, appears to be the most unique feature and makes the major contribution to the character of FSR&D. The farming household system, in its environment, is studied and viewed from the perspective of the household on the farm by household and field team members and specialists, and bottom-up hypotheses are developed to remove constraints and/or capture realistic opportunities.

Planning On-Farm Research

After having identified the more relevant problems and opportunities confronting specified groups of farmers in the research area, and developing hypotheses for improvements, the FSR&D team is ready to plan the research program. This activity should produce a work plan for research leading to the development of practices and technology that will improve the situation of these farmers. This potential for improvement becomes the basis for setting research objectives, selecting research activities and methods, coordinating the resources and efforts of experiment station staff and other supporting organizations, and outlining the FSR&D team's tasks and responsibilities (Shaner 1981a, 114).

Four general-level activities are usually carried out:

1. Laying groundwork for planning by considerations, such as: reviewing priority problems; appraising the organization's capabilities and resources; searching for relevant technologies; setting assumptions about near-term conditions; developing hypotheses for testing; establishing research collaboration.
2. Preliminary analysis and estimates of feasibility of a range of on-farm experiments. Major concerns would involve: looking for alternative solutions; further analysis of farmer conditions; developing clearer understanding of farmer's perspectives, perceptions, and probability of acceptance; estimation of compatibility with societies' goals; working toward internally consistent research designs—technically adequate and responsive to conditions likely to prevail over a broad range of application; develop "conservative" estimation values; project secondary, side and eventual consequences.
3. Consider alternative research methods and activities.
4. Finalize plans for on-farm experiments, including: setting outcome criteria; setting design; deciding on the number of farms and setting criteria for choosing farms and farmers.

From the knowledge generation-utilization paradigm point of view, a factor of major importance here is the attempt to plan high quality research-experiments and develop realistic, applicable criteria for judging success.

On-Farm Research and Analysis

With the completion of the research planning phase, the team moves to implement the on-farm research program. The team's objectives are met primarily through researcher-managed trials, farmer-managed tests and superimposed trials.

Researcher-managed trials are experiments undertaken on the farmer's farm, basically under farmer conditions, but managed by FSR&D team members to test or develop new technologies appropriate and acceptable to farmers. The researcher often tries to simulate farmer conditions by questioning, observing and having the farmers perform much of the work. Non-experimental variables are generally set or maintained to represent farmer conditions and practices. Researchers will often pay farmers for the use of their land, labor and inputs so the farmers do not bear the risk of failure.

Through this process, many existing or developed practices and technologies can be rapidly screened, high risk and more difficult and complex technologies can be tried, greater control is exercised, modifications can be rapidly incorporated, unknown characteristics of the research area can be discovered, gaps between present and potential production can be determined, and much is learned about farmers, households and communities, and usually credibility for research results are established (Shaner 1981a, 126, 149).

Farmer-managed tests are on-the-farm tests of practices or technology that have usually been through researcher trials and prove to be at least as good as present farmer practices. There are several exceptions to this general rule. Sometimes these tests are undertaken to determine how the farmer and the system respond to change. In some cases, the technology or practice appears to be overwhelmingly superior to an existing technology and is moved directly to farmer-managed tests.

For best results, farmers need to manage these tests using resources and non-experimental variable practices normally available or used by farmers without interference from the team. The team serves mainly as a resource person or advisor. In fact, the way the farmer alters the test, together with the reasons, are important test results. Such information can be the basis for modifying the technologies and identifying opportunities for further research. These tests show researchers how new technology performs under near farm conditions, how acceptable the technology is to

farmers, and provides a partial basis for projecting the
degree of adoption to other research and the target areas
(Shaner 1981a, 127).

Superimposed trials are a low-cost means of preliminary
evaluation of relatively simple changes. They are basically
superimposed on existing enterprises and practices in
technology. These trials are often single factor-variable
experiments (e.g., levels of fertilizer, insect control over
a wide geographic area so there will be no contamination,
labor-consuming or saving innovations).

Analysis of On-Farm Research. Since research trials
and farmer tests are an iterative, dynamic and continuing
process, analysis of results is a constant and continuing
activity. Analysis in FSR&D is an integrating activity in
which the team seeks to simulate the breadth of activities,
variables and considerations that farmers do intuitively.
The team usually begins the analysis by seeking to understand the household and the farming environment. After the
on-farm experiments are completed, the results are used as a
basis for judging whether technical changes represent an
improvement. That is, they want to know if a new technology
or practice produces more from a given set of resources,
meets farmers' goals with less, different or cheaper
resources, or helps stabilize inputs and outputs (Shaner
1981a, 172-173).

Usually the first and most basic step in analysis is
determining the biological, productivity results of experiments and trials. In many ways the research procedures are
similar to experiment station type research. However,
analysis procedures, variables and criteria for evaluation
may vary some. In the discussion of analyzing and drawing
conclusions from the biological, productivity outcomes of
the experiments, the following are among the terms used:
"yes-no" experiments, "how much" or level experiments,
combinations, replications, average yield, yield stage
curves, estimating benefits and costs, net benefits,
opportunity costs, sensitivity analysis, marginal rate of
return, minimum acceptable return, risk allowance.

When experimental results are biologically positive,
the team must clearly determine whether farmers have the
resources and capabilities to implement the changes and
whether the results are economically satisfactory (e.g.,
represent a satisfactory net benefit when compared with
existing farming practices). Even if all the above are
satisfactory, financial feasibility should be examined to
determine whether the farmers are able to secure cash
resources for implementing the change and subsequently will

be able to repay any borrowed money, according to the terms
of the agreement.

The team also must analyze the acceptability of the new
technology to the farmers in terms of both productivity and
household goals. This is usually done through discussion
with farmers, by observing and analyzing farmer-managed
tests and by noting acceptance rates (Shaner 1981a, 173).
In one FSR&D country program an "acceptability index" is
computed by multiplying the percentage of farmers who adopt
a new technology by the percentage of crops on their farms
to which it is applied, and dividing the product by 100. In
most cases, an index of 25 is considered high enough to
recommend the practice to extension for dissemination to
other relatively homogeneous groups within the target area
(Shaner 1981a, 201).

Analysis also is often made of the results in terms of
societies' goals and policies, for example, by efficient use
and conservation of non-renewable resources, improvement in
distribution of income, increased food available in the
marketplace, maintaining farmers in rural areas.

Where all indications are that the new technology
should interest farmers, but does not, the team should
examine its assumptions and knowledge about the farming
system, the farm household and the sociocultural
environment.

These types of continuing analyses should assist the
team in determining (1) the readiness of the improved and
new technologies for diffusion to other target audiences and
(2) the need for changes in support services, infrastructures and social environment and policy changes. Many
different concepts, measurements, analysis techniques and
operational procedures, and decision matrices are available
(and presented) to carry out the general procedures outlined
(Shaner 1981a, 30, 172-207).

Final Emphasis. In this phase of the process, the
fundamental and relatively unique characteristics of FSR&D
are carried out. R&D is carried out on the farms, basically
under farmer environment and resource conditions, and by
using farmer- and household-oriented criteria to judge
acceptability and appropriateness for dissemination, which
builds on both on-farm and off-farm knowledge and
technology.

Extension of Results

In FSR&D, R&D develops new technologies and demonstrates their worth and acceptability to a relatively small
number of farms. The extension service or similar agencies
take on major responsibility for diffusing these new
technologies to as many farmers as applicable and practical.
The complementary and changing roles between R&D staff and
extension staff is recognized during the entire R&D process.
However, it is at this stage that the major transition and
transfer of roles and responsibilities are especially
critical. Since FSR&D is a relatively new concept and to
date has concentrated on R&D, the role and strategy of
extending the application of the technology through
extension and similar agencies have not been fully
developed. However, there has been some experience and
there appear to be other logical needs that support
alternatives which are now emerging.

Probably the most important principle of successful
transfer is the involvement of extension personnel at all of
the previous stages. An attempt has been made to
demonstrate this point in the previous discussion of each of
the stages and by the description of major roles. A second
important element is the training of selected extension
personnel as FSR&D specialists and involving them in
providing the training on FSR&D and newly developed
technologies for all extension personnel at the field staff
level. A third important element is to set up coordinators'
units involving FSR&D, extension, experiment station
research and other related agencies at national and regional
levels and FSR&D-extension and similar agencies at the field
level.

There are two main new approaches emerging that play
major roles in the diffusion of appropriate technologies
developed by FSR&D: Multi-Locational Testing and Pilot
Production programs (see Figure 8.1). They are often
undertaken in sequence.

Multi-Locational Testing. As previously indicated,
target areas, subareas, and research areas were chosen to be
relatively homogeneous, but it was recognized that there
would be variations within these areas. The objective of
multi-locational testing is to test the applicability and
acceptability of the technology developed on selected trial
or test farms, in the research area and subareas.
Subsequently, this approach may also be used in other target
areas.

A team composed of FSR&D and extension staff carries out this activity. Major responsibility is with the FSR&D members and the tests are basically researcher-managed or supervised tests. Extension team members are directly involved in selecting farmers and carrying out the application and evaluation of the technology and related activities. During this multi-location testing process, team members learn about adapting technologies to fit varying conditions; attempt to identify differences in performance with causal factors; verify or revise subarea boundaries for recommendations; assist in preparing instructions for the extension agents and farmer diffusion and use of the technology; and consider the feasibility of extrapolating results to other subareas or areas or groups outside the target area (Shaner 1981a, 219-222).

Sometimes the joint team will continue testing over two or three seasons to make adaptations or to further verify the technology applicability if it represents substantial change or risks (Shaner 1981a, 222).

With proven applicability and acceptability and continuing monitoring, the technology and practices are disseminated throughout the applicable subareas, target areas, and when practical, to other delineated applicable areas.

Pilot Production Program. Once the new technologies have been tested multi-locationally and modified as necessary, pilot production programs may be initiated. A new technology suitable for a single farm may not be suitable when many farmers simultaneously adopt it. A pilot program may be designed to gain information on the capability and adequacy of such factors as inputs and input infrastructures (e.g., fertilizer, chemicals, equipment, credit, labor, information) and output structures (e.g., markets, prices, processing units and transportation).

Probably the pilot program will be coordinated by the Extension Specialist in farming systems but involve FSR&D field and regional staff and other related organizations including people from the input and marketing systems. The pilot program is carried out, and evaluated with adjustments made in the technologies and/or suggestions made for changes in the infrastructure and other environmental factors as well as in the policy area. In many cases these suggestions will have to be incorporated into policy inputs, market and related structural changes if the full benefits of the FSR&D activity are to be reaped (Shaner 1981a, 222, 223).

Other Dissemination Activities. Based on the results of the multi-locational testing and pilot production

programs appropriate technology can be implemented
throughout the target area and extrapolated and diffused in
other similar areas (see Figure 8.1).

Throughout this entire extension process and time span,
there is need for constant communication and feedback
between extension staff (and other diffusion personnel) and
FSR&D staff. Feedback is important regarding such phenomena
as applicability, acceptability, performance, environmental
factors, and innovative adaptations. Out of this extension
of technology there will probably emerge a new generation of
constraints and opportunities, changes in environment and
need for structural and policy changes. The needs for new
knowledge, including basic and applied research, must be
communicated to local, regional, national and international
research units. All of these activities can be a part of a
continuing, dynamic, iterative process leading to continued
development, improvement and use of improved and new
practices and technology to help optimize household and
society goals.

A FOOTNOTE ON THE "OLD" AND "NEW" PARADIGM

To the extent one accepts a number of the proposed
characteristics of the "new" paradigm of development and
desires to cite an empirical example of an approach that is
experiencing some success in the real world, does FSR&D
represent such an example? It does appear to have the
logical and empirical potential, and it also has
demonstrated some success in field programs which, at a
general level, incorporates: decentralization of many
research decisions; local participation; farmer involvement;
rural and agricultural orientation; a greater degree of
self-determination and less dependency at the national and
local levels; increasing self-sufficiency for low resource,
small farmers; aids in equity and distribution of rewards; a
farming system, household orientation rather than specific
commodity or practice orientation; takes account of the
physical, biological and socioeconomic environment; more
orientation toward household goals, quality of life and
basic human needs; and attempts to influence social
structure and policy.

In terms of knowledge and technology development and
use, it tries to understand the farmer-household members as
rational, motivated people within their perceived world of
reality; is cognizant of and builds on indigenous knowledge,
practice and technology; does not depend on Western

technology transfer and solutions; develops appropriate, feasible (usually labor-intensive rather than capital-intensive) and acceptable technology, mainly through on-farm experiments, trials and tests; is incremental and developmental; is disseminated after demonstrated appropriateness and acceptability, through multi-locational trials and pilot projects to relatively homogeneous target audiences.

NOTES

1. The label "knowledge generation-utilization" is used in this paper to describe a general phenomena, including discovery or accessing knowledge, through the various phases, however conceptualized, to dissemination application and use of the knowledge.

2. For attempts to summarize some of the issues and discussion of the micro and macro levels, see George M. Beal and Meheroo Jussawalla, "'Old' and 'New' Paradigms of Development: Concepts and Issues," and Meheroo Jussawalla and George M. Beal, "Development Paradigms: Old and New," both from Communication Institute, East-West Center, Honolulu, 1981.

3. Most of the information used in this paper to describe Farming Systems Research and Development is taken from the two-volume publications by Shaner, Philipp and Schmehl 1981a and 1981b. (These volumes were subsequently revised and combined into one volume by the same authors titled Farming Systems Research and Development: Guidelines for Developing Countries, Westview Press, Boulder, Colorado, 1982.) These guideline books are based on their analysis of FSR&D programs that have been carried out over approximately the last decade by international organizations and nations in approximately ten countries in Latin America, Africa and Asia. It may be noted that the author of this paper is cited as a sociological consultant in the preparation of the two volumes, drafted original copy for several sections in the text, is shown as author in the Appendices, and participated in the field testing in Guatemala of an earlier version of the guidelines with an international group of administrators and policy makers, researchers and field workers. Thus, the author should have a certain degree of familiarity with FSR&D. The author of this paper desires to give full credit to the three authors of the two-volume

guidelines and the large number of scholars, administrators, workers and peasants who contributed to the volumes. However, the author will take full responsibility for what is presented in this paper, some of which cannot be traced to the Guidelines and, in fact, might not be acceptable to the authors.

4. This section is based largely on Shaner (1981b, 466, 480).

REFERENCES

Larsen, J. K. 1981. "Knowledge Utilization: Current Issues." In The Knowledge Cycle, ed. R. F. Rich, 149-168. Beverly Hills, Calif.: Sage Publications.

Shaner, W.W., P.F. Philipp, and W.R. Schmehl. 1981a. Farming Systems Research and Development: Guidelines for Developing Countries, Vol. One: Text. Consortium for International Development, prepared for United States Agency for International Development, Washington, D.C.

Shaner, W.W., P.F. Philipp, and W.R. Schmehl. 1981b. Farming Systems Research and Development: Guidelines for Developing Countries, Vol. Two: Appendices. Consortium for International Development, prepared for United States Agency for International Development, Washington, D.C.

Shaner, W.W., P.F. Philipp, and W.R. Schmehl, eds. 1981c. Reading in Farming Systems Research and Development. Consortium for International Development, prepared for United States Agency for International Development, Washington, D.C.

Weiss, C. H. 1978. "Improving the Linkage between Social Research and Public Policy." In Knowledge and Policy: The Uncertain Connection, ed. L. E. Lynn, Jr. Washington, D.C.: National Academy of Sciences.

PART THREE

Linkages

9

Linkage: Key to Understanding the Knowledge System

Ronald G. Havelock

All systems comprise elements and their interconnections. In previous chapters we have indicated how the knowledge system can be viewed as a series of "worlds" within which communication and the transfer of all kinds of resources are relatively easy and between which communication and resource exchange is relatively difficult. These "worlds" may be separate countries or cultures, separate disciplines of knowledge, or separate social-functional concerns and responsibilities. However we may wish to divide up the whole, the key troublesome questions concern the connections between the worlds. This paper provides an analysis of connections, particularly the connections forming bridges between groups. Such connections, which may not even exist to begin with, are from slender threads and eventually have to carry tremendous information loads. It is on these bridging connections that the macrosystem depends, if there be a macrosystem serving the needs of humanity as a whole.

The term "link" is in a number of ways an appropriate descriptor for the phenomena we are about to consider. First of all, "link" implies a chain, a sequence of entities connected to one another in series and serving a common purpose. Secondly, a link is a continuous loop in which there is no end and no beginning. Thirdly, as it is configured on a chain, it has two sides and two ends. Fourth, at its two ends it interpenetrates other links or elements of some kind. Finally, the strength of the weakest link defines the strength of the chain. Thus the link-chain metaphor is apt for the knowledge system as well as for the analysis of the connection between any two subsystems or "worlds."

THE ELEMENTS OF A ONE-WAY COMMUNICATION ARC[1]

   It has been a tradition to begin analyses of communication with the formula: "who says what to whom by what
channel to what effect?" This formula has been transformed
by Berlo (1960) into the "S-M-C-R-E" model (source, message,
channel, receiver, effect) and has been employed by many
other authors with slight modifications as a way of laying
out the major factors that have to be studied. The general
utility of the model cannot be argued as it lays out some
very important dimensions in a very simple way. However,
its very simplicity is misleading because it masks some
crucial features. The single "act" of communication should
really be understood as two separate and distinct acts that
somehow have to be coordinated in space and time (Harary and
Havelock 1972). These are the act of sending a message and
the act of receiving a message. If we suppose that "A"
designates the would-be sender and "B" the would-be receiver
the configuration of a communication event is something like
Figure 9.1.
   For message x to make a successful transit from A to B,
all of the following conditions must hold:
1. A must initially possess message x and must be able to
    retain it in its original form until such a time and
    place are reached where its transit to B is physically
    possible.
2. A must have a <u>capability</u> of transmitting x into a
    compatible medium m.
3. A must have a desire (motivation) for thus transmitting
    x.
4. There must exist a medium m which is capable of
    carrying x and receiving it from As sending mechanism
    and delivering it to Bs receiving mechanism.

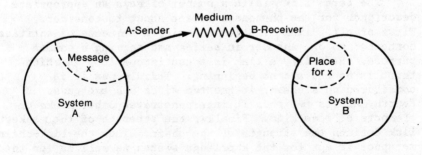

Figure 9.1 Essential elements of a communicative transfer event

5. B must exist.
6. B must have a place or space into which x can go and be retained, once received.
7. B must have the capability of receiving x from the medium m.
8. B must have the desire (motivation) to receive x.
9. A and B must be in the same space at the same time in close enough proximity that the medium m can be operative as a vehicle for the transit of x between A and B; and
10. A must transmit the message x at the moment or immediately prior to the moment at which B is set to receive.

Such a microanalysis of a single communication event might seem painfully obvious, given the fact that most of us communicate readily and almost continuously regarding whatever matters we please to whomever we please. However, this very ubiquitousness of everyday communication blinds us to the problems of unusual communication, new communication, and communication between radically different systems. Because the latter types of communication are our special concern in this paper, it is well for us to ponder these details and their implications. Let us take two examples that are hypothetical but representative of the types of knowledge transfer that might be deemed highly desirable from the point of view of improving the world knowledge system.

For the first example, let us say that a chemist working for a plastics manufacturer in Toronto, Canada, has just discovered a substance that can filter a host of life-threatening impurities out of drinking water, a substance that in Toronto at least can be manufactured cheaply in large quantities, it being in fact an otherwise wasted by-product of plastics manufacture. The chemist is A; the substance is x. Somewhere in the world, indeed at countless numbers of places, people are getting sick and dying because they either lack or cannot use this substance or some other means to purify their water. The people, the community, the leaders, or the health workers at any one of these places can be designated as B. Let us say that B is a village on the southern edge of the Sahara. Now what is the problem? Let us start with A and condition #1: when he made the discovery was he able to write it down, noting all the conditions of its production and preservation? Maybe not; maybe the implications of his discovery were not clear to him or did not appear to be very important; after all, Toronto has no water pollution problem in the city's water

system. Condition #2: obviously, A's discovery needs
considerable embellishment before it can be communicated
even to fellow chemists; then it needs to be transformed
into a practical and replicable process that can be understood by sanitary engineers and health officials; then it
has to be packaged and scaled down in such a way that it can
be adopted by a poor village; even then it has to be
translated into the language of the receiving culture and
even then quite possibly packaged for oral communication to
non-literate people. Condition #3: A must want to go to the
effort of doing all this or finding others who have both the
capability and willingness to do it. Among other things, he
will need to obtain permission and waiver of patent rights
from his company or involve his company in a marketing
venture that has little promise for major financial return
from well-heeled buyers. Condition #4: the medium in this
case is a very complex international infrastructure of
developers, manufacturers, translators, and communicators, a
mechanism that spans continents and the cultural distances
from the most highly developed to the most underdeveloped
countries in the world. Fortunately, though they are
woefully inadequate, such infrastructures do exist within
the United Nations system and within the various bilateral
and multilateral aid-giving agencies. Condition #5:
certainly many Bs do exist but not necessarily within the
awareness of chemist A. Condition #6: the village surely
will have no existing receptacle for handling the filtering
substance and may have no capability of maintaining the
practice of using it, even if it is adopted once on a trial
basis. Condition #7: the message might yet prove to be too
complicated for many villagers to understand; local folk
beliefs regarding water and the causes and nature of disease
may block comprehension. Condition #8: villagers may be
suspicious of outsiders and their innovations, and they may
have had bad experiences trying to adopt other outside ideas
at an earlier time. Condition #9: obviously A does not have
to be physically present when B is ready to listen, but A's
surrogates must be, and the village may be very remote,
inaccessible by road or telephone. Condition #10: depending
on the culture, there are good times and bad times for
receiving outsiders and their messages. Hunting season,
harvest time, holy days of all sorts intrude on the
calendar; there are times when key villagers will be
together, times when they will be scattered; times when they
will be attentive and times when they will be pre-occupied.
  Now consider a second case. This is a village
technical school which has been put together with local

resources; it emphasizes olders teaching youngers; deriving
the maximum learning from studying and working to change
local conditions; using skills already existing among
village members but now shared more widely and efficiently.
In its structure and in its outcomes, it is a successful
going concern; it works for these people and contributes
significantly to the raising of the quality of their lives.
This village is A and its school is x.[2] Condition #1: A has
the school today, and it works today so it may not exist
tomorrow for reasons having nothing to do with its worth as
an innovation or the investment of the villagers in its
survival. Condition #2: those who grow their own innovations rarely have the various talents and resources
requisite to evaluating and describing what they have done
in such a way that others in other villages even in the same
country can follow with any degree of fidelity. For this
innovation, involving as it does many components, including
complex social arrangements, condition #2 is especially hard
to meet. Condition #3: typically villagers will be proud of
such an achievement and will be quite willing to show it off
to others; this is probably not going to be a difficult
condition to meet for this innovation. Condition #4: as
noted under #2, a new school is a difficult innovation to
communicate at best. The medium might well be an outsider
with strong communicative skills and a great enthusiasm for
this type of innovation who will come to serve as the
promoter, either within the country or outside. Such
"linkers" are critical to the transfer of complex messages
between cultures, as will be discussed more fully later in
this paper. Condition #5: we might well ask, in this case,
if there is another village somewhere with the precise
configuration of needs and resources that would be suitable
as a host to this innovation. Organizational innovations
tend to be situation-specific. If there is a B village out
there somewhere, where will it be? How can it be found?
Condition #6: the x idea may be good, but B may already have
some kind of technical school, and the people who would run
the new school may be so busy they don't have time to sit
down and listen or, more difficult yet, go to another
village to observe what they are doing. Condition #7: as
complicated as it is to describe and "package" a social
innovation like a school, it is just as hard to understand
someone else's description. Condition #8: whereas A may be
proud of its own school and willing and eager to boast about
its achievements, B may well have local pride also and may
be unwilling to copy what someone else is doing. Many
cultures also resist certain configurations of vocational

training as limitations on status and upward mobility.
Condition #9: again for such an innovation the proximity
issue is perceived to be of great importance: Peru and Nepal
may in fact have a lot of things in common, but the peoples
of those two cultures will have difficulty exchanging
innovations both for real and perceived distances that
separate them. Condition #10: such innovations are likely
also to be time-bound, to be highly applicable at a certain
stage of development, irrelevant and even counter-productive
at other times. Furthermore, the number of persons and
interest groups that would have to have convergent
perceptions and views for full-scale adoption to occur make
the going especially rough for this type of innovation.

HOW THE LINK EMERGES FROM THE ARC

Thus far we have only considered unidirectional acts of
transfer, but it should be obvious that most such acts are
far from simple. Indeed, when the innovative message is
truly new and the transfer is between senders and receivers
who are initially totally unknown to each other,
consummating the act of transfer can appear to be impossibly
difficult. It is this very difficulty, however, that
creates the need for a more complex configuration, which we
call the "link." To understand how this comes about, we
need to consider in more depth what "senders" and
"receivers" are: they are, first of all, organic systems,
and as such they have capabilities of both sending and
receiving messages over a number of media. Furthermore, as
a matter of survival, they are constantly doing both,
sending and receiving, in many directions on many media, in
relation to innumerable As and Bs. Most such communication
is not particularly relevant or clarifying for our analysis
because it is highly routinized and mostly <u>closed</u>. In other
words, most input and output channels most of the time
cannot be used either to send or to receive <u>new</u> sources
because they are preoccupied or "bound" to old sources for
the transfer of familiar messages. Nevertheless there is
always <u>some excess</u> of attention span, sometimes identified
as dither or even "error" so that most channels are unbound
at least some of the time and some are unbound a good deal
of the time. This will also vary from individual to
individual, some having a higher tolerance or openness to
sending or receiving new messages, some nearly none.
One reason why some channels <u>must</u> remain open is the
fact that most human and social systems continue to have

<u>needs that go unmet</u>. If needs are unmet, the organism has a natural tendency to reach out restlessly in many directions, including the unknown.

Another reason why channels need to remain open is defensive: new stimuli can impinge upon the organism at any time from any direction. Thus defensive measures must be undertaken without notice, and these defensive measures include reaching out to find out what the stimulus is all about. This sometimes comes under the heading "curiosity," but the motivation for such forays is more directed than that word would imply. Any outside system that sends a message may be doing so for a variety of reasons, not all beneficial to the host system, and some messages sent without destructive intent may nonetheless have destructive effects.

Yet another reason for sending counter messages is the necessity of establishing trading relationships in order to receive valued resources from others; something has to be given in return. The sender must be given an incentive for continuing to send what is useful to the receiver; in many cases, but not all, a barter has to be arranged or money has to be provided. Finally, as noted at the beginning of this section, the very difficulty of making initial communicative contacts requires that the receiver initiate communication with the sender merely to align the sending and receiving apparatus of each system, to determine what medium is most appropriate and what message, if any, is welcome at this time.

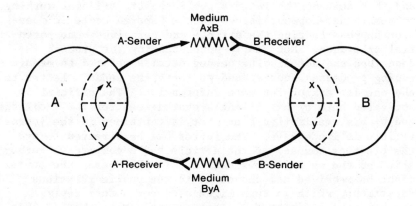

Figure 9.2 Essential elements of a communicative link

In purely formal terms, building on Figure 9.1, Figure 9.2 suggests the elements that are required to form an initial link.

As the figure suggests, a link is formed out of elements that consist of symmetrical communicative arcs: the sender and receiver reverse roles such that B also has a message, y, must have a means of communicating y, and must be willing to send y (for any of the reasons identified above). A medium must be found that is compatible both with the message and with As receiving apparatus. A must have a capability and a desire to receive message y and must have a place to put it. Finally, A must remain in the same environment with B long enough to receive the message (proximity, simultaneity).

In addition to this obvious symmetry, however, two additional important requirements have to be fulfilled before these two symmetrical transfer acts become a link: a causal connection has to be made between the act of receiving x and the act of sending y within B; and a subsequent connection has to be made between the receipt of y and the original act of transmitting x within A such that A can perceive the causal roots of receiving y in the act of sending x. It should be noted that x and y may not have any formal similarities, that the media used to transmit each message may be entirely different and unrelated, and that the time and place of the B x A transaction may be entirely different from the A x B transaction.

We may be able to bring some of this analytic discussion to life by referring once again to our hypothetical examples. Let us suppose that our Toronto chemist has managed to publish his findings in a public health journal and that some months later a public health official working on health development issues in the Saharan state in question happens to find the article and perceives some potential relevance. Not really understanding the process described and not finding needed details related to manufacturing processes, costs, and so forth, he sends a letter to the chemist asking for more information. The official is motivated both by his client's stated need for the knowledge and by his realization that what is contained in the journal article is inadequate. The letter may be directed toward the plastics company if the article had a corporate "authorship" as the sole identification. In that case, the letter might be received and channeled to the public relations department, which in turn might send out a form reply, thanking the official for his interest. Note that if this happens, a true link has not been formed because the original sender has not been informed of the letter.

In the case of the village technical school, an initial link might be formed as follows. A member of the village travels to the provincial office of education to request some special support for the purchase of new materials. While in the provincial capital, he encounters an educator from a different village whom he tells about his village's innovative school and the success it has had. The person from the second village, hoping to make some improvements back home, is intrigued by the story and asks if he can come for a visit. Again we have completed the link as the first villager acknowledges the request. Here, however, the medium used for both communication acts is the same and the distance in social and geographic terms is short. If, however, it only occurs to the second villager that he should ask about a visit after the first villager has returned home, completing the link may be next to impossible since there might be no adequate mail service and the distance traveled on foot just to make the request may hardly justify the effort.

In both these examples we have attempted to illustrate only the beginning stages of a solid inter-system bridge. In each case, the real message was not yet really transmitted in anything like its complete form, and the counter message was merely a request for further information. Nevertheless, each link seemed destined to continue on to at least one more communicative act and quite possibly several more. In subsequent sections of this paper, we will consider what happens as the interchange develops and as the messages transferred become increasingly important for both parties. Before moving on, however, it is important to note the following:

(1) all substantive linkages begin with one communicative arc for which ten special conditions must hold regarding sender, receiver, message, and medium;

(2) that communicative arc must be followed by another causally connected arc in the other direction;

(3) the essential ingredients of the resulting link hold true as necessary but usually not sufficient conditions for the evolution of subsequent stronger links;

(4) the initial communicative arcs rarely are successful at conveying the whole of a significant innovation (in fact, usually only conveying crude impressions and awarenesses of it); and

220

(5)   the initial counter-message is typically some kind
      of signal for amplification or clarification of
      the received message segment.

LINKAGE AS A NEEDS-RESOURCES DIALOG[3]

     It is axiomatic that human beings, like all other
organisms, communicate primarily, if not solely, for the
purpose of satisfying needs of one kind or another. The
more basic the need, the stronger the efforts to reach out
and acquire the resources necessary to fill that need.
Therefore one way to interpret efforts to achieve and
maintain links is an attempt to develop stable connections
to needed resources. Communication arcs emanating from the
system in need can thus be classified as need-related
communications, and communication arcs coming toward the
system in need, particularly those in response, can be
classified as resource- or solution-related communications.
Figure 9.3 is intended to illustrate this relationship.
     Note that in Figure 9.3 we have designated one system
as the user and the other as the resourcer without indicating which is sender and which is receiver. It should be
understood, however, that such labels are just as relative:
for one situation and one need, the system on the right
might be completely reversed. It could also be that they
are simultaneously in need of resources that can be provided
by the other, in which case they are both users and
resources to each other at the same time. This is the pure
barter situation; a happy circumstance, perhaps, but,
considering our previous analysis of the difficulties in
establishing arcs and links, probably a very rare one.

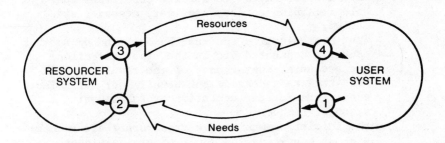

**Figure 9.3 Linkage as an inter-system dialog concerning needs and
resources**

Indeed, one of the most serious problems inherent in the needs-resources dialog is the requirement of providing incentives for resourcers that are either equivalent to those of users or at least sufficient to continue the resource flow. The resource-needs dialog can also be seen as bargaining or economic exchange. Each party in the exchange gives the other something of value that is sufficient to induce them to give an item of greater value to the recipient. The difficulty of establishing such an exchange relationship is greater when the two parties to the exchange are grossly unequal in power or resource wealth, as is typically the case when developed and developing countries attempt to form exchange relationships.

Analytically, Figure 9.3 illustrates four critical transfer points within the resource-needs dialog. Each is a "barrier"-crossing issue, either in terms of exiting from a system or entering one. Points also correspond to the sending and receiving demi-arcs illustrated in Figure 9.2. Transfer point #1 is the expression of needs. There are actually three related but distinct issues here. The first is the arousal of needs. Would-be user systems are not always either aware or concerned about certain needs that, from an outsider's perspective, are very serious. In the case of our hypothetical Saharan village, for example, high infant and child mortality may be seen as the hand of God and not something that it is either possible or appropriate to struggle against. It may take an unusual event like a flood or an invasion by another tribe to upset traditional explanations and make people open to change. Beyond arousal, there is the question of where aroused energies are to be directed. Self-reliance is a strong value in all cultures and help-seeking is usually viewed as a sign of dependence, immaturity, or weakness. We can well imagine that such inhibitions would be present for any would-be innovation seeker in the hypothetical technical school case: each community, after all, should be able to manage the rearing of its own youth, so why should we in this village go somewhere else to find a model for what we should do here? Even beyond the willingness to seek help is the issue of need articulation. Many people have trouble clearly indicating what their needs are to others; they may realize they have problems, that their system is not functioning well or as well as others are, but are yet unable to understand or to state what is wrong in ways that can be communicated effectively to others. Again the technical school case is instructive, looked at from the point of view of the potential user of this innovative development: how

will a village not having such a school be able to realize
what it is missing? The needs that such a school would
serve are many and diverse but not easily communicable
without having a clear vision of what the school would look
like. Thus we find that articulation is something that can
often come only <u>after</u> there is awareness of the resource and
what it can offer, something that would have to result from
a prior contact with the resource, a message reception of
some kind from the source. In considering this problem with
regard to small farmers in developing countries, Esman
(1974) has proposed that farmers' organizations have a very
important role to play in the articulation of needs as well
as in the diffusion of innovations and providing feedback on
such innovations to developers.

Another set of issues relates to transfer point #2 in
Figure 9.3, the entry of the need message into the would-be
resource system. Three issues in particular should be
noted, issues that correspond to those cited above for the
would-be user. First, there is the question of whether the
resourcer is open and attentive to messages coming from the
user. Do they care about the needs of others enough to take
the effort to listen? Secondly, if they do care, do they
have the capability of receiving such need messages?
Usually the more different the resourcer is from the user in
culture, role, and situation, the more difficulty there will
be in comprehending user need messages. Even if messages
are comprehended, there is yet a third resourcer problem
regarding the need message: will the resourcer be able to
connect up to the need message in meaningful ways with
resources that he has to offer?

Turning now to the resource transfer arc of Figure 9.3
there are two more potential trouble spots to consider: the
passage of resource messages out of the resourcer system
(transfer point #3) and the entry of such messages into the
user system (transfer point #4). For messages to leave the
resourcer system, the resourcer must have both the desire
and the capacity to send such messages. Our two hypothetical cases provide an interesting contrast on these two
points. For the Toronto chemist, capacity may be no
particular problem: he is fully cognizant of the details of
his invention and the technical subject matter and processes
from which it derives, but is he likely to have the desire?
The invention is outside his company's product line, and
there are no obvious potential users close at hand; thus any
return on his effort might well be a long time in coming, if
it comes at all. At the same time, his company may be
reluctant to have him publish findings that are derived from

processes in which it has a proprietary stake. In contrast,
the developers of the village technical school may have
great eagerness to tell others about their innovation for
the honor it bestows on their village and themselves.
Describing the innovation to others in anything like
adequate terms so that others can appreciate the achievement
and emulate it may be quite difficult in contrast.

Finally we should consider the problems that may arise
at the transit point #4 in Figure 9.3, the entry of the new
knowledge or resources into the user system. At least three
problems are of special importance: <u>desire</u>, <u>comprehension</u>,
and <u>application</u>. As with each other transfer point, there
must be some willingness or openness or motivation to
acquire the new resources. As we shall note in a subsequent
section of this paper, such motivation is likely to grow
over successive cycles of linking to the same resource
system, beginning merely with something we could call
"curiosity." However, after one such cycle, the user at
least must come to the recognition that the incoming message
might have some value to an internally recognized need,
whether or not the message is seen as a response to a
particular need message. Probably of our two hypothetical
cases the one that conveys the life-saving message about
drinking water has more motivational potency than the one
that tells of an improved form of schooling. Again, perhaps
in contrast, however, the message about a chemical substance
derived from plastics manufacture may be much harder for a
Saharan villager to comprehend than messages about teachers
and crafts and olders teaching youngers.

The third entry problem is probably the most difficult
and the one most persistently neglected, especially by
outside change agents. How can knowledge be applied in
useful ways to solve local problems, once it has been
accepted and understood? This is the essence of the problem
of knowledge utilization. It is likely to be a long process
involving many attempts to adapt the knowledge to meet the
local circumstances and the exact nature of the local need,
and it may end in ultimate failure even after many trials.
Let us suppose that the village has somehow managed to
understand the water purifying substance, has been
instructed in its use, and has acquired enough sample
material for a one-year tryout. Now it will have to
construct a special filtering basin and storage tanks where
water will not be recontaminated. Rules for maintaining the
system and for water usage will have to be developed and old
rules modified. Then after the year is out some means will
have to be developed for replenishing the supply on a

regular basis and so forth. Obviously, for many types of innovation the bulk of the problem is not receiving the message but putting it to meaningful and sustained use within the receiving and using social systems. Thus far in this section we have considered the meaning of the resourcer-user dialog primarily in terms of boundary-spanning issues either at the user end or the resource end. However, Figure 9.3 also poses additional issues related to the nature of "need" messages and "resources" messages and related to the media appropriate to carry them between user and resourcer. In this paper we will not attempt an elaborate classification of either, but a few observations on each should be made. First, resource and need messages are likely to fall into different categories. Resource messages cover a range from mere signals or hints that the resourcer system is capable of transmitting a certain type of resource under certain conditions all the way to packaged delivery of materials, training, personnel, instructions, and financing. How much of a message is truly needed obviously depends on the internal capacity of the user system. For our Saharan village, we might guess that a very complete package would be required; for the technical school perhaps only a reasonably full comprehension by one or two key educators or village leaders would be enough to start a process of adaptation of the school model.

Need messages also cover an enormous range, starting with mere signals that one has need for outside help. The depth, accuracy, and detail of need messages will also depend on the ability of the user to articulate needs and to differentiate levels and types of need. Need messages may also come as responses to resource messages, in which case they are typically referred to as "feedback" or "reactions." On the other hand, feedback in the sense of communication about the message or about the process of communication can come from either user or resourcer and may be sent and received over and over again.

Media can be broken down into three classes with regard to the resource-need dialog: media that are especially suited to the transfer of resource messages; media that are especially suited to the transfer of need messages; and media that are suitable to the transmission of both. In the first category are most types of mass media and mass production processes, including print and other forms of multiple copying of word messages, television, and radio. These mass processes are generally not as suitable for need communication, and they are generally poor for resource transfer steps at the application stage and after

(implementation, maintenance, sustained use). They can be
very effective, however, at creating initial understanding,
motivating first acceptance, and arousing need. Need
communication, in contrast, favors more personalized and
targetted media such as mailed correspondence, petitions,
orders, inquiries, complaints, and even protests delivered
by mail or telephone or face-to-face encounter. Such
face-to-face encounters are also the prime example of
two-way media suitable for exchange of both needs and
resource knowledge. Included in this category would be many
kinds of site visits (either to the user site or the
resource site), training sessions, and consultations. It is
generally the case that strong linkages cannot be built
without the utilization of a mix of media going both ways
and a strong dose of two-way media at critical junctures
such as the first behavioral trial of the innovation.

LINKAGE AS THE INTER-PENETRATION OF
PROBLEM-SOLVING SYSTEMS

Linkage theory takes as a starting assumption that all
persons and all cultures are problem-solving systems unto
themselves with their own internal needs and their own
internal resources as well as internal procedural routines
and connections through which problems are solved and needs
met. The Saharan village may have existed even in its
present form for many centuries with its own means of
rearing children, acquiring food, managing internal
conflict, caring for the sick and the aged, and warding off
threats from weather, animals, and unwelcome human
intruders. It may go on within certain definitions of
success in this same fashion for many years to come.
Changing the ways of this village through the intrusion of
new ideas or technologies may be of some benefit, but
experience of would-be change agents suggests that the
potential for disruption to these long-standing patterns of
self-sufficiency may bring more harm than good. This is a
frustrating and sad learning from intercultural exchange
efforts aimed at the "improvement" or the "development" of
one culture at the hands of another and with the initiative
of another.

There is also an equivalent truth about resourcers as
problem-solving systems that is even more frequently
overlooked. Let us take the plastics firm in Toronto for
which our chemist-inventor works. It probably has not been
in existence as long as that village, but it has a clear

226

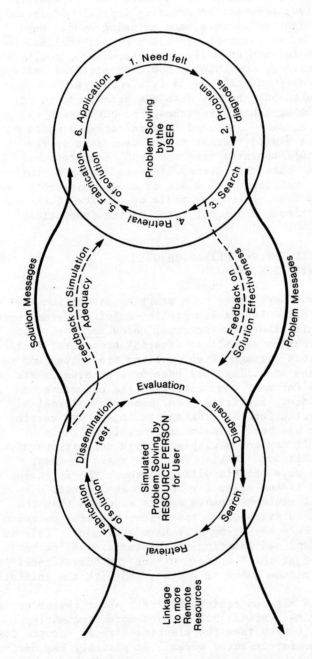

Figure 9.4 Mutual penetration and simulation of problem solving

institutional structure with an elaborate division of roles and responsibilities, many of which might inhibit the transfer of the invention to others. Yet all these rules and regulations are in place for a reason, to help this company continue to function, to keep its manufacturing processes private so that it can retain its special advantage in the marketplace, to keep its mission clear so that all members can understand it and continue to work for it, to keep everyone employed, and to keep the investors satisfied. All these organizational features contributed in one way or another toward creating the stable internal environment in which the chemist could go quietly about his work, perhaps over many years, leading to the discovery in question.

Such stalwart independence on both sides has its limitations, of course. All systems are thoroughly and continuously dependent on outside resources and outside markets for what they produce. Thus, they all have well-developed mechanisms of communication with other systems in their environment. Yet what is special about linkage theory is its explanation of how altogether new connections are formed, connections that extend perhaps to far-away resourcers and far-away users outside the normal working environment. What we are looking at is the way in which one system can send other messages that penetrate the self-protective layers and become planted in the on-going routines and problem-solving processes of the other. Figure 9.4 suggests another way of looking at the linkage relationship, this time emphasizing this aspect of system inter-penetration.

Each system is depicted as a circle. The circumference represents the many barriers that are established by all organic systems to keep things out and other things in and to preserve the integrity of the whole. The arrows inside represent internal connections between persons and/or processes and functions which constitute the operating routines of the system. The particular designations used convey the steps that might be involved in a more-or-less rational cycle of problem-solving. Note, however, that the figure is drawn to indicate only the direct self-centered problem-solving of the user system, whereas the counterpart cycle in the resourcer is a simulated cycle stimulated by the resourcer's interpretation of the user's need and appreciation of the user's circumstances.

According to Chantran (1972, as cited by Diaz-Bordenave 1974) French change agents working on development projects have long insisted that two kinds of research were necessary

228

in support of their work in rural areas: (1) studies on
farmer characteristics and environment and (2) studies on
their "technology," i.e., the ways in which they solved
problems, defined and carried out tasks, used tools, and
established methods of doing things. What Chantran and
Diaz-Bordenave were talking about is partially illustrated
in Figure 9.4. In our example of the Saharan village,
whoever would want to introduce some new water filtering
technology will have to know what these people do now about
water filtering, water acquisition, water storage and
distribution, and water use. One would also need to know
about more generic processes of decision-making and
knowledge use in the village: who makes decisions on what
issues? what are established channels by which new
knowledge is acquired from outside?

Ideally there is a counterpart requirement on the part
of would-be resource users to understand and to simulate the
problem-solving processes of resource systems, at least at
some level. This is especially the case when resource
systems are offering scientifically validated innovations
such as those emanating from the network of research centers
around the world that specialize in experimentation with new
crop varieties and growing methods for developing countries.
It is important for potential users to know, first of all,
that such innovations have a basis in the carefully measured
and tested experience of others. To have such an appreciation, the users will have to have some minimal understanding
for what scientific investigation is and how it differs from
random speculation and unmeasured experience. Even in the
most developed countries only a minority of persons have
much appreciation of what scientific knowledge is, as
distinct from other kinds of knowledge, and the value placed
upon such knowledge and its derivative products and skills
is generally not as great as it should be.

THE DEVELOPMENT OF LINKAGE OVER TIME

It is also important to understand linkage as an
iterative process involving many communicative arcs spread
over a period of time. In the early stages, the substantive
content of transferred messages may be minimal, establishing
only awareness of the other, providing only minor or symbolic or anticipatory rewards for each party. Yet such
early communicative links are essential as a basis for later
ones. They can be seen as the setting up process; the
definition of limits and capabilities on both sides; the

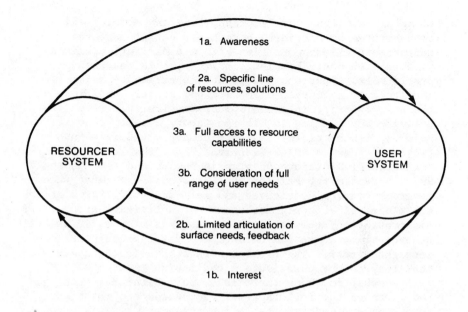

Figure 9.5   Iterations in linkage development

scope of message content and form, the media that will have
to be used, the additional resources required, and the depth
of change expected. It could be called the "contract"
phase, although the contract may be mostly unwritten and may
change as the parties get to know one another better.

Figure 9.5 suggests the pattern by which linkage is
likely to develop over time if it is successful. It should
be noted that unsatisfactory communication in either
direction at the early stages is likely to terminate the
relationship. At later stages, however, missed cues or
inadequate rewards are more likely to lead to regressions to
earlier types of communication, to recheck the lines as it
were, to make sure that earlier assumptions about the other
and about the proper means of communication with the other
are still correct.

The second major stage in the development of linkage is
the first substantial resource transaction in which problem-
relevant resources of some significance are successfully
received and tried out in the user system. This is the
stage to which most attention tends to be directed by those
who promote innovation projects around the world, particularly projects of the "campaign" variety. Kearl (1976), for

example, describes the "packaged programs model," which concentrates on providing a complete set of resource supports to client countries within a carefully defined problem area where knowledge of results is reasonably predictable. Such approaches assume extensive prior knowledge of cultural, climatic, and social conditions in the host country, in other words, considerable stage one activity and linking in linkage theory terms. A number of major instances of the approach can be cited, the Puebla Project in Mexico (Diaz-Cisneros 1974), the Intensive Agricultural Districts Program in India, and the "Masagana 99" program in the Philippines (Drilon 1974). When such programs are well-conceived and well-financed, they include all manner of supports for users and anticipate problems of implementation; they also employ a great many media as well as activation of social networks to get the essential messages across. The problem with such efforts, however, is that they do not constitute a continuing linkage relationship in which there is a truly bilateral exchange and in which the full range of user needs and resourcer resources are made available for transfer.

In reference to Figure 9.5, therefore, linkage theory would propose a third and a fourth stage. At the third stage, the two systems take account of what they have learned about each other so far and seek meaningful follow-up to make the relationship more balanced and more permanent. In the fourth stage, the systems develop a full appreciation for what they can provide for one another. There are multiple ties of different subgroups and individuals, and a variety of needs of both systems are served with "user" and "resourcer" distinctions either shifting back and forth from one to the other or perhaps disappearing. In a real sense, when this stage is reached the two systems have functionally become one.

INTERMEDIARIES: THE ROLE OF THE LINKER

The many difficulties regarding the development of linkage point strongly to the need for many kinds of mediating roles and mechanisms to assist linkage processes. Such roles may be different for different need and resource domains, and they may also be different at different stages in the growth of a relationship. We would like to begin this discussion by distinguishing between what might be called "natural intermediaries" and "specialized linkers."

The basic principle underlying natural connections is

homophily, the similarity of sender and receiver on key
characteristics related to sending and receiving capacities
and motivation, internal problem-solving, and messages held
and wanted.[4] The principle states simply that the more
similarity, the easier will be the transit of messages in
either direction. This is clearly not true in all
circumstances, of course. · For example, if two identical
systems have goals that are identical but mutually exclusive
(as in a zero sum game situation: "if I win, you must lose"
and vice versa), then effective interchange may be blocked
in spite of or even because of similarities. On the other
hand, the great majority of situations of social interaction
are not of this nature.

The pervasiveness and importance of the homophily
principle creates a paradox of great significance for
innovation communication, a paradox that has intrigued
communication theorists such as Rogers (1976) and
Granovetter (1973, 1982): the more similar two systems are
to each other, the less they will have to say to each other
that is new. Conversely, the more different two systems,
the more they will have to say to each other that is new and
perhaps useful or potentially useful for system improvement.
Let us take our first example of the Toronto chemist and the
Saharan village. The two settings are about as different
from one another as any on earth, and this makes communication between them in any direct way virtually impossible:
there are language barriers, cultural differences, differences in resources and capacities, and in social and
economic context, which are staggering. Yet one could learn
a great deal from the other. The Africans, of course, could
learn about a great many technologies and about scientific
knowledge and the development of products, about the
management of enterprises, and so forth. What could the
chemist learn? Probably he could learn a great deal about
survival processes under extreme conditions, about family
ties, human interdependence; above all, he could learn much
more about the true dimensions of the problems we face as
humanity, the needs that we must somehow someday work on
collectively so that a bountiful life can be shared by all.

What is remarkable is that we have begun in a few
instances around the world to bridge gaps as wide as the one
between the Saharan village and the chemist, and in large
part we have been able to do this through what might be
called the semi-homophilic chain. Figure 9.6a depicts the
pure homophilic situation. As in Figure 9.1, A starts with
message x but his target is not an unknown B but his
identical twin A_2. A_1 can be sure that A_2 will have both

232

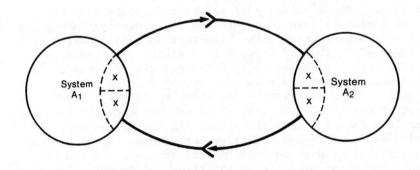

Figure 9.6a   Pure homophilic transfer arcs

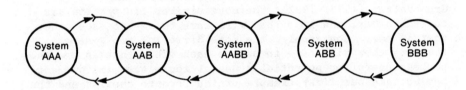

Figure 9.6b   The semi-homophilic chain

the desire and the capacity to receive the message x and
will also have a place to hold it, once it has been
received. We might imagine that A_2 is a physician who is
called to examine a patient without having his kit. Needing
a stethoscope, he acquires one from another physician
standing nearby. The two physicians in this case are
functionally homophilous with the exception that one has a
stethoscope and the other does not. There is no question,
however, that A_2 has both the need and the capability to use
the stethoscope, once he has received it. Subsequently,
having used it and recognizing that A_1 is now deprived of
it, A_2 will feel the pressure to return it and in doing so
will also have full knowledge that A_1 has both a desire and
a capacity to receive it and a place (in his kit) to keep
it, once received. Now consider Figure 9.6b. If we assume
that the desired objective is to transfer message x from
system AAA to a system with very different characteristics,
"BBB", an obvious means to this end is to have intervening
systems with characteristics partially shared with both

systems. In terms of our very different Saharan village and
Toronto chemist, a possible scenario fitting Figure 9.6b
might go something like this. The chemist publishes his
findings in a chemical journal which happens to be read by
another chemist who works in public health and specializes
in water purification. This chemist works out a practical
proposal for how the substance could be used in the water
system of a small community, and he publishes this analysis
in a public health journal. In developing his analysis, he
might well correspond with the Toronto chemist, and he might
elicit his reactions to a draft manuscript. The resulting
publication might come to the attention of a public health
official working for an international development agency,
who in turn might share it with public health representatives from the poor countries on the edge of the Sahara.
One of these officials might be especially intrigued with
the idea and might try to influence members of his own home
village to try it out. If it succeeds in this village, some
other villages might be induced to follow the example, no
doubt learning from the mistakes as well as the achievements
of the first village. Each successive link on this chain
introduces an intermediary who has some characteristics in
common with the sender and others that form a bridge to
subsequent users. It should further be noted that as the
message passes, it is transformed successively into something that is more and more directly useful and finally
use-tested before it reaches the originally designated
remote village. At the user end of the chain, it is also
important to note the likelihood, demonstrated in thousands
of diffusion studies, that most of those who ultimately
adopt an innovation will do so because other social units
with strongly similar characteristics have previously
adopted. In this case, the social unit is the village. One
village stands out as the innovator village, in large part
because it was the home or birthplace of a public health
official but also probably because its leaders were slightly
more innovative than the leaders of other villages to begin
with. In any case, it had the advantage over other villages
of having better contacts with outside knowledge sources.

If all knowledge generated in the world followed such a
smooth natural path as that hypothesized for the water
purifier, there would be little need for special interventions or social inventions to improve the process of
linkage. There is every evidence from countless empirical
studies that the "natural" process does work and works more
or less as described in the example. However, there is
another side to this story: most chains that might lead to

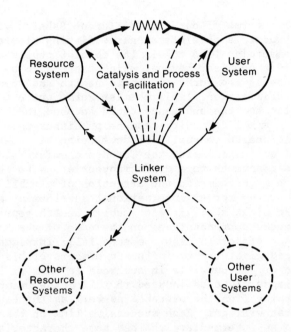

Figure 9.7   Some alternative linker functions

human benefits never get there and most others get there
long after they might have. The natural process of linkage
is generally slow, inefficient, error-prone, and costly.
Furthermore, there are many links along potential knowledge-
use chains that are either dangerously weak or missing
altogether. That is why there is a great need to provide
specialists in various linkage processes at various
strategic points along the knowledge chain.

Figure 9.7 suggests some of the ways in which the
linker role can work to improve the flow of messages along
the knowledge chain. A specialized linker can be thought of
as some intermediary person or agency who improves the flow
of messages in either direction between would-be researcher
and a would-be user. A linker can assist the process at any
point along a knowledge chain and at any point among the
several elements that go to make up a message arc and a link
as discussed in sections 1 and 2 of this paper.
Essentially, the specialized linker can either <u>substitute</u>
for weak or missing elements or can <u>strengthen</u> weak or
misdirected elements. Although the range of possibilities
for linking roles is very great, some types deserve special

comment. Eight such roles are identified here to give some
indication of the range of possibilities: (1) the relay
station, (2) the transformer, (3) the synthesizer, (4) the
locator, (5) the implementation assister, (6) the user
system mobilizer, (7) the linkage catalyst, and (8) the
linkage process facilitator.

The Relay Station

Perhaps the most simple and the most obvious linker
role is the passing on of a message in the form that it was
received. If the resourcer and the user are widely separated
or if they have very different characteristics (lack of
homophily), the relay function can be vital. A linker could
relay only resource messages or only need messages; less
typically they can relay both. A significant variation on
the relay role is the broadcaster, one who takes a single
message from one source and reproduces it to send to many
receivers. Journal and book publishers play this role.

The Transformer

Major message transfer issues relate to the suitability
of the message for the medium and for the receiving and
holding capabilities of potential users. The simplest
transformation is probably translation, where the message is
changed from one language or one medium to another. More
elaborate transformations include the reshaping of the
message in some way (e.g., to make it more interesting,
attractive, or clear for the receiver to understand).
Transformation functions apply equally to resource and to
need messages. The extent of transformation that is
required to span large differences in need and circumstance
between resourcers and users is almost always
underestimated.

The Synthesizer

As suggested in Figure 9.7, the linker may be in a
position to connect users with more than one resourcer and
to serve as a funnel for message transfer from a number of
sources. If the user receives a single transformed message,
then the linker has taken the trouble to put the two
resource messages together in some way that will be helpful

to the user. Synthesis is perhaps the most complicated and most demanding task that a linker can perform because, in effect, it is the act of creating an entirely new message in service to the user. Synthesis may also be performed by a linker using messages from the resourcer and the user. Let us take, for example, the case of the innovative technical school. An educational consultant observes the school in one country and later sees a village situation in another country where the same school configuration might work, but here there is a different climate and a different set of economic and social conditions. The skilled synthesizer will be able to read those conditions (need messages) and find the points in the school design where substitutions and alterations are required, providing the user village with a plan already partially adapted to its situation and its needs.

The Locator

Every individual person and every social unit in the world has (a) needs that are unmet and (b) resources in excess that might be helpful in meeting someone else's needs. To some extent there are "natural" networks that connect everyone with everyone else, but these networks are very weakly connected in some places, especially between cultures, and when they are present they can operate very slowly. Thus there will always be a need for linkers who merely identify needs and resources and try to match them up. The role is similar to the relay station role discussed above but involves a much more elaborate and proactive search process on both resource and need sides. It is probably most frequent to find locators who are either resource locators or need locators but not both at the same time. This is a practical matter: it is far easier to concentrate on one product line or one need domain where one can be both expert and visible and then to expend one's energies fanning out to locate the multitude on the other side. A well-functioning knowledge system requires many of both types of locator-linkers.

The Implementation Assister

In the last decade, studies of knowledge utilization have tended to become more and more concerned with what happens to knowledge after it has been received and what

happens to innovations after they have been adopted. Along
with this increased concern has also come the realization
that an important linker role is providing technical
assistance to would-be users at various stages after they
have received new knowledge, assistance with such issues as
adaptation to local conditions, gaining wider internal
system acceptance (e.g., getting the whole village to accept
the idea of a new technical school rather than just the
educational leaders), developing new skills and recruiting
personnel to maintain the innovation after adoption,
developing routines and procedures for integration within
the existing structure, and so forth. In many ways, this
has been an appropriate trend in emphasis, but it raises
some serious practical and ethical questions. On the
practical side, the further the linker goes in assisting the
client, the more costly each client relationship becomes,
and, in effect, the fewer the number of clients that can be
served. Somehow a balance must be struck between providing
effective service to individual users and providing services
to sufficient numbers of clients to make such rare services
of benefit to the many. A second practical problem is the
danger of creating excessive dependency, induced incapacity
resulting from too heavy reliance on others to perform
problem-solving tasks that the system can as well or better
perform for itself. The related ethical question resides in
the danger that the user can be corrupted or undermined in
its own problem-solving capacities and in its very integrity
as a system by the excessive intrusion of the "assister."
Developing nations are continuously and rightfully
suspicious of both the developed nations and the Soviet bloc
countries on such grounds.

The User System Mobilizer

Another type of "linkage" that can be seen from some
angles as highly intrusive on the user system is the
mobilization of concern within the user system toward the
expression of collective needs and aspirations. Here the
linker is dealing with the earliest stages of the need
communication arc, bringing people together to recognize
common needs, to articulate these needs, and to communicate
them forcefully, sometimes through strong protest actions
directed at persons or groups seen as obligated to provide
resources. Such animators are likely to be seen as "outside
agitators" by ruling elites and are generally controversial.
Nevertheless, such stimulation is probably a prerequisite in

many communities to the initiation of any resource linking
efforts.

The Linkage Catalyst

A type of linking role that can frequently be seen to
operate informally is what might be called the linkage
catalyst, someone who brings together resourcers and users
and creates happy marriages between them. Catalysts and
locators might be somewhat similar, but the catalyst is one
who gets out of the way, once the connection is formed,
mediating only at the initial stages.

The Linkage Process Facilitator

Considering the many steps and conditions necessary to
achieve inter-system linkage and the many places in the
process where something can go wrong, it would seem that
there would be a place for specialists in the process of
linking, per se. These persons would not themselves act as
locators or catalysts or technical assisters in any
substantive sense but would assist and advise on various
problems of connecting. Such consultation would presumably
start with diagnostic analysis of the current inter-system
relationship and move on to the provision of specific
guidance or training only in areas of weakness, whether
these be on the resource arc side or the need arc side, in
the message, the medium, the capabilities and motivations of
the resourcer or the capabilities and motivations of the
user system. In effect, such a consultant or trainer would
take to heart what has been said in these pages concerning
the process of linkage, applying the concepts discussed here
in diagnostic fashion and developing training and support to
strengthen connections accordingly.[5]

LINKAGE SYSTEM DEVELOPMENT

Up to this point, this paper has been largely
theoretical, although the basic principles are simple and
the connections to practical situations reasonably obvious.
The time now comes to ask where such reasoning leads us in
practical terms and in terms of understanding and improving
the functioning of the worldwide knowledge system. First of
all, it is to be hoped that the linkage construct can

provide an especially useful perspective on the knowledge system and how it works, especially on the connections between the knowledge system and the practical concerns of humanity. If it is a useful construct, then we would expect those who study the knowledge system to use it in their work and this seems increasingly to be the case. It is noteworthy, for example, that Rogers, in his latest edition of <u>The Diffusion of Innovations</u> (1983), starts his chapter on change agents with the heading "change agents as linkers" and proceeds to provide a synopsis of the needs-resources (innovations) dialog with the linkage agent as the key intermediary mechanism.

Numerous studies of change agent and agencies in action further suggest the value of specialized roles fulfilling one or more of the functions described in the previous section. Most notably the Cooperative Extension Service, which serves the agriculture and rural farm sector in the United States, is an example of a well-developed linkage system in which there are specialist roles covering many if not all of the functions identified here (see, for example, Sanders 1966 and Rogers, Eveland, and Bean 1976). Also of note is the National Diffusion Network developed in the United States in the 1970s as a diffusion-utilization linkage system for scientifically validated educational innovations (Emrick, Peterson, and Agarwala-Rogers 1977; Crandall and others 1982). Particular systems, like other innovations, probably need considerable transformation and adaptation when they are considered in other national and topical contexts, but it is interesting that studies of such systems overwhelmingly support the validity of the linkage construct and the desirability of designing intermediary mechanisms to promote linkage.

Looking to the international arena and particularly to the issues related to Third World development, there would appear to be a special need and a special promise in moving toward a knowledge resource linking network, building on elements that already exist in partial form today. Five tasks lie immediately ahead of us if we are to move constructively in this direction. First, we need to define the array of linkage functions, as we have begun to do in this paper, but to do so more thoroughly and with an attempt to reach some kind of consensus on what the categories and labels should be. To this task must be added the important research and documentation tasks of assembling what is now known under each heading. Such a knowledge base would be the first step toward developing skill training and consulting guidance within each area.

Second, we need to begin to identify a worldwide group of experienced consultants who have and are continuing to provide consultation and training on linkage processes. This group has to be made more acutely aware of their common mission in a process sense and has to be provided with means of sharing their experience.

Third, with the help of the worldwide network we need to establish training centers where linkage skills can be taught with greater competence and precision to a new generation of consultants and trainers.

Fourth, we need to begin to redesign development programs and technical assistance efforts in all fields to reflect linkage principles and the empirical research base on linkage processes.

Finally, we need to develop at the highest levels of national leadership in all countries, North—South, East—West, a macro-policy perspective that reflects the resourcer—user dialog and other linkage principles as guiding concepts and as appropriate models for international relations.

NOTES

1. Much of the analytic work supporting theoretical formulations in this and following sections was conducted under a grant from the National Science Foundation: "Formulation of New Bridges between Basic and Applied Disciplines" (Havelock, in preparation).

2. Schools exhibiting many of these characteristics have been reported in the literature from time to time, e.g., Orata 1972.

3. This concept was first developed and elaborated in Havelock 1969; it was subsequently elaborated in terms of Third World development in Havelock and Huberman 1978.

4. The homophily principle and its major correlates have been discussed at length by Rogers and Shoemaker (1971).

5. A practical handbook for linkers was developed by Havelock (1973) and alternative models for training programs by Havelock and Havelock (1973). Hood (1982) reviews recent studies in education.

REFERENCES

Berlo, D. K. 1960. The Process of Communication. New
York: Holt, Rinehart, and Winston.

Chantran, P. 1972. La Vulgarisation Agricole en Afrique et
a Madagascar. Paris: G.P. Maisonneuve et Larose.

Crandall, D. P., and Associates. 1982. People, Policies
and Practices: Examining the Chain of School Improvement. 10 vols. Andover, Mass.: The NETWORK Inc.

Crawford, R. H., and W. B. Ward, eds. 1974. Communication
Strategies for Rural Development: Proceedings of the
Cornell-CIAT International Symposium. Ithaca, N.Y.:
New York State College of Agriculture and Life
Sciences.

Diaz-Bordenave, J. 1974. "Communication and Adoption of
Agricultural Innovations in Latin America." In Com-
munication Strategies for Rural Development, ed. R. H.
Crawford and W. B. Ward. Ithaca, N.Y.: New York State
College of Agriculture and Life Sciences.

Diaz-Cisneros, H. 1974. "An Institutional Analysis of a
Rural Development Project: The Case of the Puebla
Project in Mexico." Ph.D. diss., University of
Wisconsin.

Drilon, J. D., Jr. 1974. "The Spreading of New Rice
Varieties--Then and Now." In Communication Strategies
for Rural Development, ed. R. H. Crawford and W. B.
Ward. Ithaca, N.Y.: New York State College of
Agriculture and Life Sciences.

Emrick, J. A., S. M. Peterson, and R. Agarwala-Rogers.
1977. Evaluation of the National Diffusion Network. 2
vols. Menlo Park, Calif.: Stanford Research Institute.

Esman, M. J. 1974. "Popular Participation and Feedback
Systems in Rural Development." In Communication
Strategies for Rural Development, ed. R. H. Crawford
and W. B. Ward. Ithaca, N.Y.: New York State College
of Agriculture and Life Sciences.

Granovetter, M. S. 1982. "The Strength of Weak Ties: A
Network Theory Revised." In Social Structure and
Network Analysis, ed. P. V. Marsden and N. Lin.
Beverly Hills, Calif.: Sage Publications.

_____. 1973. "The Strength of Weak Ties." American
Journal of Sociology 78, no. 6: 1360-1380.

Harary, F., and R. G. Havelock. 1972. "The Anatomy of a
Communication Arc." Human Relations 25, no. 5:
413-426.

Havelock, R. G. 1973. The Change Agent's Guide to
Innovation. Englewood Cliffs, N.J.: Educational
Technology Publications.

Havelock, R. G., in collaboration with A. Guskin and others.
1969. Planning for Innovation through the Dissemi-
nation and Utilization of Knowledge. Ann Arbor:
Center for Research on Utilization of Scientific
Knowledge, Institute for Social Research, University of
Michigan.

Havelock, R. G., in collaboration with F. Harary. Monograph
in preparation. Formation of New Bridges between Basic
and Applied Disciplines. Research study supported
under National Science Foundation Grant #DS177-17934
1977-1980.

Havelock, R. G., and M. C. Havelock. 1973. The Training of
Change Agents. Ann Arbor: Center for Research on
Utilization of Scientific Knowledge, Institute for
Social Research, University of Michigan.

Havelock, R. G., and A. M. Huberman. 1978. Solving Educational Problems: The Theory and Reality of Innovation
in Developing Countries. Paris: Unesco Press.

Hood, P. D. 1982. The Role of Linking Agents in School
Improvement: A Review, Analysis and Synthesis of Recent
Major Studies. San Francisco: Far West Laboratory for
Educational Research and Development.

Kearl, B. E. 1976. "Communication for Agricultural
Development." In Communication and Change, ed. W.
Schramm and D. Lerner. Honolulu: University Press of
Hawaii.

Orata, P. T. 1972. _Self-Help Barrio High Schools: The Story of 250,000 Students Earning Their Education and Preparing Themselves for Life._ Singapore: Eastern Universities Press.

Rogers, E. M. 1976. "Where Are We in Understanding the Diffusion of Innovations?" In _Communication and Change_, ed. W. Schramm and D. Lerner. Honolulu: University Press of Hawaii.

_____. 1983. _The Diffusion of Innovations_, 3d ed. New York: Free Press.

Rogers, E. M., J. D. Eveland, and A. S. Bean. 1976. _Extending the Agricultural Extension Model._ Stanford, Calif.: Stanford University, Institute for Communication Research.

Rogers, E. M., with F. F. Shoemaker. 1971. _The Communication of Innovations: A Cross-cultural Approach._ New York: Free Press.

Sanders, H. C., ed. 1966. _The Cooperative Extension Service._ Englewood Cliffs, N.J.: Prentice-Hall.

Schramm, W., and D. Lerner, eds. 1976. _Communication and Change: The Last Ten Years and the Next._ Honolulu: University Press of Hawaii.

10

Knowledge Utilization:
An Attempt to Relativate
Some Reified Realities

Niels G. Röling

My favorite story about knowledge generation-utilization processes concerns a group of monkeys in Japan. They live on the coast of one of the islands and are apparently quite tame: they are fed regularly with grain which is thrown out on the beach. For a long time, one could observe the monkeys carefully picking the grains out of a handful of sand, then, "knowledge generation." A clever female discovered that a handful of sand mixed with grain thrown into the water makes it very easy to scoop the grains clean from the surface. Soon others followed her, especially other females and young monkeys. Older males turned out to be quite resistant to change. Nevertheless, the discovery and subsequent utilization of the new knowledge had quite profound consequences: the group of monkeys gradually became habituated to the water and began to occupy a new ecological niche as they lost their fear and acquired a taste for seaweed.

Most cases of knowledge utilization do not, of course, involve animals but people. In fact, knowledge generation and utilization are the very essence of human development. Says Julian Huxley (1957, 44):

It appears that between five and ten million years ago, the possibilities of major improvement in the material and physiological properties of self-reproducing matter had been exhausted. The purely biological phase of evolution on this planet had reached its upper limit, and natural selection was no longer capable of producing any further large advance....beyond existing levels of organization....The new evolutionary method which became available...was the method of transmission and transformation of tradition. This

method of communication by concept and symbol provided
an additional mechanism of inheritance involving the
cumulative transmission of acquired experience, and
permitted a much speedier and in many ways more
effective type of evolutionary transformation, which we
may call cultural evolution.

According to Bronowski (1973, 35):

It took at least two million years for man to change
from the little creature with the stone in his hand,
Australopithecus in Central Africa, to the modern form,
Homo sapiens. That is the pace of biological
evolution—even though the biological evolution of man
has been faster than that of any other animal. But it
has taken less than twenty thousand years for Homo
sapiens to become the creatures that you and I aspire
to be....That is the pace of cultural evolution: once
it takes off it goes...at least a hundred times faster
than biological evolution.

MAN'S RELATIONSHIP TO THE ENVIRONMENT

Speaking thus of evolution there is a clear implication
of a dimension of progress: from foraging hunter, to nomad,
to agriculturalist, to industrialist. From being part of
nature and being able to adapt to it—and thus surviving at
the price of being captured by the environment—man moved to
control and manipulate the environment. "Man has a set of
gifts which make him unique among animals, so that, unlike
them, he is not a figure in the landscape but a shaper of
it...he did not find but made his home in every continent"
(Bronowski 1973, 13).

The relationship with the environment can thus take
two forms: adaptation and manipulation. In the former
case, man adapts his wishes to the circumstances; in the
latter, he adapts his circumstances to suit his wishes.
Development increases manipulation at the cost of
adaptation, and knowledge generation and utilization can be
seen as man's main instruments of development and evolution.
Indeed, the incredible increase in human numbers across the
globe in recent years can only be explained by the
utilization of medical and other knowledge in developing
nations which increased the control over the environment and
made it more conducive to human life.

It is from such thinking that we have also come to define man's mind as the harbinger of "reality": a representational construct which allows man to predict and control. Though we treat reality as "objective truth out there," for all practical intents and purposes, we all know that reality is a human construct while we reckon wishful thinking, ideology, doctrine, such basic drives as hunger, and our training, among the forces which shape it.

"Reality is not passively received. It does not imprint itself on the mind. It is slowly constructed through active, varied and persistent exploration, and what is learned about it is how to deal with it: what actions produce what effects on what objects" (White 1963, 186). According to Cantril (1965, 11), reality is "the pattern of assumptions which increase the correspondence between what man perceives in the environment and what his environment turns out to be when he acts within it to experience some intended consequences." According to Kelly (1963, 50), man is equipped with a representational system with which he constructs a replication of his environment with the ultimate aim to predict and control.

MAN-THE-SCIENTIST

It is for this reason that Kelly uses the scientist as his model of man: it is science which embodies the essence of man's evolutionary method through knowledge generation and utilization. Reality is as relative as a scientific model or theory, except that we tend to reify it to a point where it no longer fits the outcomes we experience. Howell (1979) has alluded to the "blinding insight syndrome" preventing us from uttering that mind-opening phrase: "let us suppose..." (Berlo 1960).

A typical example of reification, also in our training, is the circle. We are told that there is such a thing as a circle and that it has 360 degrees. In fact, the circle was invented by our ancestors in prehistoric times and arbitrarily divided into 360 degrees by Babylonian astronomers some 5,000 years ago. They arrived at this system after they had defined the year as approximately 360 days (Wilford 1981, 20). So we accept man-the-scientist who controls nature as our point of departure in discussing development, and from this reality we focus on the generation and utilization of knowledge as prime processes of development. The suffering masses of man-the-scientists in the Third World require better access to knowledge and assistance in utilizing it as prerequisites for improving their condition. Is it possible to question this reality? Have we reified it to become a blinding insight? Can we relativate it by saying: "let us suppose..."?

If we make such a bold attempt, we must again go back to the dawn of man's existence. Says Bronowski (1973, 25):

> ...And with that larger brain the ancestors of man made two major inventions, for one of which we have visible evidence and for the other inferential evidence. First the visible invention: Two million years ago Australopithecus made rudimentary stone tools where a simple blow has put an edge on the pebble. And for the next million years, man in his further evolution did not change this type of tool. He had made the fundamental invention, the purposeful act which prepares and stores pebbles for later use....The other invention is social, and we infer it by simple arithmetic. Skulls and skeletons of Australopithecus that have now been found in largish numbers show that most of them died before the age of twenty. That means that there must have been many orphans. For Australopithecus surely had a long childhood, as all the primates do: at the age of ten the survivors were still children. Therefore there must have been social organization in which children were looked after and (as it were) adopted, were made part of the community and so in some general sense were educated.

MAN-THE-VILLAGER

The stone tool is the symbol of control, of mind over matter, of man-the-scientist, whereas the second intervention, the social organization, is symbolic of a very different sort of man: the social animal, the participant in a community, the member of a tribe, the element in a social system living in a man-made environment. We shall use man-the-villager as the symbol for this second type of reality.

Where man-the-scientist emphasizes what Buber (1958) called the "I-It" relationship, man-the-villager emphasized the "I-You" relationship. The question is whether development is better served by looking at man as a potential controller of his environment or by looking at man as a member of a community living in a man-made environment. It goes without saying that such a shift in emphasis would greatly affect our definition of "reality" and the role of knowledge generation and utilization in development.

Man-the-scientist seeks to predict. He diagnoses the causes for the gap between his wants and his gets and seeks to remove them systematically. The level of his technology is the limiting factor, so we can assist him by giving technical assistance. Man-the-villager is in a different predicament. Although he too seeks to equalize his wants and gets, his methods are completely different. He cannot predict the reactions of his object of manipulation for it is reactive. He therefore relies on "intelligence" gathering, on gaming, on strategies, and to achieve what he wants he uses brute force, power, sympathy and esteem, voluntary exchange of values and love.

If man-the-scientist is the relevant model for development, the problems that the (rural) poor in the Third World experience would be reducible to the lack of control over their environment, to be solved by technical assistance to increase productivity, combat disease, harness water supplies, produce consumer goods, and so forth.

If man-the-villager is the relevant model, the problems of development would be reducible to such man-made causes as distribution of resources, lack of access. war, environmental pollution, induced poverty, oppression, exploitation, low prices and unbridled procreation.

It seems to me that the development of our mainstream civilization may have reached a discontinuity: our progress as a species is no longer served as much by further control over our environment as by increasing control over ourselves, our institutions and the consequences of being villagers with an atom bomb. Although I myself am rather firmly rooted in the man-the-scientist tradition, for my children man-the-villager seems much more relevant.

Let us suppose...that man-the-villager is a more appropriate model. What does that mean? How would such a supposition change our perspective on knowledge generation and utilization with a view to intervening to improve the condition of the rural poor in the Third World?

We could no longer assume that there is a vast reservoir of potentially useful knowledge which, if only it could be utilized, would solve most development problems, so that it is our duty to deliver this knowledge to the rural poor through a clever use of media. The problems of man-the-villager seem unsolved by a better delivery of ready-made knowledge. Instead our interventions would need to be predicated upon the following assumptions:

1. The environment upon which we intervene is man-made
and the objects of our intervention are people and
their behavior. We do not seek to teach individuals to
better control the resources available to them. rather
we seek to permanently affect social processes in
directions that seem more conducive to improving the
relative position of the rural poor. Knowledge
utilization in the case of man-the-villager is not the
individual application of some techniques, but a change
in the social system. Typically, utilization does not
lead to technical change but to organizational or
institutional change (Hesseling 1979). Realizing such
change poses a largely unsolved problem for those
interested in promoting utilization.

2. One implication is that we cannot use a blueprint
approach but must use a process approach (Sweet and
Weisel 1979). The environment upon which we intervene
is reactive, if not turbulent (Emery 1977). Therefore,
the reactions of the environment to our intervention
are unpredictable so that we cannot plan the intervention beforehand and implement it later. We must
follow a different strategy: relying on continual
intelligence gathering, we proceed in open-ended
manner, probing as we go along and building where it
seems possible and effective.

3. Knowledge utilization is not the consequence of
sock-it-to-them rationale of existing knowledge. which
is disseminated, delivered, made accessible, extended,
demonstrated and so forth. Knowledge utilization is
the consequence of linkage (Havelock 1969) between the
system having the problem and the system capable of
assembling solutions or opportunities. Both have an
essential role to play in utilization: the one provides
information on needs, constraints, available resources,
and so on. the other information on possibilities for
solving problems. Typical linkage concepts are
participation, dialogue, farming system research,
appropriate technology and user control.

4. Solving problems of the poor may be predicated upon
providing assistance in the realm of knowledge. More
often than not, however, it seems that the problems of
the rural poor involve various other elements of the
development mix, such as access to resources, capital,
markets, breaking through dependency relationships and

so forth. In fact, the rural poor are usually very much aware on which side the bread is buttered and don't need knowledge but realistic opportunities, to be provided by various combinations of the elements in the development mix.

In this respect, to overcome a serious bottleneck in promoting knowledge utilization requires the creation of effective linkages between utilizers and systems capable of providing one or more of the elements of the mix necessary to solve problems effectively. The creation of realistic and appropriate opportunities is a key challenge facing poverty alleviators today. Responding to a great many different small claims from below, coordinating different agencies each capable of dealing with part of a problem, creating responsiveness and accountability to overcome institutional imperatives, all these linkage problems seem to be key issues in knowledge utilization.

The commercial answer to such problems has been to provide uniform packages for homogeneous target groups (Kotler 1975). In agricultural development, such approaches have also been tried successfully (e.g., Ascroft and others 1973). However, such approaches have not been successful in large-scale replications because there are no rewards for agencies responsible for various elements in the mix to work together and generate appropriate packages. Instead the imperative of man-the-villager is to fight and obstruct those who encroach upon his village land.

5. Reward systems ensuring creation of opportunities for the rural poor, and especially self-sustaining linkage relationships, can only be created when the rural poor involved acquire power over opportunity-building systems. The latter must somehow be accountable to the former. Linkage only becomes a realistic concept in a balance of countervailing powers, a dynamic equilibrium between the anarchy implied by total user control and the technocracy implied by total agency control (Colin 1978).

Usually, the rural poor are poor because they lack power over anything. Accepting man-the-villager as one's reality, therefore, implies that knowledge utilization becomes very much a question of changing power relationships in the social system and of increasing the countervailing power of the rural poor vis-a-vis other groups.

For us, interested in promoting knowledge utilization, the conclusion that power is a pervasive issue when man-the-villager obtains it implies that we must seek to manipulate power relationships. It is another challenge to our creativity. Is it possible to use knowledge strategies to generate social change in this respect?

PRACTICAL GUIDELINES FOR AGRICULTURAL DEVELOPMENT

Is it possible to take these principles and elaborate more practical guidelines for promoting knowledge utilization to alleviate rural poverty? It seems possible to answer in the hesitantly affirmative because approaches are beginning to emerge which seem to respond to the realization that man-the-villager is ubiquitous.

The Power Approach

This becomes most obvious if we line up the various approaches taken when intervening in farm systems (Kearl 1978, Huizinga 1983; Haverkort and Röling 1984). The power approach assumes some means of control of the intervening party, as is the case in land-owner-tenant relationships, settlement schemes and so forth. Knowledge utilization usually is the result of central management decisions. However, the results in terms of productivity—let alone rural welfare—are often not very impressive. Furthermore, means control is usually not complete enough for effective change.

The Diffusion Approach

The diffusion of innovations approach assumes that rural people are independent decision makers, so that utilization is the result of a great number of adoption decisions. Diffusion is a spontaneous process (Rogers 1976; 1982), but its planned utilization for purposes of agricultural development is the mainstay of most extension services in the world. The "progressive farmer strategy" associated with utilizing the diffusion process has caused unjustified lack of interest in the process itself because the strategies usually assume an innovation to be equally relevant for all members of the system into which it is introduced. Extension strategies therefore, seem justified in introducing an innovation to the most progressive so that it will trickle throughout the system. Ever since the studies of the social consequences of introducing high-yielding varieties by the United Nations Research Institute for Social Development (UNRISD 1974), however, we know that differential access to resources, and not differential psychological progressiveness, must be seen as the main reason for adoption or non-adoption, so that the progressive farmer strategy acerbates disparities and stimulates that which pushes smaller farmers out of agriculture (Röling, Ascroft, and Chege 1976).

Target Group Approach

In answer to such problems, a group approach has emerged which focuses on categories of farmers which are homogeneous in terms of farming systems and/or access to resources. Therefore, one can assume that a specific package is relevant and appropriate to the specific category of farmers. Most advanced in this respect seem to be the efforts of Collinson to establish recommendation domains (CIMMYT 1979). In India, the efforts of the government to mount specific programs for small farmers administered by special agencies is testimony to the seriousness with which it seeks to tackle poverty problems.

The three approaches to agricultural development mentioned above do not provide an answer to the problems that arise if one seeks to alleviate rural poverty through knowledge utilization from a man-the-villager perspective. They largely seek technical change and seem unable to increase countervailing power among the poor.

FIVE-ELEMENT SYSTEM

The functional group or five-element system seems more appropriate in this respect, although it remains largely a promise in absence of large-scale application, however often it has proved successful on a smaller scale. The approach (Colin 1978; FAO 1979; Verhagen 1982; Röling and De Zeeuw 1983) focuses on (1) mobilization of rural people and officials and politicians so as to allow (2) organization of rural people into small functional groups and (3) training some of their members as local barefoot cadres or leaders. These functional groups are (4) provided with income-

generating opportunities, while (5) an intermediate
organization, for instance a non-government organization,
ensures that the elements function together. It is
necessary for instance, to synchronize mobilization and the
provision of realistic opportunities.

The five-element system offers modest hope in that the
confidence gained through achieving something together and
the membership in a small organization seem to allow a
spill-over of technical efficacy to social efficacy and an
assumption of countervailing power. Of course, until such
small functional groups are properly federated at higher
levels and can provide political clout and lobbying, the
fledgling self-confidence must be protected by some
political umbrella (Röling and De Zeeuw 1983).

Promoting the five-element system implies special tasks
for knowledge strategies. It is, however, only a specific
case of a much more fundamental change implied by assuming
man-the-villager.

MAN-THE-VILLAGER AND THE WIDER CHALLENGE FOR
KNOWLEDGE UTILIZATION

If we indeed accept that our survival is no longer
dependent upon technical control but upon our ability to
control the man-made universe, social processes and
ourselves, then knowledge strategies acquire completely new
tasks indeed. For survival will require that man reject the
blinding imperative of technical process and control and
accept the task of learning to control the inclinations of
man-the-villager.

We may have reached the end of what Huxley called the
"cultural revolution." Further advances of man-the-
scientist may prove infeasible if not self-destructive.
Further evolution only seems possible if we are able to
confront the neglected villager in ourselves and learn to
self-impose limits on our aggressiveness, our acquisitive-
ness, our search for power and our urge to control. It
seems that that is the real challenge for those who seek to
promote knowledge utilization. An example may illustrate
the task we face.

After the Cancun Conference in Mexico in 1981, the U.S.
secretary of the treasury claimed that it is trade, not aid,
which developing countries need. Their annual trade with
the United States, he said, was more than all aid they had
received in the past decades (Newsweek, October 26, 1981).
Indeed, in 1978, the value of U.S. manufactured exports to

developing countries (some 39 percent of total U.S. exports) was 40 billion dollars, while official development assistance in that year was 5.7 billion dollars (World Bank 1981, 156, 164).

What the Secretary did not say, however, was that the United States has large trade surpluses with developing countries, that (according to the same Newsweek article) 500,000 jobs in the United States are based on trade with non-OPEC Third World countries alone, that one in every five acres of farm land in the United States is planted with crops intended for export to the Third World, and that the trade deficits of developing countries are financed by commercial and international bank credit, while interest payments represent a constant drain of usually rural surplus from Third World countries. Most manufactured imports in developing countries, moreover, benefit not rural people but urban elites (Todaro and Stilkind 1981).

Why is this an example of the challenge we, concerned with knowledge utilization, face? For one, we cannot focus only on agricultural development in the Third World while we neglect its international context. If we are serious about knowledge utilization for rural poverty alleviation, we must also consider utilization strategies in industrial countries. Secondly, the lack of information demonstrated by the secretary and those who failed to challenge him reveals a severe shortcoming in the extent to which we have developed feedback loops and monitoring devices which make it impossible for man-the-villager to have anything but global village boundaries. In this period of discontinuity, it seems a special responsibility for the science of knowledge utilization to indicate how mass-shared realities which are rapidly becoming obsolete can be relativated and restructured.

REFERENCES

Ascroft, J., N. Röling, J. Kariuki, and F. Chege. 1973. Extension and the Forgotten Farmer. Wageningen: Agric. Univ. Bulletin van de Afdelingen der Landbouwhogeschool.

Berlo, D. K. 1960. Process of Communication. New York: Holt, Rinehart, and Winston.

Bronowski, J. 1973. The Ascent of Man. London: MacDonald Futura Publishers.

Buber, M. 1958. I and Thou. New York: Scribners.

Cantril, H. 1965. The Pattern of Human Concerns. New Brunswick, N.J.: Rutgers Univ. Press.

Centro Internacional de Mejoramiento de Maiz y Trigo (International Maize and Wheat Improvement Center) (Mexico). 1979. Deriving Recommendation Domains for Central Province, Zambia. CIMMYT Report no. 4. Nairobi: CIMMYT.

Colin, R. 1978. "Analyse comparative et problematique a partir de l'etude de quelques dossiers significatifs." Paris: UNESCO, Division for the Study of Development. Project Les methodes et techniques de la participation et developpement.

Emery, F. 1977. Futures We Are In. Leiden: Martinus Nijhoff Social Sciences Division.

Food and Agriculture Organization. 1979. Small Farmers Development Manual Vol. I and II. Bangkok: FAO, Regional Office for Asia and the Far East.

Havelock, R. G. 1969. Planning for Innovation through the Dissemination and Utilization of Knowledge. Ann Arbor: Center for Research on Utilization of Scientific Knowledge, Institute for Social Research, University of Michigan.

Haverkort, A., and N. Röling. 1984. "Six Approaches to Rural Extension." Wageningen: International Agricultural Center, International Course on Rural Extension.

Hesseling, E. 1979. Project report Guinea Bissao, Debriefing Period Small Farmers Project held at the IAC, Wageningen, The Netherlands, November 1979.

Howell, J. 1979. "Appraising Organization: Purpose, Method and Cost-Effectiveness." Paper presented at Conference on Rapid Rural Appraisal, Institute Development Studies, Brighton, Sussex.

Huizinga, B. 1983. "Veranderende Percepties in de Voorlichting: Implicatie voor Voorlichtingskundig Onderzoek in de Derde Wereld." In In de Ban van de Voorlichtingskunde, Liber Amicorum presented at the occasion of the departure of Professor van den Ban. Wageningen: Agricultural University, Department of Extension Education.

Huxley, J. 1957. Knowledge, Morality and Destiny. New York: Mentor Books.

Kearl, B. 1978. An Overview of Communication in Agriculture Projects. Development Communication Report, no. 22. May.

Kelly, G. A. 1963. A Theory of Personality: The Psychology of Personal Constructs. New York: Norton and Co.

Kotler, P. 1975. Marketing for Non-Profit Organizations. Englewood Cliffs, N.J.: Prentice-Hall.

Rogers, E. M. 1976. "Where We are in Understanding the Diffusion of Innovations." In Communication and Change, Ten Years After, ed. W. Schramm and D. Lerner. Honolulu: East-West Center Press.

Rogers, E. M. 1982. Diffusion of Innovations. New York: Free Press/Macmillan.

Röling, N., J. Ascroft, and F. W. Chege. 1976. "The Diffusion of Innovations and the Issue of Equity in Rural Development." Communication Research 3, no. 2 (April): 155-170.

Röling, N., and H. De Zeeuw. 1983. "Improving the Quality of Rural Poverty Alleviation." Final Report of the Working Party "the Small Farmer and Development Cooperation." Wageningen: International Agriculture Centre.

Sweet, C., and P. F. Weisel. 1979. "Process versus Blueprint Models for Designing Rural Development Projects." In International Development Administration, ed. G. Honadle, R. Kraus. New York: Praeger.

Todaro, M. P., and J. Stilkind. 1981. City Bias and Rural
    Neglect: The Dilemma of Urban Development. New York:
    The Population Council.

United Nations Research Institute for Social Development.
    1974. "Summary and Conclusion of a Global Research
    Project." Volume 8. In The Social and Economic
    Implications of Large—Scale Introduction of New
    Varieties of Food Grain. (8 vols., 1971-1974).
    Geneva: UNRISD.

Verhagen, C. 1982. "Cooperative Research and Planning with
    Small Farmers." Royal Tropical Institute, Interna-
    tional Cooperative Alliance and Cooperative League of
    Thailand Collaborative Research Project on Cooperatives
    for Small Farmers. Amsterdam: Koninklijk Instituut
    voor de Tropen.

White, R. W. 1963. Ego and Reality in Psycho—Analytic
    Theory: A Proposal Regarding Independent Ego Energies.
    Psychological Issues 3, no. 3, Monograph 11. New York:
    International Univ. Press.

Wilford, J. N. 1981. The Mapmakers: The Story of the Great
    Pioneers in Cartography from Antiquity to the Space
    Age. London: Junction Books.

World Bank. 1981. World Development Report 1981.
    Washington, D. C.: The World Bank.

PART FOUR

Environment

11

Understanding the Role of the Environment in Knowledge Generation and Use: A Plea for a Hermeneutical Approach

Wimal Dissanayake

In this paper, I wish to examine the relationship between the process of knowledge dissemination and the environment and urge a fundamental change in our epistemological approach to the question of knowledge dissemination. Very often we tend to regard the environment as something peripheral and marginal to issues of knowledge production and use. It is my conviction, on the contrary, that a clear understanding of the nature of knowledge generation and use cannot be gained without encountering deeply the environmental factors. In many ways, to use a phrase put into academic parlance by modern phenomenologists, it seems to me that the environment is constitutive of the meaning of knowledge that is generated and used.

This paper consists of three parts. In the first part, I have sought to examine critically the classical diffusion of innovations model, which is even today profoundly influential, and point out how both in theory and praxis it failed as a consequence of paying inadequate attention to the role of the environment in knowledge creation and use. In the second part, I have attempted to isolate three important environmental factors--the social, cultural and political--and demonstrate how critically they impinge on issues of knowledge generation and utilization. Having done that, in the third part, I have made an effort to argue the case for a hermeneutical approach to knowledge generation, diffusion and utilization so that we could take into consideration the full implications of the impact of the environment more productively, and thereby pave the way for the emergence of a more fruitful perspective on knowledge production and use.

Let us begin by defining our terms. I think, at the very outset, we need to draw a distinction between

261

information and knowledge, two terms that are frequently
deployed synonymously and interchangeably. In this paper I
use the word knowledge to signify an interrelated and
ordered body of facts as opposed to information, which
suggests a body of disconnected facts. Morss and Rich
(1980, 49) refine this concept further by distinguishing
between data bits, information and knowledge. Machlup
(1980, 8) offers some other ways of enforcing this
distinction which might have the unfortunate effect of
obfuscating more than illuminating this distinction.
Guruvitch (1971, 37) talks of ten different types of
knowledge: mystical, rational, empirical, conceptual,
positive, speculative, symbolic, concrete, collective, and
individual. Of these, in this paper, I am not so much
concerned with the mystical, speculative and individual
forms of knowledge. Or, to put it differently, I am
interested in the collectively validated and organized
knowledge.

The term "use" seems simple enough. However, when we
examine the literature pertaining to knowledge production
and use, we realize that it has been employed as an umbrella
term to cover a number of different phenomena like overuse,
underuse, nonuse, misuse, and use as well as a number of
different stages of use. These distinctions are crucial if
we wish to analyze in detail the various facets of the
concept of use. Such refinement of categorization is vital
if we are to sharpen our conceptual tools.

By environment, I mean the social, economic, cultural,
political, ideological, legal, ethical contexts within which
the process of knowledge generation, dissemination and
utilization takes place. Although for heuristical purposes
we can talk of these as distinct dimensions, we need to
remember that in the "real world" they are indeed closely
interrelated.

In order to illustrate the centrality of the environment to the process of knowledge creation and use, let us
first consider a simple model which seems to have secured
wide approval.

In this model, it seems to me that we are leaving out a very
significant component, namely the environment. The process
of knowledge generation and utilization does not take place

in a sociocultural or environmental vacuum. On the contrary, it is indeed the environment which is instrumental in
sustaining this process and investing it with meaning.
Hence, it is very important indeed that we modify this
simple model to include the environment.

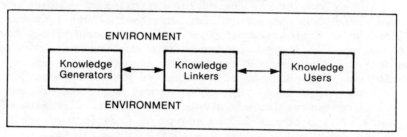

Although we are still endeavoring to win recognition
for the centrality of the environment in knowledge generation and use, nearly fifty years ago, Huxley (1934, 279) put
the case very eloquently when he said that:

> science is not the disembodied sort of activity that
> people would make out, engaged on the abstract task of
> pursuing universal truth, but a social function
> intimately linked up with human history and human
> destiny. And the sooner scientists as a body realize
> this and organize their activities on that basis, the
> better both for science and for society.

In order to enforce my point regarding the importance
of the environment in understanding the process of knowledge
creation and use, I wish to examine the early diffusion of
innovations studies. They were, in many ways, the most
influential early examples of knowledge generation, dissemination and utilization designed to achieve practical ends.
During the fifties and the sixties this tradition of
knowledge diffusion had a great impact on communication
scholars both in the developed and the developing world.
Hundreds of studies were conducted using this conceptual
framework. The work of scholars like Ryan and Gross (1943),
Beal and Bohlen (1954), Lionberger (1949), and Spaulding
(1955) served to define the area of study which came to be
known as diffusion of innovations. The attempts at diffusion of innovations using this model were by and large
successful in the United States. However, the degree of
success achieved in the developing countries was less
certain largely due, in my judgment, to the failure to take
into consideration the role of the environment in the

formulation of this theoretical framework. Interesting as
the classical diffusion of innovations studies are, with the
wisdom of hindsight we can identify a number of deficiencies
in them which spring largely from inadequate attention paid
to the impact of the environment.

Let us examine the concept of diffusion of innovations.
It was said that there were four important elements in the
diffusion of innovations (Rogers 1962). They were: (1) the
innovation, (2) its communication from one individual to
another, (3) in a social system, (4) over time. An innovation was defined as an idea perceived as new by a person
or a group of persons. By diffusion was meant the process
by which an innovation was disseminated. This diffusion
process had its origin in the source of creation and ended
with the users and adopters. A social system in this
context was defined as a group of persons who were functionally differentiated and were involved in a common
problem-solving endeavor. By adoption was understood the
decision to make use of a given innovation. Therefore, the
process of adoption ranged from the initial kindling of an
interest in an innovation to its ultimate adoption.

Scholars associated with the early model of diffusion
of innovations conceptualized this process in terms of five
different stages: Awareness-interest-evaluation-trial-
adoption. These different stages, it is interesting to
observe, were conceptualized in terms of individual effort
without paying sufficient attention to the social pressures
that impinge on these stages so powerfully.

Classical diffusion of innovations research paid much
attention to the various categories of adopters. They came
up with five categories: innovators, early adopters, early
majority, late majority, and laggards. Innovators were
supposed to be bold and prepared to experiment. Early
adopters respected change. Early majority were conscien-
tious. Late majority were skeptical, and laggards were
tradition-bound. Once again, it is interesting to observe
the fact that, despite the social system being listed as one
of the four elements in the process of diffusion of innovations, its impact did not enter in any meaningful way into
the conceptualization of the categories of adopters.

Despite the widespread influence of the classical model
of diffusion of innovations, it became evident by the end of
the sixties, that it left much to be desired by way of
theoretical formulation. Its main deficiencies can be
enumerated as follows.

1. The definition of innovation was too circumscribed
   to make it conceptually useful.

2. Attention was concentrated on specific innovations without considering sufficiently the needs and contexts of the potential users.
3. The model of communication adhered to (S---M---C---R) was unilinear, source-based and too simplistic to do justice to the complexities involved in the process of human interaction.
4. It was a research-driven and resource-based model rather than a problem-oriented and user-based one.
5. Attention was focused on the individual and his psychological make-up rather than the collectivity and the social structure.
6. The decision to adopt was regarded as the end of the process, thereby ignoring the complex issues emanating from this decision.

All these deficiencies, which vitiated its theoretical validity and practical usefulness, are attributable largely to the failure to take adequate cognizance of the impact of the environment on the knowledge generation and utilization process.

From the late fifties onward the model of diffusion of innovations as formulated by the early scholars of diffusion began to be increasingly used in development efforts in the Third World countries. And as these efforts failed far short of their objective, scholars began to have second thoughts on this model. It was strongly criticized on one important point, namely the failure to pay adequate attention to the social system within which the process operated (Beltran 1976; Diaz-Bordenave 1976). It was pointed out that the socioeconomic environment exercises a considerable influence on the behavior of individuals with regard to innovations and that the socioeconomic structure in general favored the adoption of innovations by individuals with high socioeconomic status (Rogers and Adhikarya 1979). It was demonstrated that diffusion processes were imperfect equalizers of development benefits due to unequal distribution of resources (Röling and others 1976, 63). Scholars like Esman (1974), Diaz-Bordenave (1976), and Beltran (1976) emphatically maintained that the main constraints to development are basically social cultural and not informative and that a fundamental rearrangement of society is called for if the diffusion of innovations is to be more productive and supportive of social development.

Therefore, the whole question of the failure to adopt innovations needed to be examined in a broad social framework rather than laying the blame on individual and psychological factors. As Rogers (1976) points out, the failure

of farmers to adopt innovations is due more to lack of
opportunities rather than due to their aversion to change.
Farmers with more land, more money and more knowledge can
obtain more credit, information and other inputs to adopt
technical innovations than those without. What all these
criticisms point to is the lack of adequate recognition of
environmental factors impinging on the whole process of
knowledge generation, dissemination and utilization.

Although the field of diffusion of innovations research
represented the confluence of a number of academic disciplines such as anthropology, sociology, rural sociology,
education, industrial and medical sociology, the main thrust
of these studies were psychological in nature. That is to
say, the individual rather than the collectivity received
pride of place. This propensity had its origin in even a
more fundamental epistemological premise. There are two
broad conceptions of knowledge. I should like to term them:
1. Individual-centered
2. Society-centered
The proponents of the first category would maintain
that knowledge is the product of individual effort. That is
to say, isolated and dispassionate individuals who specu-
lating and contemplating on, and experimenting with, reality
produce a body of knowledge. In this effort, there is very
little intrusion of the individual between reality and its
representation. The perception of reality is independent of
the experience, interests, propensities of the individual.
The knowledge thus produced is only a function of reality
itself. It can be tested by any individual who is able to
compare it with reality, since the property of correspondence with reality is entirely independent of the
situation wherein it was produced (Barnes 1979).

The society-centered approach, on the other hand, emphasizes the social basis of knowledge production. The
advocates of this approach maintain that knowledge is a
social and cultural product. The ideas, idea systems,
everything from day-to-day "recipe" knowledge to philosophical doctrines do not arise from some immaculate conception. Knowledge reflects, in some way, the social interests
and symbolic representations of the social structure and
history (Bailey 1975). As Elias put it quite eloquently,
ideas, knowledge, thoughts, perceptions, etc. are primarily
determined by the structures of human groups where they are
produced and not by consciousness itself, call it logic,
reason or whatever (Elias 1972). Mannheim (1960) is surely
right when he says that mental structures are differently
formed in different social and historical settings.

The early diffusion of innovations studies were largely governed by the first epistemological premise. As a consequence, very little attention was paid to the social and cultural bases of knowledge production and utilization. I have dwelled at fair length on some of the deficiencies of the classical model of diffusion of innovations, because it was the most influential model (and is so up to a point even today) of knowledge generation and use. And its central weaknesses seem to enforce rather dramatically the essential point of this paper. It is indeed true that subsequent scholars engaged in this field have chosen to emphasize more strongly the impact of the environment on what Rich (1981) refers to as the knowledge cycle. But this idea needs to be elaborated, its full implications delineated and disseminated among researchers as well as all other parties interested in the use of knowledge for social progress.

As was mentioned at the beginning of this paper, by environment I refer to the social, economic, political, cultural, legal, ethical, administrative factors that influence knowledge generation, dissemination and utilization. Clearly, all such dimensions cannot be usefully discussed or treated with any degree of justice within the narrow compass of a paper of this size. Therefore, I have decided to concentrate on three of these aspects, namely, the social, cultural and political, and through these reiterate my general plea for the need to pay greater theoretical attention to the role of the environment in the knowledge cycle.

Let us first consider the social aspect. In any consideration of the production and use of knowledge, the social matrix in which they take place needs to be studied carefully. Katz (1960, 435) says that it is as unthinkable to study diffusion without some knowledge of the social structures in which potential adopters are located as it is to study blood circulation without adequate knowledge of veins and arteries. And Rogers (1973, 77) remarks that diffusion does not occur in a vacuum; the actors involved in the spread of an innovation are members of a social system. I think it is of utmost importance that we take into consideration the social context in which knowledge is generated and used and examine its full implications.

When we talk of knowledge generation and use, we are in point of fact talking of two social systems. As Havelock (1969) points out, knowledge use represents the linkage between two systems—the one faced with a problem and the other able to delineate the options that will facilitate the resolution of the problem. In studying this interchange or

interaction one must perforce pay attention to the social
norms, values, interests, lifestyles, etc. that characterize
each system.

A number of empirical studies have shown the importance
of this fact. For example, a study conducted by Van den Ban
(1960) on the impact of modern and traditional norms on the
innovativeness of farmers in Wisconsin townships found that
township norms were an even more powerful source of influence on the decision of farmers to adopt innovations than
were such individual attributes as education and wealth.
This study established that a farmer living in a traditional
township, although he may have a higher degree of wealth and
education, was less likely to adopt an innovation than a
farmer living in a more modern township who had less wealth
and education. Similar research conducted by Saxena (1968),
Davis (1968) and Qadir (1966) in India, Nigeria and the
Philippines enforced the same point. In Sri Lanka it was
found (Dissanayake 1978) that a large percentage of the
population was aware of the compelling need for family
planning as well as of contraceptive methods, but that many
of them chose not to adopt family planning in deference to
social factors.

Rogers (1977), having explicated the relationship
between social structure and social change, identified nine
middle-range propositions drawing upon the cumulative
evidence of a large number of social scientific studies on
knowledge diffusion activities. They are:

1. Social structure acts to impede or to facilitate
   the rate of diffusion and adoption of new ideas
   through system effects.
2. Diffusion can change the social structure of a
   social system.
3. Power elites act as gatekeepers to prevent restructuring of innovations from entering a social system
   while favoring functioning innovations that do not
   immediately threaten to change the system
   structure.
4. A system's social structure helps determine the
   nature and distribution of an innovation's
   consequences.
5. Top-down change in a system, which is initiated by
   the power elites, is more likely to succeed than is
   bottom-up change.
6. Bottom-up change involves a greater degree of
   conflict than top-down change.
7. Bottom-up change is more likely to be successful at
   times of perceived crisis in a system.

8. Bottom-up change is more likely to be useful when a social movement is headed by a charismatic leader.
9. The role of the charismatic leader in a social movement decreases as the movement becomes institutionalized into a more highly structured organization.

All these propositions stress the need to examine very carefully the interrelationship between social structure and social change. In the diffusion of new knowledge what really happens is that the people in a given social system decide to effect certain changes in the social relations, social organizations that characterize that social system. Deciding to adopt an innovation amounts to deciding to effect certain changes in the social system. Therefore, when we study the process of knowledge generation, diffusion and utilization, we need to examine more and more closely what it entails in terms of the social system. Hence the centrality of the environment.

Let us next consider the impact of culture. Nelson (1981, 44) is surely right when he says that knowledge is developed in a specific cultural context. Frake (1963) defines culture as how people organize their experience conceptually so that it can be transmitted as knowledge from person to person. Clearly, the social and cultural dimensions are very closely linked, and it is only for analytical purposes that we treat them separately. When we examine the way in which new knowledge has arisen in various societies, and has been introduced to other societies, we see very clearly the shaping hand of culture. An inadequate recognition of this fact can impede the purposeful use of knowledge. Indeed, it is largely to this aspect that Rothman (1980, 20) is directing our attention when he says that on the basis of an extensive review of pertinent literature the following appear to be significant areas of dissonance between knowledge producers and knowledge appliers: conflicting values, orientations toward clients, languages, methodological assumptions, role perceptions, focal objectives and concerns, definitions of professional ethics, and identifications.

Knowledge is a product of culture. It is abstracted by means of various analytical and speculative devices from reality. And reality is a social and cultural construct. The norms and values that guide our actions, the language that we use play a very crucial role in this endeavor. Schutz (1967), Berger and Luckmann (1967), and Whorf (1956) admirably clarify this point from different angles. This notion runs deep in Western philosophical traditions. For example, Hegel's philosophy suggests that human thinking is determined culturally and historically and that it is not capable of stepping outside these boundaries. He also believed that human thought is essentially the product of a collective and not an individual endeavor and that the relationship subsisting between the human mind and its object was governed by the cultural matrix in which these entities existed. And Vico, whose ideas on history exerted a profound influence on subsequent Western thinkers, emphatically proclaimed that ideas are formed by language in the dialectical interplay between human nature and culture.

There are a number of angles from which we can examine the centrality of culture for knowledge generation and use. Let us first consider the issue of the frame of reference. In interpreting a body of knowledge that is newly introduced to another cultural system, use has to be made of a frame of reference sanctioned by that culture. In the process of doing so, the frame of reference may be altered or modified, just as much as the body of knowledge may undergo certain changes. In other words, there is a kind of dialectical interaction between newly introduced knowledge and the frame of reference sanctioned by a given culture. This is indeed a matter of great practical interest. I believe the diffusion of agricultural innovation strategies succeeded in the United States in a way that they did not in Asia partly due to the influence of the culturally agreed frames of reference which were deployed for the purpose of interpreting newly introduced knowledge.

This is closely linked to the question of legitimation. Newly introduced knowledge, if it is to be used by a community, needs to be legitimated in the eyes of that community. This is not merely a matter of explaining the "science" behind that knowledge, because all forms of knowledge have far reaching social implications. The gaining of legitimation is indeed a cultural phenomenon. Numerous studies conducted in Asia regarding the dissemination of family planning knowledge reinforce this point (Rogers 1973).

This again is closely connected to networks through which new knowledge is diffused and receives legitimization. Here, too, the role of culture is unmistakably crucial. It has been shown that knowledge when diffused through culturally accepted opinion leaders is more likely to gain a wider acceptance than when diffused through people who are less culturally esteemed, however educated and knowledgeable they may be in the field of knowledge under consideration. For example, it was found in Sri Lanka (Dissanayake 1978) that people were more likely to adopt family planning

knowledge diffused through culturally esteemed opinion
leaders like native physicians and school teachers than
knowledgeable graduates and government officials.

On the other hand, proper attention paid to cultural
factors and an imaginative deployment of them can help in
the fruitful use and adoption of new knowledge. The
Japanese experience of modernizing the country is wonder-
fully illustrative of this. Japan absorbed new knowledge
into the existing cultural fabric, while using the existing
cultural institutions to hasten this process. The way in
which the labor intensive traditional cottage industries
were harnessed, at the turn of the century, to supplement
the more modern and capital-intensive industries is but one
example of this phenomenon.

The conflict between culture and civilization is fundamental to the acceptance of new knowledge particularly in
the more traditional societies. It has been pointed out by
McIver and Page (1957) that while culture dictates the goals
and ends people cherish, civilization provides the means by
which the cultural goals are to be achieved. There is an
interesting interaction between these two elements. While
the development of civilization is stimulated by changes in
the goals of culture, the development of civilization serves
to introduce new cultural goals. This has obvious implications for knowledge utilization. Very often newly introduced knowledge placed in the hands of people in traditional
societies introduces new civilizational means which are
likely to challenge existing cultural goals. This is
potentially a conflict situation that can have beneficial or
harmful effects on society depending on the way in which it
is handled. Making use of a Mertonian typology, Röling
(1970, 77) points out the imperatives of this situation.

Mode of Adaptation	New Cultural Goal	Existing Civilization
1. Innovation	+	−
2. Ritualism	−	+
3. Retreatism	−	−
4. Rebellion	±	±
5. Conformity	+	+

Note: + means acceptance; − means rejection; ± means
rejection of prevailing values and the substitution of
new ones.

Röling says that (1) innovation is an adaptation of the existing civilization to satisfy a new cultural goal. It is often seen as an extra effort needed to complete the response to the goal. (2) Ritualism constitutes the rejection of new cultural goals so as to conform to the existing civilization. By retreatism (3) is meant the rejection of the new cultural goal and the existing civilization. It signifies a withdrawal resulting from a sense of apathy. Rebellion (4) represents the rejection of existing norms and values and their replacement by new ones. Conformity (5) signifies the adherence to both new cultural goals and the existing civilization. Although Röling adopts this typology to illustrate his point about the role of frustration in development, it serves to point out the very important relationship that exists between culture and civilization, and its implication for knowledge use.

When we discuss the impact of culture on knowledge generation and utilization we must perforce pay attention to the concept of indigenous knowledge systems. This is indeed an area that has been largely ignored in our efforts to bring about social progress through the diffusion of knowledge. Indigenous knowledge systems have been looked down upon as primitive and inconsequential. It is indeed true that much superstition and irrationality are embedded in indigenous knowledge. But at the same time, as development anthropologists and ethnoscientists are increasingly realizing, there is much in culturally nourished indigenous knowledge systems that is rational, scientific and exploitable to meet contemporary needs. Brokensha and others (1980) admirably demonstrate the need for development planners to take into consideration the accumulated knowledge and traditional skills and technology of the people among whom they work by presenting case studies from a number of Third World countries.

Bellonele (1973, 24), based on his experiences in Africa, remarks that for over ten years agricultural extension was heading in the wrong direction from the very outset, based as it was on a number of erroneous postulates. One of the most obstinate postulates was that the black peasant is endowed with a very low technical capacity. He goes on to point out that very rarely are scholars and planners able to look behind outward appearances and observe what delicate balances the African peasants have succeeded in achieving. Bellonele makes the important point that modern agronomists must be persuaded to study carefully these practices and not forget the fact that these peasants have accumulated a capital of experience which constitutes the indispensable point of departure. These remarks only underline the need to pay greater attention to the culturally fostered indigenous knowledge systems.

The imaginative use of indigenous knowledge systems, which are inextricably linked with the cultural milieu in which they operate, are important in the development effort on a number of counts. They can be briefly stated as follows:

1. Ideas borrowed from the people, and then developed and refined in the light of modern knowledge, have a far greater chance of being readily accepted than those imported from outside.

2. The use of culturally sanctioned indigenous knowledge systems promotes bottom-up development.

3. For the development effort to succeed, focus on materials alone is not adequate. Attention needs to be paid to human needs and resources. This can best be achieved through the harnessing of indigenous knowledge systems.

4. The use of indigenous knowledge systems promotes local skills and initiative.

5. The harnessing of knowledge and skills found among a people tends to increase popular participation in development efforts.

6. Greater attention to indigenous knowledge systems facilitates the adaptation of new technology to suit local needs and conditions.

Therefore, we see that the use of indigenous knowledge systems for the purpose of social development is closely associated with economic as well as psychological factors. These factors serve to emphasize the compelling need to recognize the importance of culture in knowledge generation, dissemination and utilization in matters of social development.

Let us examine next the political dimensions of knowledge production and utilization. Indeed, this is assuming greater and greater importance. Holzner and Fisher (1979, 220) state that we cannot escape from the fact that the utilization of knowledge occurs in political arenas of some kind, and that the process of interest articulation, of social and political mobilizations, cannot be omitted from inquiry. He goes on to point out that it is in these political contexts that social problems are constructed and given legitimation as problems to be resolved. I think it needs to be pointed out that all problems whether social in the narrow sense or not, have social consequences and hence this notion is valid for all problems. Rule (1971, 48)

rightly observes that there can be no definition of a
"social problem" which does not involve political judgments,
nor certainly any "solutions" to such problems devoid of
partisan interest. And he says that to pretend otherwise
merely leads to the introduction of partisan measures and
objectives in the guise of nonpolitical technocratic
"problem solving." Weiss (1978, 48) remarks that the
problems in the application of research results derives in
large measure from the various characteristics of the
political domain into which they move. Caplan (1975, 49)
observes that when determining knowledge utilization the
political implications of the findings of research appear to
dominate all other considerations.

The importance of the political dimension is to be
discerned not only in the use of knowledge, but in the
entire process of generating, packaging, disseminating and
utilizing. In the modern world, as Levi-Leleland (1976,
136) points out, the direction and priorities of knowledge
generating activities are decided at an even more elevated
level of the social apparatus and always further and further
away from the places of scientific endeavor. He says that
the ideological determinations operate institutionally much
more than individually, that is to say, far upstream or
downstream from the place where scientific production
emerges as a formulated discovery. The findings of Oasa and
Jennings (1981) are interesting from this point of view.

The importance of politics in knowledge generation,
diffusion and utilization can be analyzed from different
vantage points. Let us examine the example of diffusion of
agricultural innovations, which is one of the most vital
knowledge dissemination activities for the developing world.
The goal of this knowledge diffusion activity is ultimately
to better the conditions of the peasantry in the less
developed countries. If so, this activity has to pay close
attention to the political contexts in which this could be
achieved. In other words, those involved in such activities
must also keep in mind the broad development goals endorsed
by a given community. Or else, they must introduce these
innovations in a context that they deem most suitable for
the community. The important point, though, is that one
cannot fruitfully talk of diffusion of agricultural
innovations in isolation from the political context.

Broadly speaking there are four main rural developmental models, each with its own political bearings. They
are the technocratic, reformist, transformational, and self-
reliant models. The essential characteristics of each can
be represented in the following way.

Model	Points of Emphasis
1. Technocratic Economic growth	Increase in output
2. Reformist Social development	Income redistribution
3. Transformational Power relationships	Restructuring of society
4. Self-reliant Popular participation	Reliance on local skills and resources

When one makes use of new strategies of diffusion of agricultural innovations one must pay attention to these political considerations as well. To say that one is only interested in the diffusion activity and nothing more is to confess to an involvement in a partial and, in many ways, a futile effort.

We can examine the relationship between knowledge diffusion and the political context from a different, although not unconnected angle. It has often been said by classical diffusion of innovations theorists that some people showed less interest than others in adopting innovations mainly because they were lethargic and too tradition-bound. The political context hardly entered their calculation. However, many studies have demonstrated that wealth and power relationships have a far more significant impact on the question of adoption of innovations.

Let us consider the question of technology, which is vital to an understanding of the way in which new knowledge and skills serve to promote social development. If the poorer countries of the world are to make social and economic progress, they need to make use of technology at an ever increasing rate. And this in inextricably linked with political issues. For example, talking of agricultural technology, Bechford (1979, 208) says that technology is not neutral. It comes with the biases of the countries exporting it. It seems to affect everything, including education, people's values and the pattern of consumption mix that people aspire to achieve. He further goes on to lodge the plea that ultimately developing countries will have to develop indigenous technology to suit their particular resource endowments and the value endowments of the people. Such pleas only serve to underline the political dimensions of knowledge dissemination.

The way in which new knowledge and innovations are

closely linked to political factors is dramatically illustrated in the triumph and failures of the Green Revolution.
The essence of the Green Revolution is the transfer of the
highly fertilizer-responsive varieties and the capacity to
produce such varieties from Japan, Taiwan and the United
States and Europe to the developing countries of Asia, Latin
America, the Middle East and Africa. It is in effect a
package deal that comprises a combination of improved grain
varieties, chiefly rice and wheat, heavy fertilizer usage
and carefully managed irrigation. This was an important
innovation, and one that aimed to bring about social and
economic progress in the poorer countries of the world.
However, in consequence of inadequate attention paid to
political aspects, although the Green Revolution was instrumental in increasing the grain output, it also resulted in
social unrest and the exacerbation of regional conflicts.

On the basis of evidence from countries where the
effect of the Green Revolution was most deeply felt, it has
been remarked that the spatial distribution of the benefits
and costs of technical change has not been even. According
to this view, from a technical viewpoint, the Green Revolution is largely a biological and chemical revolution, while
from a socioeconomic point of view it has been transformed
into a commercial revolution. It has been observed that the
Green Revolution tends to increase economic inequality and
this, in turn, may aggravate social conflicts. This only
serves to point out the fact that, however well-meaning the
introduction of an innovation to developing societies may
be, if due recognition is not given to the political contexts, it can in the end prove to be self-defeating and
counter-productive.

The political dimensions of knowledge production and
utilization touch on not only the character of knowledge as
a social institution with an identifiable ethos but also on
the internal progress in the culture of knowledge. These
two aspects represent the two main currents of thinking in
the field of sociology of science, the one represented by
Merton (1945) and the other by Kuhn (1962). Merton and
others of the functionalist school examined mainly the
internal social control in science and its dependence on a
reward system. To a lesser extent, the functional relationship subsisting between science and the wider society in
which it operated were also studied. However, they failed
to appreciate adequately the cultural implications of the
growth of science. On the other hand, Kuhn's path-breaking
work facilitated the study of the internal processes of
science.

We have discussed so far some of the impact of social, cultural and political factors on knowledge production, distribution and utilization. And the one point that emerges with unambiguous clarity is that it is only by paying very close attention to the environmental factors that we shall be able to conceptualize the knowledge dissemination process in a way that would prove to be of practical value.

As the various citations and references in the body of the paper would amply indicate, this point has been duly appreciated by some of the leading thinkers in the field. However, it has not as yet been fully developed, drawing out its full implications, into a coherent model or paradigm. Larsen (1981) talks of seven models that are currently influential in the field of knowledge creation and use. They are the research, development and diffusion model, the user needs model, the social interaction model, the organization change model, the two communities model, and the interactive model. All these models, in their own ways, give recognition to the impact of the environment, some more than others. To my mind, however, in none of the models is the role of the environment explicated in a way that does justice to the full complexity of the transactions and linkages involved.

House (1981) identifies three perspectives of knowledge use. They are the technical, political and cultural. The technical perspective is still the most persuasive and dominant in the field. It emphasizes the instrumentalities of knowledge generation, distribution and utilization and conceptualizes the development effort largely in terms of technical efficiency. The political perspective has as its focus of interest the political structures and power relationships in society. The generation and utilization of knowledge is closely linked to power relations, and the proponents of this perspective stress the need to pay greater attention to this aspect as a means of understanding better and facilitating the development effort. The approach has as its focus the culturally determined meaning systems which are vitally linked with knowledge production and use. Questions of cultural domination, self-reliance, values and traditions of a given community loom large in this perspective. What is needed is an amalgamation of these perspectives. Dunn (1981, 6) is profoundly correct when he says that the technical, political and cultural perspectives are complementary in the sense that each affirms at least one plausible assumption which, viewed from the standpoint of another perspective, is either disregarded or wrongly dismissed as implausible. An attempt to construct a more comprehensive and unified model on the basis of an amalgamation of these three perspectives will enable us to redefine the role of the environment in knowledge generation, and the use of such a model would delineate more perceptively the complex linkages involved.

How can one construct such an integrated conceptual framework? This calls for a fundamental rethinking of the knowledge generation and utilization process. It is indeed true that during the last fifteen years or so, much thought and effort has been expended on conceptualizing the process of knowledge production and use. However, all those conceptualizations operate within the same basic intellectual framework namely that of transporting knowledge from one social system to the other. If we are to understand fully the issues involved in knowledge production and use, we need to break out of this framework. Such an effort, it seems to me, has still not yet been made. It is in order to facilitate this breaking out of the conventional framework that I advocate a hermeneutical approach to knowledge dissemination.

The conventional approach suggests that in knowledge dissemination what really happens is that a body of knowledge is transferred from A to B, where A and B could be either individuals or social systems. As opposed to this, I wish to suggest that in knowledge dissemination what actually takes place is a joint venture by A and B which results in the creation of meaning. In other words, knowledge is not transported, it is jointly created by knowledge "disseminations" and "users." This is indeed what a hermeneutical approach emphasizes.

Hermeneutics is generally regarded as the theory of the interpretation of meaning or the understanding of understanding. In recent times it has become extremely influential among European thinkers. Although it had its modern origin in the earlier half of the nineteenth century, it is only during the last three decades or so that hermeneutics has begun to exercise a profound influence on the imagination of many modern thinkers. The writings of Dilthey, Betti, Bultmann, Heidegger, Gadamer, Apel, Habermas and Ricoeur, among others, have contributed powerfully to the emergence of this mode of thinking. Despite the fact that there is considerable divergence of opinion among them, their thinking conforms to the basic pattern of hermeneutics, whether it be the ontological hermeneutics of Heidegger, the philosophical hermeneutics of Gadamer, or the critical hermeneutics of Habermas.

Hermeneuticists point out that in understanding and interpreting new knowledge, it is always transposed into and absorbed by the values and meaning contexts of the interpreter: One never starts with a blank or neutral mind. There is an interaction between the new body of knowledge and the interpreting mind of the receiver. What eventually results is, to use Gadamer's memorable phrase, the "fusion of horizons." As Linge (1976, xii) observes, hermeneutics has to do with bridging the gap between the familiar world in which we stand and the alien meanings that resist assimilation into the horizons of our world. It is extremely important to realize that the hermeneutical phenomenon encompasses both the alien that we strive to understand and the familiar world that we already understand.

The concept of the "hermeneutical situation" as enunciated by Gadamer is important in this regard. Gadamer takes the interpreter's boundness to his present horizons and the chasm separating him from his object to be the productive ground of all understanding. The various social, economic, political, cultural, historical and other environmental factors help to shape the present situation, which constitutes the given meaning-context for the act of interpreting new knowledge. They define the situation and context in which the receiver of new knowledge seeks to interpret it. As Gadamer points out, understanding is not reconstruction but mediation. As a consequence, the receiver does not merely recreate the intended meaning of the knowledge given, but is himself actively involved and is changed practically by the relevant elements of the knowledge.

From the point of view of hermeneutics, knowledge creation is a product of dialogue--a dialogue between new knowledge and its interpreter. Here the environmentally conditioned situation of the knowledge-receiver is an important determinant of understanding. As Gadamer remarks, hermeneutical understanding is a participation in a shared meaning. Knowledge evolves, emerges, as a result of the interpretational interaction between A and B.

The hermeneutical approach stands in striking contrast to the conventional transportational approach to knowledge that has inspired knowledge generating and utilizing thinking up till now. The hermeneutical approach, while taking into account in a very central way the crucial importance of environmental factors, paves the way for the emergence of a more meaningful perspective on knowledge production and use. It is not as if some of the leading thinkers in our field have totally ignored this aspect of knowledge dissemination. For example, Havelock (1980, 12) says that effective communication between research generator and research user is not a one-way process, but a dialogue which takes place over time, which allows a full sharing of concerns on both sides, and which allows the reshaping of the message to suit the needs, concerns, and circumstances of the receiver. However, it seems to me that we have not yet succeeded in finding a way of achieving this objective. Unless a radical change in the epistemology of knowledge dissemination, in the way that I have suggested, takes place, the chances of this happening are extremely slim. Tinkering around with the conventional transportational paradigm, however ingenious our typologizing may be, will not bring this about.

The hermeneutical approach to knowledge and meaning involves elucidating not only the symbolic system that is the subject matter of analysis but also the interpreter's frame of reference (Shapiro 1981, 132). Gadamer (1975, 238) speaks of understanding the statements of other people in terms of our own prejudices and presuppositions. He sees this as the foundation for experiencing the world. Ricoeur (1974, 51) focuses attention on the "receptivity structure" through which we experience our world. Both stress the concept of self-understanding in understanding others. This notion should form the basis of our models and paradigms of knowledge dissemination. This would provide an excellent means of breaking out of the transportational framework of knowledge generation and utilization that has dominated the field so far.

REFERENCES

Bailey, J. 1975. Social Theory for Planning. London: Routledge, Kegan Paul.

Barnes, B. 1972. Sociology of Science. Penguin Books Ltd.

_____. 1979. Natural Order: Historical Studies in Scientific Culture. Beverly Hills, Calif.: Sage Publications.

Beal, G., and J. Bohlen. 1954. "The Diffusion Process." A presentation made to the Annual Conference, Iowa Extension Services in Agriculture and Home Ecnomics, Iowa State College, Dec. 6-9, 1954.

Bechford, G. L. 1972. <u>Persistent Poverty</u>. New York: Oxford University Press.

Bellonele, E. 1973. Quoted in D. Brokensha et al., ed., <u>Indigenous Knowledge Systems and Development</u>. University Press of America.

Beltran, L. R. 1976. "Alien Premises, Objects and Methods in Latin American Communication Research." In <u>Communication and Development</u>, ed. E. M. Rogers. Beverly Hills, CA: Sage Publications.

Berger, P. L., and T. Luckmann. 1967. <u>The Social Construction of Reality</u>. New York: Anchor Books.

Brokensha, D., et al. 1980. <u>Indigenous Knowledge Systems and Development</u>. University Press of America.

Caplan, N. 1979. "The Two-Communities Theory in Knowledge Utilization." <u>American Behavioral Scientist</u> 22 (3): 459-70.

Davis, B. E. 1968. System Variables and Agricultural Innovations in Eastern Nigeria. Ph.D. dissertation, Michigan State University.

Diaz-Bordenave, J. 1976. "Communication of Agricultural Innovations in Latin America." In <u>Communication and Development</u>, ed. E. M. Rogers. Beverly Hills, CA: Sage Publications.

Dissanayake, W. 1978. A Report on Family Planning Practices in Sri Lanka submitted to the Community Development Services Centre. Colombo.

Dunn, W. N. 1981. "If Knowledge Utilization is the Solution, What is the Problem?" Occasional paper series, University of Pittsburgh.

Elias, N. 1972. "Sociology of Knowledge: New Perspectives." <u>Sociology</u> 5, no. 2: 149-168.

Esman, M. 1974. Popular Participation and Feedback Systems in Rural Development.

Frake, C. O. 1962. "The Ethnographic Study of Cognitive Systems." In Theory in Anthropology, ed. R. A. Manners and D. Kaplan. Chicago: Aldine Publishing Co.

Gadamer, H. G. 1975. "Hermeneutics and Social Science" In Cultural Hermeneutics, 2, no. 4: 38-56.

Guruvitch, G. 1971. The Social Frameworks of Knowledge. New York: Harper and Row.

Havelock, R. G. 1969. Planning for Innovation. Ann Arbor: University of Michigan Institute for Social Research.

_____. 1980. Foreword to Using Researching in Organization by Jack Rothman. Beverly Hills, CA: Sage Publications.

Holzner, B., and E. Fisher. 1979. "Knowledge in Use: Considerations in the Sociology of Knowledge Application." Knowledge 1, no. 2: 219-44.

House, E. R. 1981. "Three Perspectives on Innovations: Technological, Political, Cultural." In Improving Schools: Using What We Know, ed. R. Lehming and M. Kane. Beverly Hills, CA: Sage Publications.

Huxley, J. 1934. Quoted in B. Barnes, ed., Sociology of Science. Penguin Books Ltd., 1972.

Katz, E. 1960. "Communication Research and the Image of Society: Convergence of Two Traditions." American Journal of Sociology, 65: 435-504.

Kuhn, T. S. 1962. The Structure of Scientific Revolutions. Chicago: Univ. of Chicago Press.

Larsen, J. 1981. "Knowledge Utilization: Current Issues." In The Knowledge Cycle, ed. R. F. Rich. Beverly Hills, CA: Sage Publications.

Levi-Leleland, Jean-Marc. 1976. "Ideology of/in Physics." In The Radicalisation of Science, ed. H. Rone and S. Rone. New York: Holmes and Meier Publishers.

Linge, D. 1976. Historicity and Hermeneutics: A Study of Contemporary Hermeneutic Theory. Ph.D. dissertation. Vanderbilt University.

283

Lionberger, H. F. 1949. Low-Income Farmers in Missouri,
Their Contacts with Potential Sources of Farm and Home
Information. Research Bulletin 441, May 1949,
Missouri.

Machlup, F. 1980. Knowledge and Knowledge Production.
Vol. I. Princeton University Press.

Mannheim, K. 1960. Ideology and Utopia. London.

McIver, R., and C. Page. 1957. Society: An Introductory
Analysis. London: Macmillan Co.

_____. 1945. Social Theory and Social Structures. New
York: Free Press.

Merton, R. K. 1957. "Priorities in Scientific Discovery:
A Chapter in the Sociology of Science." American
Sociology Review, 22: 635-659.

Morss, E. R. and R. F. Rich. 1980. Government Information
Management: A Counter Report of the Commission on
Federal Paper Work. Westview Press.

Nelson, B. N. 1981. On the Roads to Modernity: Conscience,
Science and Civilizations, ed. T. E. Huff. Totowa,
N.J.: Bowman and Littlefield.

Oasa, E. K., and B. H. Jennings. 1981. The Nature of
Social Inquiry in International Agricultural Research:
A Reproduction of the American Experience at IRRI and
CIMMI. Paper delivered at Annual Rural Sociological
Society Conference, Ontario.

Qadir, A. S. 1966. Adoption of Technological Change in the
Rural Philippines: An Analysis of Compositional
Effects. Ph.D. dissertation, Cornell University.

Rich, R. F. 1981. The Knowledge Cycle. Beverly Hills, CA:
Sage Publications, 1981.

_____. 1973. "The Task of Hermeneutics." Philosophy
Today, 17: 112-128.

Ricoeur, P. 1974. The Conflict of Interpretations: Essays
in Hermeneutics, ed. D. Ihde. Evanston, Ill.:
Northwestern Univ. Press.

Rogers, E. M. 1962. Diffusion of Innovations. New York: Free Press.

_____. 1971. Communication of Innovation: A Cross Cultural Approach. New York: Free Press.

_____. 1973. "Social Structure and Social Change." In Process and Phenomena of Social Change, ed. C. Zaltman. New York: Wiley and Sons.

_____. 1975. Communication Strategies for Family Planning. New York: Free Press.

_____. 1976. Communication and Development. Beverly Hills, CA: Sage Publications.

_____. 1977. Strategies for Planned Change, ed. G. Zaltman and R. Duncan. New York: Wiley.

Rogers, E. M., and R. Adhikarya. 1978. "Communication and Inequitable Development: Narrowing the Socio-economic Gap." Media Asia 5 (5): 3-10.

Röling, N. 1970. "Adaptions in Development: A Conceptual Guide for the Study of Noninnovative Responses of Peasant Farmers." Economic Development and Cultural Change 19, no. 1: 71-85.

Röling, N., and others. 1976. "The Diffusion of Innovations and the Issue of Equity in Rural Development." In Communication and Development, ed. E. M. Rogers. Beverly Hills, CA: Sage Publications.

Rothman, J. 1980. Using Research in Organizations: A Guide to Successful Application. Beverly Hills, Calif.: Sage Publications.

Rule, J. B. 1971. "The Problem with Social Problems." Politics and Society 2 (1): 47-56.

Ryan, B., and N. Gross. 1943. "The Diffusion of Hybrid Seed Corn in Two Iowa Communities." Rural Sociology, 8, no. 1: 15-24.

Saxena, A. P. 1968. System Effects on Innovativeness Among Indian Farmers. Ph.D. thesis, Michigan State University.

Schutz, A. 1967. *Phenomenology of the Social World.* Evanston, Ill.: Northwestern University Press.

Shapiro, M. J. 1981. *Language and Political Understanding.* Yale University Press.

Spaulding, I. A. 1955. Farm Operator Time-Space Orientations and the Adoption of Recommended Farming Practices. Bulletin 330, June 1955. University of Rhode Island.

Van Den Ban, A. W. 1960. "Locality Group Differences in the Adoption of New Farm Practices." *Rural Sociology* 25: 308-320.

Vico, G. B. 1968. *The New Science of Giambattista.* Rev. translation of the 3d ed. (1744) by T. G. Bergin and M. H. Fisch. Ithaca, N.Y.: Cornell Univ. Press.

Weiss, C. H. 1978. "Improving the Linkage between Social Research and Public Policy." In *Knowledge and Policy: The Uncertain Connection,* ed. L. E. Lynn. Washington, D.C.: National Academy of Sciences.

Whorf, B. L. 1956. *Language, Thought and Reality.* New York: Wiley.

12

Information Science: Interfaces with Knowledge Generation-Utilization

Sumiye Konoshima

Most of us will agree that the generation, diffusion, possession and use of information and knowledge are necessary conditions for the advancement of societies. Recognition of this factor as being crucial for development has pushed into greater prominence the articulation of concerns and issues on information imbalance, the new world information order, technology transfer, computerized data flow across borders, and the emerging trends in the expansion of the information sector and knowledge production industries. There has been a rapid growth of the ratio of the total work force engaged in knowledge production, especially in the industrialized world. It is estimated that in Germany, Sweden, Australia, Japan, the United Kingdom, and the United States over one-third of the population are involved in knowledge production industries (Boaz 1981). The concept of an information society is entering into discussions on contemporary society more markedly.

It is within this context of the current state of society that concepts and theories of information science are developing and evolving. This chapter reviews definitions of information science and its components, and identifies key components in the information sector environment which impact knowledge generation and use.

INFORMATION SCIENCE DEFINED

Elements of many disciplines are contained within the various definitions given to information science, reflecting the interdisciplinary nature of its evolution as a field of study. These multifarious definitions incorporate key concepts which relate to the study of knowledge generation-

utilization. Of particular relevance to our general
discussion is Weiss' definition (1977, 2):

> Information science can be defined as that set of
> principles and prescriptive rules dealing with the
> organization, maintenance, and management of bodies of
> scientific, technical, and business information used in
> decision-making. It is concerned with improving the
> communication of recorded information among three types
> of individuals or groups: (1) the originator of infor-
> mation; (2) the processor of information; (3) the user
> of information. Thus, information science must be an
> organized body of knowledge based on explanatory
> principles which seek to discover and formulate in
> general terms the conditions under which facts and
> events relating to the generation, transmission, and
> use of information occur.

An important perspective on the field has also been offered
by Saracevic, who stresses the need for information science
to "study a large number of properties, processes and/or
elements and to study their interaction and their organization rather than to stress the mechanistic one-way causality
or to isolate individual causal strains" (Saracevic 1970,
20).

Common elements gleaned from a survey of definitions of
information science provide a point of reference for identifying key components in this field. These elements include:

1. Bodies of _information_ constituting particular kinds
of knowledge;

2. The organization, maintenance and management of
information;

3. The communication and transfer of these bodies of
knowledge;

4. The interrelationships and interactions of three
groups in the information system environment in the
generation, transfer and use of information; and

5. The nature and properties of information as related
to the process of accessing, transferring, communicating and
using information.

Key Components of Information Science

The following key components of information science are
identified:

1. The systems approach to information systems, which

takes into consideration the interaction between the producer, the linker/intermediary/provider and the user of information, and all of the contingencies in the system environment which influence the information system and its effectiveness;

2. The linking process between the producer/generator of information and the recipient/user, the properties of this process and how they influence the transfer/flow/receipt and use of information.

3. The entities which are linked--the producer/generator of information the information provider/broker, and the recipient/user.

4. Information--that which is being transferred, its properties, its relevance to the user, and the related factors in processing, organizing and representing it.

INFORMATION SCIENCE AND INFORMATION SYSTEMS

The major components and thrusts of information science activities center on those conditions that have to do with how best to transfer and communicate information from the source/producer/generator through the information processor to the receiver/user. The study of these conditions is approached with a holistic, systemic perspective. These components and conditions constitute the major entities of information systems. Information science examines information systems, their properties and behaviors, the processes of interaction between these entities, the properties of the interaction processes and how they influence the flow of information from the source through the linker/intermediary to the user/receiver. Thus, the central focus for information science is information systems.

Information systems are an integral part of many knowledge utilization systems. These systems range from a simple family planning collection of training materials in rural India as a small part of a family planning knowledge use system to a sophisticated, computerized international information system (AGRIS) for agriculture. Consequently, what one can learn about how information systems dictate the flow, transference and communication of information to the user/receiver can be applied directly to the study of knowledge utilization systems.

In studying information systems, information science has developed models of information-use systems. The models incorporate the elements of source/producer, transfer channel, linker and user. These elements are the same, or

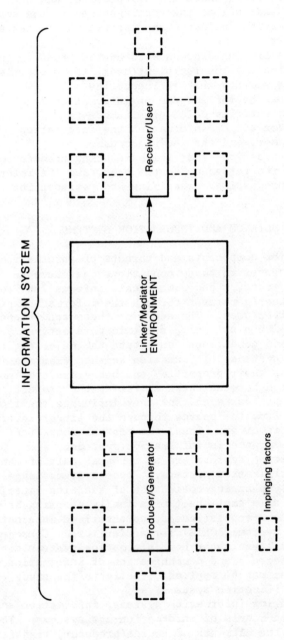

Figure 12.1 Focus of information science

at least similar, to the components of models of knowledge-use systems at the macro level. Thus, these models of information-use systems can also be considered as models of knowledge use systems at a micro-level (see Figure 12.1).

Information systems are devoted to the communication of knowledge. These systems include libraries, scientific societies, journals, information retrieval/dissemination systems, data processing systems, and so forth. They are used for diverse purposes: for political, economic and social purposes; for preservation of knowledge; for control of knowledge, for control of the explosion and growth of literature; for transmission of various signals representing information.

The efforts of information science have focused on problems related to information retrieval systems, to computers as information technology and systems, and to the problems of representing knowledge in the organization of information within the system and design of the system. There are common structural and functional elements in these information systems which relate to knowledge utilization processes. What are they and how do they relate to knowledge use?

The Systems Approach

"It is fundamental to information science to study the interaction of a large number of properties, processes and/or elements and to study their organization e.g., "whole," "system," "structure," "organized complexity" rather than to stress the mechanistic one-way causality or to isolate individual causal strains" (Saracevic 1970, 20). Information science uses a holistic approach to examine information systems in terms of relationships to larger and super-systems and to sub-systems and utilizes systems analysis (Levitan 1980).

Information science studies the information transfer process within the context of a system and all of the contingencies that bear upon this process. The system and all of its contingencies include not only the information system but also the environments of the information/knowledge-generator and the receiver/user. Variables associated with the generator and user environments interface with the transferring system and its processes and will affect the process, and in fact, whether transfer will take place.

Knowledge utilization systems also include the entities

and properties encompassed by the holistic, systems approach
of information science. Examination of the various models
of knowledge use systems indicate that the same elements of
generator, transmitter, user and their environments, and the
interrelationships and interaction processes are present.
(See Part 2 on models).

Transfer—Communication Processes

Information transfer is a basic component of
information science and a prerequisite for the design of
effective information systems. Information becomes usable
only when it is transferred.

Communication processes are fundamental to the transfer
function of information systems. Communication takes place
between the producer, information-linker, and user.
Producer/generator behavior and characteristics and the
working environment will influence what is communicated and
how knowledge and information are communicated and
transferred to the information system. User behavior and
characteristics and the context in which the user uses the
information will influence the process of transfer from the
information source to the user. The transfer function
cannot be fully comprehended if the process is studied in
isolation from the generator-user worlds. These two worlds
are integral parts of the system and the process.

If the fundamental premise that information becomes
usable only when it is transferred or communicated is
accepted, whatever the transfer mode or channel, then the
importance of analyses of factors related to the transfer
process for knowledge use theory cannot be disputed.

For some information scientists, distinction is made
between transfer and communication. Transfer takes place
when the message moves from the sender to the receiver
through a medium and the message is perceived in such form
that further action can be taken within the context of the
overall system. Communication takes place when the
information in the message is understood and appropriate
action is initiated. Communication for this group of
information scientists is a higher level process that
involves other phenomena in addition to transfer (Debons
1974).

Channels and mechanisms employed in communicating
between the three sub-systems will influence the nature,
quality, quantity and timeliness of the information
transferred.

For example, if a person-to-person channel is used via the telephone, one may have instantaneous information but certainly visual information is ruled out. The recipient will have to rely on his memory, and the quantity of information that can be absorbed will be limited. The use of mail or postal systems for transfer of information between persons in different parts of the world will certainly affect timeliness and quantity of information. If the channel or mechanism in communicating information is simply transference of information in the form generated by the producer, the recipient may have too much information to sift through to find the relevant information. The advent of computers, information networks and other communication technology has made an impact on the transfer process and on information dissemination and has mitigated many of the problems related to quantity and timeliness.

However, as we move from the informal to the more formal channels and mechanisms, different processes come into play. Modifications in the producer/user universes take place. Organizational structure, institutionalization and systems develop. Factors of the environmental context in which the information system operates will have greater influence on the flow and use of information. The economics and politics of the information system environment will dictate who can access and receive the information and what information is transferred. These factors will dictate also who communicates information/knowledge to whom and in what form (U.N. Centre on Transnational Corporations 1982).

Additional areas for further investigation of information transfer channels and mechanisms which might be fruitful for advancing information science and equally productive for the knowledge utilization field include:

1. The nature of the transmission channel, its effect on the quality and quantity of information that is transferred, and its weaknesses;

2. The study of comparative linguistics with a view to developing a common information-transfer language;

3. International and cross-national research for ensuring right-of-access to channels and mechanisms for all citizens of all nations;

4. New techniques for conversion of spoken and printed text to machine-readable forms; and

5. Man-machine interface improvements and decrease in costs for large segments of the world's population (Debons 1974).

Linker/User/Producer: The Linked Entities

The Linker/Mediator/Broker. For the information system, the principal actor is the processor of information--the linker/mediator/broker. Information science is concerned with this actor and his/her work-related behavior, the context in which he/she works, what influence these factors have on the process from generation/source of information to its use. The primary function for the information system person is to promote transfer of information from producer to user or receiver.

These linkers have particular work-related behavior which will affect the communication process to users and influence use and non-use of information. Do they publicize the existence of the information system and its services, or wait for users to come to them? How do they acquire information for the system? Do they analyze users' information needs? Do they focus on only the internal workings of the system? What do they do with the acquired information? How do they get it out to the user? How do they respond to information needs/demands?

The User. Information must be transferred or transmitted to someone or something and presumably for some manner of use. As information science delved into examining and developing information systems and services, the focus of attention began to shift to the users and their information demands, needs, articulation of needs, information-seeking patterns and application and use of information. Study of and attention to these user factors have contributed and continue to contribute to increasing knowledge on circumstances under which information/knowledge is best transmitted.

User studies in information science are conducted in order that knowledge about user behavior and characteristics and their interacting relationships with the information transfer process might be applied to improve information systems for increased probability of knowledge/information use. Users or potential users do not always articulate their information needs. Actual needs and perceived needs do not always coincide. Needs differ among different classes of users. Information-seeking patterns and formulation of queries vary. The information seeker, receiver and user may not be the same person. The information receiver may be also a non-user and merely a transmitting channel to the ultimate user. Receivers may not be the original seekers (Debons 1974). All of these variables relate to user impact on the transfer process, the performance of information systems and ultimately on the use of knowledge and information.

Although more adequate consideration of user aspects has contributed to increasing knowledge on circumstances under which information/knowledge is best transmitted, at the same time, additional problems for information systems were identified. As Kent (Debons 1974, 299) has noted: "The development and operations of information systems call for predictions as to what society (user) will be like; what words will mean; how people will act and how people will view events. Information systems do not work in the sense that recall and precision measures are not designed to read values relevant to those who would evaluate the systems". What to acquire or not to acquire and place into an information system contains the element of predicting information needs and the value of information/knowledge to the potential user. And what about unacquired information? Information and knowledge cannot be used if the information source system is a predominant or sole source and fails to include the information in its files. The selector in the information system then functions as gatekeeper and has an impact on knowledge use.

The notion then of use and non-use as a complex concept encompassing different uses of the same knowledge/information by different people for a variety of purposes is reinforced in research, not only on knowledge use systems but also in information science research.

Other problem areas in user/use studies identified as requiring further investigation are:

The characteristics of the receiver/user interface with the transmission channel; the preparation of the receiver to receive the transmitted information; nature of user feedback mechanisms and their improvement; user error-reporting devices/mechanisms for improving information transfer (Debons 1974).

The Producer/Generator. Information systems function as linkers/mediators and transmitters of information/knowledge generated by people and institutions. They interface with the producers of knowledge and the environment in which the producers work. They reflect the organizational approach of the producer-scientists-technologists and so forth to their respective fields of knowledge. These systems must take into account the disseminating patterns of producers and generators of knowledge, the channels through which knowledge and information are disseminated, and in what form. Producers and generators of information and knowledge are users as

well, but different from other users who are on the outside
of the knowledge areas. Information needs as articulated by
users are fed back to producers and generators of knowledge
who use this information to generate information to meet the
requirements of users. These variables associated with the
generation and production of information and knowledge
affect the design and organization of information systems,
what knowledge and information will be transferred, in what
form and how, and also have consequences for knowledge use.

In addition to their function not only as linkers and
mediators between producers and users of information,
information systems also serve as generators of knowledge.
This becomes evident if one examines the complex of
information activities (including organizing, ordering,
indexing, abstracting, classifying, relating and packaging)
needed to process all the bits of information into a
meaningful body of knowledge.

Information: Its Nature and Properties

The primary function of an information system is to
transfer information/knowledge from a source to a user in an
efficient and effective manner. What is being transferred
should be matched to what is needed, thereby increasing the
probability of use. This body of information or knowledge
must be represented accurately so as to impart the knowledge
content and at the same time be meaningful and relevant to
the seeker/user of the information/knowledge.

Information science examines bits of information and
the interrelationships among the information units within
specific bodies of knowledge; it attempts through analyses
to organize, structure and store information into systems to
reflect and represent the particular knowledge field.
Information science has investigated methods and ways of
expressing ideas, of converting these expressions into
storable and manipulable forms for analyzing and correlating
elements of information and synthesizing them into new
usable intelligence--in a sense, generating knowledge--and
providing meaning to the potential user or seeker of
knowledge/information. Information is not a matter of
presence or absence of facts but refers to facts assimilated
to a framework of general knowing (Debons 1974).

In recent discussions the properties of information
have been analogized in economic terms as commodities or
goods. While information has value and costs, this analogy
neglects the aspect of re-use. Information can be frozen in

time, can be "canned" and used and re-used beyond the time of production/generation and possibly eternally—unlike goods and commodities in the usual treatment in economics (Levitan 1982).

Within this economic context, the idea of information/knowledge as having value to the possessor or user and the treatment of information/knowledge as a commodity are incorporated into approaches to the study of systems. Growth in information systems appear to be correlated with economics and use in economic planning as well as with growth and development of knowledge areas and their literatures (Saracevic 1970, 696). Numerous studies have been conducted on the cost of information, the costs of designing, developing and operating information systems and on the economics of information and communication, but very few people have really addressed the question of the cost of no information/knowledge.

It would appear then that the value of information/knowledge to the user would be a factor in knowledge use and the willingness of the user to pay for its use.

Other issues on the nature and properties of knowledge fields which in turn influence potential use or non-use of knowledge are: vocabulary control, hierarchical relationships, methods of expressing ideas and concepts, ways of representing information which reflect the structure and evolving behavior of the knowledge field more precisely and in a meaningful way, and accessing mechanisms such as indexing, classification, and thesaurus development.

Information science then pays attention to the nature and properties of particular bodies of knowledge and how their properties will influence how best to organize, repackage, and represent information so that it can be retrieved, relayed, and transmitted in a meaningful way to the user. For instance, research information on the use of mass media to promote development programs as generated by social scientists is couched in technical terms and is usually replete with social science jargon. An administrator or mid-level manager or field worker for the development program will find it difficult to comprehend this information as presented by the social scientist. In fact, if access and approach to this information are only through the terminology and languages of the social scientist, the administrator, manager or potential user of the information may not be aware of its existence. As a consequence, the knowledge is not used even though it may be significant for implementation of the program.

Information Representation. Representation of information is given prominence in information science research, as discussed in the preceding paragraphs. However, there are other aspects to representation of information which need elaboration and relating to knowledge use.

The assumption is made by many information systems designers that given a good scheme for representing information, the problem of providing information to users is solved and everything else will follow the scheme. In order to develop a "good" scheme, there are particular components of information representation which must be analyzed. The results of these analyses must be taken into consideration in developing and designing the scheme. The structure of the languages, the semantic interrelationships between words in the text and as processed within the retrieval system; the relationship of individual records and their relevance unity; the organization of terminology--indexing, thesauri--in relation to the knowledge base and in terms of meaning rather than purely statistical association; structure and taxonomy of the knowledge field and interrelationships of subareas of the knowledge field--classification; comparative quality of content of the information--abstracting (Saracevic 1970). All of these components of a scheme for information representation directly affect the matching of the system with user information needs, user approach and information-seeking patterns, and potential use of the knowledge base. These components are crucial for assuring that the linking process will result in the receipt of appropriate information by the seeker/user; that the bits of information are related and belong to that body of knowledge with which the user is concerned; that the records in the information system reflect accurately the body of knowledge covered by the information base to minimize the user/seeker's being misled or misinformed; and that meaning related to the knowledge base will be transmitted to the user in understandable terms, thus providing the user with access to the knowledge/information base.

Relevance. Relevance is another important concept in information science. It includes more than just aspects related to performance internally within an information source system and more than the property of document content or document relatedness to other documents in the system. Relevance should be examined not only in terms of source but also in terms of destination (receiver/user) relevance. Judgments and measures of relevance are not simply a dichotomous decision of relevant or non-relevant. There are levels of relevance; levels contingent upon factors such as who is judging the relevance, what are the measures used to assess relevance, time when information is being sought and judgment on relevance is being made; the articulation of information needs and the ability of information systems to match up relevant information to meet those needs; the value of what is transmitted or communicated will affect judgments of relevance (Saracevic 1970). Studies of relevance have much to contribute to developing strategies for more effective information synthesis, organization and transmission, and in turn, to the body of knowledge generation and use research.

Conclusion

The key concepts and approaches outlined above would suggest that information science is a "pan-information science" which encompasses more than the flow of library documents and science and technology communication (Licklider 1974, 453). It is the foundation for a vast complex of information industries which constitute the knowledge industry. It can be considered a "super observer" who transcends and synthesizes results of functional analysis, systems analysis and reductionism and provides an integrated perspective on information units, processes, components, mapping and matching them and the systems of generators/producers of information to user systems (Levitan 1980).

However, these same concepts and approaches would suggest that there are assumptions that pertain to only a particular model or just a few of the many models of knowledge use. Information science focuses on information systems; research has concentrated on the more formal systems which deal with science and technology information. The underlying assumption of research has been that there is a body of users, who are seeking information now, or will be in the future. It assumes that information systems have evolved and have been established for these users. It has examined transfer processes and derived principles about information/knowledge use processes within the context of a purposive system with users or potential users who represent only one or only a few of the segments of the universe of information/knowledge users. Nevertheless, to the extent that the concepts and principles from information science are applied to approaches to the study of knowledge generation and use, information science will have

300

contributed to the understanding of knowledge use systems
and to the advancement of society.

REFERENCES

Boaz, M. 1981. Strategies for Meeting the Information
Needs of Society in the Year 2000. Littleton, Colo.:
Libraries Unlimited.

Debons, A., ed. 1974. Information Science, Search for
Identity. Proceedings of the 1972 NATO Advanced Study
Institute in Information Science. New York: Marcel
Dekker.

Levitan, K. B. 1980. "Applying a Holistic Framework to
Synthesize Information Science Research." In Progress
in Communication Sciences ed. B. Dervin and M. J.
Voigt, 241-273. Norwood, N.J.: Ablex Publishing Corp.

_____. 1982. "Information Resources as 'Goods' in the
Life Cycle of Information Production." Journal of the
American Society for Information Science (January):
44-54.

Licklider, J. C. 1974. "An Overview." In Information
Science, Search for Identity, ed. A. Debons, 453-457.
New York: Marcel Dekker.

Saracevic, T., comp. 1970. Introduction to Information
Science. New York: R. R. Bowker.

U.N. Centre on Transnational Corporations. 1982. Report
for the Seventh Session of the Commission on Transnational Corporations, Geneva, August 31 to September
14, 1981. New York: U.N. Economic and Social Council.

Weiss, E. C., ed. 1977. The Many Faces of Information
Science. Boulder, Colo.: Westview Press.

13

Some Ethical Considerations for Knowledge Utilization Studies: Research and Development Systems as an Example

Bruce M. Koppel

Contemporary research and development (R & D) systems are excellent examples of knowledge utilization systems. The reference may be to the significant and well-established system of land-grant colleges and experiment stations that constitute the bulk of the public agricultural research system in the United States, the pharmaceutical, electronic, and chemical industry research parks, or the military-industrial establishment. All are prime examples of a consciously designed, carefully evolved, and deliberately managed system for borrowing, generating, discovering, selecting, screening, evaluating, transforming, merging, and applying knowledge. Each year numerous professional schools in many countries turn out small crowds of R & D managers and managers-to-be, all equipped more or less with a social technology, namely, "management skills," to mobilize the knowledge generating process for specific ends. In recent years, in the United States, Japan and Europe, conferral of the title "economic leader" is measured increasingly by the vitality of R & D systems. Calls for "reindustrialization," re-evaluations of the economic justifications for environmental and occupational regulations of the workplace, strained trade relationships between the United States and other member countries of the OECD, and deep reassessments of government's role in the economy are indications of concern about the decline in American productivity and the international competitiveness of the American economy. Ultimately, such concerns are challenges to the American R & D establishment to compete more vigorously in a high-technology and recession-plagued world.

Anxieties about R & D systems have not been confined to the issues of low productivity and diminished competitiveness. There are also deeper worries about the strategies

301

R & D systems have pursued and may pursue to confront
productivity and competitiveness issues as well as other
issues (e.g., environmental conservation) that some
R & D systems have chosen largely to ignore. For example,
the current concerns about nuclear and industrial waste
disposal are direct challenges to industrial and chemical
R & D systems. Three Mile Island and Love Canal suggest to
many that some costs and risks have been excessively discounted. A string of publications beginning with Silent
Spring (Carson 1962) and Hard Tomatoes, Hard Times
(Hightower 1973) raised significant questions about the
impacts of America's agricultural research system on the
structure, sustainability, and safety of American agriculture. The current strong interest in biotechnology and
its commercial possibilities is already generating discussion on topics ranging from the probabilities and distribution of risk incidence to whether patterns of scientific
communication in the universities might be altered in
directions that insulate publicly funded research from
public accountability and weaken traditional educational
missions. The examples go on. At the least, the concerns
confirm the existence of a view that the consequences of
R & D efforts may include some costs and risks that are not
always sufficiently recognized or considered.
    The discomfort with R & D also sometimes reflects an
anxiety that the R & D ship may be without an adequate
ethical rudder, that competitiveness and productivity
objectives have effectively substituted for a more direct
relationship to social, environmental, and moral goals.
That anxiety is often portrayed by defenders of accused
R & D systems as anti-technology and, hence, profoundly
irrelevant. The portrayal is sometimes accurate, but it
would be a mistake to assume that all ethical questions
about R & D are similarly irrelevant. What may be more
appropriate to ask is whether and when such questions are
evidence more of political naivete than ethical commitment.
Some might argue, for example, that the practice of R & D is
a form of instrumental knowledge that, by definition, serves
interests other than pure understanding. Cavalieri (1981),
for example, argues that molecular biology gets into ethical
difficulties when it drifts from being science to commercial
technology. Cavalieri's professional colleagues would
probably argue that R & D cannot itself be held directly
accountable for consequences of its work—that liability
belongs with those commercial and political interests
setting the goals for R & D. I suggest that such
propositions are problematic because they ignore the complex

relationship between the practice of science, the society of
which scientists are part, and the organization of R & D.
Too often, there is a tendency to conceive the ethical
evaluation of R & D as a question of where R & D is
conducted rather than what R & D is. In any case, an
anxiety about R & D that has ethical roots usually will be
drawn to situations where it is apparent that problematic
consequences are not recognized as problematic. It is not
that such consequences are somehow accidentally ignored, but
rather that the probability of problematic consequences is
systematically discounted.

This chapter will focus on ethical concerns about
R & D. What does it mean to say that R & D is ethically
adrift? Why would R & D systems have difficulty accepting
the proposition that they are ethically adrift? What would
have to happen for R & D systems to confront more fully and,
if needed, address, the possibility of ethical drift? What
role can knowledge utilization studies play in both understanding and answering these questions? These questions
will be addressed here.

ETHICAL ISSUES FOR R & D

The basic ethical issues for R & D systems are not
obscure. They relate to the distribution of costs, risks,
and benefits between individuals, groups, and generations.
They relate to the broader social and moral values served by
the problem R & D chooses to solve, the process R & D
selects to reach a solution, and the solution itself. The
ethical aspects of R & D systems relate to accountability--
the human and moral processes through which interests and
values (such as to whom and by whom accountability is
structured) are translated into concrete social and sometimes political action. Finally, the ethical dimensions of
R & D systems as knowledge utilization systems relate very
centrally to choice, the amplification of choice, and the
enhancement of the ability of individuals and groups to
recognize and make choices. Much can be said about the
forms these issues take, but the question that might better
be asked is why it is that our R & D systems seem to run
away from such issues. What are some major attempts R & D
systems have made and are making to compensate for being
ethically adrift?

Some of the reasons contemporary R & D systems have a
hard time with ethical issues are well known. Contemporary
R & D is, with few exceptions, the organizational perfection

of reductionism. The best known manifestation of reductionism is a scientific and technological division of labor
around specializations, each premised to be part of
virtually any "normal" problem that R & D might confront.
Closely tied to that reductionism is the belief that science
(whether natural or social) involves a form of objective
knowledge that carries no ethical assumptions or political
baggage. The average bench scientist would react with
incredulity to the proposition that his or her work was
something more or other than an incremental contribution to
a knowledge of nature and the natural world and, in some
cases, an application of that knowledge to useful ends. In
this view, science and society are distinct. A scientific
discovery has no "social" content until it is specifically
used by society. Discovery is therefore a neutral activity.

When science is organized as an R & D system, can the
claims of sanctuary be sustained? A useful example of how
that question is answered is a field called the policy
sciences. Policy science is a form of R & D that attempts
to understand and prescribe for the political process
through a set of purportedly neutral analytic filters. The
emergence and content of policy is a "natural" process
subject to "laws" and "regularities" like other natural
processes. The policy scientist assumes that the political
process operates according to some lawful regularities that
can be known, regularities that are built around the interaction of interests, not values. Not surprisingly, the
regularities assumed, sought for, and found bear strong
resemblances to free market metaphors commonly used by
economists. Laurence Tribe's (1972, 75) comments are about
the policy sciences, but they are an appropriate statement
about numerous other R & D frameworks:

> One of the most persistent beliefs about policy science
> techniques...is a conviction of their transparency to
> considerations of value and their neutrality with
> respect to fundamental world views and to more or less
> ultimate ends. Although it is by now widely recognized
> that such techniques can be abused as tools in a
> disguised play for power, the myth endures that the
> techniques in themselves provide nothing beyond value-
> free devices for organizing thought in rational
> ways—methods for sorting out issues and objectively
> clarifying the empirical relationships among
> alternative actions and their likely consequences. The
> user of such techniques, the myth continues, may turn
> them to whatever ends he seeks. Ends and values, goals

and ideologies are seen as "inputs" to a machine like, and hence inherently unbiased, process of solving problems consistent with the facts known and the values posited. The machine itself, like all machines, is said to be subject to misuses but to have no imperatives of its own: only animistic thinking, we are told, can obscure its essential neutrality.

Today, many R & D systems at least acknowledge that problems may be more complex than originally thought. The energy problem and the food problem, for example, are <u>seen</u> as more than simple supply-demand problems. However, translating a wider vision into programming and organizational change is not so easy nor is it so readily attempted. Sometimes, the expanded vision is really the outer cover of an onion. At the core, there really is no expanded vision. For example, the concept of "integrated pest management" evolved in part from a perspective on the food problem that appeared to be sensitive to ecological and environmental consequences of intensive food production strategies. As developed at several universities and research centers, however, integrated pest management has become a strategy that <u>increases</u> chemical applications in agriculture and may actually aggravate the problem of environmental and ecological degradation of natural agricultural resources. Moreover, integrated pest management requires an extraordinary amount of farm-level and village-level managerial and organizational skills. Thus, as often happens, technological and social fixes remain quite secure and interchangeable at the onion's core.

In some cases, R & D systems will argue that more complexity means broader problems, and then conclude that broader problems are beyond their reach or responsibility. Here again, the reaction of the average bench scientist is illustrative. In a survey of problem choice in the agricultural sciences in the United States, Busch and Lacy (1983) found that what agricultural scientists thought were problems 'and what they actually worked on were quite distinct. Hargrove (1977) found similar patterns among scientists in the Indian agricultural research system. In both countries, scientists were not unaware of the incongruence, but to the contrary, defended it as an indication that means (their scientific skills) and ends (the problems the skills could solve) were appropriately matched. Therefore R & D systems can and should only work on their piece of the pie: but who is working on the rest of the pie? Who decides what kind of pie there will be? Which

306

problem definitions will continue to dominate? In some
cases, also, R & D systems simplify complex problems because
they believe the problems really are reducible. For
example, much money will be spent to synthesize insulin.
Yet there is no shortage of insulin. Ruth Hubbard comments:

> [W]hat we need to know in order to study the cure for
> diabetes are the causes of diabetes, which are, as with
> all other diseases, heavily influenced by social and
> environmental factors. This is not to downgrade
> diabetes as a health problem. It obviously is; it is
> among the top eight killers in this country. But we
> need to know more about its real causes, and the real
> causes are not lack of insulin.... [W]hat we don't need
> right now is a new, potentially hazardous technology
> for producing insulin that will only profit the people
> who are producing it. And given the history of drug
> therapy in relation to other diseases, we know that if
> we produce more insulin, more insulin will be used,
> whether diabetics need it or not. (Cavalieri 1981, 68)

The same might be said about interferon and cancer or
about the logic of arguing that applications of recombinant
DNA technologies to food production will solve the world's
food problems (rather than dealing with perseverence of
poverty, a factor that accounts for both low food production
and inadequate food consumption). In these situations, what
we are confronting is less deliberate concealment of
alternate problem conceptions than confidence in the R & D
system and the fixes it generates. It is a confidence born
of years of supportive social, economic and political
experience; some sophisticated conceptual frameworks and
ideologies which lead those inside and outside R & D systems
to believe the systems and their products are ultimately
efficient and even inevitable; and once in a while the
negative experiences of those who have tried to orient
themselves differently. Where the issue acquires special
ethical significance is when we ask: Who determines when
excluding or including certain problem definitions is
acceptable or unacceptable? When "who determines" is
different from "who bears the risks and costs," there may be
an ethical problem.
   In recent years, a major solution suggested for this
problem has been "interaction." The R & D system should
have more interaction with those it presumes to serve. One
must be careful about this appealing prescription. No
interaction scheme yields a necessary or inevitable

reduction in the disassociation of risks and benefits. One of the major criticisms of the land-grant system, for example, has been precisely that the system interacts too closely with agribusiness and larger commercial farm enterprises (rather than smaller family-operated farms or migrant labor households). If interaction is a path to a more ethically satisfactory R & D system, it must be because of who the interaction is with as well as the alteration of "traditional" power relationships represented in the structure of communication within the interaction. From that perspective, interaction might better be viewed as an approach to (1) improving R & D's accountability to interests and values other than those it might autonomously select; (2) identifying problems that closely resemble problems that people actually have; and (3) choosing people whose problems are, in some sense, of ethical priority. The literature on farming systems research and the earlier literature on appropriate technology are examples of this broader understanding of what interaction means for the relationship between technology (R & D) and social purpose.

In practice, even a more limited understanding of interaction, one that concentrates on aspects of problem definition, turns out to be more easily discussed than accepted. A few years ago, the International Rice Research Institute (IRRI) celebrated its 20th anniversary. An anthropologist who was a visiting staff member wrote a paper that was seen as provocative. The paper suggested that IRRI scientists might find it useful to pay attention to problems as farmers perceive them. The paper was suppressed by IRRI's leadership (thereby ensuring it would be widely read). Interaction in this case was acceptable, but not if it required restructuring communication patterns. On whose terms is interaction to occur?

Several years ago, a group of entomologists questioned whether farmers in their area knew enough about insect pests and their population dynamics to justify initiating some research on biological pest control approaches. The entomologists developed and implemented a questionnaire which sought to determine among other things if farmers could match insect names and pictures using the Latin names of the insects! At issue in this example are the terms of interaction between "science" and "indigenous knowledge." The approach chosen by the scientists was to measure the correspondence of indigenous knowledge with their science. This was, of course, a test in scientific literacy, not an evaluation of the descriptive or explanatory power of an indigenous knowledge system. The example is not atypical.

The very concept of a "scientific community" practically makes such misunderstandings inevitable. Professionalism and professional autonomy are frequently used as points of reference by scientists, as territorial markers of the scientific community. Unfortunately, such reference points do not automatically correspond with what society needs in the way of technological or social intervention (or neglect). What is equally unfortunate is that there is no simple solution to this problem of designation without representation. We might argue for more participation of farmers in IRRI's decision making because of the social origins of IRRI science. What about the social origins of the farmers' perceptions of their problems? On what basis do we accept either at face value?

Some argue that it is unrealistic to expect the bench scientist to interact with the lay public to guide his or her basic work. The argument is made that such an understanding of interaction is too literal. Interaction, it is suggested, should not be applied to individual members of an R & D organization, but rather to the R & D organization itself. Thus the question: How can R & D systems interact more satisfactorally with appropriate portions of the real world? An answer that is often given to that question is to place the responsibility with R & D management. After all, it is R & D management that generally establishes internal goals, maintains internal reward systems, and, of course, represents the organization in a diverse number of external settings.

Placing the interaction burden on R & D management is not without serious problems. Many of those problems are direct consequences of R & D's insulation, actual or assumed. In agriculture, for example, a dilemma for contemporary research management is that obtaining the broad spectrum of inputs needed to support a broader problem definition is difficult if not impossible. The contemporary R & D manager in agriculture often lacks channels to those research presumes to serve while depending for political and financial support on a different audience, but one that is well prepared to press its demands. In the United States, the strong links certain interest groups have with the leadership and funding structure of the land-grant system do much to explain what the system does and does not do, and for whom it makes those choices. The same pattern of relationships serves as evidence that the system's leadership lacks linkages, or at the least, lacks politically adequate linkages, to parts of the American population not necessarily well-represented by those interests more

experienced in using the land-grant system. In developing
countries, research system leadership may be quite adept at
rhetorically taking on social objectives (e.g., reducing
malnutrition or increasing the income of poor farmers), but
linkages of virtually any kind to the malnourished and poor
may be politically infeasible.

The R & D manager who strives to translate such
rhetoric into an operational agenda may be overwhelmed by
excessive accountability to numerous audiences with diverse,
sometimes inconsistent, and usually ill-defined goals. This
is an important point, especially in publicly supported
research systems. Even where R & D management is listening,
there is no reason to believe that the message will be one
that can be understood or one that can be readily converted
to an internal R & D work program. Arope (1977) has argued
that the agricultural R & D manager must be sensitive to
changing social goals and effectively transmit their
implications to the scientific staff. Unfortunately, the
research manager will rarely be in a position to calibrate
alterations in ethereal entities like social goals. He or
she will be too busy understanding the social goals of
various external groups making demands on the R & D organization, and simultaneously mollifying and motivating the
scientists in the organization, to give much thought to the
goals of society at large. Even where R & D leadership is
prepared to take the risks, the results may not be
rewarding.

> The laboratory cannot do all its thinking in private;
> to succeed it must have detailed interaction with some
> region of the universe it seeks to understand.
> Inevitably, it is compelled to pass through some phase
> of external visibility, at a time when its sophisti-
> cation and expertise are generally poorly formed. At
> that moment, during its days of heady anticipation,
> opponents will often attempt its assassination,
> complaining to the laboratory's overlords that it
> meddles where it has no competence. The charge of
> incompetence will be true and unanswerable, at least at
> that stage; the only defense could be on societal
> grounds, and not on professional or technical claims.
> No escape exists from this difficulty. To assume a low
> profile and say nothing controversial is to adopt
> disciplinary surrogates for motives that can only be
> described as self-preservation; the problem remains,
> alternately, to labor privately toward perfection is
> almost certainly to labor in vain (Rose 1974, 154).

Farming systems R & D efforts offer some promising examples of organizational and programmatic innovation, but the difficulties that lie ahead should not be underestimated. Farming systems research, for example, is a recognition of complexity; it is not necessarily an inevitable bridge to a better dialogue between scientists and farmers. At the same time that plant breeding has recognized the complex systemic nature of problems like photosynthetic efficiency and nitrogen fixation, specializations have proliferated to grapple with parts of those problems. Of what value is improving interaction between R & D and the public if R & D has increasing trouble talking to itself? Remember the song: "Once the rockets are up, who cares where they come down. That's not my department says Werner Von Braun." If interaction is not limited to a code of behavior for individual scientists and is not feasible if left to the ingenuity of R & D leadership, what remains is a broader alteration in R & D organization and its relationship to society at large.

Sometimes one senses that R & D managers are asking: Are we faced only by complexity or are we also facing the limits of conventional wisdom about how to organize ourselves to deal with complexity? For example, efforts are currently underway in the United States to establish a centralized computer-based National Plant Germplasm System. This would supersede the diverse state and regional germplasm collections the United States now maintains. This is an important development given the increasing potential capabilities of plant breeding due to new genetic technologies. Germplasm resources will become very important basic raw materials and on a larger scale than has been true in the past. The descriptors chosen to organize genetic information in such a system are crucial because they will represent the boundaries on what sorts of problems can and cannot be easily addressed within the system's normal operating codes. If you look, for example, at the descriptors proposed for tomatoes, what you will see are characteristics keyed to three major interests: plant protection, processing, and yield. What we find are thus descriptors that are compatible with existing breeding goals—goals associated with high-capital, high-energy agricultural strategies established essentially by tomato processors. You will not find anything that is directly linked to improved nutritional value. Nor do you find descriptors that could be easily adapted to implementing breeding goals associated with more ecologically sustainable agricultural systems. Nor do you see the representatives of such alternate interests on the scientific boards establishing the descriptors.

It is necessary to emphasize that questions that encompass recognition of greater complexity do not necessarily lead to some ethical reawakening. Such questions do not even necessarily lead to deviation from business as usual. Complexity can acquire ethical importance if confronting complexity raises questions about what terms of reference and whose terms of reference will be used to "order" the complexity. If that opportunity still yields a "business as usual" result, it may be that "business as usual" is indeed adequate. If that conclusion is controvertible, however, it does not follow that some people are deliberately conniving to exclude certain points of view. That perspective is more simple than compelling. R & D is a social process, a process that occurs in an institutional setting where trade-offs occur for many reasons and where subtle but powerful pressures operate to make it very unlikely that certain viewpoints will be expressed. Logrolling and horse trading are a feature of internal resource allocation in many R & D systems. These are bargaining arrangements in which participants are not required to seriously consider each other's aims. In organizations that are very homogeneous in terms of staff disciplinary backgrounds and specializations, that kind of exchange will usually be present, but only moderately. The homogeneity usually ensures that goals and objectives will differ more because of internal bureaucratic squabbling than because of substantive disagreements. In organizations with multiple disciplines and divergent specializations represented on a staff, logrolling will be much more common, in part as a way to reduce the probability that substantive differences will surface and come into confrontation. In that kind of communication environment, even where intentions are good, the dangers of qualitative misunderstandings are real: positions will be taken and solutions proposed as if much more were understood about how disciplines and specializations and about how society and the R & D system interact than really is.

In a broad sense, there is a public interest in what R & D systems do. In general, it is an interest that should be concerned with why R & D does what it does, how that activity can be made more socially purposeful, and whether some things that R & D does should be done at all. What is not clear is how that interest can express itself or, in practice, what it should express about itself. That is not because R & D is opposed to being ethically purposeful, but

because the communication patterns described earlier suggest
that despite the fact that everyone decides for the best,
things can go from bad to worse. These problems are not the
only cause of perverse outcomes, however. What other
dynamic processes are operating? Some are known. The
prisoners dilemma may characterize agricultural extension
systems, especially where "late adopters" are involved.
Incrementalism yields the mechanical rice transplanter in
labor surplus agricultural economies. Societal problems
like pollution and social dislocation occur not so much
because of individual or collective wickedness, but more
often because goods and bads are joint products. For
society, choosing as it does to live with the products of
R & D efforts, that creates a problem. If the bads are not
sufficiently recognized and somehow paid for, there will be
too many of them. That is an instance of the invisible hand
slapping us in the face. How can society, unable to consistently sort out the goods and bads in time, expect the R & D
system to do it? How can an R & D system take on such a
responsibility? Currently, there is increasing interest in
bureaucratic reorientation--empowerment of the poor through
new types of learning and participatory behaviors for rural
development agencies (Korten 1981). That interest and the
experience it is beginning to generate are very promising.
It suggests a direction that may be reproducible: break down
the distinction between an R & D system and "society" and
substitute interaction between the two as a route to a
proper sorting out of goods and bads in prospective forms of
social intervention. In the bureaucratic reorientation
movement, there is special emphasis on interaction with the
poor, an especially encouraging sign. Nevertheless, the
blinding temptation of a social blueprint still stands
strongly in the way. It is the blueprint, whether social or
technological, that inhibits the first aspect of interaction
noted earlier, namely, improving R & D's accountability to
interests and values other than those it might autonomously
select.

In recent years, R & D systems have experimented with a
number of approaches to dealing with these difficult uncertainties. They include: social impact assessment and social
indicators, environmental impact assessment, technology
assessment, and risk analysis as well as the more well-
established economic cost-benefit techniques. In principle,
any of these techniques could be vehicles for a considerable
sensitizing of R & D systems. Often they are. However, we
need to recognize that these methodologies often take the
form of social technologies, R & D systems of another sort,

with well-established premises, professionalization patterns, and most of the other characteristics that have caused difficulties in the R & D systems they are supposed to enlighten.

Ethical guidance for R & D is very difficult because of what R & D systems are: institutionalized and exquisitely codified knowledge utilization systems. What are especially institutionalized and codified are conceptions of what the "real" problems are, what constitutes a solution track, what kind of solution is "enough," what constitutes acceptable and recognizable knowledge, and who are qualified to make judgments about that knowledge. Broad consensus is not required on problems for that knowledge utilization system to work as it does. What is required is consensus about the system within which problems are defined. If you believe that the world consists of producers adopting new technology at different rates based on diffusion of information, you are not likely to state problems in terms of class struggle or power relationships. What is considerably more likely is that you will state problems that range from the literacy and socialization characteristics of agricultural households to extension strategies and alternate hardware communication devices. If you believe that agriculture consists of small farmers who own their land and seek to maximize profits, then your perception of problems in agricultural development will consist of those things which prevent farmers from doing as much profit maximizing as they would like. Thus, agricultural economists and engineers can make a case for the development and commercialization of a mechanical rice transplanter in terms of reducing farmer-operator costs. That transplanting in parts of Southeast Asia is highly labor-intensive and that mechanizing transplanting would leave large numbers of agricultural laborers in trouble is not seen as a crucial objection. This is not an example of people thinking of ways to cause misery for others. It is an example of people proceeding logically within a conception of a system to conceptions of problems and solutions.

A critique has been made by some which points essentially to the methods of science as the source of trouble. That is a useful insight. Certainly the methods of science divert attention from understanding the world to verifying the rules science uses to describe the world. I am not convinced, however, that a different epistemology for describing physical and social processes will necessarily yield any more satisfactory ethical knowledge or orientation. I say that for two reasons. One is that the pattern of institutionalization itself creates some quite serious problems for altering an ethical course. Very few organizations, whatever their epistemologies, are known for reacting comfortably to counterintuitive knowledge, particularly counterintuitive ethical knowledge. It is one thing for an organization to recognize that what it is doing is, in some sense, not working. It is a much more difficult task for an organization to confront, never mind acknowledge, the argument that what it does is, in some sense, "bad." Such problems are unlikely to be absent, even in "Hermeneutic Land." It is difficult in any R & D system to maintain a critical stance toward what are given as or what become conventional meaning structures. In fact, they are ideologies, belief systems that provide comprehensive guides to social reality and the place of the R & D system in that reality. As Leslie White argued several years ago, science is a way of experiencing the world. In the face of such ideologies, whatever their associated methods and techniques, a critical stance does not come easily. That is because a key characteristic of ideologies is that they are not neutral. They demand allegiance.

A second reason why changing the epistemology might not improve the probability of ethical knowledge is the question of complicity: What is the complicity of an R & D system with the very problems it purports to solve? How much autonomy does R & D really have? To what extent is it the product of larger political and economic forces? If we believe that each R & D system is historically idiosyncratic and politically autonomous, then we can bound the problem of counterintuitive ethical knowledge rather easily: it stops at the doors of the R & D system. If we cannot assume autonomy and idiosyncrasy, however, then we are talking about degrees of involvement in a larger process that conceals counterintuitive ethical knowledge. Issues like these emphasize the importance of knowledge utilization studies <u>as a critical enterprise</u>, as a form of inquiry that may have some quite important things to tell us about what kinds of ethical considerations R & D systems are capable of and perhaps what kinds of knowledge utilization systems might be capable of incorporating more thorough ethical navigation.

GETTING STARTED

Can an R & D system be critical of itself as a knowledge utilization system? To answer that, I believe it is necessary to begin by asking three questions that are crucial for understanding how ethically adrift any R & D organization is.

1. What forms does the system's conceit take?
2. With what is the system in complicity?
3. What is the system's conception of choice?

Conceit

Conceit in one sense is part of the very act of institutionalization. By institutionalization, I mean the ordering of a pattern of behaviors and meanings in a format that is recognized through some publicly identifiable symbols. The symbols differentiate the pattern from other individual examples of social interaction. The symbols can vary from broad patterns of professionalization to credentialism and uniforms. The symbols serve the dual purpose of reminding outsiders they are excluded and reinforcing the appreciation by insiders of their distinctiveness. Scientific R & D is certainly an illustration of such use of symbols to reinforce institutionalization. A key to the very meaning of science is limited access to a body of knowledge. Access to an institutionalized pattern of meanings, in this instance science, requires more or less extensive immersion in a framework of understanding. That means a science's rules for identifying, interpreting, and attributing significance to that aspect of the world it purports to understand; the rules for evaluating that understanding as knowledge; and the structure of meanings (and vocabulary) for expressing those rules in practice.

How much and in what ways do patterns of institutionalization in science influence the definition, comprehension, and acceptance of ethical knowledge? To what extent is there a conceit that confuses an ideological confirmation that what is being done is "good" for ethical knowledge that equations linking patterns of institutionalization to positive ethical characterizations are falsifiable? Such questions point to a deep characteristic of scientific R & D—a type of instrumental teleology that confers activity with axiomatic positive ethical value.

Conceit can take other forms in knowledge utilization systems. One example for R & D is the conceit of abstraction and with it an erosion of linkages to any real clear sense of social purpose. Calling abstraction a conceit is not saying that abstract tools such as models are themselves a conceit. The issue turns rather on the degree to which models are kept in perspective. Do they provide enlightened understanding of consequences, especially counterintuitive consequences, or do they create their own reality? To the extent that the answer is the latter, creating their own reality, it becomes necessary to ask: What is the degree to which models deflect accountability from consequences by denying consideration of relationships not previously encountered or anticipated? What if they are oriented instead essentially to verifying some self-contained set of rules that assume the models are ethical, in part by denying the possibility of relevant ethical knowledge outside the model's terms of reference? That denial, however made, is the conceit of abstraction—thought that is dissuaded from accountability beyond its own terms of reference. It is, in fact, thought that confuses conformity to method for accountability to ethical purpose.

It is important to state that conceit is not always blatant, just as arrogance is not always offensive. Virtually all agricultural and food research is done ostensibly for the greater good of humankind. The link between hunger and poverty is almost always acknowledged in one way or another, but rarely embraced as a central orientation. Technological fixes are substituted for social orientation; social fixes are substituted for ethical sensitivity. The latter is a special example of the conceit of abstraction. In some versions, historical determinism is used to essentially undermine the possibility of choice by assuming and then projecting a set of relationships that are not falsifiable. That form of argument disassociates behavior from responsibility. Another example is functionalism, the belief that whatever one does is "right" because one did it. What are presented as hypotheses are axioms in disguise. As I shall argue below, choice is crucial if there is to be ethical knowledge. Consequently, a substantial weakening of choice approximates a denial of ethical knowledge. Although the conceit may take the form of social or historical knowledge, it does not make the denial any less a denial.

Complicity

The issue of complicity is both obvious and subtle, complex and straightforward. At one level, the issue follows from some elementary premises. No R & D organization is completely autonomous. To argue otherwise is to propose that science is unrelated to patterns of political, economic, and cultural development and that its manifestation as R & D is random. A variety of interdependencies

ranging from external funding to the professional backgrounds of R & D staff to the historical relationships of
science to society exist and influence what R & D looks at,
how it learns, how it uses its knowledge, and how its
knowledge is used. Since such interdependencies are only
partially under R & D's control, R & D has limited autonomy.
In such cases, the complicity issue is, in essence, a search
for problematic ethical orientations attributable to forces
external to the R & D organization. However, the link
between finding interdependencies and proving complicity can
be deceptively simple and obvious.

For example, in what sense is some form of association
with evil (or good) by itself *ipso facto* evil (or good)? Is
an R & D system less able to acquire ethical knowledge about
itself if portions of its funding come from a source that is
unable to comprehend the ethical dimensions of its own work?
Conventional wisdom says "yes" if the effect of association
is to legitimize an ethically questionable funding source.
Is that still true if the funds are used for ethically
"good" purposes? The political manipulation of publicly
financed R & D is well-known and repeatedly documented by
R & D's advocates and critics alike. What we hear less
about are objectives pursued by R & D that suggest
manipulation is over means, not ends. For example, American
R & D typically pursues objectives that have the effect of
promoting stability for capital accumulation. That amounts
to a promotion of specific political interests. Serving
such purposes is not intrinsic to science; R & D does not
have to serve any single political interest. It could serve
labor; it could serve capital. What makes that a naive
statement, however, is that R & D functions in a context,
which is why American agricultural research concentrates on
increasing yields and profitability rather than something
else. Peter Buck's conclusions about the introduction of
American science into late nineteenth- and early
twentieth-century China are to the point:

> In American contexts, images of science as uniquely
> exempt from the distorting influence of social and
> political controversy had and still have enormous power
> to mediate among competing social, political, and
> scientific forces; but the images derive their symbolic
> power from the fact that our reality does not conform
> to them. In China, where American science achieved a
> considerable amount of autonomy from Chinese society
> and politics, its freedom only ensured its irrelevance.
> (Buck 1980, 236)

As noted earlier, interaction is offered as a desideratum, but it may not be terribly different from complicity. When does one become the other? The answer probably lies in what larger social and political patterns (and associated ethical assumptions) are reproduced in R & D's organization, mission, and indeed, in the very substance of scientific specialization. That raises a deeper complicity issue, one that does not revolve around behavioral linkages alone, but rather around the convergence of meaning structures. Can R & D systems working on a problem—whether that be hunger, energy, or family planning—be distinguished from that problem? Can R & D assume that it is spawned by fundamentally different social and political forces than those which generate the broader social problems R & D believes it ultimately addresses? Can R & D assume that the laboratory is a neutral medium through which the light from society's social and political conflicts passes without refraction? Belief in essential independence from a problem focuses R & D's ethical attention on what it contributes to the perpetuation of the problem.

What if R & D is part of the problem it works on? In what ways does that limit how the R & D system will see the problem, define solutions, and recognize crisis? The understanding of complicity now being suggested proposes that what at one level may be, in fact, relatively autonomous behavior at another level may be a limited vocabulary of meanings. Most crucial among those limits are those which pattern the possible varieties of recognizable ethical knowledge. An example of the form this patterning can take is provided by looking at the mushrooming number of R & D organizations concerned with contemporary resource problems. There is wide subscription to the belief that what the R & D systems are doing is not ideological. That belief reveals an essential example of how complicity in meaning structures can influence the possibility of ethical knowledge. I refer to the fallacy of secularism, the faith that a set of meanings is not value-ladden but rather states physical "facts" and their relationships. Major themes of resource-focused R & D in the United States are promoting stability (of supply and prices), reducing vulnerability (to reductions or denials of supply and rapid or dramatic escalations in prices), and improving sustainability (of resource exploitation rates or access). Actually, these are value statements that are closely tied to specific patterns of economic development. They are statements that look different when viewed globally or from the perspective of poor or weak groups both within and outside the United States. What accounts for such differences are, in part, different vested interests and win-lose profiles, but I would argue that what accounts for a larger part of the difference will not map out as simply as that. Operating also are a variety of ethical propositions about stewardship and people's responsibilities to others and to future generations.

From a knowledge utilization perspective, the complicity question as an approach to ethical orientation points towards deeper understanding of autonomy—not simply as a matter of interorganizational relationships—but also as a matter of converging meaning structures. When meaning structures have a limited ethical vocabulary and a very limited grammar for using that vocabulary, an ethical problem may exist precisely because of the difficulty of recognizing unanticipated or "unfriendly" ethical knowledge. The mechanisms of convergence can take several shapes varying from professionalization patterns to the political accommodations of R & D. What is important to remember is that convergence by itself is not inherently problematic nor is it necessarily inconsistent with the possibility of autonomously acquired ethical knowledge. Convergence becomes a problem if it is towards meaning structures that effectively and substantially reduce the likelihood of ethical knowledge.

Choice

The most important question is choice. Many R & D systems believe they do best by essentially learning to choose between given alternatives. The alternatives are supplied by widely accepted paradigms, all of which discount the plausibility of other choices; by prominent people and the folkways of invisible colleges, with whom disagreement amounts to anything from admission of stupidity to professional masochism; and by the ideologies of organizational and even national "missions," providing as they do special cloaks for a few alternatives and pariah status for any others. Ethical responsibility is juxtaposed and identified with methodology, narrow consensus, and loyalty. In such cases, the question of choice is really a question of reaffirmation. This can take several forms. Arguing against abstraction and for more grounded approaches to acquiring social knowledge can result in the substitution merely of one kind of epistemological restriction for

320

another. Altering methods for acquiring social knowledge is
hardly the last word on ethical drift; deeply problematic
still are the maintained premises of the organization,
convergence with other, particularly political, meaning
structures, and the net probabilities that what constitutes
counter-legitimating ethical knowledge can be acquired.
R & D needs to avoid the technological trap, namely, in
conceiving the social problem as being essentially one of
rational choice between given alternatives. Social
alternatives are not given. They must be created. Beyond
choice, more fundamental and more distinctively human than
choice, is the task of developing the alternatives between
which we choose. The essential social process is not of
choosing but of learning, and the most essential social
process is not learning what to choose but choosing what to
learn. There is the crux of the ethical problem for R & D.
It revolves around a critical perspective on the question:
what is knowledge? In particular, what are the possibilities of ethical knowledge given different ways of
attempting to know the world? How one attempts to know the
world is inherently problematic unless one can also pursue
ethical knowledge that the path chosen is _wrong_. Conceit
and complicity are issues that point to essentially
behavioral characteristics of knowledge utilizations
systems. So does choice, but it goes further because more
clearly than the other two issues, the issue of choice is
explicitly normative. It says: "There must be choice."
There must in particular be _ethical_ choice, a perception of
good and bad, a perception that is not defined or provided
by ways of understanding physical relationships, but
perception that is independent of how one attempts to know
the physical, social, or economic world. Ethical perception
does not mean that one must search until one finds an
ethical basis for saying: "What we are doing is wrong."
Ethical perception means instead that it is _possible_ to
reach that conclusion; as possible as it is to say: "What we
are doing is good." That is choice. What kinds of choices
do our R & D systems perceive, make, treasure, and suppress?

If knowledge utilization can point us to the critical
perspectives of conceit, complicity, and choice, then it
will have something to tell us about the ethical aspects of
R & D. However, make no mistake about it. Knowledge
utilization as a field must begin by critically questioning
its own ethical assumptions, and it must keep on
questioning. We must be honest with ourselves and recognize
that while all social scientists are (supposed to be)

neutral, most are more neutral toward some social groups, social values, and ethical goals than others.

CONCLUSION

Knowledge utilization systems are systems for organizing linkages between what is valued as information and how information that is valued can be brought to a form that is useful for those who value it. Knowledge utilization is a social process because it involves interaction and exchange behaviors among individuals and groups who are producing, processing, and consuming a commodity called knowledge. Knowledge utilization is a historical process because it is a dividing of intellectual labor that occurs over time. It is a political pattern of consumption because that process involves power relationships among individuals and groups who are exposed to different consequences from what knowledge is generated, which knowledge is utilized, by whom, and for what purposes. Knowledge utilization is an ethical process because it involves motivations and consequences that influence and structure the lives of humans today, future generations, and the natural world that humankind must share.

R & D as we know it today is a marvelous social innovation and probably the best example of what we mean by a knowledge utilization system. R & D systems continue to experiment periodically with a range of methods and processes that they hope will improve their claim to social relevance, political legitimacy, and ethical validity. Unfortunately, it is difficult to avoid the conclusion that most R & D systems would prefer to see those problems of relevance, legitimacy, and validity resolved axiomatically. Indeed, the methods and processes proposed to describe the problems, and I include here the field of inquiry called knowledge utilization, often lay claim to an especially interesting form of neutrality--ethical neutrality.

Ethical neutrality is a hoax, but not simply because the concept of value-free attribution is implausible. Neutrality is the sanctuary that methodology holds out to those who seek to know the world without having to think twice about ethical valuations. Neutrality is a hoax because it is _not_ a sanctuary, but a monastery. Rather than somehow sweeping aside ethical questions, neutrality sweeps aside ethical reservation. The broom it offers is a complex and powerful catechism for meditating on the truth of a few answers. Just as R & D will therefore have to begin an

322

attempt to get back on ethical course by understanding it is
in and of this world, so will knowledge utilization as a
field of study. The first step to recognizing that a system
is ethically adrift is acknowledging that you are in and of
the ocean. The next step is acknowledging that drifting
with the current is not moving without direction.

REFERENCES

Arope, H. A. 1977. R & D Management in the Rubber Research
    Institute of Malaysia. College, Laguna (Philippines):
    Southeast Asian Regional Center for Graduate Study and
    Research in Agriculture.

Buck, P. 1980. American Science and Modern China:
    1876-1936. New York: Cambridge Univ. Press.

Busch, L., and W. B. Lacy. 1983. Science, Agriculture and
    the Politics of Research. Boulder, Colo.: Westview
    Press.

Carson, R. 1962. Silent Spring. Boston: Houghton Mifflin.

Cavalieri, L. F. 1981. The Double-Edged Helix: Science in
    the Real World. New York: Columbia Univ. Press.

Hargrove, T. 1977. Genetic and Sociologic Aspects of Rice
    Breeding in India. IRRI Research Paper Series No. 10.
    Los Banos, Philippines: International Rice Research
    Institute.

Hightower, J. 1973. Hard Tomatoes, Hard Times. Cambridge,
    Mass.: Schenkman Publishing Company.

Korten, D. 1981. "The Management of Social Transfor-
    mation." Public Administration Review, 41, no. 6:
    609-618.

Rose, D. 1974. "New Laboratories for Old." Daedelus 103
    (summer): 143-155.

Tribe, L. H. 1972. "Policy Science: Analysis or Ideology?"
    Philosophy and Public Affairs 2, no. 1: 66-110.

PART FIVE

Research

14

Conceptualizing
Knowledge Use

William N. Dunn

As yet there is no satisfactory approach and
methodology for assessing the impact of the applied social
sciences on social problem solving. This deficit, which is
as much philosophical as it is technical, has permitted and
even encouraged ambiguous, exaggerated, or plainly false
claims about the practical role of policy analysis, program
evaluation, and other applied social science disciplines.
The crux of the problem is that studies of knowledge
utilization are, in Carol Weiss' words, "conceptually soggy"
(Weiss 1977, 11), contributing to a tangled literature which
thus far has not supplied workable definitions of knowledge
use as a dependent variable or phenomenon-to-be-understood
(Machlup 1980; Weiss 1981; Zaltman 1982). Given the
conceptual disarray that now characterizes most research in
the field, it is not surprising that knowledge use studies
yield non-comparable findings (Larsen 1981) that are based
on attempts to measure precisely a plethora of ambiguous and
poorly understood concepts. Under these circumstances,
research findings often become a justification or pretext
for affirming or denying, as the case may be, the practical
contribution of the applied social sciences to social
problem solving.

Consider the claim (Lindblom and Cohen 1979) that
policy analysis, program evaluation, and other applied
social science disciplines yield less usable knowledge than
do various forms of interactive problem solving based on
common sense, casual empiricism, and thoughtful speculation
and analysis. We will do better, according to this view, if
we supplement or displace policy research with ordinary
knowledge that "is highly fallible, but we shall call it
knowledge even if it is false. As is the case of scientific
knowledge [sic], whether it is true or false, knowledge is

knowledge to anyone who takes it as a basis for some
commitment to action" (Lindblom and Cohen 1979, 12).
Consider as well the blunt assertion that the dissemination
of policy research through "artificial" means—that is,
deliberate non-market strategies designed to facilitate the
adoption of technological and policy innovations—"is an
inappropriate solution for most problems most of the time"
(Knott and Wildavsky 1980, 541; compare Wildavsky 1979).
Finally, consider the dismal forecast that policy-related
social science research may come to dominate and corrupt the
style and ethos of the governmental system. "If the
analytical techniques produced and propagated from the
universities supersede the skills of the politician and (on
the rare but all-important occasions when it is manifested)
the wisdom of the statesman, the successful working of the
political system will be gravely jeopardized" (Banfield
1980, 3).

These critical assaults, while drawing attention to
exaggerated claims about the policy relevance of the applied
social sciences, project a deep pessimism about the
potential creative role of the policy sciences in
alleviating social problems. As Moore (1980) observes,
critics are inconsistent and perhaps disingenuous when they
maintain that the policy sciences represent a dangerous new
"fourth estate," while affirming in the same breath that the
theories, methods, and findings of the policy sciences are
so abstract, general, or superficial that they have little
practical relevance for specific policy choices. While it
is conceivable that the policy sciences are politically
innocuous in specific contexts, but politically dangerous in
general, it is also possible that policymakers and
practitioners achieve improved levels of performance by
combining the general theories, methods, and findings of the
social sciences with knowledge derived from the contingent
claims of practice.

The main purpose of this chapter is to explore
alternative criteria for conceptualizing and measuring
knowledge use. In an effort to uncover taken-for-granted
assumptions about knowledge use, the first section reviews
several contrasting metaphors that have been employed to
capture essential features of knowledge creation,
dissemination, and use. The second section, by specifying a
variety of dimensions according to which knowledge may be
classified, draws attention to the complexity of knowledge
itself. The third section, by identifying multiple
dimensions of use, highlights the additional complexity of
using such knowledge. The concluding section suggests

several principles whose consideration may contribute to a
reconceptualization of knowledge use. The core claim of the
chapter as a whole is that most past attempts to measure
knowledge use have been premature, since they have been
based on an oversimplified and misleading conception of
knowledge and its uses.

CONTRASTING METAPHORS

Social scientists and practitioners often view the use,
nonuse, misuse, and abuse of social science knowledge as
quasi-physical processes. Prevalent metaphors (House 1981;
Rogers and Kincaid 1981, 38-9) are illustrative:
  - Knowledge is carried from source to receiver like a
    bucket carries water.
  - Knowledge is transported from producer to user like
    a wheelbarrow carries sand.
  - Knowledge travels like a bullet shot at a target.
  - Knowledge is introduced like a hypodermic needle
    injects vaccine.
  - Knowledge spreads like an infectious disease.
  - Knowledge is stored like grain in a silo, books in a
    library, or bits and bytes in a computer.
  - Knowledge is manufactured like products in a
    technological or machine process.

Quasi-physical metaphors are sometimes enlarged into
allegories (extended analogies), which permit the creative
interpretation of one kind of experience in terms of the
characteristics of another. Colleague Jack Rothman (see
chap. 7), for example, employs the allegory of a lumber mill
to visualize the process of producing and using social
science knowledge:

The social science researchers have gone into the
forest of knowledge, felled a good and sturdy tree, and
displayed the fruits of their good work to one another.
A few enterprising, application-minded lumberjacks have
dragged some logs to the river and shoved them off
downstream ("diffusion" they call it). Somewhere down
river the practitioners are manning the construction
companies. They manage somehow to piece together a few
make-shift buildings with what they can find that has
drifted down the stream, but on the whole they are
sorely lacking in lumber in the various sizes and forms
they need to do their work properly. The problem is
that someone has forgotten to build the mill to turn

> the logs into lumber in all its usable forms. The logs
> continue to pile up at one end of the system while the
> construction companies continue to make do at the other
> end....there has been governmental and foundation
> support for the logging operation. There has also been
> some support for the construction companies. There has
> been almost nothing, however, for the planning and
> running of the mill.

The allegory of the lumber mill, when used as a vehicle for
creatively interpreting the process of knowledge use by
policymakers, punctuates the importance of knowledge gaps
between social scientists and policymakers, gaps that have
been identified by numerous investigators in the field. A
natural and perhaps inevitable response to the recognition
of gaps has been the use of new metaphors that express the
gap-filling potential of new social roles, including
"linkers" (Havelock 1969), "translators" (Lazarsfeld and
Reitz 1975), and "brokers" (Sundquist 1978). For Rothman
the allegory of the lumber mill does double duty, since it
calls attention to gaps between knowledge production and
use, while also suggesting a mechanism for spanning them.
Social science research and development methodology, based
on the image of a well-run lumber mill, is Rothman's
preferred mechanism for reconciling and linking social
science knowledge and practice (Rothman 1980).

Quasi-physical metaphors justifiably may be regarded as
elements of the deep structure of present-day thinking about
knowledge and its uses (Schon 1979; House 1981). Although
quasi-physical metaphors do represent one dimension of the
domain we seek to understand (it is difficult to imagine
knowledge use without libraries, information systems,
commercial and non-profit research organizations, or
articles and research reports), they are imperfect vehicles
for representing processes of knowledge use. Quasi-physical
metaphors enhance our understanding of knowledge use, while
at the same time constraining and even corrupting it.

Quasi-physical metaphors may preempt opportunities to
visualize knowledge use as a cognitive process that is at
once central to policy making but entirely inaccessible to
direct physical inspection. This lack of direct
accessibility does not mean, of course, that cognitive
processes—that is, processes based on the act or faculty of
knowing—cannot be described, classified, and measured; nor
does classification and measurement imply the irremediable
distortion of such processes. Here the analogy of modern
quantum physics is instructive, especially as conveyed in

Gary Zukav's The Dancing Wu Li Masters: An Overview of the
New Physics (1979). One of Zukav's Wu Li Masters, Albert
Einstein, wrote in 1938:

> Physical concepts are free creations of the human mind,
> and are not, however it may seem, uniquely determined
> by the external world. In our endeavor to understand
> reality we are somewhat like a man trying to understand
> the mechanism of a closed watch. He sees the face and
> the moving hands, even hears its ticking, but he has no
> way of opening the case. If he is ingenious he may
> form some picture of a mechanism which could be
> responsible for all the things he observes, but he may
> never be quite sure his picture is the only one which
> could explain his observations. He will never be able
> to compare his picture with the real mechanism and he
> cannot even imagine the possibility of the meaning of
> such a comparison (Einstein and Infeld 1938, 31).[1]

In quantum mechanics it is impossible and unnecessary to
observe relations among subatomic particles; it is
sufficient to observe their traces. The underlying
structures of subatomic phenomena are entirely inaccessible
to direct physical inspection, although their traces may be
described, classified, and measured without irremediable
distortion. (Recall that Heisenberg's indeterminacy
principle is a theory of error that maintains the
corrigibility of knowledge claims, not a theory of
indeterminism or of epistemological relativism.)

To visualize knowledge use as a cognitive process—that
is, a process related somehow to the act or faculty of
knowing—requires appropriate metaphors. Significantly,
many of these have come from areas of education, science,
and the humanities. A widely employed metaphor, drawn from
C.P. Snow's The Two Cultures and the Scientific Revolution
(1959), is what some have called the two-communities theory
of knowledge use (Caplan 1979; Rich 1979; Stokes 1978; Knorr
1981). Here the use of social science knowledge by
policymakers is interpreted metaphorically in terms of the
bi-polarization of contemporary intellectual life, the gulf
that separates literary intellectuals and physical
scientists. The two-communities metaphor is not a well-
developed theory (Dunn 1980), does permit the creative
interpretation of one kind of experience (the knowledge gap
between social scientists and policymakers) in terms of the
characteristics of another (the gulf of mutual incompre-
hension between scientists and literary intellectuals).

Yet, Snow's (1959) solution was to improve the process of
educating and training scientists and literary
intellectuals--immersing each in the culture of the
other--and to recruit the best of these to government
service. The gulf-spanning function was to be performed by
the educational system and not by systematic attempts to
pool, translate, and transfer social science research to
policymakers and practitioners.

The two-communities metaphor, by drawing attention to
the cultural basis of differences between social scientists
and policymakers, represents a bold contrast to the
quasi-physical imagery of the lumber mill. Contrasting
metaphors with more direct relevance to cognitive processes
have been offered in the field of educational research
(House 1981). One of these asks us to imagine that
knowledge use is similar to drawing and continuously
revising mental pictures or maps:

> Everyone employs a "cognitive map," that is, to define
> it metaphorically, a picture in their mind of the
> complex phenomena with which they deal. One's map of
> instructions may be very simple--certain things to be
> learned, pupils to learn the desired things. But
> teachers quickly discover that this map is too simple
> to help them identify what is wrong when the pupils do
> not learn even though they go through the activities.
> They then look for refinements in their maps,
> additional concepts that help them to understand the
> phenomena they encounter as teachers, and they will add
> and modify their maps from time to time as they become
> aware of new concepts that appear to give greater
> richness to the representation they have of the
> situation. (Tyler 1978, 96)

The clash of contemporary metaphors highlights the
complexity of processes of knowledge use. Knowledge use
cannot be satisfactorily defined as a quasi-physical
process; nor is the meaning of the concept adequately
captured by such terms as "cultural," "cognitive," "social,"
or "political." Knowledge use is all of these and more, and
it is just this multidimensionality that creates the
problem. At present we lack an adequate understanding of
what is meant by the term knowledge use, even though
knowledge, information, and research use are regularly put
forward as criteria of success (and failure) by governmental
and private bodies and citizens-at-large.

VARIETIES OF KNOWLEDGE

Contrasting metaphors make it evident that knowledge use is not a unitary concept. When we describe the uses of different knowledge "products"--for example, policy models, social indicators, or results of program evaluations--it may appear, erroneously, that we are talking about different versions of the same thing (compare Rescher 1980). Taking its uses as given, knowledge has been described in many ways:

Subscribership. Knowledge may be classified according to the persons or groups who subscribe to it. The dimension of subscribership includes such categories as "personal knowledge," "practitioner knowledge," "public knowledge," and so forth. Who affirms or certifies that something is knowledge?

Source. Distinctions may also be based on the source of knowledge. Distinctions by source include "scientific knowledge," "professional knowledge," "craft knowledge," "practice knowledge," "experimental knowledge," "ordinary knowledge." Source and subscribership should not be confused, since much professional knowledge (subscribership) is based in part on ordinary knowledge (source) (Lindblom and Cohen 1979). Where did the knowledge originate?

Object. Knowledge may also be classified according to its object. Distinctions by object include "economic knowledge," "political knowledge," "environmental knowledge." The object of knowledge should be distinguished from its subscribership and source. To what does the knowledge refer?

Benefit. Knowledge may also be classified in terms of the types of benefits expected to occur upon its acquisition. Machlup (1980), for example, distinguishes knowledge according to expected benefits which are "practical," "intellectual," "pastime," "spiritual," and "unwanted." The expected benefit of knowledge is not the same as its object, since knowledge about a particular object--e.g., the politics of budgeting--may confer benefits that are primarily intellectual (or spiritual) and only secondarily if at all, practical. Similarly, the source of knowledge is no guarantee that it will result in particular kinds of benefits, since basic research has often resulted in practical applications. What valued consequences will occur by using knowledge?

Purpose. Knowledge may be classified according to the type of purpose served by the realization of a benefit. Habermas (1972), for example, distinguishes purposes of

"control," "understanding," and "emancipation." "Practical"
knowledge (benefit) does not necessarily expand capacities
for controlling the human and material environment
(purpose), while "intellectual" and "spiritual" knowledge
(benefit) do not necessarily enlarge capacities for
understanding or self-reflection (purpose). The realization
of practical benefits by using knowledge about social
problems may distort our understanding of problems, as
experienced by victims, and reinforce tacit assumptions and
theories that blame victims for their problems (Gregg et al.
1979). What ends are served by the realization of benefits
of knowledge?

    <u>Warrant</u>. Knowledge may be classified according to the
types of assumptions that warrant its certification as
knowledge (Toulmin, Rieke and Janik 1979; Mitroff and Mason
1981). Knowledge-warranting assumptions may be empirical,
analytic, teleological, pragmatic, authoritative, ethical,
and so forth. Warrants for knowledge ("reality tests") are
organized in frames of reference that affect and are
affected by social frameworks (Holzner and Marx 1979; Weiss
and Bucuvalas 1980). These warrants represent standards,
criteria, or rules for assessing the adequacy, relevance,
and cogency of knowledge claims (Dunn 1982). The type of
warrant used to certify knowledge is potentially independent
of its subscribership, source, object, benefit, and purpose.
"Practitioner knowledge" (subscribership) may be based on
the same kinds of warrants employed by social scientists;
there is no necessary relationship between the source of
knowledge, e.g., everyday experience, and its causal
adequacy or practical relevance (Zaltman, Heffring, and
LeMasters 1982). What counts as knowledge in the first
place?

DIMENSIONS OF USE

    Once we have chosen an appropriate definition of
knowledge, an effort that surely will involve several
dimensions outlined above, we can proceed to specify what it
means to say that such knowledge is "used." This task may
seem relatively straightforward, since we can simply look at
the decisions made by users--for example, policymakers,
managers, clients, social scientists, members of
society-at-large--and determine whether such decisions are
based on a particular type of knowledge. Yet the concept of
use, like that of knowledge, is by no means a unitary one
(compare Weiss 1981). Taking knowledge as given, use has

been distinguished according to multiple dimensions:

Usership. Use may be classified according to the persons or groups who constitute users knowledge. Users may be national or local policymakers, members of professional associations, media representatives, client groups, social scientists, and so forth. While users are often knowledge subscribers, some users subscribe to knowledge for reasons that differ from those of persons who are the source of knowledge. For example, policymakers may use results of evaluation research to support their own personal or political ambitions, thus subscribing to knowledge on the basis of warrants that are quite different from those of program evaluators. Under these conditions we might speak about the "misutilization" of evaluation research (Cook, Levinson-Rose, and Pollard 1980). Who uses knowledge?

Object. Use may also be classified according to its objects, which may include recommendations, empirical generalizations, hypotheses, theories, models, concepts, assumptions, principles, ideas, and so forth. The object of knowledge use and the object of knowledge differ, since knowledge classified by object (e.g., "political" knowledge) implies nothing about the object of use (e.g., policy recommendations versus general political ideas). Choices involving different objects of use often depend on variations in expected benefits and purposes of knowledge, as well as knowledge-warranting assumptions. What elements or aspects of knowledge are used?

Directness. Use may be classified according to its directness to an original knowledge source. Use may be relatively direct, and have high "fidelity," in cases where some user reads an original report or study produced by a social scientist. By contrast, "infidelity" occurs when research findings are filtered through executive summaries and secondary written descriptions or reviews, or passed on through communications that involve little or no face-to-face interaction ("invisible colleges"). How close is use to an original knowledge source?

Temporal Proximity. Use may be classified according to its proximity in time to an original knowledge source. Apart from its directness, use may be immediate, occurring simultaneously with the creation of knowledge. For example, when subscribers are also the source of knowledge they engage in immediate use. Use may also be delayed, as when knowledge is transmitted across years, periods, generations, or historical epochs. The concept of "diffusion time" is a specific variant of temporal proximity, as is Keynes' statement that policymakers are the slaves of some defunct philosopher. How long does it take to use knowledge?

Magnitude of Expected Effects. Use may also be
classified according to the magnitude of its expected
effects. Use sometimes refers to "conceptual" and/or
"instrumental" effects, categories that are often viewed as
discrete and mutually exclusive classes. Machlup (1980)
describes thirteen elements of the state or act of knowing
which include acts of knowing that range from being
acquainted with or aware of something to being able to
explain, demonstrate, talk about, or perform some action.
What counts as use in the first place?

Composition. Use may also be classified in terms of
the composition of users. Users may be individuals, groups,
agencies, or institutions. However, it is necessary to
distinguish between individual and relational use since
policy making is a collective process, involving a system of
relations among those who have a stake in the definition and
alleviation of public problems. Individuals use knowledge,
but it does not mean that collectivities follow suit. The
"tragedy of the commons" applies to knowledge use as well as
economic behavior. Collective learning is not simply the
sum of individual uses of knowledge. What types of
individual and relational acts constitute use?

In sum, knowledge use is a complex process that may be
characterized in quasi-physical, cultural, and cognitive
terms. By specifying multiple dimensions of knowledge and
its uses we not only create new opportunities for
conceptualization and measurement, but accentuate the
difficulties and dangers of viewing the process in overly
simple terms. As we discovered in a recent effort to assess
the state of research in the field (Dunn, Holzner and
Zaltman 1983; see also chap. 16), the bulk of available
studies have not investigated, from the standpoint of
subscribers, the expected benefits, purposes, and warrants
of knowledge. In general, knowledge use studies have also
neglected questions surrounding the objects, directness,
temporal proximity, expected effects, and composition of
use. Under these circumstances, we are entitled to join
others such as Knott and Wildavsky (1980) in asking: If
knowledge use is the solution, what is the problem?

RECONCEPTUALIZING KNOWLEDGE USE

Answers to this question have assumed various forms
(Larsen 1981; Weiss 1981; Machlup 1980), all of which strive
towards a more adequate conceptualization of knowledge use.

In general, however, answers have been based on the distinction between instrumental and conceptual uses of knowledge--that is, on the basis of a twofold classification of expected effects of using knowledge (Caplan, Morrison, and Stambaugh 1975; Rich and Caplan 1976; Weiss 1977; Rich 1975, 1977, 1981). Instrumental use refers to processes where social science knowledge affects a specific decision, including behavior resulting in the adoption of specific decisions. A particularly lucid definition of instrumental use is provided in a study of the uses of 200 criminal justice evaluation research reports. Here knowledge (or information) use is defined in terms of the "decision-consequential impact" of research on "the irrevocable allocation of resources....a decision is not a 'decision to make a decision,' but rather the concrete action implied by the decision" (Larson and Berliner 1979, 2; Howard 1966).

Conceptual use, by contrast, refers to processes where social science knowledge affects processes of thinking, but without necessarily being accompanied by concrete action (Ciarlo 1981, 12). Conceptual use may involve changes in the orientation of policymakers, the justification of prior actions, the stimulation of further inquiry, the redefinition of problems, or simply "tucking suggestions away for future consideration" (Weiss 1981). Weiss (1981, 26) opting for a broad conceptual definition of use, cautions that an instrumental view of knowledge use assumes a rational theory of organizational behavior that is patently inaccurate:

> Major policy directions taken by federal departments and their component agencies and the Congress are almost never the product of rational analysis alone. They are strongly influenced by legislative politics, bureaucratic politics, constituent interests, competing claims on the federal budget, pressure groups, public acceptance, and a host of idiosyncratic elements.

Reported studies of knowledge use by policymakers (Caplan, Morrison and Stambaugh 1975; Patton et al. 1977; Weiss and Bucuvalas 1980; Rich 1981) lend much empirical support for the proposition that conceptual use is more prevalent than instrumental use. Given these results it is tempting to conclude that the use of social science knowledge by policymakers is rarely instrumental. In Weiss' words, they "do not utilize research the way they utilize a hammer" (Weiss 1981, 18).

The claim that knowledge use is primarily conceptual, and only secondarily and peripherally instrumental, has

created an inaccurate and regrettably misleading view of the
actual and potential role of social science knowledge in
policy making. Policymakers do use social science knowledge
the way they use a hammer, as do social scientists and
everyone else, even though scientific and ordinary knowledge
do not have the material integrity and solidity of a hammer.
Concepts are instruments, and it is erroneous and misleading to talk as if they belong to a class of entities
that do not function, like hammers, as means to the attainment of diverse human purposes. Thus, a central problem of
the policy sciences is determining the extent to which its
instruments—concepts, models, theories, methods,
techniques—improve the performance of practitioners.

An instrumental-pragmatic conception of knowledge use,
drawing on constructivist and activist theories of knowledge
put forth by Kelly (1955), Churchman (1971), Campbell
(1977), Rescher (1980), and others, punctuates the logical
fallacy of juxtaposing "instrumental" and "conceptual" use.
Accordingly, concepts frequently serve as means or instruments for acquiring other concepts, including new knowledge,
and for predicting, anticipating, and acting on events.
Some concepts result in action, but all action results from
concepts, consciously or unconsciously held. Thus, instrumental use is a particular type of conceptual use. The two
types cannot be juxtaposed as if they were mutually exclusive; nor can they be arranged along a continuum whose poles
occupy the same level of analysis. "Whatever involves all
of a collection must not be one of the collection"
(Whitehead and Russell 1910, 101; Watzlawick, Weakland, and
Fisch 1974, 6).

An instrumental-pragmatic perspective of knowledge use
supplies a more adequate basis for theory and research than
conceptual frameworks thus far available to investigators.
Indeed, an instrumental-pragmatic perspective suggests
several principles whose consideration may assist in
developing more appropriate ways to conceptualize and
measure knowledge use:

Requisite Conceptual Variety. Knowledge use is
composed of multiple dimensions. Expected benefits,
purposes, and underlying warrants of knowledge, when
considered along with the objects, expected effects, and
composition of use, accentuate the stunning cognitive and
social complexity of processes of knowledge use. Yet most
conceptual frameworks available in the field are based on
overly simple and misleading distinctions: scientific vs.
ordinary knowledge, basic vs. applied research, academic vs.
practical research, conceptual vs. instrumental use.

To detect and improve the practical consequences of using social science knowledge we require concepts that approximate the sociocognitive complexity of the domain we seek to understand. The field as a whole lacks this requisite conceptual variety, as is evident from the characteristics of most study designs and research procedures currently employed by investigators (chap. 16). Consequently, researchers and practitioners have limited capacities to construe, anticipate, and shape the practical uses of professional and scientific knowledge.

Vicarious Selection. All professional and scientific knowledge is embodied in some vehicle or carrier that has its own physical, cognitive, or social nature and limitations (Campbell 1977). Vehicles or carriers include the frames of reference or construct systems of the social scientist and policymaker, as well as the social system--professional associations, university departments, government agencies, "invisible" colleges and bureaus, and so forth--of which they are members. Reference frames and social systems alike function as vicars, deputies, or instruments in the quest for practical knowledge. All knowledge is mediated, indirect, and distal; no one directly apprehends a putative "real world" of practice.

To detect and improve the consequences of using social science knowledge, we require concepts that are consonant with the sociocognitive complexity of vicarious knowledge processes. Knowledge use studies rarely address the positive and negative consequences of vicarious selectors, a deficit that stems from a one-sided concentration on social and cognitive properties of individuals, groups, and organizations, as distinguished from their social and cognitive relations (compare Rogers and Kincaid 1981). Since we have only begun to investigate the organization of intrapersonal space (Slater 1977), it has been difficult or impossible to assess the practical impact of using professional and scientific knowledge.

Criterion Equivalence. When professional and scientific knowledge is abstract or general, attempts to assess its uses should be based on equally general behavioral criteria (compare Weigel and Newman 1976). The observed correlation between specific individual or collective behaviors and self-reported uses of general social science findings or policy recommendations is likely to be weak or insignificant, if only because investigators have posed the wrong question.

Thus, while concepts, models, and theories are instruments, they are abstract and general ones that may not be expected to affect single decisions in a predetermined way—although they may well affect multiple decisions indeterminately. To detect and improve the consequences of using social science knowledge, we require concepts that clearly distinguish a range of expected general and specific effects. Among these general effects are the expansion of collective learning capacities (Etheredge 1979), public enlightenment (Weiss 1977; Cohen and Weiss 1977), and the freedom to make collective choices that successfully anticipate and control events (Dunn 1983). The general theories and methods of the social sciences "comprise prior assumptions about certain realms of the events. To the extent that these events may, from these prior assumptions, be construed, predicted, and their relative courses charted, men may exercise control, and gain freedom for themselves in the process" (Kelly 1955, 22).

NOTES

1. Quoted in Zukav (1979, 8) from Einstein, A., and L. Infeld, The Evolution of Physics. New York: Simon and Schuster, 1938.

REFERENCES

Banfield, E. 1980. "Policy Science as Metaphysical Madness." In Bureaucrats, Policy Analysts, Statesmen: Who Leads?, ed. Robert Goldwin. Washington, D.C.: American Enterprise Institute for Public Policy Research.

Campbell, D. T. 1977. Descriptive Epistemology: Psychological, Sociological, and Evolutionary. Preliminary Draft of the William James Lectures, Harvard University, Spring.

_____. 1979. "A Tribal Model of the Social System Vehicle Carrying Scientific Knowledge." Knowledge 1: 181-202.

Caplan, N. 1979. "The Two Communities Theory and Knowledge Utilization." American Behavioral Scientist 2: 459-470.

Caplan, N., A. Morrison, and R. J. Stambaugh. 1975. The Use of Social Science Knowledge in Policy Decisions at the National Level: A Report to Respondents. Ann Arbor: Center for Utilization of Scientific Knowledge, Institute for Social Research, University of Michigan.

Churchman, C. 1971. The Design of Inquiring Systems. New York: Basic Books.

Ciarlo, J. A., ed. 1981. Utilizing Evaluation: Concepts and Measurement Techniques. Beverly Hills, Calif.: Sage Publications.

Cohen, D., and J. A. Weiss. 1977. "Social Science and Social Policy: Schools and Race" In Using Social Research in Public Policy Making, ed. C. H. Weiss. Lexington, Mass.: Lexington Books.

Cook, T., J. Levinson-Rose, and W. Pollard. 1980. "The Misutilization of Evaluation Research: Some Pitfalls of Definition." Knowledge 1: 477-498.

Dunn, W. N. 1980. "The Two Communities Metaphor and Models of Knowledge Use: An Exploratory Case Survey." Knowledge: Creation, Diffusion, Utilization 1, no. 4: 515-536.

_____. 1982. "Reforms As Arguments." Knowledge: Creation, Diffusion, Utilization 3, no. 3: 293-326.

_____. 1983. "Usable Knowledge: A Metatheory of Policy Research in the Social Sciences." In The Planning of Change: Readings in the Applied Social Sciences, 4th ed., ed. W. Bennis, K. Benne, and R. Chin. New York: Holt, Rinehart, Winston.

Dunn, W. N., B. Holzner, and G. Zaltman. 1983. "Knowledge Utilization." International Encyclopedia of Education: Research and Studies. Stanford, Calif.: Stanford Univ. Press.

Etheredge, L. S. 1979. "Government Learning: An Overview," In Handbook of Political Behavior, ed. Samuel Long. New York: Plenum.

Gregg, G., T. Preston, A. Geist and N. Caplan. 1979. "The Caravan Rolls On: Forty Years of Social Problem Research." Knowledge 1, no. 1: 31-61.

340

Habermas, J. 1972. "Knowledge and Human Interest." Trans. J. J. Shapiro. London: Heinemann Educational.

Havelock, R. G. 1969. Planning for Innovation Through Dissemination and Utilization of Knowledge. Ann Arbor: Center for Research on Utilization of Scientific Knowledge, Institute for Social Research, University of Michigan.

Holzner, B., and J. Marx. 1979. Knowledge Application: The Knowledge System in Society. Boston: Allyn and Bacon.

House, E. 1981. "Three Perspectives in Innovation: Technological, Political, Cultural." In Improving Schools: Using What We Know, ed. R. Lehming and M. Kane. Beverly Hills, Calif.: Sage Publications.

Howard, R. A. 1966. "Decision Analysis: Applied Decision Theory." In Proceedings of the Fourth International Conference on Operations Research, ed. D. D. Hertz and J. Melese. New York: Wiley.

Kelly, G. A. 1955. The Psychology of Personal Constructs Volumes 1 and 2. New York: W.W. Norton.

Knorr, K. D. 1981. "Time and Context in Practical Action: On the Preconditions of Knowledge Use." Paper prepared for a conference on knowledge use, University Program for the Study of Knowledge Use, University of Pittsburgh, March 18-20, 1981.

Knott, J., and A. Wildavsky. 1980. "If Dissemination is the Solution What is the Problem?" Knowledge: Creation, Diffusion, Utilization 1, no. 4: 515-536.

Larsen, J. K. 1981. "Knowledge Utilization: Current Issues." In Knowledge Cycle, ed. Robert Rich. Beverly Hills, Calif.: Sage Publications.

Larson, R.C., and L. Berliner. 1979. "On Evaluating Evaluations." Working Paper, Operational Research Center, Massachusetts Institute of Technology.

Lazarsfeld, P., and J. Reitz. 1975. An Introduction to Applied Sociology. New York: Elsevier.

Lindblom, C., and D. Cohen. 1979. Usable Knowledge: Social Science and Social Problem Solving. New Haven, Conn.: Yale Univ. Press.

Machlup, F. 1980. Knowledge and Knowledge Introduction, Volume I. Princeton, N.J.: Princeton Univ. Press.

Mitroff, I. and R. Mason. 1981. "Policy Analysis as Argument." Policy Studies Journal. Special Issue, No. 2 (1981): 579-584. Symposium on Social Values and Public Policy, ed. W. N. Dunn.

Moore, D. 1980. "Statesmanship in Policy Analysis." In Bureaucrats, Policy Analysts, Statesmen: Who Leads?, ed. Robert Goldwin. Washington, D.C.: American Enterprise Institute for Public Policy Research.

Patton, M. Q., P. S. Grimes, K. M. Gunthrie, N. J. Brennan, B. D. French and D. A. Blyth. 1977. "In Search of Impact: An Analysis of Federal Health, Evaluation Research." In Using Social Research in Public Policy Making, ed. C. Weiss. Lexington, Mass.: Lexington Books.

Rescher, N. 1980. Induction. Pittsburgh: Univ. of Pittsburgh Press.

Rich, R. 1975. "Selective Utilization of Social Science Related Information by Federal Policymakers." Inquiry 13, no. 3: 239-245.

_____. 1979. "Systems of Analysis, Technology Assessment and Bureaucratic Power." American Behavioral Scientist 22: 393-416.

_____. 1977. "Uses of Social Science Information by Federal Bureaucrats: Knowledge for Action Versus Knowledge for Understanding." In Uses of Social Research in Public Policy, ed. C. Weiss. Lexington, Mass.: Lexington Books.

_____. 1981. The Knowledge Cycle. Beverly Hills, Calif.: Sage Publications.

Rich, R., and N. Caplan. 1976. "Policy Uses of Social Science Knowledge and Perspectives: Means/Ends Matching Versus Understanding." Paper presented at the OECD

Conference on Dissemination of Economic and Social
Development Research Results, Bogota, Colombia, June
1976.

Rogers, E., and D. L. Kincaid. 1981. Communications
Networks: Toward a New Paradigm for Research. New
York: Free Press.

Rothman, J. 1980. Using Research in Organizations.
Beverly Hills, Calif.: Sage Publications.

Slater, P. 1977. Dimensions of Intrapersonal Space.
London: Wiley.

Schon, D. 1979. "Generative Metaphor: A Perspective on
Problem Setting in Social Policy." In Metaphor in
Thought, ed. A. Ortony. Cambridge: Cambridge Univ.
Press.

Snow, C. P. 1959. The Godkin Lectures. Cambridge, Mass.:
Harvard Univ. Press.

Stokes, D. E. 1978. The Federal Investment in Knowledge of
Social Problems. Washington, D.C.: The National
Research Council Study Project on Social Research and
Development, National Academy of Sciences.

Sundquist, J. 1978. "Research Brokerage: The Weak." In
Knowledge and Policy: The Uncertain Connection, ed. L.
Lynn. Washington, D.C.: National Academy of Science.

Toulmin, S., R. Rieke, and A. Janik. 1979. An Introduction
to Reasoning. New York: Macmillan.

Tyler, R. W. 1978. "How Schools Utilize Educational
Research and Development." In Research and Development
and School Change, ed. Robert Glaser. Hillsdale, N.J.:
Lawrence Erlbaum Associates.

Watzlawick, P., J. Weakland, and R. Fisch. 1974. Change:
Principles of Problem Formation and Problem Resolution.
New York: W. W. Norton.

Weigel, R. H., and L. S. Newman. 1976. "Increasing
Attitude-Behavior Correspondence by Broadening the
Scope of the Behavioral Measure." Journal of
Personality and Social Psychology 33, no. 6: 793-802.

Weiss, C. H., ed. 1977. Using Social Research in Public
Policy Making. Lexington, Mass.: Lexington Books.

_____. 1981. "Measuring the Use of Evaluation." In
Utilizing Evaluation: Concepts and Measurement
Techniques, ed. J. A. Ciarlo. Beverly Hills, Calif.:
Sage Publications.

Weiss, C., and M. Bucuvalas. 1980. "Truth Tests and
Utility Tests: Decision Makers' Frames of Reference for
Social Science Research." The American Sociological
Review 45, no. 2: 302-313.

Whitehead, A. and B. Russell. 1910. Principle Mathematica,
Volume 1, 2d ed. Cambridge: Cambridge Univ. Press.

Wildavsky, A. 1979. Speaking Truth to Power: The Art and
Craft of Policy Analysis. Boston: Cambridge Univ.
Press.

Zaltman, Gerald. 1982. "Construing Knowledge Use."
Pittsburgh: University of Pittsburgh, Program for the
Study of Knowledge Use, Working paper KU-03.

_____. 1982. Theory-in-Use Among Change Agents.
Pittsburgh: University of Pittsburgh, University
Program for the Study of Knowledge Use, July 1982.

Zaltman, G., M. Heffring, and K. LeMasters. 1982. Theory
Construction in Marketing: Some Thoughts on Thinking.
New York: Wiley.

Zukav, G. 1979. The Dancing Wu Li Masters: An Overview of
the New Physics. New York: Bantam Books.

15

Critical Variables
in Utilization Research

Judith K. Larsen

The transfer and use of knowledge is the single most important issue in today's information society. The fast pace of daily life and the inevitability of change are pervasive features of this new age; "a radical speeding up of the tempo of change is at the heart of the twentieth-century experience and has gained a powerful grip on the modern mind" (Gardner 1964).

The decline of an industrial society and the rise of an information society has clarified the fact that knowledge is power. Those who possess knowledge and know how to apply it are becoming primary forces in society. Corporations that provide "tools for the information society" (Jobs 1983) thrive, while those without this capacity are in trouble. Individuals with knowledge enabling them to develop new skills make the transition to sunrise jobs; those without such knowledge face a dismal future.

Since World War II there has been increasing interest in the ways knowledge can be shared and used. The trend is reflected in the increasing proportion of the U.S. Gross National Product that is devoted to knowledge production and application (Machlup 1962) and the discussion of knowledge transfer by many blue-ribbon committees (Russell Sage Foundation 1950; National Academy of Sciences 1978). Partly as a result of the attention of panels and commissions, there has been increasing research of the knowledge utilization itself.

Early studies of knowledge use focused almost exclusively on the knowledge alone. The studies assumed that knowledge was used when it was implemented into a program or led directly to some decision or action. If knowledge use did not occur, the explanation was a "gap" between knowledge producer and knowledge user.

Responsibility for bridging the gap was assigned either to the researcher or the potential user, depending on the views of the author (Guba 1968; National Institute of Education 1978). Studies of knowledge utilization accumulated and improved technological procedures for the transfer and use of knowledge were perfected. In spite of such efforts, it became apparent that the frequency and impact of knowledge use did not increase substantially (Caplan 1980). Therefore utilization researchers began to re-examine some basic assumptions and realized that the earlier conception of utilization as a relatively straightforward and linear activity was incorrect. A different paradigm was needed.

Knowledge utilization is a complex process involving political, organizational, socioeconomic, and attitudinal factors in addition to knowledge. Researchers realized that any serious study of knowledge use must be cognizant of the contribution--or intrusion--of such factors to eventual use. Not only do such factors influence use, they also interact with the knowledge and each other so that there is a constantly emerging process that continues to change as it goes along (Smith 1977). Utilization studies that ignored such issues and were based on simplistic paradigms produced conclusions that were incomplete if not inaccurate.

The classic model of knowledge use poses several components contributing to outcome: the knowledge, the user of the knowledge, the source providing the knowledge, and interaction among these (adapted from Hovland, Janis, and Kelley 1953). The interaction component hypothesizes that these factors are related, if not causally linked, to utilization. A basic premise is that introduction of knowledge into a system will not automatically result in utilization; that is, there is no assumption that presenting knowledge to potential users will lead in a linear fashion to utilization. Rather, utilization is conceptualized as a function of multiple factors.

The interaction component of the knowledge utilization model allows the study of several factors in relationship to utilization and examines how the factors interact in ways that contribute to or are associated with utilization. Measures are likely to include questions about the knowledge ("How do differences in complexity of the knowledge affect its utilization?"), questions dealing with the source of knowledge ("How did the user become aware of the knowledge?"), questions about the user and context ("What does the group hope to accomplish by using this knowledge?"), and questions regarding the interaction among these components ("Are different types of knowledge used in different organizations?"). Sometimes researchers collect multiple indicators. However, too often the indicators pertain to only one component of the knowledge use model. This amounts to variations on a theme. Knowledge utilization involves more than one factor; therefore to assess utilization, measures of all components in the knowledge utilization model need to be included. This chapter discusses the multiple factors influencing knowledge utilization and provides an example of a study operationalizing these factors.

THE KNOWLEDGE

The definition of knowledge in a study of knowledge utilization is critical. Historically, there was a tendency to assume that knowledge was the equivalent of the "results" of a formalized research study. Some took issue with the assumption that the results of one research effort were the same as "knowledge," and in response to this criticism, the definition of knowledge was expanded. Subsequent work has taken the understanding of utilization beyond a limited conception, and as a result the definition of what is meant by knowledge has been influenced as well.

Researchers, and to some extent, policymakers, are used to identifying information as the results of a research study having potential for influencing policy or practice. In the case of this example, knowledge might include findings from many research studies, preferably studies that were conceptually related or that elaborated on the findings of each other. In part, this elaboration responds to an important methodological consideration, namely the verification of findings. By combining the results of one study with others that are similar or at least comparable to the first, the studies are subject to some degree of replication and testing. Those findings that appear to be consistent across a number of individual studies would be expected to receive more serious attention than results of one study with no comparative data available. Therefore, generally research-based information is based on the cumulative findings of many studies.

Traditionally, the research or "scientific" community defined "related information" as the findings of previous studies (Yin et al. 1976). However, this definition is being challenged. It has become increasingly apparent that "ordinary" knowledge also plays a role in problem solving, and that to define knowledge as only that which is

research-based is to artificially limit the scope of
potentially relevant information. Lindblom and Cohen
(1979), in an excellent treatment of this issue,
differentiate between professional and social inquiry (PSI)
and ordinary knowledge. "By 'ordinary knowledge', we mean
knowledge that does not owe its origin, testing, degree of
verification, truth status, or currency to distinctive PSI
professional techniques but rather to common sense, casual
empiricism, or thoughtful speculation and analysis"
(Lindblom and Cohen 1979, 12). They discuss professional
social inquiry and conclude that much of "new" knowledge is
ordinary knowledge that is refined and highly selective.
Therefore, results of professional social inquiry are
generally not a distinctive source of information.
"We...want to suggest the relation of PSI to a mountain of
ordinary information which it cannot replace but only
reshape here and there." Many utilization studies now
include "ordinary" or "general" knowledge as well as
research-based knowledge.

Baldridge and Deal (1975) conceptualize utilization as
matching of the knowledge or technology with the
organization or user. Changes in the technology must be
accompanied by changes in the organization. This series of
actions then leads to outcomes. Further, they suggest
studying utilization through "why" questions and "under what
circumstances" questions. Results reporting utilization as
percentages "using" knowledge in a specific case are not
responsive to the study of the knowledge use process as they
conceptualize it.

THE KNOWLEDGE USER

Users include individuals, groups, and organizations.
Variables appropriate for a knowledge use study include the
activities and attitudes of users, and the extent to which
the users modify a practice or behavior, or solve a problem,
is the primary outcome. Much of the early work defining
user variables concerned individual users and attempted to
identify characteristics of those first to use a new
practice (Rogers 1962; Carlson 1965). The individual's use
of knowledge involves a complex set of personal
characteristics, such as attitudes, values, beliefs, and
goals. An individual's decisions are influenced by multiple
factors, among them the individual's awareness that
attitudes and actions may be inconsistent and attempts to
remove the inconsistency (Heider 1958; Festinger 1957), past

behaviors and incentives for repeating old patterns or for trying new ones (Hovland, Janis, and Kelley 1953), and functional and pragmatic considerations claiming knowledge can be used and understood only within the context of the individual's needs and personality (Smith, Brunner, and White 1956). Unfortunately most of the research on the individual's utilization experiences did not really focus on what happened to the user when knowledge was implemented. As research moved to the study of groups as users (Allison 1971; Janis and Mann 1977), more attention centered on the decision-making process. Studies investigated the procedure of introducing new information to a group and seeing how it decided to use it.

It is virtually impossible to conceptualize knowledge utilization without considering the situation in which the utilization occurs. Characteristics of the situation inevitably influence the pattern of utilization. For example, utilization in situations where interest and commitment are low is quite different from utilization in situations with high interest and commitment. Distinctions are made both in practice (Backer and Glaser 1979) and theory (Weiss and Bucuvalas 1977) between situations in which knowledge supports established attitudes and situations in which knowledge challenges them.

In most current research, utilization studies involve the actions of an organization or group and its resulting experience. Characteristics commonly included in such research are communication processes, decision-making strategies, organizational structure, and the like. There is an extensive literature on organizational factors influencing utilization and change (Bennis, Benne, and Chin 1969; Zaltman, Duncan, and Holbek 1973; Kelly and Kranzberg 1975). One of the classic works on contextual factors relates organizational variables to change resulting from knowledge use (Hage and Aiken 1970). After posing a large number of potentially important factors, the researchers identify seven organizational characteristics that interact most directly with new knowledge to produce change: complexity, centralization, formalization, stratification, production, efficiency, and job satisfaction. Organizations possessing these characteristics are likely to be more successful than others in using knowledge to implement change and solve organizational problems.

Only recently have studies of knowledge use followed through to determine whether an organization's problem was solved once the knowledge was used. In a study of knowledge use in state and local governments which identified ways users implemented knowledge use and problem solving, the researchers stated "there is no a priori reason to assume that (knowledge) intended to stimulate the development and use of new products and techniques by state and local governments will, in fact, contribute significantly to those governments' efforts to solve their problems as they see them; conversely, (knowledge) intended to help state and local governments solve their problems need not involve the introduction of new products or techniques" (Roessner 1979, 185). Knowledge utilization by local government users is also the topic of a study by Browning, Marshall, and Tabb (1980), who identify utilization as the local government's responsiveness to interests of local groups. The findings of their study based on Model Cities data suggest that knowledge coming from federal programs has an important but limited capacity to influence the direction of local change. Local community mental health centers were the users in a study where outcome was defined as the degree to which knowledge use assisted the organization in resolving a problem (Larsen 1982; Larsen and Norris 1982).

The emphasis in all these studies is on the group or organization's ability to use knowledge in solving problems; the studies do not assess utilization as the extent to which any one set of findings or body of knowledge is used. There is no reason to expect that any one discrete piece of knowledge will be the one that solves the user's problem. In fact, a comparison of these two distinct outcomes—use of specific knowledge and organizational problem solution—found that both are valid outcomes but are not statistically related (Larsen 1980).

All groups and organizations are located in environments that also influence utilization. The context into which the knowledge is introduced may be extremely important; users face specific local needs or problems that force them to use knowledge in different ways. Contextual factors may be more important than characteristics of the information source in determining utilization (Fullan 1980; Campeau 1978). In a recent review of the application of research and development (R & D) based knowledge to problems in educational organizations, Kane and Kocher (1980) identified several specific strategies to increase utilization: More strategies dealt with factors of organizational control than any other component. Examples include development of active local administrative support for knowledge use, procedures for developing a community "sense of ownership" of the knowledge, and emphasis on organizational identification of the need for knowledge.

Operationalizing contextual characteristics--both internal organizational variables and external factors--is a particularly difficult problem since in many cases the context may present a unique or highly unusual set of circumstances. In some ways, context varies for every case of knowledge use. Given the range of differential organizational factors and environmental factors, there will almost always be a different response to the knowledge from each user.

Some would argue that organizational response to knowledge has no universal referent, and therefore that the description of knowledge use outcome must be different for different organizations (Choi 1980). While this may be true in one sense, we suggest that it is possible to identify contextual factors relevant to knowledge use in the majority of situations and to use these to provide a common framework for knowledge use studies. Although no typology for information utilization yet has been generally accepted, likely candidates for inclusion in a classification of situations would be categories descriptive of (1) participants in the utilization process, (2) the purpose of the potential utilization, (3) beneficiaries of the potential utilization, (4) internal and external factors influencing utilization, (5) the intended nature of the utilization, and (6) an indication of the time frame.

To provide an example, let us take the first situational category, participants in the utilization process, and arbitrarily identify the following sub-categories: utilization studies involving one individual, studies involving a small group, studies involving a large group, studies involving a community, studies involving a state, studies involving a country, and international studies. Classifications such as these would facilitate needed comparisons of utilization between and among sub-categories. For example, what are the differences in utilization by communities compared with utilization in national-level policymaking? To what extent are there differences in utilization by individuals most concerned with direct implications for practice on the personal level, and utilization by decision-making groups concerned with defining national policy? It is obvious that utilization in which the individual considers personal options is different from utilization involving many special interest groups, each of which may be in opposition to the others and even with the utilization process. There are certainly differences between utilization in different situations, but there are similarities as well. To what extent are these consistent and predictable?

A review of utilization studies of organization in a number of fields reveals that there are situational categories that appear with some frequency, and which may form the basis of a typology of contexts. Examples include the size of the organization; number of staff and/or clients; location, whether urban, rural, or mixed; annual budget; number of years in operation; and the like. If researchers described the context of users in these terms, it would facilitate comparison of results across studies. That is, if results of a knowledge use study were reported as based on small, urban organizations, results of other studies on small urban organizations could be compared to them. At the same time, results of studies in large rural organizations may not be comparable.

In the absence of agreement on such a typology, the next best alternative is for researchers to provide explicit descriptions of the context in which they are conducting their knowledge use study (Wolek and Griffith 1979). Further, the researcher should deliberately limit the research to one contextual area and select samples from that one domain (Berman 1980). This type of contextual clarification would be responsive to a recognized need in the field (Larsen 1980) and would go a great way to clear up some of the confusion resulting from imprecise descriptions of users.

THE KNOWLEDGE SOURCE

Change agents are considered by many to be an effective way of facilitating the knowledge use process (Fullan 1980; Backer and Glaser 1979; Havelock and Havelock 1973; Rothman, Erlich, and Teresa 1976; Sieber 1972). Speaking to the value of outside knowledge sources, Lippitt, Watson, and Westley (1958, 10-11) pointed out that although dynamic systems "reveal a continuous process of change," it is equally true that "systems exhibit a high degree of stability, constancy, or rigidity in many aspects of their operation and organization." User groups, they continue, often are unable to change these stabilized and sometimes inappropriate patterns and "outside help—a change agent—is needed."

Havelock and Havelock's review of the change agent reveals the lack of agreement on how active this role should be. One position states, "This type of relationship calls for restraint and a non-directive stance by the consultant and a withholding of advice, expert information, and a minimum of programming for the consultee" (Havelock and Havelock 1973, 11). The opposite perspective finds, "The change-agent consultant is an active participant and collaborator, and a conveyor of knowledge about the process of change itself" (Havelock and Havelock 1973, 61). Other propositions state still different views about a change agent and call for alternate approaches and strategies.

If utilization is conceptualized in inclusive terms, the literature describing change agent strategies for facilitating utilization and change is relevant. However, one of the problems with this literature is the absence of criterion measures for determining outcomes. Much of the literature is limited to manuals or training guides recommending certain activities. There is very little research relating change agent activities to quantitative outcomes. Those measures that are employed usually assess general attitudes of users toward the knowledge source and ignore behavioral indicators of utilization. The methods most frequently used to collect outcome measures are questionnaires and interviews with users (Lippitt and Lippitt 1978); inspections and site visits to assess impact are infrequent.

A study of local organizations by Larsen (1982) illustrates the use of quantitative measures assessing impact of change agents in the knowledge use process. Utilization was defined as the implementation of information provided by a change agent. Data on the extent of utilization were collected through direct observation and interviews of users. Additional indicators of outcome included degree of organizational problem solution and future interest in information use. While this study suggests one way of assessing the relationship of utilization and the knowledge source, there is a clear need for more attention to the conceptualization and development of such measures.

INTERACTION

Indications of outcome should be collected from multiple sources and preferably sources that possess different perspectives (Windle, Majchrzak, and Flaherty 1979). It is not sufficient to base conclusions regarding knowledge use on the responses of one group of users. Clearly knowledge use is a complex process and involves differing perspectives. All of them may be equally valid, but all of them may be different.

A study by Yin and others (1976, vi) takes the interaction of components into account. In research on innovations in state and local services, outcome in implementing technological innovations was defined in terms of four conditions: "Each condition represents a different combination of the degree to which an innovation was found beneficial--i.e., produced a service improvement--and the degree to which it was incorporated into the daily activities of the local agency." The four conditions involved situations in which: (1) an innovation produces a service improvement and is incorporated, (2) an innovation does not produce an improvement and is not incorporated, (3) an innovation produces an improvement but is not incorporated, and (4) an innovation does not produce an improvement but is nevertheless incorporated. Initial determination of outcome centered on the characteristics of the innovation that were associated with service improvement and incorporation. Next, outcome was perceived in terms of contextual factors, and then, in terms of process variables. This broad conception of outcome allowed the study to include a range of innovations and also a range of organizational and contextual factors. Whereas historically studies have dealt with outcome as the use of one innovation or set of research findings across several sites, this broader conception of outcomes includes the aggregate experience of many different types of innovations in many different sites. Therefore, outcome was able to incorporate attributes of the innovation with attributes of the organization and context.

Another example of a study in which utilization is conceptualized as interactive is the innovation-decision model suggested by Downs and Mohr (1976). They suggest that for each organization, two or more innovations be studied. The decision of the organization regarding each specific innovation or idea forms a separate piece of data; the unit of analysis therefore is the information and the organizational decision taken in conjunction. The use of this approach allows the identification of organizational factors, both primary and secondary, that differentially affect utilization, and it allows a similar identification of information factors and the way in which these interact.

Bingham (1978) used the innovation-decision model in research on innovation utilization in local government. Studying decisions in cities, he used two innovations, one product innovation defined as the innovation requiring the adoption of a physical product and one process innovation requiring a change in method. Outcomes included factors affecting local government decisions, factors affecting the

utiliz ation of specific innovations, and the "linkage
sequence or process of innovation adoption" (1978, 178).

A major study of federal programs supporting
educational change (Berman and McLaughlin 1975) presents
another study of knowledge use process. Three outcomes were
identified in this study: perceived success--the relative
extent to which project participants believed that goals
were achieved; change in behavior--the type and extent of
change in user behavior as perceived by the participants;
and fidelity of implementation--the extent to which the
project was implemented as originally planned. These
outcomes represented the users as well as the information.

While the broader conceptualiz ation of utiliz ation in
interactive studies has had an expanding influence, it is
not without its difficulties. In general, these knowledge
use outcomes are relatively ill-defined. Specification of
interactive alternatives has not progressed as far as
definitions of outcomes for studies focusing on users,
knowledge, or the knowledge source.

TEMPORAL V ALUES

The influence of time on utiliz ation has been ignored
by most researchers. Theoretical models of information use
and organiz ational change generally describe stages in the
implementation process, thus implicitly acknowledging time.
Such models usually state that at some point knowledge
enters the user's awareness, is considered, begins to be
implemented, and eventually becomes integrated into an
ongoing program or behavior. It appears obvious that
knowledge utiliz ation takes time, however few models or
research studies include time as a variable influencing the
utiliz ation process. A study of knowledge utiliz ation could
include several rounds of data collection at different
points in time, and each would yield completely different--
and correct--findings. It is almost certain that different
outcomes would be identified at each point in the
utiliz ation process.

The influence of time can be treated in both a
descriptive and causal sense. The descriptive function is
perhaps most obvious--different characteristics of the
information and the user will be important at different
points in the utiliz ation process. V iewed in this context,
time provides a benchmark against which to note variations
in utiliz ation. Time can also be a causal factor. The
utiliz ation outcome commonly called discontinuance is

dependent on time (i.e., discontinuance cannot occur until some amount of time has passed).

If extended over a long period of time, adoption of new knowledge could be expected to become routinized (Yin et al. 1976) or to lose its distinguishing characteristics as it melts into the organization's ongoing program. Backer and Glaser (1979) found that programs lasting over time typically change in format and operation. These findings suggest that the nature and extent of utilization occur in a predictable sequence. Implementation may be followed by discontinuance, discontinuance by readoption, and rejection by later adoption (Havelock 1969).

The limited data available on the relationship of time and knowledge utilization indicate that time has an impact (Rich 1977; Ciarlo 1975) and that there appear to be systematic shifts in knowledge use over time. Rich (1977) poses the presence of two waves or cycles of utilization, the first being specific documentable use of information and the second being primarily conceptual in nature. Strommen and Aleshire (1979) found that time was a major factor in utilization decisions of large organizations; if new information were introduced after the year's program had been set, the information was disregarded regardless of its merit. Likewise, cycles of bureaucratic decision making and policy revision determine the type of information used in the public sector.

The influence of time in information use mandates a longitudinal methodology as the approach of choice for collecting useful outcome data (Tornatzky and Fergus 1980). A series of outcome indicators collected at different points in time also allows process variables to be incorporated in a structured manner and avoids the problems of selective recall found in retrospective studies.

EXAMPLE OF OPERATIONALIZING CRITICAL VALUES

Variables defined in the literature as important in utilization research sometimes seem difficult to apply in actual studies. An example of a study that operationalized and applied critical variables may help in this translation process. A good case in point is a study of knowledge use in local organizations. The study focused on local mental health organizations and how they used knowledge to implement changes in their programs. Community health centers were faced with a mandate to introduce new programs for their clients and to improve old programs—in short, to implement major changes in their organizations. In some cases, knowledge about how to make these changes was lacking. A major problem, simply stated, was how to facilitate the use of new knowledge among local mental health organizations.

A basic assumption of the research was that the introduction of new knowledge into an organization would not automatically result in its utilization or in problem solution. The interaction model discussed previously poses several factors contributing to utilization: the knowledge, the user, the source of knowledge, and the interaction of these factors. As operationalized in this study, the knowledge source was an expert consultant, the knowledge was information provided by the consultant, and the users were staff of community health centers.

The study investigated utilization resulting from consultation in community health centers throughout the United States. A representative sample of 80 centers was randomly assigned to the treatment condition (N=39) or control condition (N=41). The basic intervention used in the treatment condition was program-oriented consultation. Each center in the treatment group identified the topic of consultation, and an experienced consultant with expertise in that area was selected. Consultants were chosen from throughout the country with the assistance of the National Council of Community Mental Health Centers. Three criteria were established for selecting consultants: (1) they must have been trained and experienced in consultation, (2) they must have worked in a mental health center, and (3) they must have been acknowledged experts in specific program areas. Eighteen experts, each visiting two or three centers, met with staff and provided information on the topic, both research-based information and general information.

Standardized data collection procedures were applied at four points: prior to the consultation, during the consultation, and both four and eight months following the consultation. Centers in the control group requested consultation but none was provided as part of the study. Data from these centers were collected at the same time as the treatment groups with the exception that the second collection (that is, during consultation) did not occur.

Each expert was accompanied by a trained observer who had the responsibility for collecting data. One of the activities of the observer was to collect data on specific information or ideas provided by the expert. To do this, the observer kept a careful record of each idea suggested,

and at the end of the visit, the observer and expert
reviewed the list. This allowed the expert to approve the
list and to suggest rewording of some ideas to insure they
represented the original intent. A list of these ideas was
left with the staff, a copy given to the consultant, and a
copy retained by the observer.

The follow-up interviews identified information that
was selectively noted and used and information that was
disregarded or not used. The interviewer went through the
list of ideas sequentially, probing on each to determine
whether the information was used, and if so, how. In all
organizations, follow-up interviews were conducted with more
than one staff member. If the responses of two individuals
generally confirmed each other, the observer determined a
summary score for each of the ideas. If two respondents
differed in their opinions, a third individual was
interviewed. If no agreement was apparent from three
interviews, a fourth person was interviewed and so forth
until the discrepancy could be resolved and one score was
determined, representing the general consensus.

Outcome was differentiated into three types of non-
utilization and four types of utilization. The categories:
. Information considered and rejected
. Nothing done; no decision made about the information
. Information still under consideration
. Steps taken toward implementing the information
. Information partially implemented
. Information implemented completely as presented
. Information implemented and adapted to fit user's
  needs

Information: The Knowledge

Information in this study was defined as the ideas or
suggestions provided to an organization by an expert
consultant. Information included both the results of
professional scientific inquiry (Lindblom and Cohen 1979)
and ordinary knowledge. One of the requirements imposed for
selection of consultants was that the individuals be experts
in their content area. The rationale for this criterion was
that experts are more likely to be familiar with both
research-based information and ordinary information. To
limit the definition of information to research-based
results would not have been responsive to the needs of
practice-directed mental health centers, nor characteristic
of real-world information exchange.

It is obvious that not all ideas are equal. Some require considerable work and planning on the part of the user, while others are simple and straightforward. Simple frequency counts of use therefore have limited value. The study addressed this problem by collecting data on variables describing each idea. Characteristics providing a general estimate of the "quality" of the idea are:

- Number of people required
- Cost of implementing the idea
- Time required
- Trialability
- Complexity

Community Mental Health Center: The User

A major element in the study was the user organization. Studies reported in the literature have identified large numbers of significant variables describing user characteristics related to information use. One recent summary (Roessner 1981) reported 73 characteristics found to be significantly related to agency and program modifications by various research studies. If we wanted to be comprehensive, the researchers could have included in the study only those variables found to be important in related research, and still have had far too many. Consequently, our problem was one of excluding variables from a list of potentially important characteristics. The process we used was to review studies considered to be "classics" in the field, noting the variables found to be related to information use. Those most frequently identified were used in this study. They include the following:

Demographic Variables

- Region of the country (South, West, Midwest, Northeast)
- Metropolitan status (urban, rural, mixed)
- Budget (in thousands of dollars)
- Number of full-time employees
- Number of part-time employees
- Year in staffing grant
- Tenure of director (in years)
- Number of years center has been in operation

Organizational Attitudes

- Receptivity of leaders
- Experience using a consultant
- Staff preparation for consultation
- Past success with consultation

Contextual Characteristics

The Consultant: Information Source. Few studies quantitatively assess the relationship of consultant characteristics with information use. Most research is based on personal observation, and the results are often very general. Findings from the literature suggest the consultant should be all things to all people. Consultants are told to provide direction but to listen well; to encourage staff to participate but to give them plenty of directed input; to gather background information on many factors but to identify a limited topic for consultation; and then to be empathetic, responsive, encouraging, interested in the consultees, warm, and sympathetic. While not denying that all these are important characteristics, it is such an extensive list that most consultants find no specific recommendations to apply in a particular situation. If all these activities are good things to do, which have the highest priority?

From the literature and from our previous research, we identified demographic variables and behavioral characteristics that appeared to be most important. The variables are presented below:

Demographic Variables
- Geographical location
- Gender
- Ethnic group
- Professional training

Characteristics
- Supportive
- Knowledgeable
- Clarified problem
- Presented multiple suggestions
- Presented details of solutions
- Summarized outcomes of suggestions
- Encouraged participation
- Maintained focus
- Passed along relevant information
- Attended to organization's situation
- Prepared
- Active

Conclusion

It should be noted that the research presented in this example was designed to study only certain utilization issues at the local level. The approach presented here may not be appropriate to utilization research at the macro level. There are other variables such as the study of the media, extension service, and written communication strategies that would be necessary for research at the macro level and must be included in such studies. The current example is not intended to be a comprehensive model, but provides an example of one approach.

Results from this study indicate that information is used and used frequently by local organizations. Three-fourths of the ideas were used or considered; only 25 percent had been disregarded. More specifically, 25 percent of the ideas had been used after four months—19 percent implemented exactly as presented by the consultant and 6 percent implemented with adaptations. Almost half of the ideas (49 percent) were being planned or considered. One-quarter of the ideas had not been used—nothing had been done with 16 percent, and 9 percent had been considered and rejected.

Using any type of knowledge requires the individual or the organization to make a commitment in terms of time and energy. In the current study, all information was rated on a difficulty scale that combined measures of time, staff, and cost. Nearly 80 percent of the ideas that were used required three or more staff and at least 40 hours of staff time to implement them, suggesting that planning for utilization is time-consuming and requires the involvement of staff at many levels and with different types of skills.

Information or an innovation is presented to a potential user and the user either adopts or fails to adopt the complete package. Findings from this study indicate that complete utilization is more likely to occur with information that is relatively easy to implement. Only one-quarter of the information implemented completely as presented was above average in difficulty level. Evidently information completely implemented often is straightforward and can be incorporated into the organization's program with little disruption.

Information that was considered but then rejected by the organization tended to be relatively difficult to implement. If this is the case, implementation may be beyond the organization's resources and utilization may be virtually impossible. Therefore, a non-utilization decision may be a correct and positive outcome for these organizations.

A major finding of the study is that information utilization takes time; at least, utilization of information designed to be relevant to program concerns in community mental health centers takes time. This study found that implementation was still underway eight months following presentation of the information. How much longer the implementation process may last is not known.

Perhaps information utilization can occur quickly—in a few months—if the information is simple to understand and easy to put in place. However, when dealing with public organizations such as schools, health agencies, or governmental units, there are few situations in which program changes are simple or easy to put in place. Using information in real-world programs requires a lengthy process of negotiation, planning, try-outs, establishing support, and consolidation.

Utilization is complex, incorporating elements of the information and the user. Utilization—and non-utilization—can occur in several forms. This research begins to address alternative outcomes and factors influencing those outcomes. However, investigation of these issues must be expanded and applied in different contexts before definitive conclusions can be drawn.

REFERENCES

Allison, G. T. 1971. Essence of Decision: Explaining the Cuban Missile Crisis. Boston: Little, Brown & Co.

Backer, T. E., and E. M. Glaser. 1979. Methods for Sustaining Innovative Service Programs, Final Report. Los Angeles, Calif.: Human Interaction Research Institute.

Baldridge, J. V., and T. E. Deal, eds. 1975. Managing Change in Education Organizations. Berkeley, Calif.: McCutchan Publishing Corp.

Bennis, W. J., K. D. Benne, and R. Chin. 1969. The Planning of Change. New York: Holt, Rinehart & Winston.

Berman, P. 1980. "Toward an Implementation Paradigm of Educational Change." Paper prepared for the National Institute of Education, March 1980.

Berman, P., and M. W. McLaughlin. 1975. Federal Programs Supporting Educational Change. Santa Monica, Calif.: Rand Corp.

Bingham, R. D. 1978. "Innovation, Bureaucracy, and Public Policy: A Study of Innovation and Adoption by Local Government." Western Political Quarterly 31, no. 2 (June): 178-205.

Browning, R. P., D. R. Marshall, and D. H. Tabb. 1980. "Implementation and Political Change: Sources of Local Variations in Federal Social Programs." Policy Studies 8, no. 4, Special no. 2: 616-632.

Campeau, P. L., J. L. Binkley, D. G. Hawkridge, and P. G. Treadway. 1978. Evaluation of Project Information Package Dissemination and Implementation, First year report. Palo Alto, Calif.: American Institutes for Research.

Caplan, N. 1980. "What Do We Know About Knowledge Utilization?" New Directions for Program Evaluation no. 5: 1-10.

Carlson, R. O. 1965. Adoption of Educational Innovations. Eugene, Oreg.: Center for Advanced Study of Educational Administration.

Choi, T. 1980. "Governance of University Hospitals." Mimeographed paper.

Ciarlo, J. 1975. "Personal Communication." Reported in H. David and S. Salasin, "The Utilization of Evaluation." In Handbook of Evaluation Research, ed. E. Struening and M. Guttentag. Beverly Hills, Calif.: Sage Publications.

Downs, G. W., and L. B. Mohr. 1976. "Conceptual Issues in the Study of Innovation." Administrative Science Quarterly 21, no. 4 (1976): 700-714.

Festinger, L. 1957. A Theory of Cognitive Dissonance. New York: Row & Peterson.

Fullan, M. 1980. "The Role of Human Agents Internal to School Districts in Knowledge Utilization." Prepared for the Program on Research and Practice. NIE.

Gardner, J.W. 1964. Self-Renewal. New York: Harper and Row Publishers.

Guba, E. G. 1968. "Development, Diffusion and Evaluation." In Knowledge Production and Utilization in Educational Administration, ed. T. L. Eidell and J. M. Kitchel. Eugene: Center for the Advanced Study of Educational Administration, University of Oregon.

Hage, J., and M. Aiken. 1970. Social Change in Complex Organizations. New York: Random House.

Havelock, R. G. 1969. Planning for Innovation Through Dissemination and Utilization of Knowledge. Ann Arbor: Center for Research on the Utilization of Scientific Knowledge, Institute for Social Research, University of Michigan.

Havelock, R. G., and M. C. Havelock. 1973. Training for Change Agents. Ann Arbor: University of Michigan.

Heider, F. 1958. The Psychology of Interpersonal Relations. New York: Wiley and Sons.

Hovland, C., I. Janis, and H. Kelley. 1953. Communication and Persuasion. New Haven, Conn.: Yale Univ. Press.

Janis, I., and L. Mann. 1977. Decision-Making. New York: Free Press.

Jobs, S. 1983. Remarks at Annual Meeting of Apple Computer, Inc. Cupertino, Calif.

Kane, M., and A. T. Kocher. 1980. "The Dissemination and Utilization of Educational R&D in the United States." Paper presented at the Conference, the Political Realization of Social Science Knowledge, Institute for Advanced Study, Vienna, Austria, June 1980.

Kelly, P. and M. Kranzberg. 1975. Technical Innovation: A Critical Review of Current Knowledge, Vol. I. Atlanta: Georgia Institute of Technology.

Larsen, J. 1980. "Knowledge Utilization: What Is It? An Essay." Knowledge: Creation, Diffusion, Utilization 1, no. 3: 421-422.

_____. 1982. Information Utilization and Non-Utilization. Palo Alto, Calif.: American Institutes for Research.

Larsen, J., and E. Norris. 1982. The Impact of Consultation. Palo Alto, Calif.: American Institutes for Research.

Lindblom, D. E. and D. K. Cohen. 1979. Usable Knowledge: Social Science and Social Problem Solving. New Haven, Conn.: Yale Univ. Press.

Lippitt, G. and R. Lippitt. 1978. The Consulting Process in Action. La Jolla, Calif.: University Associates.

Lippitt, R., J. Watson and B. Westley. 1958. The Dynamics of Planned Change: A Comparative Study of Principles and Techniques. New York: Harcourt, Brace and World.

Machlup, F. 1962. The Production and Distribution of Knowledge in the United States. Princeton, N.J.: Princeton Univ. Press.

National Academy of Sciences. 1969. Behavioral and Social Science Survey Committee. The Behavioral and Social Sciences: Outlook and Need. Englewood Cliffs, N.J.: Prentice-Hall.

National Academy of Sciences. National Research Council. 1978. "The Federal Investment in Knowledge of Social Problems." Vol. 1 of Study Project on Social Research and Development. Washington, D.C.: NAS.

National Institute of Education. 1978. Reflections and Recommendations. Fourth annual report of the National Council on Educational Research.

National Science Foundation. 1969. National Science Board. Special Commission on the Social Sciences. Knowledge Into Action: Improving the Nation's Use of the Social Sciences. Washington, D.C.: NSF.

Rich, R. F. 1977. "Uses of Social Science Information by Federal Bureaucrats: Knowledge Use for Action Versus Knowledge for Understanding." In Uses of Social Research in Public Policy, ed. C. Weiss. Lexington, Mass.: Lexington Books.

Roessner, J. D. 1979. "Federal Technology Policy: Innovation and Problem Solving in State and Local Governments." Policy Analysis 5, no. 2: 181-200.

_____. 1981. Personal communication.

Rogers, E. M. 1962. Diffusion of Innovations. New York: Free Press.

Rothman, J., J. L. Erlich and J. G. Teresa. 1976. Promoting Innovation and Change in Organizations and Communities. New York: John Wiley and Sons.

Russell Sage Foundation. 1950. Effective Use of Social Science Research in the Federal Services. New York: Russell Sage Foundation.

Sieber, S. D. 1972. Incentives and Disincentives for Knowledge Utilization in Public Education: A Systhesis of Research. Prepared for the Research and Educational Practices Program, NIE.

Smith, M. B. 1977. "A Dialectical Social Psychology? Comments on a Symposium." Personality and Social Psychology Bulletin 3, no. 4: 719-724.

Smith, M. B., J. S. Brunner, and R. W. White. 1956. Opinions and Personality. New York: John Wiley and Sons.

Strommen, M., and A. Aleshire. 1979. Effecting Utilization: The Experimental Use of Consultants, Phase II Report. Minneapolis: Search Institute.

Tornatzky, L. B., and E. O. Fergus. 1980. "Innovation and Diffusion in Mental Health: The Community Lodge." In Community Mental Health: A Behavioral-Ecological Perpective, ed. A. M. Jeger and R. Slotnick. New York: Plenum.

Weiss, C. H., and M. J. Bucuvalas. 1977. "The Challenge of Social Research to Decision-Making." In Using Social Research in Public Policy-Making, ed. C. Weiss. Lexington, Mass.: Lexington Books.

Windle, C. and E. W. Flaherty. 1979. "Indirect Services: Consultation, Education and Interagency Relationships." In Evaluation in Practice, ed. G. Landsberg and others. NIMH. [DHEW Publication No. (ADM) 78-763.]

Windle, C., A. Majchrzak, and E. W. Flaherty. 1979. "Program Evaluation at the Interface of Program Echelons." In Translating Evaluation into Policy, ed. R. Rich. Beverly Hills, Calif.: Sage Publications.

Wolek, F. W., and B. C. Griffith. 1979. "Policy and Informal Communication in Science and Technology." Science Studies 4: 411-420.

Yin, R. K., K. A. Heald, M. E. Vogel, P. D. Fleischauer, and B. C. Vladeck. 1976. A Review of Case Studies of Technological Innovations in State and Local Services. Santa Monica, Calif.: Rand Corp.

Zaltman, J., R. Duncan, and J. Holbek. 1973. Innovations and Organizations. New York: John Wiley and Sons.

16

Studying Knowledge Use:
A Profile of Procedures
and Issues

William N. Dunn

Societies have long been concerned with research on the impact of public and private policies, a concern that may be roughly but conveniently dated to the emergence of empirical policy research, including censuses and social surveys, in nineteenth-century Europe and North America. Yet it is only recently that members of scientific and policy-making establishments, first in the industrialized countries and later in much of the rest of the world, have directed attention towards research on the production, dissemination, and utilization of policy-relevant knowledge. This historic turn towards research on knowledge utilization, signalled by such terms as "knowledge society" (Machlup 1962), is punctuated by the titles of books published over the last forty and more years: Knowledge for What? The Place of Social Science in American Culture (Lynd 1940), The Production and Distribution of Knowledge in the United States (Machlup 1962), Knowledge and Power (Lakoff 1966), Public Knowledge (Ziman 1968), Knowledge Application: The Knowledge System in Society (Holzner and Marx 1979), Usable Knowledge: Social Science and Social Problem Solving (Lindblom and Cohen 1979), Universities and the International Distribution of Knowledge (Spitzberg 1980), and the Knowledge Cycle (Rich 1981b).

Systematic research on processes of knowledge creation, diffusion, and utilization is a distinctively modern enterprise. While the intellectual history of previous centuries discloses many important theoretical antecedents, particularly in the fields of history and philosophy of science (e.g., Laudan 1977) and the sociology of knowledge (e.g., Remmling 1967), these theoretical antecedents have been somewhat peripheral to recent research on knowledge use.

While the sociology of knowledge has been centrally
concerned with the social origins and determinants of
intellectual productions, only secondarily, if at all, have
contributors to this discipline focused on the consequences
of applying intellectual productions to problems of
practice. Consequently, some have called for a sociology of
knowledge applications, a classic sociology of knowledge
"turned upside down" (Holzner 1978, 8), one that emphasizes
the need for a basic social science of the applied social
sciences (Weiss and Bucuvalas 1980, 25-6, 271-72; Holzner
and Marx 1979). Similar basic research programs rooted in
the psychology and economics of knowledge applications,
respectively, have been set forth in major contributions by
Campbell (1977) and Machlup (1980).

The majority of available knowledge use studies have
not been significantly shaped by these or other basic
research perspectives. Instead, they have drawn primarily
from research on planned social change, marketing, and the
communication innovations (Havelock 1969; Glaser, Abelson,
and Garrison 1976; Meehan and Beal 1977; Zaltman 1979;
Rothman 1980a). Accordingly, the bulk of knowledge use
research has been oriented towards the translation of social
science knowledge into guidelines for the improvement of
practice, rather than towards a balanced program of basic as
well as applied research on processes of knowledge use.
While there are important exceptions to this generalization,
some of which are reviewed below, the field as a whole has
been dominated by applied research whose overriding purpose
is the immediate satisfaction of needs of policymakers and
practitioners.

In the past twenty and more years there has been a
dramatic increase in such applied studies. Glaser (1976)
estimates that there are as many as 20,000 citations to
literature on knowledge use and planned change, a figure
that is likely to double by the mid-1980s. As a field of
study, knowledge use has its own professional journal,
Knowledge: Creation, Diffusion, Utilization, established in
1979. In the last decade, issue-specific studies have been
undertaken in areas of education, mental health, criminal
justice, community development, information management, and
general program evaluation and policy analysis (Glaser 1976;
Weiss 1977; Rich 1981a; Ciarlo 1981). Concurrently,
governmental and private bodies have emphasized both the
importance and need for improvements in the utilization of
the stock of knowledge available for social problem solving
(e.g., National Science Foundation 1969; Social Science
Research Council 1969; National Academy of Sciences 1978).

Thus, it is no longer necessary, as once it may have
been, to justify the study of knowledge use. Yet many
important theoretical, conceptual, and methodological issues
have not been satisfactorily addressed by researchers in the
field (Larsen 1981; Conner 1981; Weiss 1981; Rich and
Goldsmith 1983; Dunn and Holzner 1982):

- What do we mean by knowledge when we attempt to
  measure its uses by policymakers, practitioners,
  and other stakeholders in the alleviation of
  practical problems?
- How should we conceptualize and measure the uses
  of knowledge and how are these uses related, if at
  all, to characteristics of knowledge itself?
- What research paradigms, strategies, and
  procedures are available to make more plausible
  inferences about the uses of knowledge in complex
  practice settings?

Questions posed above suggest a range of pressing
methodological problems confronting those who study, and
thereby seek to improve, processes of knowledge use. The
present chapter seeks to define, clarify, and suggest ways
to alleviate such problems by comparing and contrasting a
range of knowledge use studies conducted in recent years.
The first section presents a profile of such studies, while
the second provides an inventory of many of the most important research procedures employed to date. The concluding
section offers an overall assessment of methodological
strengths and limitations of research conducted to date.

A PROFILE OF KNOWLEDGE USE STUDIES

Studies reviewed below are identified in the course of
a multiyear project supported by the National Institute of
Education (Dunn and Holzner 1982). The selection of
studies, as well as methods and techniques employed in their
conduct, grew out of consultations with members of a
national network of knowledge use researchers. In addition,
we searched the Social Science Periodical Index and the
Social Science Citation Index and examined available
bibliographic resources such as those by Glaser (1976) and
Rich (1981a). A computerized bibliographic search was also
conducted, yielding items which appeared between 1969 and
the present in the Current Index to Journals in Education.
Finally, a flexible form of snowball sampling was employed
to contact researchers who had been identified through the
bibliographic search.

One major aim of the project was to investigate the range of study designs employed to conduct research on knowledge use. For this purpose we constructed study profiles describing key methodological characteristics of research in the field. In all, profiles were constructed for some forty studies whose key methodological dimensions are reviewed below.

Unit of Analysis

A key decision in knowledge use studies is the selection of an appropriate unit of analysis. Since much knowledge use research is concerned with assessing the effects of social science research on policy decisions, it is important to recognize that such decisions are made within organized collectivities or systems. In studying the impact of knowledge use on collective decisions made within a network of actively communicating decision makers, it is often essential to obtain data about the respondent's relationships with other individuals. Aggregated individual responses (e.g., responses to questions about the number of times a given research report influenced an individual's decision) may provide an inaccurate and misleading picture of the direct and indirect processes through which research is used, contributing to different forms of the individualistic (atomistic) fallacy—that is, invalid inferences about collective properties based on the aggregation of non-relational data obtained from individuals. For these and related reasons Weiss (1981, 28-31) has drawn attention to alternative methodological approaches that focus on the effects of research on policy decisions, policy issues, persons and organizations. Each of these four approaches has special limitations associated with the unit of analysis adopted for study.

Individuals or aggregates of individuals are the unit of analysis in almost all of our set of knowledge use studies. Typical of these many studies is research reported by Hall, George, and Rutherford (1979) in which the investigators administered a questionnaire designed to assess the concerns of individual users and nonusers about the implementation of particular educational innovations. By contrast, Yin and Gwaltney (1981), in their study of regional educational agencies, focus on cases of interorganizational collaboration as the unit of analysis. This study, focusing as it does on relations among organizations as well as individuals, is not representative

of the vast bulk of studies (Weiss and Bucuvalas 1980; Rich
and Goldsmith 1983; Caplan, Morrison, and Stambaugh 1975)
that focus on individuals or aggregates of individuals as
units of analysis.

Sampling

Few reported studies employ random sampling, with the
bulk of research conducted with convenience or purposive
samples of individuals, organizations, or documents.
Typical of the few studies in which random sampling is
employed is research on the uses of market research reported
by Zaltman and Deshpande (1980). This study, designed to
explore factors that influence the use of market research by
managers and researchers, was based on a self-administered
questionnaire completed by 176 randomly selected
respondents.

By contrast, most other studies employ some type of
convenience or purposive sampling. Dunn and Swierczek
(1977), for example, selected a purposive (theoretical)
sample of 67 cases of planned change and knowledge use
reported in available literature. Their purpose was to
generate grounded theories of knowledge utilization and
planned change by analyzing the effects of some 12 factors
(e.g., type of organization, societal type, mode of
intervention, task environment, focus of change) on the
adoption and effectiveness of innovations. A similar
strategy of purposive sampling has been employed by Gregg
and others (1979) to select and analyze 698 cases of social
problems research and by Yin and others (1976) to select and
analyze 140 cases of technological innovation in state and
local governments.

Research Design

Studies reflect a diversity of research designs ranging
from case studies and cross sectional analysis to
quasi-experiments conducted in representative contexts of
practice. Some case studies are based on prior theory,
while others are not. For example, Firestone and others
(1981), exploring through naturalistic observation the
transfer of educational research into instructional practice
in five schools, began with no explicit theory of knowledge
use. By contrast, Yin and Gwaltney (1981) examine three
regional educational agencies, attempting to explain

processes of knowledge use in terms of prior theories about
the effects of complex patterns of collaboration and
exchange. Case studies comprise more than one-third of our
set of knowledge use studies.

A sizeable group of knowledge use studies are based on
quasi-experimental designs. Typical of this group, which
accounted for nearly one half of profiles, is research on
the managerial uses of evaluation research reported by Weeks
(1979). Following initial telephone contacts, questionnaires were sent to 76 program evaluators who supplied data
about their involvement in different phases of evaluation,
as well as their methodological preferences, decision context, and the degree to which evaluation findings were
applied to specific program decisions. A similar quasi-
experimental design, but one conducted under real-time
conditions, is Rich's study (1981b) of the use of information provided by the National Opinion Research Center under
the NSF-sponsored Continuous National Survey. Larsen (1982)
also reports a unique real-time field experiment where
research-based ideas, suggestions, and recommendations were
introduced into community mental health organizations.

The remaining studies were cross-sectional or longitudinal designs exploring retrospectively a multiplicity of
factors affecting the utilization of research. This latter
group includes studies of the impact of social science
research on decision making in state legislatures (Mitchell
1980), studies of the sources of information used by
congressional staff members (Florio, Behrmann, and Goltz
1979), and studies of the uses of social science research by
federal, state, and local policymakers (Caplan, Morrison,
and Stambaugh 1975; Weiss and Bucuvalas 1980; Rich and
Goldsmith 1983).

Research Methods

The prevailing method for obtaining data in knowledge
use studies is the self-administered questionnaire.
Approximately one-half of studies employed questionnaires,
while the use of content analysis, naturalistic observation,
and interview schedules characterizes the remainder of
studies. Only one-quarter of all studies employed
multivariate techniques to analyze data, while little more
than 20 percent of studies were qualitative in the specific
sense that they sought to capture the underlying contextual
meanings attached to knowledge and its uses. A small
proportion of studies employed multiple methods.

Definition of Use

A central problem of knowledge use studies is defining what is meant by "use." The most widely used definition in the field is one that distinguishes between conceptual and instrumental uses of knowledge (Rich 1975; Caplan, Morrison, and Stambaugh 1975; Weiss 1977). Generally, conceptual use refers to changes in the way that users think about problems, while instrumental use refers to changes in behavior, especially changes that are relevant to decision making. While many unresolved difficulties continue to plague this twofold distinction (Weiss 1981, chap. 17 below), many knowledge use studies continue to employ it. Instrumental use, for example, tends to imply that respondents are single decision makers, notwithstanding the collective or systemic nature of organizational decision making. Given these and related difficulties it is striking that more than two thirds of studies define use in primarily instrumental terms, with the remainder stressing either conceptual or symbolic aspects of knowledge use.

Reliability and Validity

Knowledge use studies, while they are based heavily on the use of questionnaires whose reliability may be readily assessed, are frequently based on procedures with unknown or unreported reliability and validity. Over half report no reliability data, while validity data are unavailable in more than two-thirds of the studies. Given the fact that knowledge use studies are intimately related to the assessment of cognitive (subjective) properties of many kinds, the absence of information about the reliability of procedures and the validity of constructs (e.g., instrumental and conceptual use) represents a serious unresolved problem of most research in the field.

INVENTORY OF RESEARCH PROCEDURES

A second major aim of the project was to identify new or promising procedures for conceptualizing and measuring knowledge use. Since books, articles, and reports typically do not provide adequate descriptions of research procedures, it was necessary to contact many researchers directly. More than 100 investigators were contacted by letter or phone and asked to provide a description of the procedures they had

employed to conduct their research project, including copies
of interview protocols, questionnaires, and coding schema.
An original pool of some 200 candidate-procedures was[1]
eventually narrowed to a smaller set of 65 procedures[1] that
were compared, contrasted, and evaluated according to a
standardiz ed abstracting procedure (the number of procedures
exceeded that of studies because some methods have not been
used in knowledge use studies proper). Each abstract
provides information about the author(s), availability,
purpose, variables, description, development,
reliability/validity, and administration of a particular
procedure (Dunn, Dukes, and Cahill 1982).

Some of these procedures, while they had not been
employed in knowledge use studies proper, were included in
the inventory because of their potential importance for
conceptualiz ing and measuring knowledge use. The remainder
of this section describes three types of procedures--
naturalistic observation, content analysis, questionnaires
and interview schedules--as well as several scales and
indices. While it is not possible to describe each
procedure in detail, abstracts of questionnaires, interview
schedules, and content analysis schema are available in Dunn
and Holz ner (1982).

Naturalistic Observation

Procedures for making naturalistic observations in
field settings have certain general advantages (Denz in
1970), including the development of concepts and hypotheses
that are grounded in the subjectively meaningful
experiences of persons studied. While Weiss (1981) has
identified participant observation as one of four major
approaches to the study of knowledge use, such procedures
for naturalistic observation are rarely employed in
knowledge use studies. Questionnaires and interview
schedules, as noted above, remain the dominant method of
investigation.

Even where naturalistic observation is reported as a
major element of knowledge use studies (Firestone et al.
1981; Louis, Rosenblum, and Molitor 1981), procedures may be
insufficiently specific, orderly, or regular to permit
applications by other investigators. Consequently,
procedures for naturalistic observation, while they appear
to be particularly appropriate for eliciting contextually
meaningful observations, cannot always be reproduced by
other investigators or examined as part of an external audit

that helps ensure the methodological accountability of
research findings (Guba 1981). Recent work by Huberman and
Miles (1982) has contributed innovative procedures for the
analysis of qualitative data, procedures that have been
described by their authors as methods of "grounded data
reduction." Relatedly, Rothman, Teresa, and Erlich (1977)
have developed a log reporting form that may be used to
monitor and assess concepts or practice guidelines. The log
reporting form, in contrast to relatively unstructured forms
of naturalistics observation, is readily reproducible in
various research contexts.

Content Analysis

A range of content analysis procedures is available for
studying processes of knowledge use. These procedures may
be employed with various kinds of documents, including
research reports, case materials, and other records of
experience. Content analysis procedures permit longitudinal
and cross-sectional studies of patterns of knowledge
production in the applied social sciences (Gregg et al.
1979; Rothman 1974), exploratory analyses of factors
associated with the adoption of innovations, planned change,
and knowledge use (Yin et al. 1976; Dunn and Swierczek 1977;
Dunn 1980), and investigations of the cognitive structures
and strategic decisions of policymakers (Huff 1982; Axelrod
1976).

Different content analysis procedures have produced
divergent or conflicting findings about processes of
knowledge creation, dissemination, and use. Whereas Rothman
(1974) finds that much social science research yields
consensus findings that may be translated into practice
guidelines (compare Rogers and Shoemaker 1971), Gregg and
others (1979) report substantial consensus among
investigators who have unknowingly or deliberately produced
false or misleading conclusions about major social problems,
including racial discrimination, rape, and substance abuse.
Whereas Rothman (1974) stresses the importance of the
methodological adequacy of research findings, Dunn (1980)
finds no relation between the technical quality of research
(e.g., adequacy of research designs), and its utilization.
Whereas Yin and others (1976) find that factors associated
with the implementation of innovations are critical to their
adoption, thus raising doubts about research, development,
and diffusion as an approach to innovation (compare Havelock
1969), the efficacy of this latter approach is generally

supported by Rothman (1974). Since Huff (1982) takes the
individual decision maker as the unit of analysis, her
finding that a complex network of causal attributions shapes
strategic decisions is not directly comparable to results
produced in content analysis studies where cases of
research, planned change, or knowledge use are the units of
analysis.

Questionnaires and Interview Schedules

At least 30 different questionnaires and interview
schedules have been employed to study various aspects of
knowledge use. Some questionnaires and interview schedules
(Hall et al. 1975; Weiss and Bucuvalas 1980; van de Vall and
Bolas 1982) are relatively structured, since they contain
fixed-choice and scale items, while others are relatively
unstructured. Relatively unstructured questionnaires and
interview schedules (Rothman 1980a; Mitchell 1980; Rich
1981b) include open-ended questions and, in some cases,
involve a recorded or transcribed record of responses to a
general question or decision-evoking scenario or vignette
(Voss, Tyler, and Yengo 1983). A number of questionnaires
are sufficiently flexible that they may be self-administered
or used in interview settings. A cross section of
questionnaires and interview schedules, constructed to
illustrate the variety and richness of available procedures,
is provided below according to three categories of
procedures: relatively structured, semi-structured, and
relatively unstructured. This categorization is for
convenience only, and there are points at which particular
procedures fall at the boundary between two categories.
Relatively Structured Procedures. Relatively
structured procedures allow respondents little freedom in
devising responses to questions. In their survey of
characteristics of evaluation research, Bernstein and
Freeman (1975) analyze responses obtained from 236
self-administered questionnaires completed by directors of
evaluation projects conducted in areas of education, health,
welfare, manpower, income security, public safety, and
housing. The mailed self-administered questionnaire
includes several classes of items: characteristics of
researchers, research organizations, and target populations,
information about programs being evaluated, methods for
assessing their impact, and information about plans for
disseminating and utilizing findings. The Bernstein and
Freeman study, which documents the diversity of evaluation

research projects, rates research quality in terms of "generally accepted" standards (e.g., quasi-experimental design, random sampling, use of multivariate techniques for conducting social science research).

Relatively structured procedures have also been employed to obtain information about diverse perceptions of research quality. In contrast to Bernstein and Freeman's "common" standards of research quality, Weiss and Bucuvalas (1980) attempt to assess characteristics of social science research studies that are perceived by respondents themselves to make such studies useful for decision making. Weiss and Bucuvalas designed an interview schedule which, administered to a stratified random sample of 250 mental health decision makers and researchers, required scale responses to 29 descriptors of research characteristics. Responses to these items were then factor analyzed, yielding four major factors: research quality, conformity with user expectations, action orientation, and challenge to the status quo. These factors are believed to "represent underlying constructs that people use in describing research" (Weiss and Bucuvalas 1980, 73).

A number of other studies have used relatively structured procedures to obtain reported levels of research use. Dickey (1980), for example, measured levels of research use by developing a Guttman scale on the basis of responses obtained from the directors of 54 educational evaluations conducted in Minnesota. Similarly, Johnson (1980) measured the use of evaluation research by constructing a Guttman scale designed to measure conceptual and instrumental use in a network of academics and decision makers concerned with the administration of justice. Dickman (1981) employed a four-item scale designed to assess the impact of research on recommendations to adopt various types of changes in social programs in two counties in Southern California.

In one of the most comprehensive research programs undertaken to date, Hall, George, and Rutherford (1979) have employed a questionnaire with 35 items designed to assess the concerns of users and nonusers about the implementation of specific innovations in education and other areas. Seven stages of concern--ranging from simple awareness to a concern with collaboration in implementing an innovation or exploring new alternatives--have been related to six levels of use of innovations (Hall et al. 1975). In contrast to the stages of concern (SoC) questionnaire, the levels of use (LoU) interview schedule yields information that is subsequently coded and rated by multiple observers. The eight levels of use range from nonuse to routine use, refinement, integration, and renewal. Finally, these two procedures may be employed with an innovations configurations checklist (ICC) that supplies information about the elements of a particular innovation that have entered into the practice of users and affected their behavior.

Other relatively structured procedures involving self-administered questionnaires have been developed by Strommen (1982) to measure components of the Davis-Salasin AVICTORY model (Davis and Salasin 1975), by Nelson and Kirst (1980) to determine the sources, modes, and uses of research by state educational policymakers, by Pelz and Horsley (1981) to assess the utilization of research in nursing practice, by Rothman (1980a) to measure the extent to which specific products of social research and development are utilized by intended users, by Weeks (1979) to assess the managerial use of evaluation research, by Hood and Blackwell (1976) to assess factors governing the market for educational research and development, and by Zaltman and Deshpande (1980) to explore factors that promote and retard the effective use of market research by product managers. The development of most of these self-administered questionnaires followed pilot-testing efforts based on focused interviews.

Semi-Structured Procedures. Semi-structured procedures, as the term suggests, lie somewhere between relatively structured and relatively unstructured questionnaires and interview schedules. Semi-structured procedures thus allow an intermediate degree of freedom in responding to questions. Caplan, Morrison, and Stambaugh (1975), in their study of 204 policymakers occupying key positions in federal departments, agencies, and commissions, used an interview schedule composed of open-ended and closed-ended questions. Interviews, each lasting an average of one and one-half hours, yielded data in several categories: awareness and self-reported use of social science information; evaluation of the worth and objectivity of data, research methods, and measurement procedures; beliefs and attitudes about social science research and factors governing its uses in policy making; interest in social indicators as a means for the scientific measurement of the quality of life; and respondents' personal and educational background, employment history, and career plans. This study, based upon a two-communities theory of knowledge use (Caplan 1979), documents the diverse criteria employed by policymakers and social scientists to assess and act on social science research.

Semi-structured procedures have also been employed in other studies of policymakers and practitioners. Bigelow and Ciarlo (1976) obtained data from managers of community mental health centers through two procedures: a decision-making questionnaire with fixed-response items concerning political pressures, structures, and goals; and an information utilization questionnaire consisting of four open-ended items regarding the use of a specific body of program-relevant data. Cohen (1980), in a study of factors governing the use of psychotherapy outcome research, used mailed questionnaires requiring scale responses to a set of 24 desirable characteristics of research as well as open-ended questions in which respondents were asked to provide five or fewer "crucial" and "extremely important" characteristics of research. Seidel (1981) also used a mix of open-ended and closed-ended items to measure relationships between perceived research quality, perceived usefulness, and organizational incentive systems.

Madey and Stenner (1980), adapting the delphi technique to study the use of policy research by national and local policymakers, employ a six-stage process to acquire and code data on the diverse expectations and information needs of persons with different perspectives. Florio, Behrmann and Goltz (1979) use focused interviews and a self-administered questionnaire to investigate the sources of information used by congressional staff members and to assess the relative importance and value of educational research in various phases of the policy-making process. Rich and Goldsmith (1983) employ similar semi-structured procedures to measure the use of mental health policy research by 479 national, state, and local policymakers. This study, one of the largest conducted to date, required responses to forced choice and open-ended questions concerning the type of information used (e.g., service vs. financial information), the type of use (e.g., conceptual vs. instrumental), political and organizational constraints, and other factors. Finally, van de Vall and Bolas (1982), in their study of 120 client-oriented applied research projects in the Netherlands, constructed an overall policy impact scale composed of responses to questions posed in semi-structured interviews with policymakers and researchers.

Relatively Unstructured Procedures. Relatively unstructured procedures allow respondents maximum freedom to respond to questions, while ensuring that the same procedures can be reproduced in diverse settings. In her unique real-time field experiment, Larsen (1982) investigated the uses of 788 program-relevant research

findings, ideas, or suggestions in 39 local mental health
organizations. Seeking to assess the uses of information
passed from mental health experts (consultants) to potential
users (staff members), this study required that each
consultant be accompanied by a trained observer who recorded
findings, ideas, and suggestions provided to staff members.
Follow-up telephone interviews were subsequently conducted
at four months and eight months to determine the extent to
which information had been utilized. A seven-point ordinal
scale was used to code interview responses.

Relatively unstructured procedures have also been used
to measure innovation configurations (Heck et al. 1979), to
assess the impact of social science research on legislative
decision making (Mitchell 1980), to investigate factors
related to the uses of information supplied to policymakers
through the NSF-supported Continuous National Survey (Rich
1981b), to study factors related to the utilization of
federal health evaluations (Patton et al. 1977), and to
explore factors related to the uses of research by 12 local
departments in and around London (Rothman 1980a). While
each of these studies is based on focused interviews, Voss,
Tyler, and Yengo (1983) employ relatively unstructured
procedures to investigate individual differences in problem-
solving styles among experts and novices confronted with
ill-structured policy problems. Respondents were given a
general policy question (e.g., one asking for a solution to
problems of low agricultural productivity), and their
responses (protocols) were coded in terms of a model of
argument developed by Toulmin (1958) and used in other areas
of policy research (Mitroff and Mason 1981; Dunn 1981) and
research utilization (Dunn 1982). The protocol analysis
produced graphic representations of the structure of
arguments employed by experts and novices and measures of
the complexity of their individual argument chains. Experts
devoted a relatively large proportion of their protocol to
problem representation and proposed relatively few but
complex solutions. By contrast, novices spent little time
on problem representation and proposed numerous simple but
unrelated solutions, thus failing to grasp the systemic
nature of problems.

Scales and Indices

Procedures reviewed above include various scales and
indices designed to measure knowledge use. A selective
overview of these scales and indices follows.

Information Utilization Scale. The information utilization scale contains seven ordinally ranked categories. A research (Larsen 1982) finding, idea, suggestion, or recommendation is placed in one of these categories and assigned a rank value:

(1) Considered and Rejected: Some discussion takes place but the information is rejected.

(2) Nothing Done: No action, not even discussion, is taken.

(3) Under Consideration: The information is not used but is being discussed and considered.

(4) Steps Toward Implementation: While the information is not used, the decision to do so has been made and initial planning steps have been taken.

(5) Partially Implemented: Certain features of the information have been used while others have been discarded.

(6) Implemented as Presented: The information is used in the form in which it was originally presented.

(7) Implemented and Adapted: The information is modified or adapted to fit the local situation.

Larsen does not report reliability or validity data for this scale.

Stages of Concern (SoC) Scale. The (SoC) scale (Hall, George and Rutherford 1979) includes seven stages at which users and nonusers of innovations express different kinds of concerns. The SoC questionnaire consists of 35 statements. Respondents use a Likert-type scale to mark each statement according to its perceived truth. The seven stages are:

(1) Awareness: Little concern or involvement with the innovation.

(2) Informational: General awareness of the innovation and interest in its substantive aspects.

(3) Personal: Perceived personal uncertainty about the relationship of the individual to the innovation.

(4) Management: Attention focused on the introduction.

(5) Consequence: Attention towards the impact of the innovation on subordinates and co-workers.

(6) Collaboration: Attention diverted towards cooperation and coordination with co-workers in implementing the innovation.

(7) Refocusing: Exploration of alternative innovations as replacements.

The SoC questionnaire has been extensively validated. Internal consistency reliability coefficients (Cronbach's alpha) for the seven stages range from .64 (awareness) to

.83 (personal) and have a median of .76 (n=830). Test-
retest correlations for the seven stages have a median value
of .82 (n=171). The validity of the SoC scale has been
assessed through confirmatory factor analysis, which yields
factor scores for each stage ranging from .67 (awareness) to
.96 (management).

Levels of Use (LoU) Scale. The LoU scale (Hall et al.
1975) measures eight levels of use of innovations:

    (0) Nonuse: Potential user has little or no knowledge
        of the innovation.

    (1) Orientation: User gathers information about the
        innovation.

    (2) Preparation: User prepares for initial use of the
        innovation.

    (3) Mechanical: User directs attention to day-to-day
        use of the innovation.

    (4) Routine: User stabilizes the application of the
        innovation.

    (5) Refinement: User varies the application of the
        innovation.

    (6) Integration: User combines application of
        innovation with activities of colleagues to
        achieve collective impact.

    (7) Renewal: User reevaluates the quality of use of
        the innovation.

Data for the LoU scale are acquired through personal interviews which are taped and rated in terms of the eight levels
of use. Interrater reliabilities with two raters ranged
from 65 to 70 percent agreement in initial applications of
the scale. The LoU scale, which measures the adoption and
implementation of innovations, was designed to be used in
conjunction with the SoC scale, which measures individual
feelings or concerns about innovations. These scales are
also intended for use with the innovations configurations
checklist (Heck et al. 1981), which measures individual
variations in the selection and adaptation of components of
an innovation.

Evaluation Utilization Scale. The evaluation utilization scale (Johnson 1980) was developed through a standard
Guttman scalogram analysis of questions pertaining to conceptual use (thinking about or planning to use evaluation
methods or results) and instrumental use (actually using or
suggesting to supervisors the use of evaluation products).
This scale is composed of seven types of forced-choice
questions, the first three of which seek to measure
conceptual use:

(1) Beliefs in Outcome Evaluation: Whether the
     findings produced in a particular evaluation
     research project(s) are believed to be useful to
     respondents and their agency.
(2) Beliefs in Process Evaluation: Whether respondents
     have verbally spoken against or in favor of the
     conduct of process evaluation in their agency or
     in another agency.
(3) Plans to Use Evaluation Processes or Outcomes:
     Whether respondents have made specific plans to
     use evaluation processes, procedures, or findings
     in their agencies.
(4) General Use of Evaluation Research: Whether
     respondents have used non-particular findings to
     obtain funding or to justify existing programs.
(5) Particular Adaptive Use of Evaluation Research:
     Whether respondents have used particular findings
     to develop programs.
(6) Particular Use of Formative Evaluation Procedures:
     Whether respondents had presented or suggested
     that a formative evaluation procedure be used to
     evaluate other programs.

The reliability of the evaluation utilization scale was
assessed through a Guttman analysis of responses obtained
from a convenience sample of 75 criminal justice decision
makers. Reported coefficients of reproducibility and
scalability are .94 and .73, respectively. A similar
10-item evaluation utilization scale has been developed by
Weeks (1979), who reports a test-retest reliability
coefficient of .84 (n=21).

     Research Utilization (RU) Index. The RU index (Pelz
and Horsley 1981, 133-34) is a composite index composed of
responses to the question: "We are interested in knowing how
often you have engaged in the following research activities
in the past year." The response scale required answers in
the form of the frequency of activities (ranging from zero
to five or more times a year) in five areas:
(1) You reviewed research literature in an effort to
     identify new knowledge for use in your practice.
(2) You evaluated a research study to determine its
     value for practice.
(3) You transferred the knowledge included in the
     results of the research studies into useful
     practice activities.
(4) You planned for the implementation and evaluation
     of new research-based practices.

(5) You discontinued or rejected a practice activity
     because of knowledge included in the results of
     research studies.

The internal consistency reliability (Cronbach's alpha) for
the RU index was .87, computed on the basis of responses
from approximately 1,500 nonstaff nurses in 32 Michigan
hospitals.

Depth of Utilization Scale (DUS). The DUS measures the
degree to which a product of social research and development
(e.g., a handbook for human service practitioners) is
actually used (Rothman 1980b, 200). In contrast to scales
and indices described above, each of which focuses on the
individual as the unit of analysis, the DUS is designed as a
measure of aggregate use that may be attributed to diffusion
and dissemination strategies of different kinds. Questions
in the depth-of-utilization questionnaire are forced-choice
items referring to nonuse ("I did not receive a handbook"),
conceptual use ("After examining the handbook I seriously
considered applying it to my practice"), and behavioral use
("I partially implemented a specific action guideline").
The scale is expressed in the form of a depth-of-utilization
ration (DUR) represented by the "aggregate utilization score
for all respondents exposed to a given diffusion approach
aggregate score for that subsample of respondents" (Rothman,
in press). Hence,

$$DUR = \frac{\text{aggregate utilization score}}{\text{maximum utilization score} \times N}$$

where the aggregate utilization score is the sum of reported
utilization scores for N respondents, the maximum
utilization score is the sum of all items, and N is the
number of respondents in a target group. While the DUR was
calculated on the basis of a nine-point scale, any number of
items might be combined to create a normalized maximum
utilization score. Rothman does not report reliability
data, although coefficients of reproducibility and
scalability, as well as internal consistency reliability
(Cronbach's alpha), may be readily calculated for the DUS.

Overall Policy Impact (OPI) Scale. The OPI scale is
designed to assess the impact of research on organizational
decision making (van de Vall and Bolas 1982). The OPI scale
is composed of four subsets of scale items:

(1) Manifest Impact: identifiable spinoffs in
     decisions or policy measures from the research
     project at the following steps of policy
     formation:

      [ ] initiating a policy
        [ ] advising
        [ ] co-deciding
      [ ] preparing a policy
        [ ] advising
        [ ] co-deciding
      [ ] executing a policy
        [ ] advising
        [ ] co-deciding

(2)   Stage Impact: Identifiable spinoffs in decisions or measures at the following stages of research:
    [ ] formulating the problem
    [ ] operationalizing the problem in terms of research procedures
    [ ] sampling and collecting data
    [ ] analyzing data
    [ ] informal discussions with client
    [ ] translating research into policy recommendations
    [ ] follow-up recommendations
    [ ] correcting or adjusting recommendations
    [ ] other

(3)   Certainty Impact: Identifiable spinoffs in decisions or measures regarding:
    [ ] perception of the problem
    [ ] explanation of causes of problem
    [ ] assessment of severity of problem
    [ ] dissolution of problem

(4)   Latent Impact: Identifiable spinoffs in decisions or measures related to:
    [ ] postponing a decision
    [ ] enhancing rank-and-file participation
    [ ] increasing awareness of problem
    [ ] enhancing policymakers' status
    [ ] establishing information monopoly
    [ ] preventing policy error

Overall policy impact scores are calculated by summing the totals of the four component subscales. The manifest impact subscale is weighted by step (initiation = 3, preparation = 2, executing = 1) and role (advising = 1, co-deciding = 2), resulting in values that range from 1 (executing-advising) to 6 (initiating-co-deciding). Weights for the stage impact scale range from zero (no stage impact) to 10 (correcting or adjusting recommendations) or 11 (additional or other stage impact). The certainty impact scale ranges from zero (no certainty impact) to 4 (dissolution of problem). Similarly, latent impact values range from zero (no latent impact) to 6

(preventing policy error). Internal consistency reliability
is estimated at .61 (Cronbach's alpha) for all items in the
OPI scale, while an average convergent validity coefficient
of .57 was obtained by correlating OPI scores of researchers
and policymakers involved in 120 applied research projects.

AN OVERALL ASSESSMENT

The main purpose of the preceding sections was to
compare and contrast principal methodological features of
recent research on processes of knowledge use. This review
made no attempt to identify factors that shape processes of
knowledge use, partly because such factors are reviewed
elsewhere in this volume (Larsen, chap. 15), but also
because available research yields no consistent empirical
support for claims that particular classes of factors--
economic, political, social, organizational, behavioral,
attitudinal--affect the creation, diffusion, and utilization
of knowledge in decisive and practically significant ways.

There are many reasons for the inconsistency or
instability of research findings, many of which stem from
conceptual and methodological problems documented by Downs
and Mohr (1976), Weiss (1977, 1981), Berman (1981), Miles
(1981), Larsen (1981), Dunn and Holzner (1982), and Huberman
and Miles (1982). This concluding section provides an
overall assessment of recent research on knowledge use by
exploring the extent to which the field as a whole has
responded to these problems.

The Problem of Criteria

In terms of what criteria should we define and measure
knowledge use? Answers to this basic question, as we have
seen above, assume a variety of forms. For some investigators, knowledge use is principally conceptual, defined and
measured in terms of mental processes of various kinds,
while for others knowledge use is represented and measured
in terms of overt behavior. Weiss and Bucuvalas (1980), for
example, define and measure knowledge use in terms of
judgments about research usefulness that are shaped by
subjective criteria ranging from technical quality and
action-ability to conformity to prior expectations.
Similarly, Caplan, Morrison, and Stambaugh (1975) and Caplan
(1979) put forth a two-communities theory of knowledge use
that also rests on subjective criteria, since research

usefulness is defined and measured in terms of culturally
dependent standards. While several other investigators
define and measure use according to subjective criteria--
that is, criteria that are based on respondents' conceptions
of what counts as usable knowledge--the majority of studies
define and measure use primarily in terms of the overt
behavior of individuals and organizations.

With the exception of several observational studies
(Firestone et al. 1981; Rothman, Teresa, and Erlich 1977;
Louis, Rosenblum, and Molitor 1981; Yin and Gwaltney 1981),
studies of overt behavior rely exclusively on respondents'
reports. Consequently, generalizations about individual,
group, and organizational behavior are based on questionnaire and interview data that are themselves shaped by the
subjective states of respondents. For example, it is
difficult to determine whether responses to questions about
"instrumental" use are based on a common conception of
research and its uses among diverse respondents. This
semantic indeterminacy of responses is particularly acute
when we consider that the reliability and validity of many
procedures designed to measure instrumental use are
unreported and perhaps unknown.

Hence, what has been termed the criterion problem
pervades most studies of knowledge use conducted to date.
Well-articulated formal definitions of knowledge use have
thus far been conspicuously absent, while a central
difficulty of available definitions is their
oversimplification of criterion dimensions. The distinction
between conceptual and instrumental use, while it provided
an initial focus for early studies, such as Rich (1975),
Rich and Caplan (1976), and Weiss (1977), oversimplifies and
thereby conceals a number of important dimensions according
to which knowledge and its uses may be classified and
measured (chap. 14). Instrumentally focused definitions of
use, for example, generally neglect properties related to
the expected benefits, purposes, and underlying assumptions
of knowledge and its uses. Even those studies based on a
conceptual definition of use focus mainly on surface
properties of knowledge, taking for granted the meaning of
knowledge, research, or information.

The Multiattribute Problem

Why does knowledge vary in perceived relevance,
adequacy, and cogency? This question calls attention to the
fundamentally interpretive character of processes of
knowledge use, processes in which different stakeholders

attribute multiple and frequently conflicting meanings to
knowledge and its uses. These meanings typically arise from
diverse sets of assumptions that are organized in terms of
cognitive maps (Huff 1982; Axelrod 1976), frames of
reference (Holzner and Marx 1979; Weiss and Bucuvalas 1980),
or construction systems (Dunn 1983; Kelly 1955).
Consequently, processes of knowledge use are structured by
the ways that policymakers, practitioners, and social
scientists themselves anticipate or predict events, such
anticipation being a function of collective as well as
individual reference frames and of the coordinative social,
political, and administrative contexts in which they are
established, maintained, and changed.

In a more restricted and operational sense, frames of
reference include what have been called truth and utility
tests (Holzner and Fisher 1979; Weiss and Bucuvalas 1980).
Truth tests are decision rules for assessing the adequacy of
knowledge claims, while utility or relevance tests delineate
an appropriate domain of inquiry or action. Cogency tests,
by contrast, establish the relative force or confidence
required of knowledge in particular circumstances.

Concepts of truth, relevance, and cogency do not
exhaust the classes of standards available to assess
knowledge and its uses. Each of these broad classes of
"reality tests" may be divided into additional categories,
such as causal, pragmatic, ethical, and so forth (Dunn
1982). Yet the specification of these and other
categories--including "conceptual" and "instrumental" use,
"science-based" and "ordinary" knowledge, "professional
social inquiry" and "causal empiricism"--is a product of the
meanings and subjective judgments of researchers, and not of
those to whom such categories are applied. Thus, for
example, it is rather doubtful that policymakers and
practitioners share the same constructs and assumptions as
those which underlie many studies described in preceding
sections.

What is needed are procedures that will generate
classificational schema or typologies that differentiate
criteria actually employed to assess knowledge, as
distinguished from criteria that are imposed on research
contexts by investigators. Such procedures would facilitate
efforts to map the universes of meaning surrounding the uses
of knowledge, including processes of innovation, and improve
now limited capacities to explain the impact of social
science knowledge on policymaking and professional practice.

Formal typologies of truth tests and utility tests are
not easily translated into procedures that elicit constructs

that actually comprise individual and collective frames of reference. While factor analysis, principal components analysis, and multidimensional scaling may be employed to reduce item-response to discrete constructs (Weiss and Bucuvalas 1980), the aggregation or averaging of responses to questions whose content was specified in advance by researchers tends to diminish capacities to identify unique or distinctively organized systems of personal constructs (Slater 1977). Data reduction procedures also limit opportunities to investigate structural properties of reference frames—differentiation, complexity, integration, permeability—that are central to questions of knowledge synthesis, individual and collective learning (Dunn 1983), and practical problem solving (Voss, Tyler, and Yengo 1983).

The Transactional Problem

How can we conceptualize and measure knowledge transactions? Generative typologies of truth and relevance tests, while important for mapping the universe of meaning surrounding processes of knowledge use, would not deal with the distribution of tests among individual and collective actors. Multiple and potentially conflicting truth and relevance tests may be applied by the same person, while the structure of individual as well as collective frames of reference may change over time as a result of the dynamics of social relations among stakeholders in the policy process. What is now unclear about processes of knowledge use, generally and in settings of public policy, is the extent to which changes in frames of reference affect and, in turn, are affected by structures and processes of policy making.

It is possible and desirable to visualize this problem as analogous to a single coin with two porous and semi-permeable surfaces, the "social" and the "cognitive." Processes of knowledge use, according to this formulation, may be viewed as sociocognitive relations among actors involved in generative reciprocal acts, that is, cognitively structured (filtered, mediated, processed, interpreted, construed) feedback that transforms and is transformed by structures and processes of policy making. The essential property of such sociocognitive relations is that they involve subject-subject and subject-object relations that cannot be decomposed or reduced to erstwhile independent dimensions conveniently labelled as "social" and "cognitive," "instrumental" and "conceptual," or "behavioral" and "attitudinal." At this point, in fact, it seems wise to

avoid certain established but perhaps prematurely specified
constructs employed to label, categorize, and generalize
social processes, including "stages of innovation,"
"linker," "loosely coupled system," "knowledge transfer,"
and so forth. The empirical validity of these constructs,
and the causal models in which they are often embedded, is
at present doubtful or lacking (Berman 1981; Miles 1981).

A recognition of the contextual, relational, and
generative properties of knowledge use has promoted
significant shifts in the language research. For example,
the terms interaction, exchange, and transfer have been
replaced with that of transaction (Bauer 1964; Zaltman
1979), while the term receiver has been discarded in favor
of transreceiver (de Sola Pool 1973). Yet existing
methodologies for studying knowledge use do not adequately
specify generative reciprocal processes involving cognitive
as well as social processes. While recent contributions to
theory and research on communication networks recognize the
importance of distinguishing contextual and referential
meanings (Rogers and Kincaid 1981, 1-78), there have been
few attempts to develop systematic and reproducible
procedures for identifying organized configurations of
assumptions, constructs, or criteria applied by members of
different sociocognitive networks.

Processes of knowledge use are structured not only by
differences in individual and collective frames of
reference, but also by variations in individual network
proximity and overall network connectedness that occur over
time (Rogers and Kincaid 1981, 319-21). In this specific
sense network dynamics represent structured transactions
with interpretive, relational, and generative properties.
Thus, for example, changes in transactions among large
numbers of policy stakeholders may be studied with methods
of network analysis that permit investigators to identify
specialized roles (e.g., liaisons, bridges, linkers,
brokers) and structures (e.g., dyads, cliques, systems) and
to develop and apply indices for measuring such key
properties of roles and structures as density, distance, and
connectedness. Methods of procedure (e.g., survey
sociometry) are now available to collect network data to
process and analyze it with packaged computer programs
(e.g., NEGOPY and CONCOR).

Despite advances in the methodology of network
analysis, few investigators have attempted simultaneously to
study social and cognitive properties of communications
networks. Needed is some kind of epistemic or cognitive
network analysis which focuses on manifest and latent

cognitive structures and describes the dynamics of reciprocal changes in social interaction and individual and collective frames of reference (Dunn, Bangs, and Rahmanian 1981). This kind of network analysis, by focusing on cognitive as well as spatial and social determinants of network linkages, will permit the systematic investigation of individual and collective learning, processes that so far have eluded students of knowledge use.

The vast majority of knowledge use studies conducted to date have employed methods that are inappropriate to the investigation of generative reciprocal processes. As is evident from study profiles described in the first section of this chapter, nearly all studies take individuals or aggregates of individuals as units of analysis. With the exception of a few field studies (Louis, Rosenblum, and Molitor 1981; Firestone et al. 1981; Yin and Gwaltney 1981) that have other methodological limitations, including those discussed above in connection with the criterion and multiattribute problems, the bulk of research has failed to investigate relational and systemic properties of knowledge use. Consequently, the substance, organization, and texture of cognitive and social relations have rarely been preserved. Instead, sociocognitive relations have been processed, in Rogers and Kincaid's words (1981, 39), through various "methodological shredders" which tear respondents from their distinctive contents of intrapersonal and relational space: "It is a little like a biologist putting his or her laboratory animals through a hamburger machine and looking at every hundredth cell through a microscope; anatomy and physiology get lost; structure and function disappear and one is left with a cell biology" (Barton 1968; Rogers and Kincaid 1981, 39).

Conclusions

Systematic research on processes of knowledge use is a distinctively modern enterprise. The majority of recent studies, however, have not been consciously shaped by theory and research in the sociology, economics, and psychology of knowledge applications or, more broadly, by a basic interdisciplinary social science that seeks to examine the practical consequences of applying scientific and professional knowledge. Instead, the field of knowledge use has been oriented towards the translation of social science knowledge into guidelines for the improvement of practice. Thus, knowledge use studies are appropriately characterized

in terms of applied rather than basic research on the uses
of scientific and professional knowledge.

The applied research orientation of knowledge use
studies, most evident in the attention directed toward problems of utilizing evaluation research, has brought mixed
blessings. While an applied research orientation has
created greater sensitivity to the costs and benefits of the
social sciences, thus punctuating their practical role in
social problem solving, this same orientation has often
constrained researchers from examining basic theoretical,
conceptual, and methodological issues. By comparing, contrasting, and evaluating a range of knowledge use studies
conducted in recent years, this chapter has attempted to
define, clarify, and suggest ways to resolve some of these
issues.

REFERENCES

Axelrod, R., ed. 1976. _Structure of Decision_. Princeton,
N.J.: Princeton Univ. Press.

Barton, A. 1968. "Bringing Society Back In: Survey
Research and Macro-Methodology." _American Behavioral_
Scientist 12: 1-9.

Bauer, R. 1964. "The Obstinate Audience: The Influence
Process from the Point of View of Social Communication." _American Psychologist_ 19: 319-28.

Berman, P. 1981. "Educational Change: Toward An Implemen-
tation Paradigm." In _Improving Schools: Using What We_
Know, ed. R. Lehming and M. Kane. Beverly Hills,
Calif.: Sage Publications.

Bernstein, I., and H. Freeman. 1975. _Academic and Entre-_
preneurial Research: The Consequences of Diversity in
Federal Evaluation Studies. New York: Russell Sage
Foundation.

Bigelow, D., and J. Ciarlo. 1976. "The Impact of Thera-
peutic Effectiveness Data on Community Mental Health
Center Management." In _Evaluation Studies Review_
Annual, Vol. 1, by G. V. Glass. Beverly Hills, Calif.:
Sage Publications.

Campbell, D. T. 1977. <u>Descriptive Epistemology: Psychological, Sociological, and Evolutionary.</u> Preliminary draft of the William James Lectures, Harvard University, Cambridge, Massachusetts, Spring, 1977.

Caplan, N. 1979. "The Two Communities Theory and Knowledge Utilization." <u>American Behavioral Scientist</u> 22, no. 3: 459-470.

Caplan, N., A. Morrison, and R. J. Stambaugh. 1975. <u>The Use of Social Science Knowledge in Policy Decisions at the National Level: A Report to Respondents.</u> Ann Arbor: Center for Research on Utilization of Scientific Knowledge, Institute for Social Research, University of Michigan.

Ciarlo, James, ed. 1981. <u>Utilizing Evaluation: Concepts and Measurement Techniques.</u> Beverly Hills, Calif.: Sage Publications.

Cohen, L. 1980. "Methodological Prerequisites for Psychotherapy Outcome Research: A Survey of Clinical Psychologists." <u>Knowledge: Creation, Diffusion, Utilization</u> 2, no. 2: 263-272.

Conner, R. 1981. "Measuring Evaluation Utilization: A Critique of Different Techniques." In <u>Utilizing Evaluation Concepts and Measurement Techniques,</u> ed. J. Ciarlo. Beverly Hills, Calif.: Sage Publications.

Davis, H., and S. Salasin. 1975. "The Utilization of Evaluation." In <u>Handbook of Evaluation Research,</u> ed. E. L. Struening and M. Guttentag. Beverly Hills, Calif.: Sage Publications.

Denzin, N. K. 1970. <u>The Research Act.</u> Chicago: Aldine.

de Sola Pool, I. 1973. "Communication Systems." In <u>Handbook of Communication,</u> ed. I. de Sola Pool and W. Schramm. Chicago: Rand McNally.

Dickey, B. 1980. "Utilization of Evaluation of Small-Scale Innovative Educational Projects." <u>Educational Evaluation and Policy Analysis</u> 2, no. 6: 65-77.

Dickman, F. B. 1981. "Work Activities, Settings, Methodologies and Perceptions." Knowledge: Creation, Diffusion and Utilization 2, no. 3: 375-387.

Downs, G. W., and L. B. Mohr. 1976. "Conceptual Issues in the Study of Innovation." Administrative Science Quarterly 21, no. 4: 700-73.

Dunn, W. N. 1980. "The Two Communities Metaphor and Models of Knowledge Use: An Exploratory Case Survey." Knowledge: Creation, Diffusion, Utilization 1, no. 4: 515-536.

_____. 1981a. "If Knowledge Utilization is the Solution, What is the Problem?" Pittsburgh: University Program for the Study of Knowledge Use, University of Pittsburgh, October 1981.

_____. 1981b. Public Policy Analysis: An Introduction. Englewood Cliffs, N.J.: Prentice-Hall.

_____. 1982. "Reforms as Arguments." Knowledge: Creation, Diffusion and Utilization 3, no. 3: 293-326.

_____. 1983. "Usable Knowledge: A Metatheory of Policy Research in the Social Sciences." In The Planning of Change: Readings in the Applied Social Sciences, ed. W. Bennis, K. Bennne, and R. Chin. New York: Holt, Rinehart, Winston.

Dunn, W. N., and B. Holzner. 1982. "Knowledge Use and School Improvement: Conceptual Framework and Design." Vol. II of the Final Report to the National Institute of Education, Methodological Research on Knowledge Use and School Improvement.

Dunn, W. N., and F. Swierczek. 1977. "Planned Organizational Change: Toward Grounded Theory." Journal of Applied Behavioral Science 13, no. 2: 135-157.

Dunn, W. N., M. J. Dukes, and A. G. Cahill. 1982. "Measuring Knowledge-in-Use: A Procedural Inventory." Volume III of the NIE-funded Final Report (see Dunn, W. N., and B. Holzner).

Dunn, W. N., R. Bangs, and H. Rahmanian. 1981. Studying Knowledge Networks. Pittsburgh: Program for the Study of Knowledge Use, University of Pittsburgh.

Firestone, W., et al. 1981a. "Knowledge Use and Local School Improvement." Philadelphia: Research for Better Schools.

Firestone, W., et al. 1981b. Annual Report on Study of Regional Educational Service Agencies: Fiscal Year 1981. Philadelphia: Research for Better Schools.

Florio, D., M. Behrmann, and D. Goltz. 1979. "What Do Policymakers Think of Educational Research and Evaluation? or Do They?" Educational Evaluation and Policy Analysis 1, no. 6: 61–87.

Glaser, E. M., H. H. Abelson, and K. N. Garrison. 1976. Putting Knowledge to Use: A Distillation of the Literature Regarding Knowledge Transfer and Change. Los Angeles: Human Interaction Research, National Institute of Mental Health, Rockville, Md., 1976.

Gregg, G., T. Preston, A. Geist, and N. Caplan. 1979. "The Caravan Rolls On: Forty Years of Social Problem Research." Knowledge: Creation, Diffusion and Utilization 1, no. 1: 31–61.

Guba, E. 1981. "Criteria for Assessing the Trustworthiness of Naturalistic Inquiries." Educational Communication and Technology Journal 29, no. 2 (Summer): 75–91.

Hall, G., A. George, and W. Rutherford. 1979. Measuring Stages of Concern About the Innovation: A Manual for Use of the SoC Questionnaire. Austin: Research and Development Center for Teacher Education, University of Austin.

Hall, G., S. Loucks, W. Rutherford, and B. Newlove. 1975. "Levels of Use of the Innovation: A Framework for Analyzing Innovation Adoption." Journal of Teacher Education 26, no. 1: 52–56.

Havelock, R. G. 1969. Planning for Innovation Through Dissemination and Utilization of Knowledge. Ann Arbor: Center for Research on Utilization of Scientific Knowledge, Institute for Social Research, University of Michigan.

Heck, S., S. Stiegelbauer, G. Hall, and S. Loucks. 1981. Measuring Innovation Configurations: Procedures and Applications. Austin: Research and Development Center for Teacher Education, University of Austin.

Holzner, B. 1978. "The Sociology of Applied Knowledge." Sociological Symposium 21: 8-19.

Holzner, B., and E. Fisher. 1979. "Knowledge-in-Use: Considerations in the Sociology of Knowledge Applications." Knowledge: Creation, Diffusion and Utilization 1, no. 2: 219-244.

Holzner, B., and J. Marx. 1979. Knowledge Application: The Knowledge System in Society. Boston: Allyn and Bacon.

Hood, P., and L. Blackwell. 1976. The Educational Information Market Study. San Francisco: Far West Labs.

Huberman, A., and M. Miles. 1982. "Drawing Valid Meaning From Qualitative Data: Some Techniques of Data Reduction and Display." Paper prepared for a Symposium on Advances in the Analysis of Qualitative Data Annual Meeting, American Educational Research Association, March, 1982.

Huff, A. S. 1982. "Discovering Strategic Patterns from Documentary Evidence." (Mimeo)

Johnson, K. 1980. "Stimulating Evaluation Use By Integrating Academia and Practice." Knowledge: Creation, Diffusion, Utilization 2, no. 2: 237-262.

Kelly, G. 1955. The Psychology of Personal Constructs Vol. 1 and 2. New York: W. W. Norton.

Lakoff, S. A. 1966. Knowledge and Power. New York: Free Press.

Larsen, J. K. 1981. "Knowledge Utilization: Current Issues." In The Knowledge Cycle, ed. R. F. Rich. Beverly Hills, Calif.: Sage Publications.

_____. 1982. Information Utilization and Non-Utilization. Washington, D.C.: American Institutes for Research in the Behavioral Sciences.

Laudan, L. 1977. Progress and its Problems: Towards a Theory of Scientific Growth. Berkeley and Los Angeles: Univ. of California Press.

Lindblom, C., and D. Cohen. 1979. Usable Knowledge: Social Science and Social Problem Solving. New Haven, Conn.: Yale Univ. Press.

Louis, K., S. Rosenblum, and J. Molitor. 1981. Strategies for Knowledge Use and School Improvement. Cambridge: ABT Associates.

Lynd, R. S. 1940. Knowledge for What? The Place of Social Science in American Culture. Princeton, N.J.: Princeton Univ. Press.

Machlup, F. 1962. The Production and Distribution of Knowledge in the United States. Princeton, N.J.: Princeton Univ. Press.

_____. 1980. Knowledge and Knowledge Induction, Volume I. Princeton: Princeton Univ. Press.

Madey, D., and A. J. Stenner. 1980. "Policy Implications Analysis: A Methodological Advancement for Policy Research and Evaluation." Paper presented at the meeting of the Education Research Society, Arlington, Virginia.

Meehan, P., and G. Beal. 1977. Knowledge Production and Utilization: A General Model, Third Approximation. Sociological Report No. 138. Ames: Department of Sociology and Anthropology, Iowa State University.

Miles, M. B. 1981. "Mapping the Common Properties of Schools." In Improving Schools: What We Know, ed. R. Lehming. Santa Monica, Calif.: Sage Publications.

Mitchell, D. 1980. "Social Science Impact on Legislative Decision Making: Process and Substance." Educational Researcher 9, no. 10: 9-19.

Mitroff, I., and R. Mason. 1981. "Policy Analysis as Argument." Symposium on Social Values and Public Policy, ed. W. N. Dunn. Policy Studies Journal Special Issue, no. 2: 579-584.

National Academy of Sciences. National Research Council. 1978. "The Federal Investment in Knowledge of Social Sciences." Vol. I of the Study Project on Social Research and Development. Washington, D.C.: NAS.

National Science Foundation. 1969. Knowledge into Action: Improving the Nation's Use of the Social Sciences. Washington, D.C.: NSF.

Nelson, L., and M. Kirst. 1980. Information Preferences of State Education Policymakers. Stanford: Institute for Research on Education Finance and Goverment.

Patton, M. Q., P. S. Grimes, K. M. Guthrie, N. J. Brennan, B. D. French, and D. A. Blyth. 1977. "In Search of Impact: An Analysis of Federal Health, Evaluation Research." In Using Social Research in Public Policy Making, ed. C. Weiss. Lexington, Mass.: Lexington Books.

Pelz, D., and J. A. Horsley. 1981. "Measuring Utilization of Nursing Research." In Utilizing Evaluation, ed. J. A. Ciarlo. Beverly Hills, Calif.: Sage Publications.

Pool, I. de Sola. See de Sola Pool, I.

Remmling, G. W. 1967. Road to Suspicion: A Study of Modern Mentality and the Sociology of Knowledge. New York: Appleton-Century-Crofts.

Rich, R. 1975. "Selective Utilization of Social Science Related Information by Federal Policymakers." Inquiry 13, no. 3: 239-245.

Rich, R., ed. 1981a. The Knowledge Cycle. Beverly Hills, Calif.: Sage Publications.

_____. 1981b. Social Science Information and Public Policymaking. San Francisco: Jossey-Bass.

Rich, R., and N. Caplan. 1976. "Policy Use of Social Science Knowledge and Perspectives: Means/Ends Matching Versus Understanding." Paper presented at the OECD Conference on Dissemination of Economic and Social Development Research Results, Bogota, Colombia, June 1976.

Rich, R., and N. Goldsmith. 1983. "The Utilization of Policy Research." In The Encyclopedia of Policy Studies, ed. S. S. Naggel. New York: Marcel Dekker.

Rogers, E., and D. L. Kincaid. 1981. Communications Networks: Toward a New Paradigm for Research. New York: Free Press.

Rogers, E., and F. Shoemaker. 1971. Communication of Innovations: A Cross Cultural Approach. New York: Free Press.

_____. 1974. Planning and Organizing for Social Change: Action Principles from Social Science Research. New York: Columbia Univ. Press.

Rothman, J. 1980a. Using Research in Organizations. Beverly Hills, Calif.: Sage Publications.

_____. 1980b. Social R and D: Research and Development in the Human Services. Englewood Cliffs, N.J.: Prentice-Hall.

Rothman, J., J. G. Teresa, and J. Erlich. 1977. Developing Effective Strategies for Social Intervention: A Research and Developmental Methodology. Springfield, Va.: National Technical Information Service.

Rothman, J., J. G. Teresa, T. L. Kay and G. C. Morningstar. 1983. Marketing Human Service Innovations. Beverly Hills, Calif.: Sage Publications.

Seidel, A. 1981. "Underutilized Research." Knowledge: Creation, Diffusion, Utilization 3, no. 2: 233-248.

Slater, P. 1977. Dimensions of Intrapersonal Space. London: Wiley.

Social Science Research Council. 1969. The Behavioral and Social Sciences: Outlook and Need. Englewood Cliffs, N.J.: Prentice-Hall.

Spitzberg, I., ed. 1980. Universities and the International Distribution of Knowledge. New York: Praeger.

Strommen, M. 1982. Five Shaping Forces. Minneapolis, Minn.: Search Institute.

Toulmin, S. 1958. The Uses of Argument. Cambridge: Cambridge Univ. Press.

van de Vall, M., and C. Bolas. 1982. "Using Social Policy Research for Reducing Social Problems: An Empirical Analysis of Structure and Functions." Journal of Applied Behavioral Sciences 18: 49-67.

Voss, J., S. Tyler, and L. Yengo. 1983. "Individual Differences in Solving of Social Science Problems." In Individual Differences in Cognition, ed. R. F. Dillon and R. R. Schmeck. New York: Academic Press.

Weeks, E. C. 1979. "The Managerial Use of Evaluation Findings." In The Evaluator and Management, ed. H. C. Schulberg and J. M. Jerrell. Beverly Hills, Calif.: Sage Publications.

Weiss, C., ed. 1977. Using Social Research in Public Policy Making. Lexington, Mass.: Lexington Books.

Weiss, C. 1981. "Measuring the Use of Evaluation." In Utilizing Evaluation: Concepts and Measurement Techniques, ed. J. A. Ciarlo. Beverly Hills, Calif.: Sage Publications.

Weiss, C., and M. Bucuvalas. 1980. "Truth Tests and Utility Tests: Decision Makers' Frames of Reference for Social Science." The American Sociological Review 45, no. 2: 302-312.

Yin, R., and M. Gwaltney. 1981. "Knowledge Utilization as a Networking Process." Knowledge: Creation, Diffusion and Utilization 2, no. 4: 555-580.

Yin, R. K., K. A. Heald, M. E. Vogel, P. D. Fleischauer, and B. C. Vladeck. 1976. A Review of Case Studies of Technological in State and Local Services. Santa Monica: Rand Corporation.

Zaltman, G. 1979. "Knowledge Utilization as Planned Social Change." Knowledge: Creation, Diffusion and Utilization 1: 82-105.

Zaltman, G., and R. Deshpande. 1980. "The Use of Market Research: An Exploratory Study of Manager and Researcher Perspectives." Occasional Working Paper KU-111. Cambridge: Marketing Science Institute.

Ziman, J. 1968. Public Knowledge: The Social Dimension of Science. New York: Cambridge Univ. Press.

Implications for Policy and Social Change

17

Perspectives on Knowledge Use in National Policy Making

Carol H. Weiss

What are reasonable expectations for the use of social science research in national policy making? How much influence has research had on policy in the past? What can we realistically expect in the future? The answers depend on how we conceptualize the key terms in the discussion. All too often the imagery that underlies "social science knowledge utilization in policy making" is simplistic or muddled, or both.

A review of the literature discloses that different authors have meant very different things in discussions of research utilization. Part of the reason for the recent disenchantment with social science as a guide to policy may well derive from the varied and often unrealistic images of what the "use of social science" means. Let me describe the varieties of meanings that scholars have, implicitly or explicitly, associated with the concept.

RESEARCH UTILIZATION

The Knowledge-Driven Model

The first image of research utilization is probably the most venerable in the literature and derives from the natural sciences. It assumes the following sequence of events: basic research leads to applied research leads to development leads to application. The notion is that basic research discloses some opportunity that may have relevance for public policy; applied research is conducted to define and test the findings of basic research for practical action; if all goes well, appropriate technologies are developed to implement the findings; whereupon application occurs (Havelock 1969 provides for a detailed description).

Examples of this model of research utilization generally come from the physical sciences: biochemical research makes available oral contraceptive pills; research in electronics enables television to multiply the number of broadcast channels. Because of the fruits of basic research, new applications are developed and new policies emerge (Comroe and Dripps 1976).

The assumption is that the sheer fact that knowledge exists presses toward its development and use. However well or poorly this model describes events in the natural sciences, in the social sciences few examples can be found. The reasons appear to be several. Social science knowledge is not apt to be so compelling or authoritative as to drive inevitably toward implementation. Social science knowledge does not readily lend itself to conversion into replicable technologies, either material or social. Perhaps most important, unless a social condition has been consensually defined as a pressing social problem, and unless the condition has become politicized and debated and the parameters of potential action agreed upon, there is little likelihood that policy-making bodies will be receptive to the results of social science research.

I do not mean to imply that basic research in the social sciences is not useful for policy making. Certainly many social policies and programs of government are based, explicitly or implicitly, on basic psychological, sociological, economic, anthropological, and political scientific understandings. When they surface to affect government decision, however, it is not likely to be through the sequence of events posited in this model.

The Problem-Solving Model

The most common concept of research utilization involves the direct application of the results of a specific social science study to a pending decision. Implicit in this model is a sense that there is a consensus on goals. It is assumed that policy-makers and researchers tend to agree on what the desired end state shall be. The main contribution of social science research is to help identify and select appropriate means to reach the goal.

The evidence that social science research provides for the decision-making process can be of several orders. It can be qualitative and descriptive (e.g., rich observational accounts of social conditions or of program processes). It can be quantitative data, either on relatively soft indicators (e.g., public attitudes) or on hard factual matters (e.g., number of hospital beds). It can be statistical relationships between variables, generalized conclusions about the associations among factors, even relatively abstract (middle-range) theories about cause and effect. Whatever the nature of the empirical evidence that social science research supplies, the expectation is that it clarifies the situation and reduces uncertainty, and therefore, it influences the decision that policymakers make.

In this formulation of research utilization, there are two general ways in which social science research can enter the policy-making arena. First, the research antedates the policy problem and is drawn in on need. Policymakers faced with a decision search for information from pre-existent research to delimit the scope of the question or identify a promising policy response; the information can be called to their attention by aides, staff analysts, colleagues, consultants, or social science researchers. Whether the best and most relevant research reaches the person with the problem depends on the efficiency of the communications links. Therefore, when this imagery of research utilization prevails, the usual prescription for improving the use of research is to improve communication with policy makers.

A second route to problem-solving use is commissioning social science research and analysis to fill the knowledge gap. The assumptions, as with the search route, are that decision makers have a clear idea of their goals and a map of acceptable alternatives and that they have identified some specific informational needs to clarify their choice. This time decision makers engage social scientists to provide data, analytic generalizations, and possibly the interpretations of these generalizations to the case in hand by way of recommendations. The process follows this sequence: definition of pending decision leads to identification of missing knowledge leads to acquisition of social science leads to research leads to interpretation of the research for the decision context leads to policy choice.

The expectation is that research generated in this type of sequence, even more than research located through search procedures, will have direct and immediate applicability and will be used for decision making. If the research goes unused, the prescription to improve utilization that arises from this imagery is to increase government control over both the specification of requested research and its conduct in the field. If the research had actually met decision makers' information needs, it is assumed, it would have been used.

Even a cursory review of the fate of social science research, including policy research on government-defined issues, suggests that these kinds of expectations are wildly optimistic. Occasional studies have direct effect on decisions, but usually on relatively low-level, narrow-gauge decisions. Most studies appear to come and go without leaving any discernible mark on the direction or substance of policy. It probably takes an extraordinary concatenation of circumstances for research to influence policy decisions directly: a well-defined decision situation, a set of policy actors who have responsibility and jurisdiction for making the decision, an issue whose resolution depends at least to some extent on information, identification of the requisite informational need, research that provides the information in terms that match the circumstances within which choices will be made, research findings that are clear-cut, unambiguous, firmly supported, and powerful, that reach decision makers at the time they are wrestling with the issues, that are comprehensible and understood, and that do not run counter to strong political interests. Because chances are small that all these conditions will fall into line around any one issue, the problem-solving model of research use probably describes a relatively small number of cases.

However, the problem-solving model remains the prevailing imagery of research utilization. Its prevalence probably accounts for much of the disillusionment about the contribution of social science research to social policy. Because people expect research use to occur through the sequence of stages posited by this model, they become discouraged when events do not take the expected course. There are, however, other ways in which social science research can be "used" in policy making. These alternative models are discussed below.

Interactive Model

Those engaged in developing policy seek information not only from social scientists but from a variety of sources-- administrators, practitioners, politicians, planners, journalists, clients, interest groups, aides, friends, and social scientists, too. The process is not one of linear

order from research to decision but a disorderly set of
interconnections and back-and-forthness that defies neat
diagrams. All kinds of people involved in an issue area
pool their talents, beliefs, and understandings in an effort
to make sense of a problem. Social scientists are one set
of participants among many.

Donnison (1972) describes this interactive model of
research use in the development of two pieces of legislation
in Great Britain. He notes that decisions could not wait
upon completion of research but had to be made when
political circumstances compelled.

> Research workers could not present authoritative
> findings for others to apply; neither could others
> commission them to find the "correct" solution to
> policy problems: they were not that kind of problem.
> Those in the four fields from which experience had to
> be brought to bear [politics, technology, practice, and
> research] contributed on equal terms. Each was expert
> in a few things, ignorant about most things, offered
> what he could, and generally learnt more than he could
> teach. (Donnison 1972, 527)

In this model, the use of research is only one part of
a complicated process that also uses experience, political
insight, pressure, social technologies, and judgment. It
has applicability not only in face-to-face settings but also
in the multiple ways in which intelligence is gathered
through intermediaries and brought to bear. It describes a
familiar process by which decision makers inform themselves
of the range of knowledge and opinion in a policy area.

Political Model

Often the constellation of interests around a policy
issue predetermines the positions that decision makers take,
or debate has gone on over a period of years and opinions
have hardened. At this point, decision makers are not
likely to be receptive to new evidence from social science
research. For reasons of interest, ideology, or intellect,
they have taken a stand that research is not likely to
shake.

In such cases, research can still be used. It becomes
ammunition for the side that finds its conclusions congenial
and supportive. Partisans flourish the evidence in an
attempt to neutralize opponents, convince waverers, and

bolster supporters. Even if conclusions have to be ripped out of context (with suppression of qualifications and of evidence "on the other hand"), research becomes grist to the mill.

Social scientists tend to look askance at the impressment of research results into service for a position that decision makers have taken on other grounds. They generally see it as an illegitimate attempt to "use" research (in the pejorative sense) for self-serving purposes of agency justification or personal aggrandizement. However, using research to support a predetermined position is research utilization, too. It would seem to be neither unimportant nor improper. Only distortion and misinterpretation of findings are illegitimate. To the extent that the research, accurately interpreted, supports the position of one group, it gives the advocates of that position confidence, reduces their uncertainties, and provides them an edge in the continuing debate. Since the research finds ready-made partisans who will fight for its implementation, it stands a better chance of making a difference in the outcome (Weiss 1973).

Tactical Model

Use of research, irrespective of its conclusions, is a tactic in bureaucratic politics. For example, there are occasions when social science research is used for purposes that have little relation to the substance of the research. It is not the content of the findings that is invoked but the sheer fact that research is being done. Government agencies confronted with demands for action may respond by saying, "Yes, we know that's an important need. We're doing research on it right now." Research becomes proof of their responsiveness. Sometimes government agencies use research to deflect criticism. By claiming that their actions were based on the implications and recommendations of social science research studies, they may try to avoid responsibility for unpopular policy outcomes. Support for a research program can also become a tactic for enhancing the prestige of the agency by allying it with social scientists of high repute. Some agencies support substantial amounts of research and in so doing, build a constituency of academic supporters who rally to their defense when appropriations are under congressional review.

Enlightenment Model

Perhaps the way in which social science research most frequently enters the policy arena is through the process that has come to be called "enlightenment" (Crawford and Biderman 1969; Janowitz 1972; Weiss 1977b). Here it is not the findings of a single study nor even of a body of related studies that directly affect policy. Rather it is the concepts and theoretical perspectives that social science research has engendered that permeate the policy-making process.

There is no assumption in this model that decision makers seek out social science research when faced with a policy issue or even that they are receptive to, or aware of, specific research conclusions. The imagery is that of social science generalizations and orientations percolating through informed publics and coming to shape the way in which people think about social issues. Social science research diffuses circuitously through manifold channels—professional journals, the mass media, conversations with colleagues—and over time the variables it deals with and the generalizations it offers provide decision makers with ways of making sense out of a complex world.

Rarely will policymakers be able to cite the findings of a specific study that influenced their decisions, but they have a sense that social science research has given them a backdrop of ideas and orientations that has had important consequences (Caplan, Morrison, and Stambaugh 1975). Research sensitizes decision makers to new issues and helps turn what were non-problems into policy problems. A recent example is child abuse (Weiss 1976). Conversely, research may convert existing problems into non-problems (e.g., marijuana use). Research can drastically revise the way that policymakers define issues (e.g., acceptable rates of unemployment), the facets of the issue they view as susceptible to alteration, and the alternative measures they consider. It helps to change the parameters within which policy solutions are sought. In the long run, along with other influences, it often redefines the policy agenda.

The notion of research utilization in the enlightenment mode has a comforting quality. It seems to promise that, without any special effort, truth will triumph. The enlightenment process, however, has its full share of deficiencies. When research diffuses to the policy sphere through indirect and unguided channels, it dispenses invalid as well as valid generalizations. Many of the social science understandings that gain currency are partial, oversimplified, inadequate, or wrong. There are no procedures for screening out the shoddy and obsolete. Sometimes sensational research results, however incomplete or inadequately supported by data, take the limelight. As an environmental researcher has noted, "Bad science, being more newsworthy, will tend to be publicized and seized on by some to support their convictions" (Comar 1978). The indirect diffusion process is vulnerable to oversimplification and distortion, and it may come to resemble "endarkenment" as much as enlightenment.

Moreover, the enlightenment model is an inefficient means for reaching policy audiences. Many vital results of social science research never penetrate to decision-making centers. Some results take so long to come into currency that they are out-of-date by the time they arrive, their conclusions having been modified, or even contradicted, by later and more comprehensive analysis.

Finally, recent reviews of research on poverty, income, unemployment, and education suggest that social science research has not led to convergent conclusions (Aaron 1978; Cohen and Weiss 1977). As more studies are done, they often elaborate rather than simplify. They generate complex, varied, and even contradictory views of the social phenomena under study, rather than cumulating into sharper and more coherent explanation. The effect may be to widen and enrich our understanding of the multiple facets of reality, but the implications for policy are less simple and clear-cut. When diverse research conclusions enter the policy arena, the direction they provide for policy is confused. Advocates of almost any policy prescription are likely to find some research generalizations in circulation to support their points of view.

Research as Part of the Intellectual Enterprise of the Society

A final view of research utilization looks upon social science research as one of the intellectual pursuits of a society. It is not so much an independent variable whose effects on policy remain to be determined as it is another of the dependent variables, collateral with policy--and with philosophy, journalism, history, law, and criticism. Like policy, social science research responds to the currents of thought, the fads and fancies, of the period. Social science and policy interact, influencing each other and being influenced by the larger fashions of social thought.

It is often emerging policy interest in a social issue
that leads to the appropriation of funds for social science
research in the first place, and only with the availability
of funds are social scientists attracted to study the issue.
Early studies may accept the parameters set by the policy
discussion, limiting investigation to those aspects of the
issue that have engaged official attention. Later, as
social science research widens its horizons, it may
contribute to reconceptualization of the issue by policymakers. Meanwhile, both the policy and research colloquies
may respond, consciously or unconsciously, to concerns
sweeping through intellectual and popular thought ("citizen
participation," "local control," spiraling inflation,
individual privacy). In this view, research is one part of
the interconnected intellectual enterprise of the time.

SOCIAL SCIENCE KNOWLEDGE

If "research utilization" has meant different things to
different people, so too has "social science knowledge."
Within the confines of the social science disciplines,
scholars engage in critical analysis of the shortcomings and
ontological limits of the knowledge that the social sciences
reveal. However, when they discuss issues of research
utilization, these same scholars often seem to make the
assumption that social science knowledge is objective,
factual, dispassionate truth. In these discussions, social
science knowledge stands in opposition to the kinds of
information and misinformation that government officials
commonly rely upon, which are assumed to be partial, biased,
incomplete, self-serving, and politically compromised.
Presumably no responsible social scientist would hold that
the results of social science research are comprehensive,
free of value premises, or valid for all seasons. As Cherns
(1972, 18) said in a related context, "We tend to have
sophisticated ideas about it when we discuss it in terms of
'sociology of knowledge,' but to revert to simplistic models
when we are arguing about 'application' and 'applied
research.'"
What do the social sciences offer the decision maker?
They provide (1) broad theoretical perspectives for
organizing and making sense of complex social phenomena,
such as functionalism, Marxism, and Keynesianism; (2)
empirically based generalization, of the sort compiled by
Berelson and Steiner (1964) that seem to have fairly wide
applicability—although not without exceptions; (3) sets of

concepts that serve to categorize events and processes in useful ways, e.g., social stratification, supply and demand, bureaucratic politics; (4) specific sets of findings, e.g., school systems that adopted "exemplary programs" marketed by federal staff with the support of federal dollars almost inevitably adapted the programs to suit local constraints (Berman and McLaughlin 1978); and (5) facts, e.g., population counts, voting data.[1]

It has become commonplace to recognize that even at the level of "facts," data are shaped by value assumptions in their definition and collection. Thus, arguments about the accuracy of the unemployment rate concern the exclusion of the "discouraged" unemployed who are no longer actively seeking jobs and the part-time employed who would prefer full-time jobs.

At the level of specific findings, the validity and reliability of conclusions depend not only on the methodological rigor of the study that produced them but also on its conceptual orientation. We are fully aware that research conclusions at their best do not represent mirror images of some reality "out there"; as Merton (1968) aptly noted, despite the term's latinate origins, data are not "given" but created. The cogency of explanations and interpretations of social phenomena depend in large part on the orienting schema and the selection of appropriate explanatory variables.

Social science research does not yield a single uncompromised truth. As we are all well aware, different investigators studying the same events often come up with divergent—even conflicting—conclusions. Sometimes the discrepancies are attributable to different underlying perspectives (see Cohen and Weiss 1977 for differences in the research of psychologists, sociologists, and anthropologists on desegregation), sometimes to differences in the variables studied, sometimes to differences in measures and measurement, sometimes to differences in conditions at the sites studied, sometimes to temporal changes, sometimes to divergent standards of judgment.

Furthermore, many social science research results fail to hold up over time. As conditions change, the middle-range generalizations of an earlier period shrivel. For example, much of the research on the determinants of voting behavior done in the 1950s and early 1960s is now obsolete. Lindblom and Cohen (1979, 51) consider it a possibility that the obsolescence of social science conclusions proceeds at a faster rate than their growth. Hope for a progressively expanding body of verified knowledge may be an idle dream.

What is it that transforms the findings of a social science research study (careful, systematic, but still somewhat tenuous) into the grandiose category of "knowledge" (that can be ignored only at the relevant user's peril)? How does a knowledge claim come to be accepted as knowledge?

In the social sciences, where compatibility with higher-order propositions is not a reasonable touchstone and replication does not always serve, the best approximation to an answer is probably: Knowledge claims are certified by the agreement of experts. Knowledge is that which other social scientists consensually accept as knowledge. Since social scientists acknowledge the fragility and the time- and situation-bound character of most research, there are serious questions about what it is that we expect government officials to plug into their decisions.

It seems likely to me that the findings of a single study, however carefully done, rarely qualify as knowledge. Information, yes. Useful, illuminating, suggestive, vision-expanding, problem-alerting, reality-testing, provocative, more systematic and less distorted than most competing sources of information, worth taking account of, yes. Does it supply the "solution" to the problem? Probably not very often—at least not in the sense of an objectively "right" answer. Even a series of studies on the same topic—even a series that converges on the same findings—may appropriately be kept on hold for a time. The studies that found that women who were raped often triggered the rape by their provocative behavior were merely indicating the pervasiveness of underlying biases; the studies on the "risky shift" in group decision-making behavior were exhibiting identical flaws in their methodological apparatus.

What social science may appropriately offer to decision makers are, first, statistical data and data series, which orient decision makers to conditions in the social world. Although some of the series stand in need of improvement, they provide maps of the social terrain that are useful for anyone venturing forth—especially for purposes of rearranging the landscape. Second, the findings and generalizations from research, evaluation, and policy analysis are usually worth attending to, although some social scientists' expectations that these should be accepted uncritically are patently unreasonable.

A third contribution that the social sciences can make is their conceptual apparatus. Notions of social movements, reference groups, school climate, social support networks, informal communications structures, the electoral

imperative, help decision makers interpret their own past
behavior and consider potential courses for the future.

Fourth, middle-range generalizations from the social
sciences also have an impact. Cause-and-effect linkages
postulated by the social sciences (e.g., family
disorganization is a cause of children's poor school
performance, or alternatively, poor school performance is
caused by teachers' low expectations for pupil achievement
and their consequent unwillingness to maintain adequate
standards in the classroom) underlie selection of strategies
of intervention. While "commonsense" theories about the
origins of social problems continue to be influential in
decisions about appropriate interventions, even the adages
of folk wisdom tend to be dressed up these days in the
trappings of social science. And when they are, they become
amenable to test--under differing circumstances and with
progressively better methodological and statistical tools.

This leads to a fifth contribution from the social
sciences--their methodology of inquiry. The systematic
methods of study that the social sciences employ have been
widely applied to governmental problems. Staff offices have
been created to conduct or support social experiments,
evaluations of policy and programs, and policy analyses of
proposed initiatives. Even beyond these specific efforts,
in the broader work of analysis and planning there is wide
recognition of the need for careful formulation of
questions, explication of hypothesized relationships,
unbiased data collection, and sophisticated modes of
analysis. Although much remains to be done to improve the
level of methodological practice, the models provided by the
social sciences represent a standard by which government
analyses are judged. Finally, the social sciences offer a
critical perspective on agency operations. By bringing
variant perspectives to bear on the problems of the time,
they provide a challenge to traditional assumptions
underlying agency programs and an infusion of new ideas for
improving practice. Every agency in time becomes ingrown
and routinized, and bureaucratic calcification constrains
the range of the possible. Ideas from social science,
however incomplete their empirical basis, represent a vital
contribution. They help agencies to rethink their actions
and to consider new ways of accomplishing their mission.

In sum, inquiry into the uses of social science in
public policy making need not be restricted to search for
applications of specific findings. A series of recent
studies (Caplan, Morrison, and Stambaugh 1975; Weiss with
Bucuvalas 1980; Alkin, Daillak, and White 1979; Patton et

al. 1977; Berg et al. 1978) has indicated that immediate and direct application of findings to decisions is a relatively uncommon event, but the wider and more diffuse consequences of social science are significant. If we alter our conceptualization of the "knowledge" that social science contributes to the policy arena, we will be better able to understand the phenomenon of utilization. On the one hand, we need to become more modest in claiming the status of "knowledge" for every empirical finding of every study that every social scientist conducts; correlatively, we need to learn greater respect for the knowledge that derives from practice, experience, professional judgment, and in Lindblom's (1977) term, social interaction. On the other hand, we need to look more widely at the range of concepts, ideas, and implicit or explicit theories about human behavior that seep from the social science disciplines into the arenas of public policy formation. They often have far-ranging consequences for the construction of policymakers' maps of social reality and therefore for the agendas they set and the policies they consider.

In a recent study, my colleagues and I asked a sample of federal, state, and local decision makers in mental health agencies about their uses of social science research, and their responses suggest the gamut of ways in which they find research helpful (Weiss with Bucuvalas 1980). A small proportion of them cited the use of research findings in the making of decisions, but this response was given by only 7 percent of respondents. Among the other uses they mentioned were the following:

Continuing education. Some people look upon social science research as a medium of communication for keeping up with the professional field. They read research to find out about problems, opportunities, emerging issues, and the range of subject matter that research addresses.

General programmatic guidance. Many people report that social science research gives general direction to their ongoing work. They are interested in evaluation studies that indicate the kinds of interventions that work, so that they can aim their programming along similar lines. They look to assessments of needs to inform them about the kinds of people who need services. They examine trends in residential mobility, labor force participation, public attitudes, and so forth to identify possible new areas for programming. Although their review of research is not linked to specific decisions either current or pending, they believe that research informs their actions in general ways.

Ritual. A few people report that they use research to

give scientific gloss to their plans and reports. Organizations tend to prize rational procedure and scientific method, and they sometimes expect references and citations, particularly in planning documents. Staff members obligingly go through the ritual.

Legitimation. More often, decision makers report using social science research to bolster the position they want to take. Research, in these cases, is not only decorative; it becomes a means of persuasion. A case that is supported by good research is expected to be more authoritative than a case based on staff judgments alone, and therefore decision makers use research to legitimize their arguments.

Uncertainty reduction. Research is used not only to justify decision makers' prefabricated positions; it is also used to shape the fabrication before the position hardens. Decision makers report that they use research to clarify their thinking during the taking of a position, and further to assure themselves that what they are doing has empirical support. Research helps to reduce the uncertainties and doubts that surround the policy issue.

Sensitivity to new concepts and perspectives. Some people indicate that social science research helps to provide them with new insights or it challenges the concepts that they have been taking for granted. Although research is not likely to overturn their conceptual formulations overnight, they find it useful for overcoming the mustiness of traditional organizational premises and for sensitizing them to new ways of looking at old problems. When additional research reinforces the new patterns of thought, the cumulative effect may be a reshaping of their understanding of events--with a consequent effect on agendas and priorities.

Some writers have made a distinction between instrumental uses of research--where findings are applied directly to a decision--and conceptual uses--where findings shape the users' understanding of the issue (Caplan, Morrison, and Stambaugh 1975; Rich 1977; Weiss 1977a; Pelz 1978). Utilization is probably better conceptualized as a continuum. At one end are the rare examples of immediate application of research to decision making; these shade gradually into less direct uses leavened with judgment; at the other end, social science research is used diffusely to affect general understandings of social phenomena. When relevant information and ideas are available from systematic study, agency staff are likely to give them at least passing attention--and depending on the nature of the research and its implications, perhaps a great deal more. Whether we can measure all the diverse and diffuse effects of research on subsequent actions is problematical. One of the most striking learnings from recent research is that even when people cannot remember the name of a single study or any research results at all, many of them are convinced that their actions are being influenced by the stream of research to which they are (through an assortment of channels) continually exposed.

POLICY MAKING

Clearer understanding of our assumptions about research utilization and about social science knowledge will help us develop more sensible views of the place of social science in policy formulation. Perhaps even more crucial is a deeper awareness of the nature of the policy-making process. Only when we understand the complex routes through which policy proposals emerge, the large and shifting set of actors who stir the policy pot (Meltsner 1976), and the many competing sources of information and interests that vie for influence, will we be able to put social science influence into proper perspective.

In common parlance, people think of policy making as a rational process. They tend to see the making of policy as involving (1) an issue (a problem, an opportunity, or a routine selection among alternatives) which faces (2) a group of people authorized to take action on such issues, who (3) generate or activate a set of options for resolving the issue, (4) weigh the relative advantages and disadvantages of at least some of the options (with more or less explicit calculation of costs and benefits), and (5) make a choice. Laymen and analysts tend to agree that important policy events take shape in this manner through this sequence of stages. And of course, they do.

This is not the only way, however, that important policy-determining choices are made. Many consequences of fateful order come about in the absence of this kind of rational chronology and, in fact, in the absence of the main presuppositions embedded in the standard concept of decision making. Organizations do things—and fail to do things—without pre-existing goals, purposiveness, consistency, rationality, boundedness of participants, time, and events, or calculation.

Consider "nondecision" in the sense that Bachrach and Baratz (1963) have familiarized the term. Many issues never come up for decision because dominant values or

organiz ational procedures keep them off the agenda. As
Schattschneider (1960, 71) noted, "Some issues are organiz ed
into politics while others are organiz ed out." Bachrach and
Baratz (1962, 1963, 1975) have stressed that in non-
decisions, nothing so gross as conscious choice by self-
interested elites is involved. Rather, community values,
myths, precedents, rituals, and institutional procedures
determine what is—and what is not—to be decided.
Taken–for–granted nonconscious assumptions "effectively
prevent certain grievances from developing into full–fledged
issues which call for decisions" (Bachrach and Baratz 1963).

In many cases, issues are present and dealt with—but
they are dealt with in similarly implicit ways rather than
through overt confrontation. The actors do not define the
issue as a decision situation but as a temporary incon-
venience. They cope with it by invoking custom, precedent,
and standard operating procedures. If necessary, they
redefine the event to fit the cases with which they are
familiar, and once having resorbed the event into accustomed
categories, they follow traditional practice. There is a
lack of consciousness about their (positive) acts analogous
to the (negative) inaction of nondecisions.

There are a variety of ways in which organiz ations take
action without going through a "decision–making process."
One of the most common is to base decisions on implicit
rules. An application for funding by a community group is
turned down by a federal agency because "we don't fund non-
governmental bodies" (although nothing in the statutes pre-
vents it). The force of custom is powerful partly because
it protects the organiz ation from the disruptions of change,
but also in part because it routiniz es decisions and therefore efficiently simplifies action without the need for
doz ens of discrete decisions based on the individual merits
of each case.

Another way in which organiz ations act is through
improvisation. No general "issue" is attended to; a single
event comes up that requires response. In coping with the
concrete event, officials use their experience, judgment,
and intuition to fashion a response. The improvised response becomes a precedent, and when similar—or not so
similar—questions come up, the response is uncritically
repeated. Consider the federal agency that receives a call
from a local program asking how to deal with requests for
enrollment in excess of the available number of slots. A
staff member responds with off–the–cuff advice. Within the
next few weeks, programs in three more cities call with
similar questions, and staff repeat the advice. Soon what

began as improvisation has hardened into policy.

A further route to organizational action without decision is through a series of actions and reactions. People in many different offices each take steps, which trigger moves by other staff in other offices, which set off the next moves, and so on--all unconcerted and uncoordinated. The sequence of well-advised or bumbling moves can add up to major shifts in policy. (Through such a series of reactions, the great powers stumbled into the disaster of the First World War.) The many independent accommodations lead to a result that no one planned or anticipated.

Probably even more common is the decision that "happens" as a side effect of other decisions. Nobody is paying explicit attention to the issue at hand, but the unintended consequences of actions taken for other purposes effectively set policy. A town that adopts strict environmental regulations to preserve open spaces, coastline, and water in effect limits the influx of new residents. Without conscious consideration, it "decides" to keep out lower-income and minority families. Or a state agency with insufficient office space moves to an available suburban location that happens to be poorly served by public transit. In so doing, it in effect "decides" to reduce the number of inner-city employees, even while its equal opportunity office is trying to increase minority representation on staff.

As a final example of the undecided decision, there is the ready-made solution looking for a window. Advocates have some policy proposal that they want to see implemented. They take advantage of any situation that seems to call for action to promote their pet solution. Thus, for example, people who want the organization to institute a computerized record system can find any organizational problem a suitable opportunity for computerizing the record system--overrun of budget, client complaints, vacancies in staff positions, boundary contests with other agencies. The decision to computerize does not follow from analysis of the problem but rather takes advantage of some current issue or impasse in order to do something that people want to do.

These examples illustrate that organizational decisions occur in a variety of ways that bear little relationship to so-called rational models. Implicit in the rational models are five components that do not always appear in real-life decision making:

1. purposiveness - a set of values or goals or utilities that the organization is attempting to attain or maximize

424

2. boundedness of time, actors, and events – a
    demarcated period during which a defined set of
    actors with acknowledged responsibility consider
    possible courses of action
3. calculation – consideration of the aptness of
    various actions for dealing with the problem
    situation and achieving desirable results
4. perceived significance – a sense that potential
    consequences are important
5. realization that a decision is being made –
    subjective awareness by the actors that they are
    participating in the making of a decision

At the extreme, all five components may be very low.
Many people in many offices, over long periods of time, may
deal with many facets of a policy problem as part of the
business of "doing their job." Only in retrospect can they
look back and recognize that the many small disconnected
steps that they took, without design or calculation,
effectively foreclosed some significant options and advanced
others. Without their explicit recognition of goals,
problems, or likely consequences, they in effect
participated in bringing about a major shift in policy.

In some cases, some components may be high and others
low (e.g., boundedness may be high while purposiveness and
calculation are low). In such a case, an identifiable set
of actors deals with events in a brief span of time, but
their sense of purpose is low and they pay little attention
to weighing the advantages and disadvantages of competing
choices. For example, a city that faces the necessity of
cutting its budget decides to apply an across-the-board
reduction to all agencies, without consideration of
municipal priorities or of alternative budget-cutting
schemes. Customary practice--and avoidance of interagency
politicking and dissension--determine the outcome. In other
cases, other elements of rational decision making may be
high or low. Probably only when all five elements are
relatively high is the situation unequivocally recognized as
"decision making."

Following the path-breaking work of Herbert Simon
(1945), scholars have been chipping away at rational models
of decision making for a generation. They have steadily
narrowed the assumptions of rationality (predetermination of
goals, maximization of utilities, comprehensive calculation
of all possible alternatives, etc.) and introduced notions
of bounded rationality, satisficing, factored problems,
sequential attention, and incremental adjustment. Examined
in the hard light of day, organizations are seen to deal

with facets of problems, make limited searches for
alternatives, and settle for solutions that are "good
enough." Avoiding uncertainty is a major aim, and
organizations (and subunits within organizations) tend to
cling to routines and prevailing myths, and to make do with
available problems of action whenever they can.

James March and his colleagues have capped the
withdrawal from traditional assumptions with their "garbage
can model" of decision making. In their formulation, four
streams flow along almost independently—a shifting stream
of participants, a stream of problems, a stream of
solutions, and a stream of choice opportunities. A decision
is an outcome of these "several relatively independent
'streams' within an organization" (March and Olsen 1976, 26)
—or the retrospective <u>interpretation</u> of the conjunction of
these streams. When a choice opportunity arises, the
organization is expected to produce behavior that can be
called a decision. The problems and solutions ("garbage")
that the currently active participants dump into the choice
opportunity ("garbage can") fortuitously becomes (or can be
interpreted as) the decision.

I was alerted to the vitality of such perspectives by a
study I conducted about the uses of social science research.
In preparing for interviews with upper-level decision
makers, we pretested a question that asked respondents to
describe the kinds of decisions that they made on their
jobs. The question caused them acute discomfort. Even
though respondents held positions of considerable authority
in federal, state, and local agencies, many of them insisted
that they did not make decisions. They proposed, planned,
reviewed, drafted, conferred, advised, revised, criticized,
wrote, supervised—but <u>decided?</u> That was not a word that
made sense to them in the light of their daily activities.

Review of their responses suggests that three
conditions mainly account for the disavowals of
decision-making authority: (1) the dispersion of
responsibility over many offices and the participation of
multiple actors in decision making, so that no one
individual feels that he or she has a major say; (2)
division of authority among federal, state, and local levels
in the federal system; (3) the series of gradual and
amorphous steps through which many decisions take shape.

Obviously in large organizations, decisions on complex
issues are almost never the province of one individual or
one office. Many people in many offices have a say, and
many participants become involved in ongoing deliberations.
In addition, legislative action is often required for major

shifts in direction, and legislative appropriations are
needed for major increase in activities. Staff in the
agencies are sensitive to the preferences and expectations
of the legislature. However influential their own proposals
and actions turn out in fact to be, they are conscious of
the recurrent approvals and signoffs that must be maneuvered
within the department and the modifications that can be
introduced during the legislative process. In fact, they
seem to be more conscious of the power of others--whether or
not it is exercised--than they are of the influence of their
own actions.

Given the slow and cumbersome process through which
proposals often travel, many organizational members are not
fully aware of the influence they have. They make a
proposal and see nothing happen for months. Even if the
proposal is eventually adopted with only minor
modifications, they may lose sight of the connection between
what they proposed and what eventually happens, and when a
series of adaptations is made, they seem to conclude that
they have little power in the system.

Officials at the top echelon can be equally convinced
that they do not make decisions. From the top of the
hierarchy, it often looks as though they are presented with
a fait accompli. Accommodations have been reached and a
decision negotiated by people in the many offices below, and
they have little option but to accept it. Only rarely, and
with the expenditure of a considerable amount of their
political capital, can they change or reject it. To them
the job often looks like rubber-stamping decisions already
made. Thus, the division of authority leaves each
participant largely unaware of the nature and extent of his
or her contribution.

The federal system adds further indeterminacy. In many
policy areas, responsibility for decision making is
distributed up and down the governmental system. Federal
officials receive their mandate from the Congress, which
passes legislation and determines appropriations, and from
the president and his departmental appointees, who give
policy direction. They have the authority to write
guidelines and pass money down to state agencies, which
decide about services. State officials receive federal
funds hedged about with federal requirements and receive
additional requirements from the state legislature. They
have limited scope for planning and for selecting local
operating agencies to receive the funds. The local agencies
receive the funds ringed around by such tight constraints
from federal and state regulation that they see little scope

for "decision." They do what they are allowed to under the weight of the rules. Thus, fragmentation of responsibility is not only horizontal but vertical.

The final set of reasons that our interviews revealed for unease with the concept of decision derives from the nature of bureaucratic work. Many problems and issues are dealt with simultaneously, and consideration of each one goes on over a protracted period of time. Each person takes small steps (writes a memo, answers an inquiry, edits the draft of a regulation, gives consultation), each of which has seemingly small consequences, but over a period of time, the many small steps accumulate and coalesce. Almost imperceptively a decision has come about without anyone's awareness that he or she was deciding.

The importance of this discussion for the "utilization of social science knowledge" is that decisions made without conscious deliberation (and the associated characteristics of purposiveness, boundedness, significance, and decision awareness) are unlikely to draw upon research in conscious and formal ways. When people are only vaguely aware that what they are doing will affect an organizational decision, they are hardly likely to seek out research to inform their actions. When they do not see the consequences of a decision as important in terms of dollar obligations, effort, or social impact, they are apt to make do with the knowledge they already have. Without a clear sense of purpose or of the relative fit of alternative strategies for achieving that purpose (at times, without the realization that there are alternative strategies), the shifting stream of actors who shape the course of policy is unlikely to consult research, let alone commission new research, to aid them in optimizing their decision.

INFORMATION, IDEOLOGY, AND INTERESTS

In closing, let us acknowledge that policy is not based on knowledge alone. Policy making is first and foremost a political process, where the major task is to arrange an accommodation among competing interests. It is usually less important to reach some scientifically "best" policy than it is to reach a decision that at least minimally satisfies the demands of the multiple ideological and interest constituencies in the nation.

Policy positions taken by policy actors are the resultant of three sets of forces: their ideologies, their interests (e.g., in power or prestige), and the information they have. Each of these three forces interacts with the others in determining the participants' stance in policy making. Observers who expect the subcategory of information that is social science research to have immediate and independent power in the policy process, and who bitterly complain about the intrusion of "politics" (i.e., interests and ideologies) into the use of research, implicitly hold a distorted view of how decisions are made. Moreover, their normative view—that research should have direct effects on policy—proposes an imagery of appropriate policy making that I believe is untenable and (if it should ever be realized) dangerous.

An emphasis on the representation of ideology and interests in decision making is not meant to suggest that information is unimportant, particularly if the information suggests that politically acceptable policies have counterproductive effects. Nor is it intended to say that the current share of research information in the amalgam represents an optimal pattern. What I do propose is that an understanding of the nature of political decision making is essential to an understanding of the place of research.

NOTES

1. The categories are adapted from R.K. Merton, "The Bearings of Sociological Theory on Empirical Research," in Social Theory and Social Structure (1968), p. 140.

2. See Allison 1969; Cohen and March 1974; Coleman 1957; Crecine 1969; Cyert and March 1963; Heider 1958; Jacobsen 1964; Lindblom 1965; Long 1958; March and Simon 1958; Steinbruner 1974; Thompson 1967; and Weick 1969.

REFERENCES

Aaron, H. 1978. Politics and the Professors. Washington, D.C.: Brookings.

Alkin, M. C., R. Daillak and P. White. 1979. Using Evaluations: Does Evaluation Make a Difference? Beverly Hills, Calif.: Sage Publications.

Allison, G. T. 1969. "Conceptual Models and the Cuban Missile Crisis." American Political Science Review 63, no. 3: 689-718.

Bachrach, P., and M. S. Baratz. 1962. "Two Faces of Power." American Political Science Review 56, no. 4: 947-952.

_____. 1963. "Decisions and Non-Decisions: An Analytic Framework." American Political Science Review 57, no. 3: 632-642.

_____. 1975. "Power and Its Two Faces Revisited: A Reply to Geoffrey Debriam." American Political Science Review 69, no. 3: 900-904.

Berelson, B., and G. Steiner. 1964. Human Behavior: An Inventory of Scientific Findings. New York: Harcourt Brace Jovanovich.

Berg, M. R., J. L. Brudney, T. D. Fuller, D. N. Michael, and B. K. Roth. 1978. Factors Affecting Utilization of Technology Assessment Studies in Policy-Making. Ann Arbor, Michigan: Institute for Social Research, University of Michigan.

Berman, P., and M. McLaughlin. 1978. "Federal Programs Supporting Educational Change." Vol. III of Implementing and Sustaining Innovations. Santa Monica, Calif.: Rand Corporation.

Caplan, N., A. Morrison, and R. Stambaugh. 1975. The Use of Social Science Knowledge in Policy Decisions at the National Level: A Report to Respondents. Ann Arbor: Institute for Social Research, University of Michigan.

Cherns, A. B. 1972. "Social Sciences and Policy." In Social Science and Government: Policies and Problems, ed. A. B. Cherns, R. Sinclair, and W. Jenkins. London: Tavistock Publications.

Cohen, D. K., and J. A. Weiss. 1977. "Social Science and Social Policy: Schools and Race." In Using Social Research in Public Policy Making, ed. C. H. Weiss. Lexington, Mass.: Lexington Books.

430

Cohen, M. D., and J. G. March. 1974. Leadership and Ambiguity: The American College President. New York: McGraw-Hill-Carnegie Commission on the Future of Higher Education.

Coleman, J. S. 1957. Community Conflict. New York: Free Press.

Comar, Cyril. 1978. "Bad Science and Social Penalties." Science 200, no. 4347: 1225.

Comroe, J. H., Jr., and R. D. Dripps. 1976. "Scientific Basis for the Support of Biomedical Science." Science 192, no. 4235: 105-111.

Crawford, E., and A. D. Biderman. 1969. "The Functions of Policy-Oriented Social Science." In Social Scientists and International Affairs, ed. Crawford and Biderman. New York: Wiley.

Crecine, J. P. 1969. Governmental Problem Solving: A Computer Simulation of Municipal Budgeting. Skokie, Ill.: Rand McNally.

Cyert, R. M., and J. G. March. 1963. A Behavioral Theory of the Firm. Englewood Cliffs, N.J.: Prentice Hall.

Donnison, D. 1972. "Research for Policy." Minerva 10, no. 4: 519-36.

Havelock, R. G. 1969. Planning for Innovations Through Dissemination and Utilization of Knowledge. Ann Arbor: Center for Research on Utilization of Scientific Knowledge, Institute for Social Research, University of Michigan.

Heider, F. 1958. The Psychology of Interpersonal Relations. New York: Wiley.

Jacobsen, K. D. 1964. Teknisk hkelp og politisk struktur. Oslo: Universitetsforlaget.

Janowitz, M. 1972. "Professionalization of Sociology." American Journal of Sociology 78 (July): 105-35.

Lindblom, C. E. 1965. The Intelligence of Democracy. New York: Free Press.

_____. 1977. _Politics and Markets_. New York: Basic Books.

Lindblom, C. E., and D. K. Cohen. 1979. _Usable Knowledge: Social Science and Social Problem Solving_. New Haven, Conn.: Yale University Press.

Long, N. 1958. "The Local Community as an Ecology of Games." _American Journal of Sociology_ 64, no. 3 (November): 251-61.

March, J. G., and J. P. Olsen. 1976. _Ambiguity and Choice in Organizations_. Bergen-Oslo-Tromso: Universitet-forlaget.

March, J. G., and H. A. Simon. 1958. _Organizations_. New York: Wiley.

Meltsner, A. J. 1976. _Policy Analysts in the Bureaucracy_. Berkeley: Univ. of California Press.

Merton, R. K. 1968. _Social Theory and Social Structure_, enlarged ed. New York: Free Press.

Patton, M. Q., P. S. Grimes, K. M. Guthrie, N. J. Brennan, B. Dickey French, and D. A. Blyth. 1977. "In Search of Impact: An Analysis of the Utilization of Federal Health Evaluation Research." In _Using Social Research in Public Policy Making_, ed. C. H. Weiss. Lexington, Mass.: Lexington Books.

Pelz, D. C. 1978. "Some Expanded Perspectives on Use of Social Science in Public Policy." In _Major Social Issues: A Multidisciplinary View_, ed. J. M. Yinger and S. J. Cutler. New York: Free Press.

Rich, R. F. 1977. "Use of Social Science Information by Federal Bureaucrats: Knowledge for Action versus Knowledge for Understanding." In _Using Social Research in Public Policy Making_, ed. C. H. Weiss. Lexington, Mass.: Lexington Books.

Schattschneider, E. E. 1960. _The Semi-Sovereign People_. New York: Holt, Rinehart and Winston.

432

Schuman, H. 1975. "Race Relations: Some Policy Implications, Proximate and Remote, of a Negative Finding." In Social Policy and Sociology, ed. N. J. Demerath III, O. Larsen, and K. F. Schuessler. New York: Academic Press.

Simon, H. A. 1945. Administrative Behavior. New York: Free Press.

Steinbruner, J. D. 1974. The Cybernetic Theory of Decision. Princeton, N.J.: Princeton Univ. Press.

Thompson, J. 1967. Organizations in Action. New York: McGraw-Hill.

Weick, K. E. 1969. The Social Psychology of Organizing. Reading, Mass.: Addison-Wesley.

Weiss, C. H. 1973. "Where Politics and Evaluation Research Meet." Evaluation 1, no. 3: 37-45.

_____. 1977a. "Using Social Research in Public Policy Making. Lexington, Mass.: Lexington Books.

_____. 1977b. "Research for Policy's Sake: The Enlightenment Function of Social Science Research." Policy Analysis 3, no. 4 (Fall): 531-545.

Weiss, C. H., with M. J. Bucuvalas. 1980. Social Science Research and Decision-Making. New York: Columbia Univ. Press.

Weiss, J. 1976. "Using Social Science for Social Policy." Policy Studies Journal 4, no. 3 (Spring): 236.

18

Knowledge Utilization
as Planned Social Change

Gerald Zaltman

Knowledge utilization might be considered a relatively new field in the sense that most people currently concerned with knowledge utilization have become so involved rather recently. It would not be surprising to find that most scholars in the history of the social sciences who have ever worked seriously in this area are still actively engaged in the area. In terms of diffusion theory, innovators in the acquisition or adoption of the idea that knowledge utilization is a critical issue in science span a considerable period of time in the history of the social sciences. Only recently, however, has the field moved into the first major growth phase in which so-called early adopters begin to commit themselves to an idea. Yet, viewed in another way, knowledge utilization might be considered as a type of innovation; knowledge utilization as belonging to the more established field of social change. This is the view elaborated below.

KNOWLEDGE AS AN INNOVATION

The term innovation is central to knowledge utilization phenomena. An innovation is an idea, practice, or material artifact perceived as new by a potential user or adopter. An item of knowledge may be perceived as new by potential users. In this sense, knowledge itself is an innovation. The literature on planned social change generally focuses on the artifacts or overt expressions of knowledge—that which results from the implementation or translation of knowledge into action. I, however, shall distinguish between an innovation that has a manifestation as a program, service or physical object and an innovation that does not have such an

433

434

overt expression, or that may be the basic research idea
underlying an overtly expressed innovation.

A knowledge innovation is an idea that is perceived as
valid; it is a mapping of experienced reality (Holzner 1968)
that is new to the person doing the mapping. Such innovations may be derived from common sense, as described by
Geertz (1966; 1975) and Lindblom and Cohen (1979), or
through the methods of conventional science. Considerable
effort has been expended in trying to understand how the
characteristics of innovations affect their use. This work
is summarized in several sources (Rogers 1983; Lin and
Zaltman 1973; Zaltman and Duncan 1977). One of the most
intriguing advances in our thinking in this area concerns
the process of reinvention, whereby existing innovations are
modified, sometimes substantially, by users to fit unique
circumstances.

The significance of this concept and of other work on
the nature or character of innovations for knowledge
utilization is beginning to be developed (Glaser, Abelson,
and Garrison 1976). The way in which the characteristics of
knowledge (that is, the characteristics of innovations)
influence the dissemination and use of knowledge is
especially important at the storage stage and at the stages
where knowledge is translated into action implications and
those implications implemented. The work on reinvention
suggests that research and development (R & D) continues at
the implementation stage, but at the hands of "users" rather
than "producers." This idea further suggests that the R & D
literature is relevant at the implementation stage as well.
Current research has begun to explore how various attributes
of knowledge innovations (e.g., new research and the packaging of knowledge) affect their adoption and implementation
(Weiss and Bucuvalas 1978; Dimaggio and Useem 1979).

The concept of social change is also important. Rogers
(1973) refers to social change as an alteration in the
structure and functioning of a social system brought about
by innovation. Zaltman and Duncan (1977) refer to change in
terms of relearning. In either case, the use of knowledge
may affect the structure and functioning of a social system
and involve relearning. When this occurs, the knowledge
utilization process may be validly viewed as a social change
process. The effective transfer of knowledge from one
person or agency to another is an instance of innovation,
adoption and diffusion. As knowledge and its use diffuse
through a population, social change may occur. Thus, many
instances of intended knowledge utilization are instances of
planned social change. What we know from the larger

literature about conducting planned social change might be
brought to bear on the task of transferring and implementing
knowledge. Thus, the works of Davis (1973), Rothman (1974;
1976), Fairweather, Sanders, and Tornatzsky (1974), Blum
(1974), Lippitt (1973), Rogers (1983), and many others
become very relevant.

To summarize, what is new about knowledge utilization
as a field of study is that the topic has just now begun to
attract a significant number of scholars seriously committed
to acquiring a better understanding of this complex
phenomenon. While knowledge utilization is, in this
restricted sense, a new topic, it is also part of a
well-established and broader topic: social change. It is
important, therefore, that the development of the knowledge
utilization area not proceed without sensitivity to the
larger field of social change. By being sensitive to
various concepts, findings, and issues in the field of
social change—especially planned social change—workers in
the knowledge utilization field may advance intellectually
more rapidly than otherwise might be possible.

The field of planned social change is most clearly
relevant to knowledge utilization when we adopt the
perspective of a purveyor or disseminator of knowledge such
as: (1) a government agency attempting to have its
sponsored research considered and used by a nongovernment
constituency, (2) a consultant concerned with having his or
her advice accepted by a client, or (3) an independent
researcher who believes his or her research findings imply
an important change in practice which should be heeded by
service providers or policymakers in some public or private
sector setting. Perhaps evaluation researchers are the most
cognizant of all social scientists of this overlap between
knowledge utilization and planned social change. Short
examples involving evaluation research will be cited
throughout this article.

PLANNED SOCIAL CHANGE AND THE PROCESS
OF APPROXIMATION

How might the field of planned social change facilitate
the development of the knowledge utilization field? One
contribution may be a lessening of what Kaplan (1964) calls
the "paradox of conceptualization," or what Jones (1974)
calls "Catch 23." In order to have good concepts, it is
necessary to have a good theory; before having a good
theory, it is necessary to have good concepts. The paradox

is resolved by a process of approximation. An improvement
in concepts (or theory) leads to an improvement in theory
(or concepts) and so on. The area of knowledge utilization
is in a fledgling state in terms of both concepts and
theory. There is very little by way of concepts or theory
to offer guidance for understanding the phenomena with which
we are concerned, or to offer guidance in research design
and data collection. (Consider the difficulties which
currently exist in conceptualizing and making operational
for measurement purposes one of the central dependent
variables—knowledge use.) Given the present growth stage
of the field, we could hardly expect a different situation.
The field of planned social change offers a number of
concepts and propositions that may greatly facilitate the
process of approximation in the field of knowledge
utilization and thus hasten its conceptual and theoretical
development.

The remainder of this essay will address various
concepts in planned social change. Consistent with the
notion of planned social change, I shall adopt the
perspective of a knowledge advocate or knowledge transfer
agent, such as a consultant. Knowledge advocates are
persons actively concerned with having an item of knowledge
(judged by some criteria as valid and reliable) accepted and
used in some specified way by others. They are thus a type
of change agent. The concepts reflected here will be
presented with simple propositions which are used merely to
illustrate how the concepts might be useful. The
propositions presented are recasts; they are knowledge
utilization-specific versions of propositions having at
least modest support in different planned change settings.
They are presented partly because their support in different
settings provides a type of convergent support for their
possible relevance to knowledge utilization. Applying these
concepts and testing the relations between or among them in
a knowledge utilization setting should yield a reformulation
of some of these propositions, but however much the
propositions may change in structure after testing, most
concepts the propositions contain are likely to remain as
relevant as before.

Many of the concepts presented here may be found in one
or more models of planned social change. Aspects of the A
VICTORY model suggested by Davis (1973) are especially
prominent. This model specifies several fundamental
conditions accounting for the attainment of planned change
program goals. Support in planned change settings for the
various guidelines and propositions in this article may be

found in several sources, including Rogers (1983), Zaltman and Duncan (1977), Zaltman, Florio and Sikorski (1977), Rothman (1976), and Brady and Isaac (1975).

The basic approach of this article involves four activities:

(1) Identifying social change practices that appear to work. These will be called guidelines.

(2) Identifying the proposition(s) from which a particular guideline appear(s) to be derived. All propositions are presented in an "other things being equal" spirit.

(3) Identifying the concepts found in separate propositions.

(4) Concluding with a particular perspective on knowledge utilization suggested by these concepts which differs from the conventional construct of the knowledge utilization process.

Proinnovation Bias and Nonpositive Knowledge

A proinnovation bias has been observed in the planned change literature (Rogers 1976). This bias refers to an implicit value judgment that innovation is good and, hence, that there is something basically good about being an early adopter of innovations and something bad about being a later adopter. This is illustrated by the common use of the somewhat pejorative term "laggard" to refer to the last group of people to adopt an innovation in contrast to the more positive term "innovator" for those who adopt first. It would not be surprising to find a comparable bias concerning knowledge utilization. On the surface, if this bias does exist, it would be difficult to fault. For a given decision, the use of knowledge is better than its nonuse, and scientifically based knowledge is at least as important to use as experientially based or common-sense knowledge. The difficulty, analogous to the difficulty it poses in the planned change field, is that this bias stresses the study of the diffusion of positive knowledge and factors contributing to its acceptance.

Positive knowledge refers to knowledge that involves a specific solution to a problem. Research showing that a particular social service innovation works well and should be continued or used more widely and research suggesting that one teaching aid is superior to another for a specific pupil audience and instructional purpose are examples of positive knowledge. Knowledge advocates are primarily concerned with positive knowledge. Nonpositive knowledge is knowledge or research that (1) indicates that a currently operating social service program, teaching aid, or policy is not supported by scientifically valid and reliable data, but (2) a sound knowledge base for formulating a substitute program or policy is not offered. An illustration of nonpositive knowledge is found in gerontology. A large array of public and private sector programs and policies are based on the assumption that chronological age is a good measure of aging among the adult population. However, recent biological and social research on aging indicates that chronological age is not associated with aging except at age ranges far beyond conventional retirement age. These studies clearly suggest that chronological age should not continue to be used as a basis for many program and policy decisions related to aging. However, these studies do not suggest good alternative summary measures of aging; they do not offer a substitute for the measure of aging they have shown to be invalid.

The utilization of nonpositive knowledge may not be the same as the utilization of positive knowledge. The analogy in planned social change would be diffusing resistance to change and diffusing the discontinuance of an innovation, as opposed to diffusing positive attitudes toward change or acceptance of change. In this instance, the knowledge advocate is concerned with diffusing an awareness of ignorance. Moreover, the implementation of this ignorance requires ceasing to use a criterion (such as chronological age) that was previously believed well-founded, but not replacing the criterion with one that is equally convenient to use. Thus, the following guideline is suggested: The strategies and tactics employed for diffusing nonpositive knowledge may differ from those used in diffusing positive knowledge. Implicit in this guideline is the idea that two different social dynamics are involved; resistance to change will be much greater in the instance of nonpositive knowledge. This suggests the following proposition: The greater the preponderance of nonpositive knowledge in a particular research endeavor, the less likely that knowledge is to be accepted, and perhaps, the less likely such research is to be undertaken if a high level of nonpositive knowledge is anticipated. Interestingly, most of the studies in social gerontology that have been critical of the use of chronological age as a measure of aging did not anticipate this particular significant conclusion at the outset of the research.

Attribute Gaps

A large number of attributes have been identified which appear important in influencing the acceptance of innovations. For example, Lin and Zaltman (1973) have identified nearly two dozen attributes found relevant to the adoption and diffusion of innovations. However, often so-called attribute gaps will occur. An attribute gap is the discrepancy between a user's actual perception of an attribute or characteristic of an item of knowledge and how that user would prefer to perceive that attribute. The greater the sum of all attribute gaps, the less likely a user is to adopt the knowledge. Thus, we have the following guideline: It is necessary to determine which attributes of an item of knowledge are most salient to users and whether significant discrepancies or gaps exist. This requires preliminary testing of an innovation.

The notion of designing knowledge to fit user preferences may be a difficult one for knowledge producers and purveyors to accept if they fail to distinguish between knowledge content and knowledge format. Even so, the notion of presenting a given item of knowledge in a way that is not compatible with our own social construction of reality is an uncomfortable one. However, the likelihood of acceptance of an item of knowledge may be enhanced regardless of its content if the different needs of different audiences are considered. Indeed, the data are more likely to meet utility tests and truth tests if this is done. Consider a statement given to colleagues and to me in an interview with a senior executive of a leading U.S. corporation:

> Most major products in our corporation have champions, i.e., people who are committed to the concept. There are also champions on the other side, i.e., those who are opposed to the product. We find it desirable to meet with both sets of champions separately...to extract an understanding of what we in market research can accomplish. _We try to negotiate with them what they will accept as supporting or negative evidence so that, when it comes back, either way we won't have any arguments_ (italics added).

The possibility of knowledge content being altered by an oversensitivity to user needs is, of course, real. The same study that elicited the above quote also yielded the following statements from two different research suppliers:

We whitewash the negative facts.

We might try to soften negative results, but in general, it is joked about much more than it's practiced. Sometimes, however, it _is_ necessary to put the best possible face on the data for the client.

The concept of pretesting information for purposes of enhancing its value and acceptance is not widely practiced in knowledge utilization settings. A sophisticated illustration of knowledge testing is provided by the research staff of a major insurance company. Prior to the actual collection of survey data, the staff constructed tables containing randomly generated data called prototype data. The exact tables and statistical analyses the staff anticipated using in their final report were then presented to the major users in the firm. This study was a sensitive one in terms of internal firm policies, and users were asked separately whether the kind of data, manner of presentation, and analysis would be helpful to them. As a consequence of this trial presentation, many changes were made in the questions to be asked in the survey, as well as in the plans for the subsequent presentation of the data. It should be added that the same users also had been consulted earlier in the initial drafting of the survey instruments. However, the trial presentation of the prototype data produced still more precise and useful research questions, as well as improvements in the reporting of the data.

Not all attribute gaps require an alteration in the innovation itself. An attribute gap may exist because of an inaccurate perception of understanding of the nature of an innovation. An appropriate knowledge advocate's response would be not to alter the knowledge format, but to design communication efforts to correct the misperception. Thus, innovation testing leading to the early identification of attribute gaps may also increase the effectiveness of communication strategies and tactics designed to increase the acceptability of given knowledge attributes.

Knowledge Effects

Traditionally, innovations have been studied in terms of their perceived attributes. An interesting additional perspective has been suggested which focuses on the effects of innovations (Koontz 1976). A guideline is suggested by this perspective: Knowledge advocates should attempt to develop knowledge that is perceived to have both incremental and preventive effects. An elaboration is necessary here. Incremental innovations increase the frequency of some desired event. The increment may produce a level of satisfaction not previously experienced, or it may simply reestablish or reinstate a previously experienced level of satisfaction. Preventive innovations are adopted to avoid some unpleasant event. A preventive innovation may (1) directly eliminate the possibility of an unpleasant event, e.g., immunization; (2) detect the possibility of an unpleasant event, e.g., a dental checkup; or (3) keep an unpleasant event from being as serious as it otherwise might be, e.g., use of a seat belt. Koontz suggests that innovations with incremental effects will be adopted more rapidly than innovations with preventive effects. Furthermore, innovations having both incremental and preventive effects will be adopted more rapidly than an innovation having only an incremental or preventive effect. During the innovation-testing phase of a preventive (incremental) innovation, the knowledge advocate should be alert to clues for incremental (preventive) effects which may be incorporated into the design of the innovation.

The implications of these ideas for a knowledge advocate are straightforward. In addition to determining whether an item of knowledge can be readily communicated, can be used on a trial basis, is compatible with particular constructions of reality, and so on, it is also important to understand the potential increments and preventive effects of knowledge. For example, in certain business decision areas, research reported in journals (as opposed to research specifically commissioned by a firm) having clear incremental effects is more readily used than research that is preventive in nature. Certain fields of research emphasize one type of effect. Organizational renewal research in education appears to stress preventive effects, while curriculum or learning psychology research stresses incremental effects. Research in both contexts might be more readily used if it stresses combination effects—that is, both incremental and preventive effects.

Audience Differentiation

Another innovation-related guideline is: If discernibly different user groups exist, consideration should be given to the need for correspondingly differentiated knowledge. It may be necessary to design

different versions of an item of knowledge to maximally
satisfy different user characteristics. The more important
these user characteristics are to the use of knowledge and
the less alterable these characteristics are, the more
important knowledge differentiation is in design and
development activities. This guideline appears to be
derived at least partially from the following proposition:
The more readily users can be segmented on the basis of
different clusters of attribute gaps, the more desirable
knowledge differentiation is. For example, one user
subgroup may perceive significant attribute gaps involving
divisibility and reversibility. A less complex presentation
of knowledge would be offered the first user group, or it
might be presented with smaller chunks of information over a
longer period of time. The second group might be offered
the component of knowledge that may be implemented on a
restricted basis with little enduring impact if the
knowledge is later disproven and no longer followed.
Another proposition is related to this guideline: The
greater the level of knowledge testing among users, the
greater the ability to determine the desirability of
knowledge differentiation. The ease of user segmentation is
only one determinant of the desirability of knowledge
differentiation. The ability of knowledge advocates to
offer differentiated knowledge is another determinant. The
ability of knowledge advocates to do this must be determined
through the testing of differentiated knowledge among users.

The Construction of Reality by Organizations

The decision to acquire and use knowledge and the
implementation of knowledge occur in social settings.
Social settings profoundly influence the way in which
individuals and groups map their experience of reality and
thereby define what constitutes knowledge for them. (For an
excellent discussion of this view, see Holzner and Marx
1979, chap. 4.) A lack of understanding of the
sociological, psychological, and political determinants of
reality construction on the part of a knowledge advocate may
lead to an underutilization or even misutilization of
knowledge. An obvious guideline for the knowledge advocate
is to identify these determinants and understand their
impact on the acquisition and implementation of knowledge.
The notion of knowledge as a sociological construct is
especially intriguing when an organization rather than an
individual is defined as the user. Substantial research

exists concerning the adoption of innovations by
organizations. Much of this research has focused on the
impact of structural characteristics on the adoption and
implementation processes. Structural factors may well
influence the way in which reality is construed as well as
how knowledge is acquired and utilized. There is very
little research, however, which addresses the interaction
between organizational structure (one set of determinants
affecting the social construction of reality) and knowledge
acquisition and use. Three groups of propositions are
suggested below relating to the acquisition of knowledge,
the use of knowledge, and the fit between knowledge
attributes and organizational structure.

Structure and Knowledge Acquisition
(1) The more complex an organization is, the more
easily knowledge is acquired.
(2) The less formalized an organization is, the more
easily knowledge is acquired.
(3) The less centralized an organization is, the more
easily knowledge is acquired.

Structure and Knowledge Utilization
(1) The more complex an organization is, the more
difficult it is to use or implement knowledge.
(2) The less formalized an organization is, the more
difficult it is to use or implement knowledge.
(3) The less centralized an organization is, the more
difficult it is to use or implement knowledge.

Interaction Between Organization Structure and
Attributes of Knowledge
(1) Knowledge having a potential impact on many
aspects of an organization is less likely to be
used by complex organizations and will involve a
more protracted decision process than less
pervasive knowledge. This is particularly true
when the organization tends more toward a
collective decision-making process than toward an
authoritarian process.
(2) Knowledge with unique relative advantages for
different subgroups within complex organizations
will be more likely to be used than knowledge
having a unique relative advantage for only one
subgroup within an organization. This is particularly true in the case where the knowledge must
be accepted by an authority outside the group.
(3) The more divisible knowledge is among
organizational subsystems, the more likely it is
to be tried by a complex organization.

(4)   The more formalized an organization is, the more
      likely it is to have a mechanism for dealing with
      radical knowledge.
(5)   The more formalized an organization is, the more
      necessary it is to make knowledge divisible and
      reversible.
(6)   The greater the degree of commitment that
      knowledge required and the more formalized the
      organization is, the longer the decision-making
      period and the less likely it is that full use of
      the knowledge will occur.
(7)   Knowledge requiring strong and widespread
      commitment for effective use is likely to be more
      successful when decision making is more
      centralized.
(8)   Highly centralized decision-making structures are
      more important and less efficient the less
      divisible, the less reversible, and the more
      pervasive knowledge is, particularly in a complex
      social structure where coordination among subunits
      may be weak.

The above propositions illustrate the types of ideas
that need to be explored for a better understanding of how
organizations construct reality and respond to new
knowledge. Until such an understanding is obtained, we
cannot fully understand how individual decision makers use
knowledge. A major issue which should be considered is
whether the above propositions are differentially true or
true for different reasons in public sector versus private
sector settings.

User Ability to Acquire and Implement Knowledge

Knowledge advocates should provide users with the
ability to convert favorable attitudes regarding knowledge
into actual behavior if this ability does not already exist.
Users cannot be expected to adopt an item of knowledge if
they do not have the skills or other resources to implement
the logical behavioral consequences of being open to the use
of knowledge. For example, research provided by an
evaluation of an organizational development program may
conclude that the program should be continued, but with an
additional component including survey feedback techniques.
Members of the organization may be generally open to this
recommendation (knowledge that a program works well in
specific ways), but may not possess the skills required for

the design and use of survey feedback techniques. If the
evaluation research consists of a conclusion that an innovation is required for the effective continuance of the program and this conclusion is to be utilized to benefit the
organization, then provision must be made to provide the
skills required by the innovation. As an example of this
guideline in another setting, a sharp debate is taking place
among various nutrition experts, food industry groups, and
the Federal Trade Commission concerning nutrient labeling on
food containers and in food advertising. All groups agree
that favorable attitudes exist among consumers toward information which would improve their nutrition. Nutritionists
and industry groups are arguing that consumers do not have
the basic ability to translate nutrient information
(knowledge) into appropriate meal-planning behaviors and
would react negatively to this information. The FTC claims
that the ability gradually will be acquired if it does not
already exist and that, rather than causing consumers to
ignore the nutrient information, provision of such data will
encourage consumers to seek the necessary additional knowledge to use the provided information. Either position may
be correct or incorrect, but both clearly address the issue
of user ability to acquire and implement knowledge.

Two concepts are central in the guideline: The
diagnosis of user knowledge-handling abilities and user
ability-building. A proposition behind this guideline could
be: The greater the diagnosed inability of users to accept
knowledge, the more the knowledge advocate should focus on
building those abilities.

Consider another guideline: Knowledge advocates should
distinguish between user inabilities that can be altered and
those that are relatively fixed and to which they must
adapt. For example, if users lack knowledge concerning the
effective utilization of an innovation, the knowledge
advocate may attempt to manipulate users' knowledge levels
directly through various kinds of instructional efforts. If
the evaluation of an organizational development program
suggests the use of survey feedback (a knowledge utilization
technique itself), then selected members of the organization
could be released from their duties to receive training in
survey feedback techniques. If, on the other hand, users
seriously lack the necessary financial resources to adopt an
innovation, the knowledge advocate should probably accept
this user inability as fixed and adapt the financial
requirements of the innovation to this constraint. For
example, a school's budget may not permit the hiring of
substitute teachers in order to release several full-time

teachers from classroom duties to participate in a training seminar lasting a number of days. If evaluation research indicates that another somewhat costly component is less effective than the survey feedback component promises to be, then that other feature might be dropped or deemphasized and the resources reallocated to the hiring of substitute teachers.

At least two social change concepts seem central to this guideline: The alterability of user inabilities and the adaptability of the innovation. The underlying proposition for this guideline appears to be: The more unalterable a user's inability is, the more knowledge advocates should focus on innovation-related alterations and less on user-related alterations. That is, if users cannot be quickly instructed in the statistical tools used in the analysis of the data, then perhaps these tools should not be presented to users. The "research" presented would consist of conclusions or recommendations only and not the tools of analysis leading to the conclusion.

Rationalistic Bias

Knowledge advocates should not assume that what is perceived to be scientifically rational to them also will be viewed as rational by users. For example, knowledge producers and advocates may place high value on conventional truth tests, while users may value rather different attributes of knowledge. Knowledge advocates and users often do not share common values and hence have different perceptions about the rationality of accepting an item of knowledge. A knowledge advocate may propose using an external evaluation researcher to assess a program if methodological expertise in evaluation research is lacking within an organization. This is a rational action for a knowledge advocate. If, on the other hand, decision makers within the user organization perceive this suggestion as threatening to the extent that the evaluation research process is less within their control with an outside evaluator and the research products could be very detrimental to the decision makers (for example, in terms of a loss of community support), then it is quite rational for the decision makers to resist the participation of an external evaluation researcher. For knowledge advocates, the user's rationale is the most important one on which to base their actions.

Two basic concepts involved in this guideline are

disparities between the value systems of knowledge advocates and users and knowledge advocates' assumptions about user rationality. These concepts suggest the following proposition: The greater the disparity between knowledge advocate and user value systems, the more salient the issue of a rationalistic bias should be. (Again, rationalistic bias refers to the knowledge advocates' assumptions that what is rational to them must also be rational to potential users.)

An intriguing study by Weiss and Bucuvalas (1978) identifies several different frames of reference users may employ for evaluating items of knowledge: relevance, research quality, conformity to user expectations, action orientation, and challenge to the status quo. Their results suggest that academic researchers may underestimate the value that decision makers place on the scientific quality of research and overestimate the value placed on research that supports the status quo. Such a misreading of user values also would be illustrative of the point made here. It is also of interest to know when particular frames of reference or value sets will be more dominant than others for users. This guides the knowledge advocate in determining which frame of reference to stress. Other research in progress (Deshpande and Zaltman 1982) focusing on business managers suggests that concern with scientific validity decreases as users' concern with action implications increases, and increases as user research expertise increases.

Innovation–User Compatibility

Knowledge advocates should exercise considerable effort to enhance the compatibility of the innovation with existing values, beliefs, and attitudes among users. This guideline follows our earlier discussion. In the case of resistance to an external evaluation researcher, the knowledge advocate may be able to demonstrate to a user organization that the use of a more expert and objective external researcher may produce research that is less likely to elicit a negative evaluation of a program by community leaders.

This guideline implies research by knowledge advocates and the use of research to enhance innovation–user compatibility. The following proposition appears to underlie this guideline: The greater the level of information acquired about the user's value system as it related to knowledge utilization, the greater the ability of

knowledge advocates to develop knowledge in a way that is
compatible with that value system. The concepts in this
proposition are related to those in the last: for example,
the greater the level of knowledge acquisition effort
expended, the more likely knowledge advocates are to learn
about discrepancies between their value systems and those of
their users. Another proposition is also suggested: The
more concerned knowledge advocates are with the avoidance of
a rationalistic bias, the greater their ability to (and
probability of) develop(ing) knowledge in a way that is
compatible with their users' value systems. For example, a
few large firms are experimenting with unique management
information systems designed to present information in a
format that is most compatible with each manager's
preferences. A manager who prefers information in the form
of bar charts, for example, may sit at a computer console
and request data about certain industry trends. His user
code clues the computer to present the data in the form of
bar charts. A colleague in the same firm whose preference
is for regressions will receive the same data in the form of
regressions. Still another manager may receive a path
analytic diagram of the same data if that manager's code
indicates a preference for this type of analysis. Thus, the
information systems present knowledge in a manner that is
compatible with each manager's unique data format
preferences.

Knowledge Needs

Knowledge advocates should clearly establish for users
the connection between the advocated knowledge and a felt
need or concern experienced by potential users, which may
require providing considerable information. A knowledge
advocate may determine that goal-free evaluation research is
appropriate for a specific program currently in operation in
a user organization and would like to gain acceptance of
this idea by the user. This type of research might be
especially appropriate when unanticipated program effects
could occur (Scriven 1972, 1973). However, the user
organization, while committed to having an evaluation
component, may not understand what goal-free evaluation
research is. Equally important, the user organization may
not be sensitive to the importance of knowledge about the
potential unanticipated program effects. In either case,
educational efforts by the knowledge advocate are necessary
to demonstrate that this type of knowledge or research

(goal-free evaluation) is desirable. This guideline appears
to be derived from the following relationship: The more
information is provided about the direct relevance of an
item of knowledge to a user need, the earlier the knowledge
will be adopted. Despite the idea being so obvious, it is
probably one of the more flagrantly ignored in practice,
perhaps because of a rationalistic bias on the part of
knowledge advocates.

Premature Use

Knowledge advocates should think in terms of optimum
rather than minimum time for securing the adoption of an
item of knowledge. Time refers to the speed (fast or slow)
of the adoption and diffusion processes. Even when rapid
adoption is possible, it may be fruitful to delay actual
adoption. For example, if user expectations about a
research finding are unrealistically high and adoption is
immediate, early disappointment is likely. Disappointment
is more likely when the basic validity of the knowledge or
research is given less attention than the implications of
the research once implemented. In this instance, the limits
of the knowledge may not be fully understood, and hence the
higher the likelihood of applying knowledge that is not
especially applicable to the user's setting or that is not
sufficiently valid or reliable from a traditional scientific
view. The idea of having science courts has been advanced
to reduce this likelihood, but--however valid and reliable
the knowledge is from a scientific standpoint--there is
still the distinct possibility that unintended dysfunctional
consequences may occur following its implementation. Such a
case warrants trial implementation (Campbell 1971) or
perhaps "social consequences courts" whose unique task would
be to identify possible unintended dysfunctional
consequences of an item of knowledge prior to its
translation into social policy. Here, too, the idea of
withholding knowledge runs counter to the inclination of
knowledge producers and disseminators, especially for
problem-oriented knowledge production.

Many examples that indicate that the minimum possible
time for adoption of knowledge is not always the best time
share in common the dysfunctional post-adoption consequences
which should be addressed in advance of actual user
adoption. Consider an organizational change based on the
results of evaluation research. For various reasons,
utilization of the research results may be resisted or

implemented in a way that renders the change ineffective.
This may dampen enthusiasm for utilizing evaluation research
in the future in the same organization.

Coordination with Other Events

Knowledge advocates should be sensitive to ongoing
events that may adversely or propitiously affect the
decision to adopt knowledge, or that may adversely or
propitiously affect the use of knowledge after adoption. It
may be propitious, for example, for knowledge advocates to
delay introducing knowledge if it appears that "trapped
administrators" might be replaced soon by a critical mass of
"experimental administrators" (Campbell 1971). This
principle is most commonly articulated regarding events over
which the knowledge advocate has little, if any, control.
It an ongoing event has a positive impact, then knowledge
advocates might find it wise to time the introduction of an
item of knowledge or the encouragement of its adoption with
that event. Conversely, an adverse event may cause
knowledge advocates to delay the introduction of an item of
knowledge or delay any final decision making by the user.
The above guideline appears to be partially founded in
the next proposition: The more impact an ongoing and
essentially uncontrollable event is perceived to have on an
adoption decision, the more salient the timing of user
knowledge adoption. Another proposition underlying this
guideline is: The more impact an ongoing and essentially
uncontrollable event is perceived to have on the user's
attitude, the more salient the timing of the introduction of
an item of knowledge.
Knowledge advocates should be sensitive to possible
future events that may have a favorable or unfavorable
impact on attitudes toward knowledge and its adoption. If
an anticipated future event is perceived by knowledge,
knowledge advocates may wish to delay introducing the
knowledge until that event occurs or is more imminent. If
the event would have a negative impact, introduction of the
knowledge well before the event would seem appropriate.
Similarly, knowledge advocates may wish to delay active
decision making by users until an expected favorable event
occurs. Again, if the event is expected to have a negative
impact on the decision, decisions prior to that event should
be encouraged.
An example was used earlier indicating that the
implementation of evaluation research results might be timed

with an approaching turnover in program administrators. Whether the implementation would be delayed or speeded up would depend on whether administrators of the "trapped" sort were being replaced by experimentally oriented administrators or vice versa.

The last guideline appears to be based on two propositions: (1) The greater the perceived degree of impact (favorable or unfavorable) of an unanticipated and uncontrollable future event on users' attitudes toward an item of knowledge, the more salient the issue of the timing of that knowledge's introduction. (2) The greater the perceived degree of impact (favorable or unfavorable) of an anticipated and uncontrollable future event on users' decision making, the more salient the issue of the timing of when users actually make that decision.

Consider another guideline: Knowledge advocates should consider how past events, such as past efforts to satisfy the relevant need, may influence user response to an item of knowledge. This guideline appears to be derived from the following proposition: The greater the perceived degree of impact (favorable or unfavorable) that related past events have had on users, the more salient the issue of timing in the introduction of an item of knowledge.

Performance Gaps

Knowledge advocates should determine whether potential users are experiencing a significant discrepancy between their present well-being in the area into which the item of knowledge falls and what they feel their well-being should be. The greater this discrepancy, the greater the felt need to change. The discrepancy between a present and a desired state is sometimes referred to as a "performance gap," a label that is preferred over "felt need."

Whether or not a significant performance gap (or felt need) is experienced influences users' motivations to consider an item of knowledge. This, in turn, should influence the knowledge advocate's decision whether or not to introduce knowledge to those users. If knowledge advocates are committed to introducing knowledge and a performance gap is not experienced, it is important for knowledge advocates to know whether to enhance the experience of a performance gap by (1) attempting to lower users' satisfactions with their present state, or (2) increasing their sense of what their state of well-being should or could be.

The first item of knowledge to be introduced might be
knowledge derived from discrepancy evaluation research such
as Provus (1971) has strongly advocated for use in
education. Discrepancy evaluation research might well be
considered as a predecessor knowledge base for other types
of knowledge. One such "following" knowledge base might be
an ongoing evaluation research program. Knowledge
advocates, however, must be able to demonstrate that the
knowledge resulting from evaluation research can close a
performance gap. This brief discussion suggests that
knowledge advocates should think in terms of bundles or
clusters of knowledge, perhaps presented in sequence, as an
appropriate response to user performance gaps. How much of
the bundle of knowledge is necessary depends on how acutely
the user is experiencing a performance gap.

Whether or not users are perceived by knowledge
advocates to be experiencing a performance gap influences
such strategic decisions as whether or how an item of
knowledge should be introduced. Knowledge advocates'
perceptions of their users' performance gaps influence
weightings given to various strategy selection criteria
concerning the introduction of an item of knowledge.
However, it appears that knowledge advocates will be more
proactive (more outreach-oriented, more persuasive) in their
strategies the less they perceive users to be experiencing a
performance gap.

A basic proposition that emerges from this discussion
is: the smaller the user-experienced performance gap
determined by knowledge advocates, the more salient
proactive diffusion will be to knowledge advocates. Again,
this appears most prevalent when knowledge advocates
themselves feel a need to introduce an item of knowledge.
Thus, the following proposition must be added: The lower
the knowledge advocates' need or obligation to introduce an
item of knowledge, the less salient proactive diffusion
strategies will be. Simply put, these last two propositions
say that the less people want to use knowledge, the more
knowledge advocates will want to convince them that they
should use knowledge, unless knowledge advocates themselves
do not have a strong need for people to use knowledge.

Knowledge advocates should exercise great care in
identifying and assessing the knowledge-related performance
gap that users experience. This guideline warns against
identifying the wrong performance gap. It also suggests
that the magnitude of the performance gap be carefully
assessed and compared with other knowledge needs that users
may have. These warnings or suggestions, if heeded, can

help avoid the error of responding to the wrong performance
gap. A performance gap could be "wrong" in several senses:
it is not the one that underlies a problem, it is not of a
serious absolute magnitude, or there are alternative, more
serious performance gaps that the knowledge advocate could
address more meaningfully.

Selecting the most appropriate performance gap to
address requires the careful acquisition of knowledge about
users. Careful data collection and evaluation or
interpretation are especially important when the user's
problem circumstances which suggest a performance gap are
unclear. Thus, this guideline appears to be derived from
the following proposition: The greater the acquired level
of knowledge about user circumstances, the more precise the
definition implies a lower likelihood of responding to the
wrong knowledge need or performance gap. The proposition
assumes that the acquired knowledge about user circumstances
relating to performance gaps will be carefully evaluated.

Resistance

Knowledge advocates should use the display of user
resistance as an opportunity to acquire additional knowledge
about the user. Being attentive to the presence of
resistance and the way resistance manifests itself may yield
many new insights into user circumstances that might not be
obtained otherwise (Davis 1973). These insights may be
helpful in responding to present or future resistance
concerning other knowledge.

This guideline suggests the following propositions:
The greater the study of actual resistance, the greater the
acquisition of knowledge about user circumstances. Also,
the greater the study of actual resistance, the greater the
acquisition of knowledge about users' personal value
systems.

"The (knowledge advocate) should distinguish between
sources of resistance that can be overcome in the short run
and those that can be overcome only in the long run or
perhaps not at all" (Zaltman, Florio, and Sikorski 1977,
313). Some sources of resistance, such as those rooted in
very basic belief and value systems or in strongly
functioning norms, cannot be altered directly by changing
the user in some way. Other sources of resistance, such as
inappropriately perceived threats, may be altered directly
by providing the user with more accurate information
indicating that the knowledge will not have the worrisome

effect. Those sources of resistance that cannot be altered readily by changing the user may require altering knowledge advocates' behaviors.

Two basic concepts appear to be involved in these guidelines. One is the alterability of a cause of resistance, and another is the alterability of the knowledge advocate's behavior. The more unalterable a cause of resistance is through manipulation of user circumstances, the more consideration knowledge advocates should give to manipulation of their behavior or programs to be more consonant with circumstances causing user resistance. An objection to this proposition on nontechnical grounds may lie in an implication that knowledge advocates should try to alter users or their circumstances before altering their own activity. This is not intended as a suggestion, although it is a frequent practice.

Knowledge advocates should consider the expression of resistance to be an accurate indication of the absence of a perceived performance gap or knowledge need. Knowledge advocates should be as willing to terminate a knowledge diffusion effort on the basis of real or anticipated resistance as they are to launch or continue such an effort on the basis of real or anticipated favorable responses to the knowledge. Resistance may be healthy. It is not necessarily something to be overcome or adapted to. This guideline is based on the next proposition: The greater the level of resistance (real or anticipated), the greater should be the knowledge advocate's willingness to terminate the knowledge diffusion effort.

Knowledge advocates should be very clear in identifying for users the intended benefits of an item of knowledge. For example, if evaluation research is being advocated for an organization, a clear statement should be made about what type of evaluation research is proposed and what type of insights it is likely or unlikely to yield. This lowers the likelihood of user uncertainty, ambiguity, and subsequent disappointment. Intended benefits, however, are not necessarily those users want or associate with a given type of knowledge. Knowledge advocates may introduce knowledge for one reason, while users adopt it for a different reason. This does not mean users should not adopt knowledge for reasons other than those proposed by knowledge advocates. Rather, it means users should have a clear understanding of what the knowledge advocates' perceptions of benefits are. Research should not be conducted without regard for who key policymakers are and what their understanding is of policy issues and related research questions (Corwin and Louis

1982). This may prevent unrealistic expectations from developing or inappropriate use of the knowledge. This guideline suggests the following proposition: The greater the discrepancy between users' and knowledge advocates' perceptions of the benefits of an item of knowledge, the more active knowledge advocates should be in identifying the benefits intended.

Knowledge should not be diffused without prior evaluation of its benefits, nor should it be diffused without a prior plan for evaluating its actual benefits and costs. Benefits and costs are considered here in both their nonfinancial and financial aspects. Research evaluating the consequences of knowledge use seems especially appropriate when the benefits and costs are not clear-cut and are not likely all to be in the expected and intended direction. This guideline appears to be based in part on the notion of uncertainty about benefits and costs. The less control knowledge advocates have over the nature of the benefits and costs, the more essential it is to have an evaluation plan. (This does not mean that it is unimportant to have an evaluation plan if benefits and costs are clear-cut or are controllable.) The next proposition appears to underlie this guideline: The more uncertain knowledge advocates are about the nature of the benefits and costs of an item of knowledge, the more important it is that their evaluation plan allow for second-order consequences. Second-order consequences are those benefits and costs that go beyond those intended by knowledge advocates.

Knowledge Disavowal

Several topics discussed thus far have touched upon an issue that merits more explicit discussion. This issue or phenomenon may be labelled knowledge disavowal. Knowledge disavowal refers to the more or less deliberate avoidance of information that, if encountered, could cause the receiver to make a difficult or unpleasant change. It is suggested here (and argued more fully in Zaltman 1983) that knowledge disavowal phenomena not only rival knowledge use phenomena in importance but that the two sets of forces co-mingle or interact so that an understanding of one requires an understanding of the other. Knowledge disavowal includes avoiding exposure to information that is outside individual or organizational "comfort zones." It also includes the dismissal of information when exposure does occur. Many different facets of knowledge disavowal have been studied and are reviewed elsewhere (Zaltman 1983). What is important for the change agent to understand is that surprising information, even of a positive sort, is often rejected (Deshpande and Zaltman 1982); that clear-cut evidence supporting a particular action may through processes of biased assimilation (Lord, Ross and Lepper 1979) be readily reinterpreted to be supportive of the opposite position; and that a widening of client comfort zones may be required when presenting information that contradicts client assumptions, expectations and decision rules. Ideas that are new to clients are often "new" because of deliberate—but not always consciously so—efforts by the client to keep them hidden (Westrum 1982). Introducing knowledge under this set of circumstances poses a rather different kind of challenge.

SUMMARY: KNOWLEDGE TRANSACTION VERSUS KNOWLEDGE TRANSFER

The various concepts identified in this article and especially their expression as guidelines and propositions display an orientation that has the user as the major focus if not the starting point in knowledge utilization. This user orientation stands in sharp contrast with the more common "product" orientation present in most knowledge utilization studies. That is, an item of knowledge is perceived by a knowledge producer or advocate as being relevant to a user need. Attempts are then made to gain awareness, acceptance, and use of that item of knowledge among users. In contrast, a user orientation stresses much more understanding of user abilities, circumstances, and values in advance of the knowledge production and dissemination process. This notion suggests a rather different construal of the knowledge utilization process than is conventionally found in the literature and in practice.

The various social change guidelines and associated concepts that have been recast in this article are those practiced by highly successful change agents in a broad array of organizational and individual settings. As indicated above, they are expressive of a user orientation. In fact, if there is one factor that more than any other distinguishes successful from unsuccessful planned social change programs, it is a strong user orientation in which change agents and clients engage in an active exchange or transaction process. This suggests that it might be more useful to think of knowledge utilization as an exchange or transaction process involving at least two active parties—producers or disseminators and users. The term knowledge transfer implies a unidirectional flow of knowledge with a passive user. Before stating what knowledge exchange or transaction implies in contrast, let us recall the definition of knowledge used here. Knowledge is the mapping of experienced reality (Holzner 1968). The reality that is experienced consists of (1) common-sense or ordinary information and (2) information produced by traditional science or professional social inquiry. Knowledge advocates and users have their own knowledge consisting of data, skills, and perspectives. Knowledge advocates and users should exchange aspects of their data, skills, and perspective that are relevant to the problem area. The exchange or transaction would occur with regard to such activities as need assessment and problem diagnosis, translation of needs into research questions, actual conduct of inquiring or research, development and use of storage and retrieval systems, translation of research, and evaluation of the actual use of the research or knowledge. This view also implies more user responsibility and activity for these activities as well as much more user sensitivity among knowledge advocates.

REFERENCES

Blum, H. L. 1974. Planning for Health. New York: Human Sciences Press.

Brady, I., and B. Isaac. 1975. A Reader in Cultural Change, Vols. I and II. New York: Wiley.

Campbell, D. 1971. "Reforms as Experiments." Urban Affairs Quarterly 7, no. 2: 133-171.

Corwin, R. G., and K. S. Louis. 1982. "Organizational Barriers to the Utilization of Research." Administrative Science Quarterly 27, no. 4: 623-640.

Davis, H. R. 1973. "Change and Innovation." In Administration and Mental Health, ed. S. Feldman. Springfield, Ill.: Charles C. Thomas.

Deshpande, R., and G. Zaltman. 1982. "Factors Affecting the Consumption of Market Research: A Path Analysis." Journal of Marketing Research 19, no. 1: 14–31.

Dimaggio, P., and M. Useem. 1979. "Decentralized Applied Research: Factors Affecting the Use of Audience Research by Arts Organizations." Journal of Applied Behavioral Science 15, no. 1: 79–94.

Fairweather, G. W., D. H. Sanders, and L. G. Tornatzsky. 1974. Creating Change in Mental Health Organizations. New York: Pergamon.

_____. 1966. "Religion as a Cultural System." In Anthropological Approaches to the Study of Religion, ed. M. Banton. London: Tavistock.

Geertz, C. 1975. "Common Sense as a Cultural System." Antioch Review 33, no. 1: 5–26.

Glaser, E., H. H. Abelson, and K. N. Garrison. 1976. Putting Knowledge to Use: A Distillation of the Literature Regarding Knowledge Transfer and Change. Los Angeles: Human Interaction Research Institute and the Mental Health Services Development Branch, NIMH.

Holzner, B. 1968. Reality Construction in Society. Cambridge, Mass.: Schenkman.

Holzner, B., and J. H. Marx. 1979. Knowledge Application: The Knowledge System in Society. Boston: Allyn and Bacon.

Jones, C. O. 1974. "Doing Before Knowing: Concept Development in Political Research." American Journal of Political Science 18, no. 1 (February): 215–228.

Kaplan, A. 1964. The Conduct of Inquiry. New York: Chandler Publishing.

Koontz, V. L. 1976. "Determinants of Individuals' Levels of Knowledge and Attitudes Towards and Decisions Regarding a Health Innovation in Maine." Ph.D. diss., University of Michigan.

Lin, N., and G. Zaltman. 1973. "Dimensions of Innovations." In Processes and Phenomena of Social Science, ed. G. Zaltman. New York: Wiley.

Lindblom, C. E., and D. K. Cohen. 1979. Usable Knowledge: Social Science and Social Problem Solving. New Haven, Conn.: Yale Univ. Press.

Lippitt, G. L. 1973. Visualizing Change: Model Building and the Change Process. Fairfax, Va.: NTL-Learning Resources Corporation.

Lord, C., L. Ross, and M. R. Lepper. 1979. "Biased Assimilation and Attitude Polarization: The Effects of Prior Theories on Subsequently Considered Evidence." Journal of Personality and Social Psychology 37, no. 11: 2098-2109.

Provus, M. 1971. Discrepancy Evaluation. Berkeley, Calif.: McCutchan.

Rogers, E. M. 1973. "What Are the Opportunities and Limitations in the Linking of Research With Use?" Paper presented at the International Conference on Making Population Family Planning Research Useful, Honolulu, Hawaii, 1973.

_____. 1976. "New Product Adoption and Diffusion." Journal of Consumer Research 2, no. 4: 290-301.

_____ 1983. Diffusion of Innovations, 3d ed. New York: Free Press.

_____. 1974. Planning and Organizing for Social Change: Action Principles from Social Science Research. New York: Columbia Univ. Press.

Rothman, J. 1976. Promoting Innovation and Change in Organizations and Communities: A Planning Manual. New York: Wiley.

_____. 1972. "Pros and Cons About Goal-Free Evaluation." Evaluation Comment 3, no. 4: 1-8.

Scriven, M. 1973. "Goal-Free Evaluation." School Evaluation: Politics and Process. Berkeley, Calif.: McCutchan.

Weiss, C., and M. J. Bucuvalas. 1978. "Truth Tests and Utility Tests: Decision-Makers Frames of Reference for Social Science Research." New York: Columbia University, Center for Social Sciences.

Westrum, R. 1982. "Social Intelligence About Hidden Events." Knowledge: Creation, Diffusion, Utilization 3, no. 3: 381–400.

Zaltman, G. 1983. "Knowledge Disavowal." In Producing Useful Knowledge for Organizations, ed. R. H. Kilmann, K. W. Thomas, D. P. Slevin, R. Nath, and S. L. Jerrell. New York: Praeger.

Zaltman, G., and R. Duncan. 1977. Strategies for Planned Change. New York: Wiley-Interscience.

Zaltman, G., D. Florio, and L. Sikorski. 1977. Dynamic Educational Change. New York: Free Press.

PART SEVEN

Future Prospects

19

Some Key Issues

George M. Beal,
Wimal Dissanayake,
and Sumiye Konoshima

We are dealing with a newly developing field. We have presented one "slice" of the state of the art, a very limited version of that originally planned by those attending the conference and outlining a potential book. Our emphasis has been on what we believed to be some of the basics: defining the field, some of the current model-constructs, an exploration of linkages, research alternatives to further develop the field, a recognition of the importance of the rapidly changing environment in which all of this is occurring, and two perspectives on knowledge use. It is hoped this will aid in providing a base for dialogue and next steps forward.

A number of important issues have been raised by the authors of the chapters. There are many additional issues. There follows a discussion of what we believe to be among the more important issues.

CLARIFYING THE FIELD

There is need for further definition and clarification of the field. Clarification and elaboration need to be carried out both in terms of what already existing areas of conceptualization are subsumed within its parameters (e.g. linkages, adoption-diffusion) as well as the field's interface with related conceptualizations such as information science and information management. Continued conceptualization and definition of knowledge and knowledge utilization appear to deserve special attention.

MODELS AND CONSTRUCTS

From those within the field, as well as critics of the field, many issues are raised about the attempts to develop models and constructs. There is general agreement that at this stage of development there is no generally accepted overarching, overriding, integrating theoretical framework for the field or the development of models. However, it may be argued that the models-constructs presented in this book are attempts in that direction and could at least provide a basis for constructive critique and attempts at improvements. One specific criticism often raised is that the various model proponents tend to go their independent ways without attempts to interact, codify, find common ground and integrate. The utility of holding a second conference involving leading model proponents and other interested parties should be considered. Certainly the journal, Knowledge: Creation, Diffusion and Utilization could be used more effectively to present and to facilitate dialogue regarding model-construct development and testing.

Some argue that present conceptualization and model building are not of a high enough level of theorizing to make it possible to generalize or apply to a wide range of real-world situations. Others would argue, as one reviewer did, that what we have in the field is a number of "...theoretical essays which may or may not have any relation to the empirical-action world."

Others put forth a number of reasons why they believe it is probably impossible to develop generally applicable knowledge generation-utilization models. They argue that differences in the political, the philosophical and value orientation (e.g., authoritarian vs. participatory, research vs. user driven) make it impossible to generalize. Along the same line of reasoning is the argument that operating systems tend to be culture- and situation-bound. Others say the level of resources, such as number and quality of staff (actors), technology, and finances, exercise major influences and limit the system's action alternatives, thus making generalization improbable. And the type of knowledge utilization target audiences may have an overriding influence on knowledge generation utilization strategies and processes (and at least inferred models or constructs). That is, they will vary depending on whether the target audience is individuals, organizations, institutions, policymakers, administrators or consumers.

In any case, there seems to be agreement that there should be closer linkages between theory and model building and empirical world action and research. Whether models are inductively or deductively derived, the operationalization, application, testing and modifying (or rejecting) of models in different situations and under different conditions should be a continuing interactive process—a process found infrequently in the field to date.

A promising area for investigation might be to identify common elements that are found in the existing models, and variances, to see if indeed there are generally applicable models. This volume, as well as this field of study, has derived models primarily from agriculture and education. Perhaps, other areas should be investigated to strengthen model construction.

RESEARCH

This brings us to the importance of increased emphasis on research—holistic research that tests the applicability of existing models, that is formative in that it is sensitive to appropriate modification of existing models, and that emphasizes inductive model construction and perhaps field theory methods.

The chapters on research by Dunn and Larson go far in pointing out and clarifying many of the problems and issues in research and suggest some steps to overcome those problems. For those who believe it is possible to move toward more explanatory, quantitative, causal models of knowledge utilization there is a great need for further work to delineate main explanatory or causal variables, clearly define and develop measures for them and test the models with empirical data. However, much is left to be done in further understanding, clarifying, applying and testing what they suggest as well as delineating other issues and alternatives for attacking them. For example, the measurement of knowledge utilization should be a high priority on the research agenda.

UTILIZATION

From one perspective, the ultimate test of knowledge dissemination, in fact of the entire field, is the degree to which knowledge is used effectively to prevent and/or solve problems. More effective knowledge utilization by all user groups is a crucial issue. Carol Weiss points out that probably the worst record is with policymakers and

administrators. Great amounts of resources are put into
conceptualizing, developing, testing and carrying out
strategies to secure knowledge use by retail consumer
groups. Nothing comparable exists in planning and actions
to secure knowledge use by policymakers and administrators.
A fruitful area of investigation might be the extent to
which information as opposed to ideology and interests
influence policymaking decisions.

The record of knowledge use by professional change
agents appears to be somewhat better. Perhaps this is
partially due to conceptualizations such as Rothman's
product development and Zaltman's social action. Certainly
there is need for increased creativity and planning and
knowledge development, testing and dissemination in this
area.

There is one aspect of knowledge utilization that
should be of special interest to those in this field,
namely, the use of the knowledge from the field of knowledge
generation-utilization, i.e., use of knowledge gained from
the field of knowledge utilization in planning
knowledge-utilization strategies. Only a limited number in
the field appear to have placed high priority on organizing,
packaging, disseminating, testing and securing use of the
knowledge from the field by many audiences who should be
able to improve their effectiveness through its use.

MANAGEMENT OF SYSTEMS

Knowledge generation-utilization systems and their
subsystems are often treated as abstract systems, "something
out there," that are not seen in their empirical reality.
Thus information creation and accessing, packaging,
dissemination and utilization are seen in terms of
functions, processes and activities. In reality,
institutions, and more specifically agencies and
organizations (formal and informal), are often the main
actors in the entire process. How they are structured and
managed may be one of the most important factors in
determining the ultimate utility of knowledge
generation-utilization systems. Little specific attention
is given to how to effectively organize and manage these
systems.

ETHICS

The importance the editors of this book attach to
ethics as a part of the development of the field is
indicated by the inclusion of Bruce Koppel's chapter on
ethics. The issue is not only what are the ethical
considerations in knowledge generation and utilization but
who has the responsibility for pointing out, focusing
attention, and becoming involved in monitoring their
application to ongoing activities. More specifically, what
is the role of those in the field? The generation, the use
of and benefits derived from knowledge cannot be divorced
from the institutional power structure, ideology and the
economics of the system. These aspects have strong ethical
implications and must be taken into consideration.

A FINAL WORD

As can be seen from this book, the field of knowledge
generation-utilization has developed a body of knowledge
that should be of great immediate use to those who play many
different roles in the knowledge-information business, from
policymakers to practitioners. In these final comments the
editors have stated what they believe to be some of the main
issues facing the field. Pointing out issues has utility
only to the degree that those working in, or joining, the
field will tackle these issues to help move the field
forward toward being more coherent, powerful and useful.
Perhaps then in its own small way it can increase its
contribution to more effective generation and accessing,
management, dissemination and utilization of timely and
appropriate knowledge, to contribute positively to desired
social and economic development and help prevent and
ameliorate personal, institutional, societal and world
problems.